Studies in Digital Politics and Governance

Editors-in-Chief
Norbert Kersting, Institute of Political Science, University of Münster, Münster, Germany

Karen Mossberger, School of Public Affairs, Arizona State University, Phoenix, AZ, USA

This book series examines how and why digital technologies matter for democracy – whether in terms of coordinating social movements, elections, e-government, or digital inclusion. Relevant topics include, but are not limited to, digital democracy, electronic voting, online participation and civic engagement, and electronic campaigning. The series also covers studies on the impact of information technologies on policy issues such as smart cities and the applications of information technologies in a diverse range of areas, such as public health, education, and cybersecurity.

Studies in Digital Politics and Governance (DPG) welcomes monographs and edited volumes from a variety of disciplines and approaches, such as political science, public administration and computational sciences, which are accessible to academics, decision-makers and practitioners working at governmental and non-governmental institutions.

More information about this series at http://www.springer.com/series/16070

Leonhard Hennen • Ira van Keulen •
Iris Korthagen • Georg Aichholzer •
Ralf Lindner • Rasmus Øjvind Nielsen
Editors

European E-Democracy in Practice

Editors
Leonhard Hennen
Institute of Technology Assessment
and Systems Analysis
Karlsruhe Institute of Technology
Karlsruhe, Germany

Ira van Keulen
Rathenau Instituut
The Hague, The Netherlands

Iris Korthagen
Netherlands Court of Audit
The Hague, The Netherlands

Georg Aichholzer
Institute of Technology Assessment
Austrian Academy of Sciences
Vienna, Austria

Ralf Lindner
Fraunhofer Institute for Systems
and Innovation Research
Karlsruhe, Germany

Rasmus Øjvind Nielsen
The Danish Board of Technology Foundation
Hvidovre, Denmark

ISSN 2524-3926   ISSN 2524-3934 (electronic)
Studies in Digital Politics and Governance
ISBN 978-3-030-27183-1   ISBN 978-3-030-27184-8 (eBook)
https://doi.org/10.1007/978-3-030-27184-8

This book is an open access publication.

© The Editor(s) (if applicable) and The Author(s) 2020
Open Access This book is licensed under the terms of the Creative Commons Attribution 4.0 International License (http://creativecommons.org/licenses/by/4.0/), which permits use, sharing, adaptation, distribution and reproduction in any medium or format, as long as you give appropriate credit to the original author(s) and the source, provide a link to the Creative Commons licence and indicate if changes were made.
The images or other third party material in this book are included in the book's Creative Commons licence, unless indicated otherwise in a credit line to the material. If material is not included in the book's Creative Commons licence and your intended use is not permitted by statutory regulation or exceeds the permitted use, you will need to obtain permission directly from the copyright holder.
The use of general descriptive names, registered names, trademarks, service marks, etc. in this publication does not imply, even in the absence of a specific statement, that such names are exempt from the relevant protective laws and regulations and therefore free for general use.
The publisher, the authors, and the editors are safe to assume that the advice and information in this book are believed to be true and accurate at the date of publication. Neither the publisher nor the authors or the editors give a warranty, express or implied, with respect to the material contained herein or for any errors or omissions that may have been made. The publisher remains neutral with regard to jurisdictional claims in published maps and institutional affiliations.

This Springer imprint is published by the registered company Springer Nature Switzerland AG.
The registered company address is: Gewerbestrasse 11, 6330 Cham, Switzerland

Acknowledgements

This book had its origins in a research project commissioned and funded by the European Parliament's Panel for the Future of Science and Technology (STOA). We would like to thank the STOA Panel, the STOA Bureau and the STOA Secretariat for initiating and accompanying the underlying research project.

Our thanks also go to Gianluca Quaglio from the STOA Secretariat and to Bruno Kaufmann and Robert Krimmer for their valuable comments and recommendations.

Finally, we would like to thank Julie Cook for a thorough English language check of the manuscript.

Contents

1 **Introduction**... 1
  Leonhard Hennen, Iris Korthagen, Ira van Keulen, Georg Aichholzer,
  Ralf Lindner, and Rasmus Ø. Nielsen

Part I   The State of Scholarly Discussions

2 **E-Democracy: Conceptual Foundations and Recent Trends**...... 11
  Ralf Lindner and Georg Aichholzer

3 **E-Democracy and the European Public Sphere**............... 47
  Leonhard Hennen

4 **Experience with Digital Tools in Different Types
  of e-Participation**...................................... 93
  Georg Aichholzer and Gloria Rose

Part II   Case Studies

5 **Introduction to the Case Study Research**................... 143
  Ira van Keulen and Iris Korthagen

6 **Parliamentary Monitoring**............................... 151
  Iris Korthagen and Hade Dorst

7 **Informal Agenda Setting**................................ 163
  Ira van Keulen and Iris Korthagen

8 **Formal Agenda Setting (National and Local Level)**............ 177
  Iris Korthagen, Gloria Rose, Georg Aichholzer, and Ira van Keulen

9 **Formal Agenda-Setting (European Level)**................... 209
  Gloria Rose, Ira van Keulen, and Georg Aichholzer

10 Non-binding Decision-Making 237
Iris Korthagen, Casper Freundlich Larsen, and Rasmus Ø. Nielsen

11 Binding Decision-Making 273
Kerstin Goos and Iris Korthagen

Part III Conclusions

12 Assessing Tools for E-Democracy: Comparative Analysis of the Case Studies 295
Iris Korthagen and Ira van Keulen

13 Options for Improving e-Participation at the EU Level 329
Rasmus Ø. Nielsen, Leonhard Hennen, Iris Korthagen, Georg Aichholzer, and Ralf Lindner

About the Editors and Authors

Georg Aichholzer is a senior researcher, sociologist and freelance collaborator of the Institute of Technology Assessment (ITA), Austrian Academy of Sciences. He has ample research and teaching experience in social studies of technology and technology assessment, especially on electronic governance, electronic democracy, digital change and the future of work.

Hade Dorst is a PhD candidate at the Copernicus Institute of Sustainable Development at Utrecht University and is involved in the Horizon2020 project 'Naturvation' on the governance and innovation of urban nature-based solutions. Previously, she worked as a researcher at the Rathenau Institute on themes such as urban innovation and smart cities, including digital democracy.

Casper Freundlich Larsen studied political science and government at Aarhus University. He worked as project assistant at the Danish Board of Technology Foundation in 2016. He is currently employed as academic officer at the Danish Agency for Digitisation.

Kerstin Goos studied communication science with a focus on sociology and social research at the University of Hohenheim (Stuttgart) and at the Aarhus University in Denmark. Kerstin Goos has participated in several European research projects, especially in the field of innovation, responsible research and innovation and public participation. After 6 years as a researcher at the Competence Center Emerging Technologies at the Fraunhofer Institute for Systems and Innovation Research, she is currently responsible for the implementation of EU projects in the field of urban innovation and cross-sectoral collaboration and digitization at the non-profit high-tech business network CyberForum e.V. in Karlsruhe.

Leonhard Hennen has a PhD in sociology. He was project manager at the Office of Technology Assessment at the German Parliament, which is run by the Institute of Technology Assessment, Research Centre Karlsruhe, Germany. He was responsible for projects on genetic testing, technology controversies, sustainable development and research policy, neuro-science and society, E-democracy and others. He participated in several European projects on concepts and methods of technology assessment. Since 2006, he has been coordinator of the European Technology Assessment Group (ETAG; www.itas.fzk.de/etag). ETAG is set up by a group of European Scientific Institutes active in the field of technology assessments, which carry out TA studies on behalf of the European Parliament.

Ira van Keulen is since 2009 senior researcher and parliamentary liaison at the Rathenau Instituut. She specializes in digital democracy and evidence-informed politics and has been involved before in projects on converging technologies and human enhancement. Ira studied sociology at the University of Groningen and at the Graduate Center of the City University of New York. In her work, she has always focused on the interaction between technology and society. As a liaison for the entire institute, Ira is responsible for ensuring that the work of the Rathenau Institute is plugged at the right time, with the right parliamentarians, at the Dutch House of Representatives and the Senate.

Iris Korthagen has a PhD in public administration. Since March 2019, she has been working as a senior researcher at the Netherlands Court of Audit. Previously, she has been a researcher at the Rathenau Instituut for four years, specializing in topics such as digital participation, disinformation, science journalism and smart cities. Iris has also worked for the Council for Social Development (Raad voor Maatschappelijke Ontwikkeling) on projects about nudging and journalism. Her PhD research focused on the roles of media and media logic in decision-making in networks. Iris studied cultural studies (BA) and philosophy (BA) at the Erasmus University Rotterdam and gained her master's degree in research in public administration and organizational science (MSc) at the University of Utrecht.

Ralf Lindner is a senior researcher at the Fraunhofer Institute for Systems and Innovation Research (ISI) in Karlsruhe and coordinates the institute's technology assessment activities. He received his degree in political science and economics from the University of Augsburg and completed graduate work at the University of British Columbia (Vancouver) and postgraduate studies at Carleton University (Ottawa). His doctoral dissertation focuses on the application and integration of digital networks in the communication strategies of intermediary organizations. Since more than a decade, he has been working on numerous research projects focusing on the political and societal impacts of ICT. In addition to his research in the area of new media and society, Ralf Lindner has specialized in the analysis of science, technology and innovation policy and governance.

Rasmus Øjvind Nielsen has an MA in philosophy from the University of Copenhagen and is currently a PhD candidate in public administration from the Roskilde School of Governance in collaboration with the DBT, where he serves as a project manager. He specializes in institutional analysis and issues regarding the conditions for policy development and public engagement. He has been involved in the development of the GlobalSay platform for online democratic debate and previously participated in the development of the World Wide Views methodology for ICT-mediated multi-site public deliberation.

Gloria Rose is a human ecologist and junior scientist at the Institute of Technology Assessment (ITA) of the Austrian Academy of Sciences. She has contributed to projects on digital tools in the areas of participative and direct democracy, nanotechnology governance, the safe-by-design concept, robotics and the potential of temporary housing as niche innovations.

Chapter 1
Introduction

Leonhard Hennen, Iris Korthagen, Ira van Keulen, Georg Aichholzer, Ralf Lindner, and Rasmus Ø. Nielsen

Abstract The introductory chapter provides an overview of the volume 'European e-Democracy in Practice'. The focus of the volume is on the exploration of the conditions needed to realise the democratic potential of the broad scope of tools, instruments and procedures to strengthen the ties between established processes of representative democratic decision-making and its constituencies, with a particular view to political communication and decision-making at the European level. Part I of the book provides the outcome of a broad literature review covering the scholarly debate on the achievements and potentials of e-democracy and its relevance for policymaking on the EU level. Part II of the book presents 22 case studies on the use of e-participation tools at the local, national and European levels which were carried out to learn about best practices and major challenges and problems of e-participation in practice. Finally, Part III provides a systematic comparative analysis of the case studies, and based on this analysis and the findings of the literature review, options for improving e-participation at the EU-level are discussed.

L. Hennen (✉)
Institute of Technology Assessment and Systems Analysis, Karlsruhe Institute of Technology, Karlsruhe, Germany
e-mail: leonhard.hennen@kit.edu

I. Korthagen
Netherlands Court of Audit, The Hague, The Netherlands

I. van Keulen
Rathenau Instituut, The Hague, The Netherlands
e-mail: i.vankeulen@rathenau.nl

G. Aichholzer
Institute of Technology Assessment, Austrian Academy of Sciences, Vienna, Austria
e-mail: aich@oeaw.ac.at

R. Lindner
Fraunhofer Institute for Systems and Innovation Research, Karlsruhe, Germany
e-mail: ralf.lindner@isi.fraunhofer.de

R. Ø. Nielsen
The Danish Board of Technology Foundation, Hvidovre, Denmark
e-mail: rn@tekno.dk

© The Author(s) 2020
L. Hennen et al. (eds.), *European E-Democracy in Practice*, Studies in Digital Politics and Governance, https://doi.org/10.1007/978-3-030-27184-8_1

The political significance of new means of communication via the Internet has been under discussion for many years, and we can observe widely established use of these means in everyday political exchange and policymaking. Until the 1990s, this discussion featured far-reaching expectations that the new media would induce a fundamental change in existing power relations and hierarchical modes of policymaking by giving the citizens a say (e.g. Rheingold 1993). As an open space for political exchange accessible to everybody, the Internet has been held by many to have the potential to function as a remedy against the crisis of representative democracy. This is represented by phenomena such as the citizenry's disenchantment with politics, the decrease in turn-outs for democratic elections or the failure of the political party system to provide for responsiveness regarding the expectations and needs of the constituency.[1] E-participation, as a generic term covering a wide range of formats, to intensify and increase direct communication among citizens as well as between citizens and political institutions and policymakers was widely seen as a way to improve the deliberative quality of political opinion formation and the legitimacy of decision-making. Among the numerous contributions to the discussion of these democratic innovations, the International Political Science Association's (IPSA) Research Committee 10 on 'Electronic democracy'[2] has been occupying an outstanding position in e-democracy research since its creation in 2007 (Kersting 2012). E-voting, e-participation and e-governance have all been considered as possible supports in the search for solutions for democratic shortcomings at the European, the national and the local levels of policymaking alike. The option to render the political system more accessible to average citizens via e-participation in particular would strengthen the ties between the sovereign, the citizens and their political representation—both governments and policymakers.

1.1 State and Perspectives of e-Democracy

E-democracy and e-participation are widely applied terms which describe a broad scope of practices of online engagement of the public in political decision-making and opinion forming (UN 2016). As regards theoretical concepts of democracy, e-democracy is mostly based on models of participatory and deliberative democracy. However, far-reaching expectations of a fundamental reform of modern democracy, through the application of online tools for political participation and public discourse, are vanishing after two decades of e-democracy. Van Dijk (2012) concludes that the primary achievement of e-democracy has been a significant improvement in access to, and the exchange of, politically relevant information. Evidence on the realisation of e-democracy supporting public debate, deliberation and community

---

[1]For an account of the history of scholarly and political debate of a renewal of democracy, see Lindner et al. (2016b).

[2]https://www.ipsa.org/research-committees/rclist/RC10

building was mixed, and—most disappointing from the perspective of direct democracy—'*no perceivable effect of these debates on decision-making of institutional politics*' was detected (Van Dijk 2012: 53 ff). Furthermore, he found e-participation was largely confined to the initial and the final stages of the policy cycle and rarely allows for entries into the core stages of decision-making and policy execution. This is more or less in line with the UN report on e-participation (UN 2016), which states that there is a modestly growing focus on citizen involvement in policymaking. Although the initial high expectations have to be adjusted, e-democracy and e-participation have changed communication between citizens and governments in many beneficial ways, for example, by providing better and faster access to all kinds of public information for citizens, procedures of e-consultation or e-budgeting. There is no doubt that e-democracy when applied in the right way and with a dedicated political will can induce beneficial participatory or deliberative elements to the standard procedures of representative democracy.

The sobering effects that have accompanied the developing practice of, for example political online discussions or online public consultations have been increased by the emergence of the political downside of many-to-many communication made available via the Internet, especially with social media becoming a central element of the new electronic 'public sphere'. In contrast to early expectations of the emergence of a new deliberative mode of democratic exchange instigated by the Internet's ability to enable citizens to intervene in politics in a way that would improve the quality of political debate, the actual technical realisation of direct social interaction among dispersed persons and publics appears to have developed into a media of distortion, disenabling substantial and serious exchange of knowledge and opinions, according to the standards of deliberative democracy. Three main tendencies stand out from the use of social media in political campaigning and political communication: the manipulation of publics through the spread of doubtful, discriminating, sometimes hate-based information; the use of Internet-generated personal data to provide target groups with tailor-made information fitting their specific preferences and expectations; and the enclosure of sub-publics into their prefabricated worldviews and perspectives in 'Internet echo chambers', with Internet-based communities willingly excluding themselves from all pieces of knowledge that might unsettle or destabilise their shared worldviews. This is not an openness of discourse to all possible actors and perspectives, but an enclosure into exchanges among the like-minded: It is not deliberation dedicated to exchange of arguments in the interest of finding consensus or sorting reliable from non-reliable information and perspectives, but deliberate manipulation of discourse by inducing false or one-sided information. And this is not bottom-up self-organisation of debate, but top-down feeding and steering of public discourse by political actors who are assisted by the exploitation of private data and the software-based production and spread of selective or prefabricated news.

The book does not ignore these negative tendencies. They are taken account of especially in Part I. The authors, however, hold that there still is a vast potential to enable rational political interaction and improve the participatory quality of the political process via Internet communication. The focus of the present volume is the exploration of the conditions needed to realise the democratic potential of e-participation, that is of the broad scope of tools, instruments and procedures to strengthen the ties between established processes of representative democratic decision-making and its constituencies, that is citizens as individuals or as organised civil society. This is done with a particular view at the potential of e-participation for political communication and decision-making at the European level. The European Union (EU) and its institutions began to think about fostering their responsiveness to the European citizenry by means of public consultations more than a decade ago, for which the new options of electronic media have a particular importance (EC 2005).

It is not only digitalisation (technology push) that has advanced e-participation. Nowadays, many European citizens are invited, especially by their local governments, to be more involved. At the same time, citizens themselves actually want to be more involved. The UN report (2016: 3) states that *'advances in e-participation today are driven more by civic activism of people seeking to have more control over their lives'*. But at the same time people appear to distance themselves from actively observing and monitoring politics, let alone active forms of engagement, and they do not feel as if their voice counts or their concerns are taken into consideration. For example, in the European Social Survey (ESS 2014), the majority of the respondents gave a negative response to the question: *'How much would you say the political system in your country allows people like you to have a say in what the government does?'* And in almost all European countries there was an increased number of respondents who disagreed with the statement that the European Parliament takes the concerns of European citizens into consideration. These and other developments appear to indicate a crisis of the political system, with particularly serious features at the European level due to what has been called the *'democratic deficit'* of the EU. EU politics, as executed by the European Commission and the European Council, is a transnational phenomenon suffering from a lack of direct democratic legitimation and responsiveness to European citizens. The executive and administrative branches of the European Union's political system are enacted and controlled by a multilevel system of policymaking which is only indirectly controlled and legitimised by the European constituency. Thus, there is a particular need on the side of the EU to foster its own legitimisation by strengthening ties with the European citizenry. And e-participation is one means that has been in the focus of EU institutions to help in this respect.

1.2 Design of the Study and Layout of the Book

In line with the above-mentioned significance of e-participation for the European level of policymaking, the present volume is based on a study that has been carried out on behalf of the European Parliament's Panel for the Future of Science and

Technology (STOA)[3] and has been carried out by the European Technology Assessment Group (ETAG, www.itas.kit.edu/etag.php), a consortium of eight European Institutes active in the field of Technology Assessment. The study—at the request of STOA—was set up to investigate how to continue with e-democracy at the EU level in a way that supports public debate, deliberation and community building and has an impact on political decision-making. The two central research questions were

- What are the conditions under which e-participation tools and procedures can successfully facilitate different forms of citizen involvement in decision-making processes?
- And how can we transfer these tools—and the conditions which make them successful—to the EU level?

The study was commissioned by the European Parliament and was completed in 2017. It has been revised and updated for publication in this volume. The study was a follow-up of a previous investigation into the potentials of e-public, e-participation and e-voting that was carried out on behalf of STOA in 2011 (see Lindner et al. 2016a). This volume provides an update of the review of the scholarly debate on e-democracy and e-participation provided by the 2011 investigation. It also dives deeper into the investigation of practical cases of e-participation in order to draw lessons (especially for application at the EU level) on the potentials and restrictions for it to support participatory decision-making, as well as on its success factors in terms of political framework conditions and practical design and management of e-participatory 'tools'. We start from the viewpoint that e-democracy, especially e-participation, is one of several strategies to support democracy, democratic institutions and democratic processes and spread democratic values. The main objective of e-democracy is the electronic support of legitimate democratic processes and it should be evaluated on these merits. In other words, e-democracy is additional, complementary to, and interlinked with the traditional processes of democracy (Council of Europe 2009: 11). The design of the study consists of three elements that are reflected in the structure of the book.

Part I is dedicated to the discussion of the state of scholarly debate and research on the scope and perspectives of e-democracy in terms of the broad scope of formats of political communication via the Internet. This comprises a discussion of conceptual issues of e-democracy and visible recent trends of Internet-based political communication with regard to its democratic impacts and effects (Chap. 2), followed by a reflection on the state of debate on the necessity for, as well as the possibility of, developing a transnational European public sphere and the potential of Internet-

---

[3]STOA (www.europarl.europa.eu) is a panel of 15 members of the European Parliament with a mission to support the European Parliament in matters of foresight and assessment of technological developments and their societal effects and political implications. The authors would like to thank the members of the STOA Panel, as well as the scientific staff of the STOA Secretariat, for initializing and accompanying the underlying research project. It goes without saying that the arguments and opinions purported in this volume are solely those of the authors and do not reflect in any way official positions of the European Parliament.

based communication formats to contribute to public deliberation beyond national public spheres (Chap. 3). Finally, literature on the current practice of e-participation in the context of policymaking is discussed in order to reflect current experiences on the democratic potential of e-participation and lessons learned regarding success and failure. The review covers the broad scope of e-participation in different formats, such as e-information, e-petitions, e-initiatives, e-campaigning, e-deliberation, e-consultation, e-budgeting and e-voting (Chap. 4). Part I is based on a systematic review covering relevant literature that has been published from 2011 to 2016. The systematic review is based on a search for a relevant set of topics with specific search terms using the Thomson Reuters database (Web of Science Core Collection), SCOPUS (an abstract and citation database of peer-reviewed literature including conference proceedings) and *U::search* (the online library search engine of the University of Vienna). In addition, relevant journals from 2011 to 2016 were examined and a search was carried out via Google Scholar to identify grey literature. As a result of the different search strategies, around 3600 significant references were identified. Via several filtering steps, this large volume of literature has been reduced to a library of the most relevant core literature consisting of around 400 titles. Where necessary, this body of literature has been updated for the publication of this book.

Part II presents 22 case studies on the use of e-participation tools at the local, national and European levels. These were carried out to establish a basis for the identification of best practices and major challenges and problems to be dealt with in e-participation, as well as to reach conclusions with regard to the application of e-participatory procedures at the EU level. The selected cases relate to different political and governmental levels (local, national, European), enable citizen involvement at different stages of political decision-making (agenda setting, decision-making and monitoring), and are possibly suitable for implementation and use at the EU level in order to counteract the deficit in European democratic processes. The case studies are based on desk research and 45 interviews with organisers and researchers of the respective e-participation processes. Detailed information about the selection of cases, the design of the case studies as well as the comparative analysis is given in the introduction to Part II of this volume.

Part III represents the concluding chapters of the book. The first chapter depicts the results of the systematic comparison of the case studies. The case studies are compared in a crisp-set Qualitative Comparative Analysis (QCA). Addressing the main research question, the comparison identifies those conditions under which digital tools can successfully facilitate different forms of citizen involvement in decision-making processes. Success means that the citizen involvement has led to either impact on decisions or impact on political or policy agendas. The most important factors for successful e-participation identified in the report are a close and clear link between e-participation processes and a concrete formal decision-making process and transparency about the intended contribution of the participatory processes' outputs to the overall decision-making process. Feedback to the participants about what has been done with their contributions is an indispensable feature of the process. Moreover, a participative process should not be limited to one event but should be embedded in an institutional 'culture of participation'. E-participation must be accompanied by an effective mobilisation and engagement strategy, involving communication instruments tailored for different target groups. To realise these conditions in practice requires serious investment (in terms of both time and costs) and the commitment of all actors involved: digital participation—as the comparison reveals—is not a quick fix.

The second concluding chapter in Part III discusses options for improving e-participation at the EU level. This analysis is based on the review of the state of research on the use of e-participation delivered in Part I of the book and on the results of the qualitative comparison of the case studies (Part II). Rather than an attempt at systematically presenting and evaluating all logically possible applications of the tools which were analysed in the case studies, the aim was to use the findings from the case studies to identify the 'low-hanging fruits', that is those changes or additions to EU-level participation mechanisms that might make a significant difference without demanding changes to existing mandates. In order to support this approach, a group of experts with EU-institutional and non-governmental stakeholder backgrounds were gathered for a day of co-creation, discussing ideas to improve existing participatory tools at the EU level and options for going beyond these tools, for example, by adopting some of the tools described in the case selection in this report. Among the options discussed with regard to improving and expanding the EU's e-participation practice are (1) to start experimenting with participatory budgeting in relation to the EU Regional and Social Funds, (2) to expand online engagement with MEPs beyond petitions, (3) to create a platform for monitoring member state actions during Council decisions, and (4) to explore the possibilities for crowdsourcing policy ideas for the European Commission. Beyond particular options for innovative approaches to e-participation at the EU level, it was found to be most urgent to overcome the obvious weaknesses regarding follow-up and learning efforts on the side of responsible organisers, in the interest of improving existing mechanisms and the development of new ones. The core question for a strategy of improving participation while staying within existing formal frameworks seems to be: What is the common unifying vision? As long as each of the existing mechanisms and experiments remain stand-alone mechanisms with discrete functions and implementation programs, e-participation will hardly become more transparent to the average citizen. The currently separate efforts of different institutions and services to open up European decision-making should begin to build on one another, rather than carving out separate corners of what might appear to citizens to be yet another bureaucratic universe. Working towards a coherent European e-participation infrastructure, including, for example, a one-stop shop for e-participation to provide synergy between the EU institutions, is regarded as the most urgent task.

References

Council of Europe. (2009). *Recommendation CM/Rec(2009)1 of the Committee of Ministers to Member States on electronic democracy (e-democracy)*. Accessed 06.02.2019, from http://www.coe.int/t/dgap/democracy/Activities/GGIS/CAHDE/2009/RecCM2009_1_and_Accomp_Docs/Recommendation%20CM_Rec_2009_1E_FINAL_PDF.pdf.

EC – European Commission. (2005). *The Commission's contribution to the period of reflection and beyond: Plan-D for Democracy, Dialogue and Debate*. Communication from the Commission to the Council, The European Parliament, the European Economic and Social Committee and the Committee of the Regions, COM (2005) 494 final, Brussels.

ESS – European Social Survey. (2014). *European Social Survey Round 7 Data*. Data file edition 2.2. NSD - Norwegian Centre for Research Data, Norway – Data Archive and distributor of ESS data for ESS ERIC. doi:https://doi.org/10.21338/NSD-ESS7-2014.

Kersting, N. (Ed.). (2012). *Electronic democracy*. Opladen, Berlin, Toronto: Barbara Budrich Publishers.

Lindner, R., Aichholzer, G., & Hennen, L. (Eds.). (2016a). *Electronic democracy in Europe. Prospects and challenges of e-publics, e-participation and e-voting*. Cham: Springer.

Lindner, R., Aichholzer, G., & Hennen, L. (2016b). Electronic democracy in Europe: An introduction. In R. Lindner, G. Aichholzer, & L. Hennen (Eds.), *Electronic democracy in Europe. Prospects and challenges of e-publics, e-participation and e-voting* (Vol. 2016, pp. 1–20). Cham: Springer.

Rheingold, H. (1993). *The virtual community: Homesteading on the electronic frontier*. Reading, MA: Addison-Wesley.

UN. (2016). *United Nations e-government survey 2016*. Accessed 06.02.2019, from http://workspace.unpan.org/sites/Internet/Documents/UNPAN97453.pdf

van Dijk, J. A. G. M. (2012). Digital democracy: Vision and reality. In I. Snellen, M. Thaens, & W. van de Donk (Eds.), *Public administration in the information age: Revisited* (pp. 49–61). Amsterdam: IOS-Press.

Open Access This chapter is licensed under the terms of the Creative Commons Attribution 4.0 International License (http://creativecommons.org/licenses/by/4.0/), which permits use, sharing, adaptation, distribution and reproduction in any medium or format, as long as you give appropriate credit to the original author(s) and the source, provide a link to the Creative Commons licence and indicate if changes were made.

The images or other third party material in this chapter are included in the chapter's Creative Commons licence, unless indicated otherwise in a credit line to the material. If material is not included in the chapter's Creative Commons licence and your intended use is not permitted by statutory regulation or exceeds the permitted use, you will need to obtain permission directly from the copyright holder.

Part I
The State of Scholarly Discussions

Chapter 2
E-Democracy: Conceptual Foundations and Recent Trends

Ralf Lindner and Georg Aichholzer

Abstract Lindner and Aichholzer provide an introductory overview of the theoretical and conceptual foundations of electronic democracy, thereby providing analytical insights on the interplay between Internet-based communication and democratic processes. To this end, different normative views, aims and approaches of e-democracy are presented and systematically related to the central tenets of the main models of democracy. As e-participation plays an essential role in most conceptions of e-democracy, a typology of Internet-based citizen involvement is developed, thereby structuring the diversity of e-participation practices. Given the growing relevance of Web 2.0 and social media, the chapter discusses to which degree they are able to support core democratic functions of public communication—namely public critique, legitimation, and integration—by exploring the effects of social media usage on the quality of deliberation, political activism and political behaviour. In view of phenomena such as "personalised politics", echo chambers and deliberate misinformation, the authors call for effective political, educational and regulatory responses to the democratic challenges social media increasingly pose.

2.1 Organisation and Theoretical Framework

This chapter provides an introductory overview of the basic concepts, which will be applied in the ensuing chapters of this volume. This includes a brief introduction of the key characteristics of liberal, participatory and deliberative democracy, with the aim of providing conceptual orientation regarding the different concepts of e-democracy that will be dealt with in greater detail in this book. A comprehensive account and discussion of the rich political and theoretical debates on democracy is

---

R. Lindner (✉)
Fraunhofer Institute for Systems and Innovation Research, Karlsruhe, Germany
e-mail: ralf.lindner@isi.fraunhofer.de

G. Aichholzer
Institute of Technology Assessment, Austrian Academy of Sciences, Vienna, Austria
e-mail: aich@oeaw.ac.at

neither feasible in the context of this analysis, nor would such an exercise advance our understanding of potentially fruitful e-democratic practices in Europe. The chapter continues with a conceptual examination of the democracy-related potential of new information and communication technologies (ICT) and explicates the various dimensions of e-democracy, before it turns to the anchoring of participatory democracy in European Union (EU)-level legal frameworks. We continue with an assessment of social media, which are increasingly receiving political and scholarly attention (Sect. 2.2). As the role of social media for e-democracy is currently the focus of both research and political debate, the relevance of social media for political communication is also dealt with briefly in the chapter on the European public sphere (Chap. 3) and is presented with regard to its potential for e-participation in the chapter on "digital tools" (Chap. 4). Apart from touching on specific aspects of social media, we deem it to be necessary to enter into the more general discussion on the expectations and the (assumed or observable) potential of social media to induce fundamental changes to political communication, which can be regarded as introducing new modes of the political or the public sphere. The chapter on conceptual foundations is closed by summarising the most relevant findings and conclusions.

It was a challenge to present the results of the literature review, covering the broad scope of articles and books and at the same time delivering a concise and concentrated text. For this purpose, we aimed to avoid lengthy introductions of basic concepts (e.g., the public sphere) as far as possible, as this has already been dealt with in Lindner et al. (2016b). We also tried to avoid repetition of discussions or controversies already expanded upon in this previous publication.

2.1.1 Introduction of Basic Concepts

Since the early days of the World Wide Web, the idea of using new media for political participation and democratic practices has been framed as novel, modern and highly innovative. While these claims seem justified with regard to the information and communication technologies, which enable Internet-based democratic processes, it is important to keep in mind that the different proposals for electronic democracy draw on—explicitly or implicitly—well-established concepts of democratic theory. In this sense, the normative views, aims and approaches represented by the different conceptualisations of e-democracy are based on, and can thus be traced back to, the fundamental tenets of democratic theory. As is the case with any normative conception of democracy, each variant of Internet-based democracy is driven and inspired by a specific understanding of an ideal-typical view of the political community and the political decision-making process. What are the main objectives of democracy? Depending on the normative position, the answers to this question will be quite different. Some views of democracy put their main emphasis on a high degree of representativeness, others promote the protection of fundamental rights and freedoms, while others strive for inclusive and comprehensive involvement of citizens (Schmidt 2008: 236f.). With the aim of clarifying these conceptual and normative relationships, the following will provide a brief overview of the main models of democracy.

If the discussion of procedural variants and details are set aside in favour of a higher-level of abstraction, the large number of different normative understandings of democracy can be related to the essence of three ideal-typical models of democracy: the liberal, the republican (or participatory) and the deliberative model (cf. Habermas 1992; Held 2006; Lembcke et al. 2012: 16–26; Schmidt 2008: 236–253; Schultze 2004: 125). These three models can be distinguished according to their diverging assumptions of human nature, the ascribed role of the individual in relation to society and citizenship, and the understanding of civil liberty. The following overview of the three main models is mainly based on Habermas (1992).

2.1.1.1 The Liberal Model of Democracy

Most democratic systems in the world are based on key elements of the liberal model. A chief characteristic of this model is its strong emphasis on procedures. Instead of attempting to realise a predefined form of society, this model concentrates on processes and institutions that ensure generally binding decision-making. By and large, the democratic process is conceptualised as a market-like competition between strategic actors, such as interest groups, political parties and elites. The citizen is conceptualised as a consumer whose political participation is more or less limited to the periodic expression of individual preferences. Processes of political will-formation, based on public debate and learning, do not receive heightened attention in this model. Thus, the political will of the democratic entity is understood as the result of the interplay of competing interests and the aggregation of individual voter preferences. In the liberal model, the status of the citizen and his/her private sphere are protected by a number of fundamental, defensive rights against arbitrary state intrusion.

2.1.1.2 The Republican or Participatory Model

Compared to the liberal model, the participatory model of democracy is highly demanding for its citizens. It requires a community which shares a broad set of common values and citizens who are able and willing to overcome the pursuit of individual interests in favour of an orientation towards the common good. The model's understanding of the political reaches far beyond mere procedures for collective decision-making. Instead, the political process is conceptualised as the central medium through which society is constituted and becomes aware of itself as a community. Here, the liberal model's scepticism towards political participation is replaced by the primacy of citizen involvement. Collective processes of will-formation between free and equal citizens are seen as a value in itself, and participation is understood as a holistic and integral feature of life. The state is assigned primarily with the function of guaranteeing processes of inclusive involvement and not so much the protection of individual rights.

2.1.1.3 The Deliberative Model of Democracy

The deliberative model is closely related to the participatory model but incorporates important elements of the liberal model. A specific and demanding understanding of the communication conditions under which processes of public will-formation are performed lies at the centre of this third ideal-typical model. It is a result of a critical analysis of both the liberal and the participatory models: While the first privileges individual autonomy in order to prevent the "tyranny of the majority", the second puts popular sovereignty on centre stage. Instead of pitching individual rights and popular sovereignty against one another, both aims receive equal weight in the deliberative model. The decisive integrative step is the establishment of sophisticated conditions for rational and fair public deliberation. Ideally, these conditions should include openness to all potential participants and points of view, reasoning and equal and free speech. In contrast to the participatory model, this procedural orientation does not require a far-reaching ex ante agreement on a certain form of society or other substantive sources of legitimacy, such as the nation or a founding myth. The questions of which norms should be constitutive for the community are referred to the processes of public deliberation. At the same time, the deliberative model incorporates constitutionalism and the guarantee of individual rights and freedoms. Thus, in the deliberative model, political power remains tied to the institutions of the constitutional state and its established procedures for decision-making. The idea of popular sovereignty is realised through rational deliberations in the public sphere and in the networks of civil society organisations, which exercise their communicative power to influence the political decision-making system. In Chap. 3, the role of the public sphere for the democratic process is outlined in greater detail.

In comparative terms, both the participatory and the deliberative models see participation as a value in itself. Or put differently, they place the main focus on the input side of democratic decision-making, sharing the hope of changing the political process through more, inclusive and better participation and deliberation, ultimately aiming to "democratize democracy" (Schmidt 2008: 236ff.). In contrast, the liberal model is preoccupied with the output dimension, aiming to achieve stability and efficient decision-making.

The main differences of these and related models can be mapped in a two-dimensional space, depicting the chief aim of the democratic process (efficiency vs. inclusiveness) and the preferred mode of decision-making (indirect/representative vs. direct/plebiscitary) (Fig. 2.1). The three main models of democracy can be located in this two-dimensional space according to their basic normative orientations. Other sub-variants of democracy, such as competitive, participative or libertarian democracy, and so on, can be grouped around the three models accordingly (Lindner et al. 2010: 12).

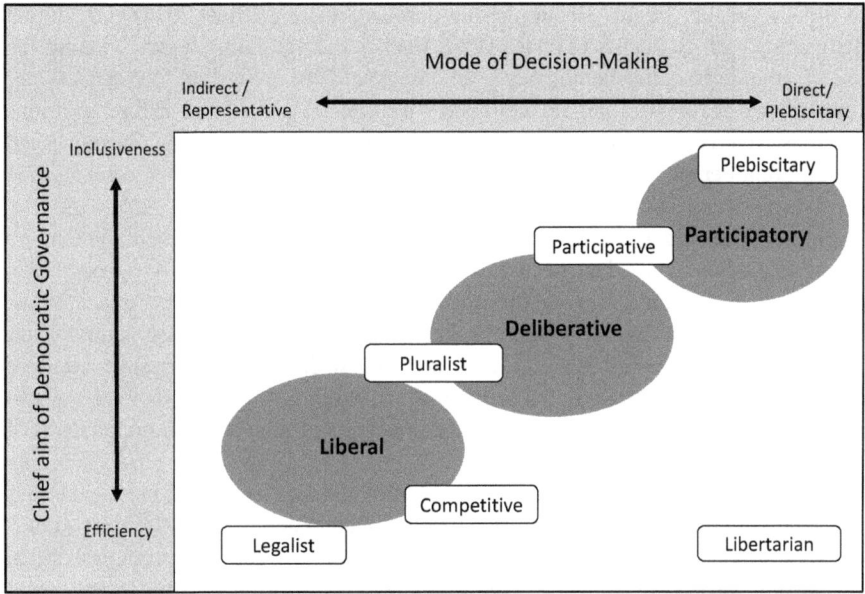

Fig. 2.1 Models of democracy: Aims and preferred mode of decision-making. Source: Based on Lindner (2007: 80) and van Dijk (2012: 51ff.)

The purpose of the two-dimensional space is to provide some basic orientation with regard to the different understandings of democracy in general and the Internet-based variants in particular:

> Arguably, preferences for a certain model of democracy will most likely determine the type of e-democracy a proponent seeks to establish. For instance, if a promoter of e-democracy belongs to the supporters of deliberative democracy, he or she will probably prefer a mix of representative and plebiscitary modes of online democratic decision-making and put special emphasis on Internet-based discussion fora, whereas members of the liberal camp are likely to favour forms of online participation that reflect the principles of representative democracy. Against this background, the disappointment about the e-democratic practices of governments which is frequently expressed by observers and promoters of e-democracy can be better understood and put into perspective. (Lindner et al. 2010: 14).

2.1.2 The Concept and Definition of e-Democracy

Since the early 1960s, futurists and scholars alike have heralded new ICT as carrying massive potential to transform existing practices of political communication and political systems (cf. McLuhan 1964). Over the years, reflections gave rise to a fast-extending interdisciplinary discourse and a continuously growing, meanwhile enormous body of literature dealing with a wide range of issues and implications of ICT for the political process in both theory and practice. Umbrella terms most often used to signify the subject are "electronic or e-democracy" (cf. Schaal 2016) and "digital democracy" (cf. Hague and Loader 1999; Hacker and van Dijk 2000a), whereas the use of the terms "teledemocracy" (cf. Becker 1981), "virtual democracy" or "cyberdemocracy" was largely confined to earlier stages of the debate. Various attempts have been made to structure the historical evolution of this discourse and the different perspectives (cf. Hagen 1997; Vedel 2006; Lindner 2007; Oblak Črnič 2012; Santos and Tonelli 2014).

However, despite the long history of these concepts and the ideas behind them, no common nomenclature has been developed to date, and generally agreed upon definitions are lacking. Among the numerous more or less different conceptions, one can discern definitions with a normative flavour as well as more neutral ones. And each of these definitions can be associated with one of the basic models of democracy outlined above. In the following, we will briefly review some of these to establish the basic concepts and outline the conceptual framework for our analysis of digital tools and systems.

A collection of contributions, which focus both on theoretical and practical issues involved with the relationship between new media and democracy, offers an authoritative starting point (Hacker and van Dijk 2000a). The editors introduce "digital democracy" as the key concept, providing a definition with normative ingredients:

> Digital democracy is the use of information and communication technology (ICT) and computer-mediated communication (CMC) in all kinds of media (e.g. the internet, interactive broadcasting and digital telephony) for purposes of enhancing political democracy or the participation of citizens in democratic communication. (Hacker and van Dijk 2000b: 1)

Just a few lines later they rephrase this conceptualisation in more neutral terms: "We define digital democracy as a *collection of attempts to practise democracy without the limits of time, space and other physical conditions, using ICT or CMC instead, as an addition, not a replacement for traditional 'analogue' political practices*."

In a more recent contribution, van Dijk (2012: 51) provides a more concise version of the earlier definition: "Digital democracy can be defined as the *pursuit and the practice of democracy in whatever view using digital media in online and offline political communication*. The online–offline distinction should be added because political activities are not only happening on the internet ..." (p. 51f.).

Both Hacker and van Dijk argue in favour of the term "digital democracy" as preferable to all other related concepts for various reasons. However, this does not mean that digital democracy will replace the use of traditional communication media and face-to-face communication. Empirically, various combinations of virtual and traditional media are currently the most commonly observed. Although they decline the term "electronic democracy" for being too general (since some old media of broadcasting or telephony were also electronic), other more recent conceptions suggest "electronic or e-democracy" as synonymous terms for "digital democracy". For example, Päivärinta and Øystein's (2006: 818) conception sounds very similar: "*E-democracy refers to the use of information and communication technology (ICT) in political debates and decision-making processes, complementing or contrasting traditional means of communications, such as face-to-face interaction or one-way mass media."*

Coleman and Norris (2005) also confirm the preference for "e-democracy" as the key concept. Having presented a range of definitions of e-democracy, they point out an essential commonality and opt for a wide, again normative, understanding of the notion: *"A common thread ... is the assumption that e-democracy has something to do with the use of information and communication technologies (ICT) to enhance democratic structures and processes"* (p. 6ff.) ... *"E-democracy is both top-down and bottom-up; it is both about the institutional processes of hierarchies and the more fluid arrangements of networks"* (p. 32).

In view of the different definitions and terminologies presented in the literature, we will use the terms "e-democracy" and "digital democracy" interchangeably as key concepts in our analysis of digital tools and systems for strengthening participatory and direct democracy.

A milestone among political frameworks on e-democracy is the Council of Europe's Recommendation of the Committee of Ministers to Member States on electronic democracy (e-democracy). Its core consists of 12 recommendations, including the following two basic ones: *"The Committee of Ministers, in accordance with Article 15.b of the Statute of the Council of Europe [...]. Recommends that Member States: 1. consider making use of the opportunities afforded by e-democracy to strengthen democracy, democratic institutions and democratic processes; 2. consider and implement e-democracy as the support and enhancement of democracy, democratic institutions and democratic processes by means of ICT, and linked to the engagement and re-engagement of citizens in democracy; [...]"* (Council of Europe 2009: 5, 7). The Appendix to Recommendation CM/Rec (2009)1 includes a long list of 80 "Principles of e-democracy" and 102 "Guidelines". To mention two fundamental principles: *When introducing or taking steps to improve electronic democracy, stakeholders should take account of the following principles of e-democracy:*

- *E-democracy, as the support and enhancement of democracy, democratic institutions and democratic processes by means of ICT, is above all about democracy. Its main objective is the electronic support of democracy.*
- *E-democracy is one of several strategies for supporting democracy, democratic institutions and democratic processes and spreading democratic values. It is additional, complementary to, and interlinked with traditional processes of democracy. Each process has its merits: none is universally applicable. ..."* *(Council of Europe* 2009*: 11).* Among the guidelines the document also points out different "sectors of e-democracy" (including further explications in later paragraphs): *"E-democracy encompasses, in particular, e-parliament, e-legislation, e-justice, e-mediation, e-environment, e-election, e-referendum, e-initiative, e-voting, e-consultation, e-petitioning, e-campaigning, e-polling and e-surveying; it makes use of e-participation, e-deliberation and e-forums* (Council of Europe 2009: 15).

Building on these contributions, we can briefly summarise our use of the two key concepts of e-democracy and e-participation as follows: We understand e-democracy as the practice of democracy with the support of digital media in political communication and participation. E-participation encompasses all forms of political participation, making use of digital media, including both formally institutionalised mechanisms and informal civic engagement.

2.1.3 Democracy-Related Potential of Information and Communication Technologies

Debates on e-democracy have essentially been nourished by various expectations about the potential of new ICT to substantially change the conditions of political communication and democratic practices. The numerous claims that have been made about effects of new ICT on democracy have been concisely summarised by Hacker and van Dijk (2000b: 4) as follows:

1. *ICT increases the scale and speed of providing information. This helps create more informed citizens;*
2. *Political participation is made easier and certain obstacles like apathy, shyness, disabilities, time, etc., can be lessened;*
3. *CMC creates new ways of organizing with subject-specific groups for discussion, cheap distribution costs, etc.;*
4. *The Net allows new political communities to arise free from state intervention;*
5. *A hierarchical political system becomes more horizontal by increasing political CMC;*
6. *Citizens will have more voice in creating agendas for government;*
7. *CMC will help remove distorting mediators like journalists, representatives and parties;*
8. *Politics will be able to respond more directly to citizen concerns as ICT and CMC enable a kind of political marketing research; and*
9. *ICT and CMC will help resolve problems of representative democracy such as territorial bases of constituencies, etc.*

However, the relationship between the use of new technologies and democratic politics is more complex and contested, since assessments of effects on democracy depend on the model of democracy they relate to. From early on, a polarity of perspectives can be observed in different shapes: Van Dijk (1999: 44ff.) contrasts views, which expect a strengthening of direct democracy and a rebirth of the Athenian agora with the views of defenders of representative democracy who fear the turn to a *push-button-democracy*. Others point to the dichotomy between expected improvements in the responsiveness of political institutions and the enhancement of direct citizen participation in public affairs versus fears of diminishing deliberation and an impoverishment of the political debate (Dutton 1999: 222). Van Dijk (2012: 50ff.) observes four waves of utopian visions:

1. The "teledemocracy" perspective in the 1980s, for example, Barber (1984), expecting increased equality in access to information, more active public participation and debate and stimulating electronic polling and voting.
2. "Virtual community" perspectives in the early 1990s, for example, Rheingold (1993) with hopes of regaining community experience lost in modernisation processes.
3. Visions of a "new democracy" around the turn of the century, expecting a broadening of participation in democratic processes through Internet-supported means.
4. Currently popular "Web 2.0" or social media perspectives, heralding an increase of citizen engagement in policymaking and democratic life in a great variety of new formats.

In contrast to these highly optimistic visions of new media effects, various dystopian perspectives, which depict potential risks to democracy, have been articulated (cf. van Dijk 2012: 50ff.): For example, rather pessimistic expectations with regard to direct democracy in view of the complexity of modern societies; digital tools would speed up deliberation to a superficial level; they would support populism, increase information inequality, and be incapable of countering a basic lack of political motivation among the citizenry; the Internet would even be more concentrated than traditional media and the ease of placing messages on the Internet would not be matched by similar options of being heard. Finally, a serious threat that has been gaining special attention in connection with dramatic events of political extremism in the recent past is the increased radicalisation and mobilisation potential of the Internet (von Behr et al. 2013). In addition to social media's role in generating "echo-chambers", hypothesised causal mechanisms for such effects include the lowering of transaction costs and promoting homophilous sorting, that is, allowing birds of a feather to flock together (cf. Farrell 2014). Such outcomes can be strengthened by a so-called "filter bubble" (Pariser 2011), created by search algorithms, which select results on the basis of information on prior search behaviour and exclude results which disagree with the user's preferences and viewpoints.

The various conceptions of democracy introduced above (Fig. 2.1) are further differentiated into six ideal-typical sub-models or variants with different views of the roles and implications of new media by van Dijk (2012: 51ff.):

1. *Legalist Democracy*: The classical Western-type procedural view of democracy as defined by the constitution and other basic laws. The role of new media is mainly to enhance information provision by appropriate measures and information retrieval by citizens.
2. *Competitive Democracy*: Parties and leaders competing for the electorate, focused on representation and efficient decision-making. The primary use of ICT is for information and election campaigns.

3. *Plebiscitary Democracy*: Puts forms of direct-democratic decision-making such as plebiscites and referenda centre stage. Here, ICT is pivotal for holding online polls, referenda and discussions.
4. *Pluralist Democracy*: Pluralism in political processes and discussion is seen as most important, combining practices of direct and representative democracy. There are plenty of options for support by ICT, especially for discussions and debates. *Deliberative democracy* shares much with the pluralist model and focuses still more on open and free exchange on political issues. The importance of digital media is especially seen in their functions for online discussions.
5. *Participative Democracy*: The focus is on promoting active citizenship, political opinion formation on a broad scale, based on the principle of combining direct and representative democracy. ICT is important for many functions, from public debates and education to all kinds of participation, access for all being a value.
6. *Libertarian Democracy*: Shares some views with the pluralist and plebiscitarian visions and focuses *on autonomous politics by citizens in their own associations* (p. 53). Digital media are especially relevant in their networking functions, among others even bypassing institutional politics with Web 2.0 applications and content generated and shared by citizens.

These models are mapped on the two-dimensional space of democratic processes and modes of decision-making provided in Fig. 2.1.

Today, the concept of e-democracy, at least in terms of online engagement of the public in political decision-making, draws mainly on the concepts of participatory democracy and deliberative democracy. Advocates of participatory democracy emphasise the intrinsic value of political participation and its contribution to the social integration of liberal societies. In contemporary liberal democracies, however, political participation is primarily realised in the form of parliamentary and representative democratic systems, in which formal participation of the demos is largely concentrated on casting votes in elections. As outlined above, from the perspective of liberal democratic theory, the instrumental functions of political participation—legitimate selection of representatives, legitimate distribution and limitation of political power, and efficient decision-making—are in the foreground. The relation between citizen participation and democratic legitimacy must also be seen in the light of Scharpf's (1999) distinction between input and output legitimacy: the former depends on mechanisms linking decisions in the political system to the citizens' will, the latter on policy outcomes, which effectively achieve the goals of a common concern.

Since the mid-1990s, and reinforced with the advent of Web 2.0, libertarianism and a normative individualism, based on the ideal of voluntaristic individual action, have become more and more influential. In the current debate on e-democracy, two concepts have gained increasing importance: "*wikidemocracy*" and "*liquid democracy*" (cf. Schaal 2016). Noveck (2009), who has elaborated on wikidemocracy in depth, uses the terms "collaborative democracy" and "wikigovernment" largely synonymously to refer to this concept. Digital media play a crucial role in these models, since they stand for new, highly decentralised modes and procedures of decision-making, which have only become possible on a large scale through the Internet. Wikidemocracy as well as liquid democracy are normatively based on the vision of a voluntarist, network-type collaboration of peers, in which the co-creation of ideas and content is a guiding ideal. The idea of decentralised "peer networks" as the cornerstone of a new political worldview, named "peer progressivism", has been elaborated and propagated to become a new social movement by Steven Johnson (2012).

Views of *wikidemocracy* imagine citizens as individuals engaged in multiple networks, either from a communitarian perspective as new forms of community-building, or in a liberal-libertarian version with a focus on decentralised organisation mediated by ever increasing capacities of information processing. In the latter view, participation is primarily seen as being of instrumental value, autonomy-enhancing and bringing about better collective decisions. According to Schaal (2016: 287), the innovative contribution of *wikigovernment,* as coined by Noveck (2009), is to democratise the throughput sphere of policymaking in liberal-representative democracies, for example, in the specification of laws and decrees, supported by the Internet and "civic software", such as wikis. The idea is to raise the epistemic quality of decisions by using the "wisdom of crowds". However, two critical points include the violation of the principle of political equality because of the involved issue-dependent restriction of participants, and unresolved issues of privacy and data protection (Schaal 2016: 294 f.).

Liquid democracy has received some public attention, especially in Germany (Adler 2018), propagated as a software-based model of internal opinion formation by the Pirate Party (see Chap. 9). The concept of liquid democracy, however, has potential beyond party politics as an innovative model of democratic decision-making, which bridges direct and representative democracy by rendering the boundary between representation and direct democratic input more "liquid". Rooted in the theory of delegated voting, this model only became realisable with the emergence of Web 2.0 technologies and is based on the principle of delegating one's voice to other people of trust. In contrast to classical representation, this form is conditional, plural, limited by issue or time and reversible. In all political decisions, every citizen can decide between direct use of his/her voice or delegation (Schaal 2016: 292). Proponents of this model regard it as an adequate response to two problems: to use competent delegates to improve decision quality, and to counter political alienation by a relationship of trust. Criticisms brought forward against the liquid democracy model include insufficient theoretical elaboration, the tension between demands of aggregative and deliberative democracy, and the lack of viable suggestions for its institutionalisation.

2.1.4 Dimensions of e-Democracy

E-democracy, as defined above, represents a wide variety of uses of ICT in support of democratic communication, and includes all levels and modes of involvement of the public (individual citizens, informal groups and civil society organisations). The scope reaches from more passive modes of involvement, such as social media or online monitoring for purposes of informing oneself about developments in society, making processes of decision-making and underlying documents accessible and transparent, to more active and cooperative modes, such as involving citizens in decision-making by providing for online voting procedures as well as online spaces for public consultation, debate on salient political issues and co-writing of political documents.

Various attempts have been made to bring some structure into the diverse forms and functions of ICT use in democratic practice.

For example, van Dijk (2012: 54 f.) provides a table listing 13 categories of *eParticipation* across five stages of the policy cycle (however, this includes two categories of *eGovernment services* because his concept of *eParticipation* goes beyond e-democracy and extends to the relationship of citizens with public administrations). Santos and Tonelli (2014: 6) suggested another set of concepts for describing e-democracy, adding a number of *sectors*, such as *e-legislation*, *e-parliament* or *e-polling*, which can be regarded as subcategories. Hoff and Scheele (2014) provide a theoretical framework that can be used to analyse all types of political and administrative web applications and demonstrate its potential with an analysis of e-democracy at the local level in Denmark.

Speaking of electronic or in short "e-participation", we prefer an understanding of Internet-based political participation in the wider sense, including both formally institutionalised mechanisms and informal civic engagement. An elaborate conceptual and empirical analysis by Gibson and Cantijoch underlines the multidimensional nature of e-participation. *(O)ffline types of political engagement are re-emerging online* (Gibson and Cantijoch 2013: 714), which tend to include more and more social-media based political activities (e.g. posting to political blogs), and also lead to novel forms of engagement such as combined offline and online participation.

Lindner et al. (2016a) distinguished three overarching dimensions of e-democracy by separating issues of the electronic public sphere (in brief: e-public) from issues of electronic participation (e-participation) in its manifold forms, and electronic voting (e-voting) as a category sui generis. The e-participation landscape was structured by level of participation (information, communication and collaboration), relevance across the policy cycle (problem definition, agenda setting, decision-making and policy formulation, policy implementation, policy evaluation), and top-down organisation (government-centric) versus bottom-up (citizen-centric). Top-down forms are initiated, organised, implemented or sponsored by governments, whereas bottom-up types of e-participation are activities initiated or carried out by citizens and civil society actors (Aichholzer and Strauß 2016: 59–62). Related concepts in use are the distinction between *invited* versus *uninvited* participation (cf. Wehling 2012). Kersting uses two similar concepts, "invented" and "invited space", and offers a useful model integrating a variety of online and offline participation formats divided into four different political spheres: participation in representative democracy,

Table 2.1 Functions, types and tools of e-participation

Function of Citizen Involvement	Type of E-participation	Tools
Monitoring	• E-information • E-deliberation • E-complaints	• Tools for monitoring, questioning and advising political representatives
Agenda setting	• E-petitions • E-initiatives • E-campaigning	• Citizen initiatives • E-petition
Decision-making	• E-consultations • E-participatory budgeting • E-voting	• Crowdsourcing for law proposals • Crowdsourcing for policymaking • Internet consultation, collaborative decision-making within political parties • Consultative participatory budgeting • Participatory budgeting • E-voting

participation in direct democracy, deliberative participation and demonstrative participation (Kersting 2013: 272 f.).

For the purposes of structuring the diversity of e-participation practices, we suggest a simple threefold structure of major digital tools used in different types of participation, serving different functions of citizen involvement, as displayed in Table 2.1.

This conceptualisation of the dimensions of e-democracy was applied to guide the literature review as well as the selection of good practice cases for the case studies. The different types of e-participation have been categorised according to their most typical function in citizen involvement but can also play a role for a different function.

2.1.5 Participatory Democracy in European Union Legal Frameworks

Long-term trends of a transformation of political participation, together with a persistent distance and mistrust of EU citizens towards EU institutions, have called for suitable counterstrategies. Starting more than a decade ago, important steps have been taken in order to better connect European institutions and representatives with the European citizenry and civil society (Lindner et al. 2016b: 7–9). Various reforms claiming to open European governance to civil society and improve opportunities for participation at EU level have since been initiated. An early document of this strategic turn, the White Paper on European Governance, succinctly summarises the goal:

> Democratic institutions and the representatives of the people, at both national and European levels, can and must try to connect Europe with its citizens. This is the starting condition for more effective and relevant policies. (...) The White Paper proposes opening up the policy-

making process to get more people and organisations involved in shaping and delivering EU policy. It promotes greater openness, accountability and responsibility for all those involved. (EC 2001: 3).

The Treaty of Lisbon has put special emphasis on strengthening democratic elements in the EU. It has, among other things, introduced the European Citizens' Initiative (ECI) as an EU-wide instrument of participatory democracy with the potential to stimulate public debate on European issues and to involve European citizens and organised civil society in policymaking at the EU level. As a key element within the architecture of participatory democracy, it complements the general commitment to representative democracy in the institutions of the EU. Table 2.2 presents a summary of the Treaty's formal provisions for direct participation in the democratic life of the EU.

In addition to the ECI, which occupies a central position, the main features of the EU's provisions for participatory democracy are enshrined in explicit citizens' rights for direct participation, in petition rights for every citizen, as well as in the obligations of EU institutions to provide for horizontal and vertical civil dialogues and consultation procedures.

Table 2.2 A holistic view of participatory democracy elements enshrined in EU norms

Art 10.3 TEU/Art 15 TFEU "Citizen Centered Democracy" Every citizen shall have the right to participate in the democratic life of the Union. Decisions shall be taken as openly and as closely as possible to the citizens.	Art 11.1 TEU "Horizontal Civil Dialogue" The institutions shall, by appropriate means, give citizens and representative associations the opportunity to make known and publicly exchange their views in all areas of Union action.	Art 11.2 TEU/Art 16 TFEU "Vertical Civil Dialogue" The institutions shall maintain an open, transparent and regular dialogue with representative associations and civil society.
Art 11.3 TEU "Consultation Procedure" The European Commission shall carry out broad consultations with parties concerned in order to ensure that the Union's actions are coherent and transparent.	Art 11.4 TEU "European Citizens' Initiative" (...) one million (...) of (7) Member States may take the initiative of inviting the EC, within the framework of its powers, to submit (...) where citizens consider (...) to implement treaties.	Art 17.1 TFEU "Spiritual Dialogue Partners" The Union respects and does not prejudice the status (...) of churches and religious associations or communities in the Member States.
Art. 17.2 TFEU "Secular Dialogue Partners" The Union equally respects the status under national law of philosophical and non-confessional organisations.	Art. 17.3 TFEU "Dialogue of Values" Recognising their identity and (...) contribution, the Union shall maintain an open, transparent and regular dialogue with these churches and organisations.	Art 24 TFEU/Art. 44 ChFR "Petition Right" Every citizen shall have the right to petition the European Parliament (...). Every Citizen shall have the right to apply to the Ombudsman (...).

TEU consolidated version of the Treaty on European Union, *TFEU* consolidated version of the Treaty on the Functioning of the European Union, *ChFR* EU Charter of Fundamental Rights
Source: Pichler (2011: 22)

The role of public participation and citizen engagement in EU governance has clearly grown in importance over the past decade. Major steps were the introduction of participatory democracy as a principle into the Constitutional Treaty, signed in Rome in December 2004, and of the relevant Article on the European Citizens' Initiative—although without its original heading of "Participatory Democracy"—into the Lisbon Treaty; an upswing of "civil society" consultations, increasingly via the Internet, through a so-called *transparent consultation mechanism* by European institutions; the EC's launch of a "Plan D for democracy, dialogue and debate" in 2005 aiming to *go local, listen to and engage with citizens*; a White Paper on the European Communication Policy with a similar mission; two large-scale meetings for exchange between civil society organisations and MEPs in the European Parliament in 2007 and 2009 ("European Agora"); the launch of a Green Paper on the European Transparency Initiative; and a proposal for a Directive on the European Citizens' Initiative (cf. Saurugger 2010; EC 2010). In 2011, the European Parliament held Citizens' Agora processes on "The Economic and Financial Crisis and New Forms of Poverty" and, in November 2013, a "Citizens' Agora on Youth Unemployment". This noteworthy upgrade of participatory elements represents a major shift in the governance regime of the European Union.

According to Saurugger (2010), a *participatory turn* emerged in the official discourse at EU level during the 1990s and was gradually transformed into a norm in basic documents and into governance reform programmes. However, the actual quality and scope of the postulated *participatory turn* is still contested and is ambiguous in its implementation. It is questionable whether the turn has effectively taken place to the same extent in practice as in rhetoric (Kohler-Koch and Quittkat 2013; Lindner et al. 2016b). Nevertheless, the participative democracy discourse has also found some manifestations in the Member States, as traditional governance regimes have been questioned and participatory elements have received more attention there. The upgrading of participation at both EU and national levels has not only been a reaction to perceived "democratic deficits" and a widening cleavage between citizens and EU institutions. There is also a growing demand for the knowledge and expertise required to cope with increasing problem complexity in the multilevel governance of advanced societies. This change encourages citizen participation because of the benefits of inputs, which are functional for enhanced problem-solving and the quality of decisions. Some commentators argue that participation has even become both a moralising discourse, expecting responsible citizens to actively contribute to problem-solving, and a normative discourse, treating participation as a means to cure the alienation between governments and the governed (Smith and Dalakiouridou 2009: 3; Jessop 2003). The thriving availability of new electronic means is certainly reinforcing the upswing of the participation discourse and to some extent also participation practice at the EU level.

2.2 Web 2.0 and Social Media: Threats and Promises for Democratic Discourse

2.2.1 Introduction

The debate about the democratic or political effects of new Internet-based modes of communication has always been characterised by a polarisation between far-reaching positive and optimistic expectations on the one side, and pessimistic expectations of detrimental effects on democratic structures and processes on the other. This discursive feature also applies to discussions around the most recent format of Internet communication, which is the use of social media by all kinds of political actors. Particularly in view of the campaign dynamics in a number of recent elections and referenda, most notably the 2016 referendum on UK's membership of the European Union and the US presidential elections of 2016 (Schill and Hendricks 2018), social media are currently receiving additional political and scholarly attention.

The focus of this section is the relationship between the use of social media, political communication and democratic politics in general. In accordance with the identified literature, special emphasis will be directed towards citizen participation, the role of interest groups, social movements, politicians/parliamentarians and potentially damaging effects for discourse and democratic institutions. The relevance of social media will also be briefly touched upon from a specific perspective in the following chapter on the European public sphere (Chap. 3) and in the chapter dedicated to a differentiated exploration of the scope of "tools" available for e-participation activities (Chap. 4).

The question of social media's impact on and relevance for political communication and democracy is triggered by a number of phenomena: Firstly, social media are the newest wave of socio-technical innovation in the field of Internet-based communication, making available new and different kinds of opportunities for users to interact online (Boulianne 2015: 524). Secondly, social media and social networking sites attract extremely high user numbers. The social networking site Facebook has over 1 billion users worldwide. Youtube, Facebook, Wikipedia, Twitter and Instagram are among the most popular platforms in the world (Alexa 2019). And thirdly, numerous political events involving social media have heightened interest in the interplay of politics and the use of social media for political purposes (Gibson 2014: 2; Sandoval-Almazan and Gil-Garcia 2014: 365). With regard to political upheavals, protest movements and campaigns, such as the anti-government Zapatistas in Mexico, the anti-capitalist "Battle in Seattle", the "outraged" protests in Spain, or the Arab Spring, many observers have concluded that social media were an important, if not even decisive, factor for the political efficacy of these movements (della Porta et al. 2006; Khamis 2011; Khondker 2011; González-Bailón et al. 2013; Herrera 2014). On the other side of the coin, the same social media increasingly seem to be gateways for and platforms of authoritarian, anti-democratic tendencies, manipulation and surveillance (Fuchs 2018;

Schill and Hendricks 2018; Carty 2015; Bradshaw and Howard 2017; Postill 2018; Wardle and Derakhsan 2017).

As with previous media innovations, the rise of social media quickly spurred hopes for democratic renewal. Particularly, the open and collaborative features of many Web 2.0 applications prompted debates about the new media's transformative and democratic potential (Loader and Mercea 2011: 757). As would be expected, the initial discussions about social media's impact on democratic politics fell into opposing camps of enthusiasts and pessimists (Price 2013; Margetts 2019), echoing the basic patterns of utopian and dystopian expectations about the role of the Internet in the 1990s and early 2000s (Lindner 2007; Lindner et al. 2016a). At this point however, there seems to be considerably more disagreement about the role of social media in the political sphere than in most areas in the field of Internet research. Both theoretical and conceptual contributions, as well as empirical investigations, often deliver contradictory claims and lines of reasoning, making it particularly difficult to identify a common ground of understanding in the field. Both pessimistic and optimistic accounts find support (Skoric et al. 2016: 1818). One reason for this deep disagreement within the academic literature might be that the discussions about the role of social media in democratic politics are facing higher levels of complexity compared to the debates of the 1990s. Since then, the media landscapes have become far more developed, and the new media today are both highly entangled with traditional mass media, and deeply embedded in daily practices, increasing the difficulties for analysts to capture their impact (Dahlgren 2013: 1).

In fact, social media have strongly transformed the way people use the Internet, taking advantage of new possibilities to connect, interact and exchange information (Price 2013: 520). In comparison, social media allow for the undemanding, fast establishment and maintenance of online social networks and personal ties. The structural characteristics of the new Internet ecology (Skoric et al. 2016: 1818) enable forms of decentralised production and co-creation of content, ideas, discussions and novel forms of online network organisations (Bennett 2008; Reichert 2013). From the perspective of information exchange and political discourse, the importance of quasi-personal ties between peers, which are a key characteristic of social media, have important implications for the acceptance of information exchanges: Information and news received from someone a user knows is more likely to be accepted, believed and trusted than information from other sources (Carty 2015). While the removal of traditional gatekeepers can have empowering effects for citizens, especially for underrepresented groups, information and discursive contributions from social media peers can also be manipulated. Bradshaw and Howard (2017) show how governments and government-sponsored groups worldwide are engaged in actively influencing information exchange and debates in social media by applying a broad range of methods, ranging from content generation, establishment of fake user accounts to forms of computational propaganda. In the following, the key debates on the role of social media in political communication and democratic politics, as represented in the relevant academic literature, will be summarised. After providing an overview of the main theoretical and conceptual lines of reasoning, the research findings related to social media's impact on political engagement will be presented.

2.2.2 Key Tenets of the Debate About Social Media's Role in Political Communication

To a large extent, the interest in social media and their potential impact on political communication and democracy has to be understood in the context of the broader discussions about liberal democracy and what many would label as a crisis. The challenges faced by contemporary democracies include declining civic and political engagement, declining party loyalty and low turnout rates, growing cynicism, a sense of decreasing political efficacy, and a seemingly rising attractiveness of anti-liberal and anti-democratic tendencies. At the same time, new, alternative forms of political engagement outside the formal representative institutions—sometimes labelled as *counter publics* or *alternative politics*—seem to be thriving (Carty 2015; Herrera 2014; Margetts et al. 2015; Imhof et al. 2015; Lindner et al. 2016b; Voss 2014; Grofman et al. 2014; Macková 2014).

Against this background, many argue that social media have the potential to cure democratic ills, revive citizens' involvement in politics or even contribute to new forms of democratic organisation. These accounts are primarily based on specific features and characteristics of social media. Most importantly, social media are credited with the ability to foster horizontal communication, making it easier to connect individuals and groups online, support diversity and provide spaces for opinion formation beyond and independent from established institutions (Dahlgren 2013; Imhof 2015). Loader and Mercea (2011: 762) identified further impacts of social media on political communication and democratic politics. These include the power of collaboration and sharing, as demonstrated, for instance, by Wikileaks, or the increasingly blurred divisions between mainstream news media and social media as the large media corporations rely more and more on political blogs and other forms of user-generated content (also Imhof 2015: 16; Jenkins 2006).

Inspired by the technical opportunities offered by social media, some authors view the new virtual spaces as media for creative, playful identity constructions and self-constitution. With regard to the political sphere, these accounts are closely related to characterisations of social media as spaces which facilitate dialogue and democratic participation (e.g. Benkler 2006; Bruns 2008). Imhof (2015: 16) diagnosed a broadly accepted expectation among many authors that social media will realise a global democratic participatory culture. Others, however, counter that the availability of these communicative capacities will not automatically change patterns of political engagement. Political participation is the result of the complex interplay of different factors, of which access to digital media may be only one (Dahlgren 2013; Vowe 2014). What is more, empirically, activities related to politics are extremely rare compared to dominant activities aimed at sociality, entertainment and consumption. In addition, more and more empirical evidence is emerging to show the detrimental effects of social media use on democratic processes. These include charges of social media's role in increasingly polluting the information ecosystem with fake news, hate speech and aggressive propaganda, and accusations of creating filter bubbles (Pariser 2011) and echo chambers that threaten constructive public deliberation (Margetts 2019) and facilitate forms of anti-democratic populism and authoritarianism (Postill 2018; Fuchs 2018).

This brief overview touched upon different contentious areas of debate in the literature. In the following, two of these themes will be presented in greater detail.

2.2.3 Redefining the Political Towards Personalised Politics?

While few dispute that the characteristics of online communities and discursive spaces facilitated by social media differ significantly from the types of communicative exchanges constituting the public sphere (at least in its ideal-typical, theoretical guises, see Chap. 3), the literature debates the question of established understandings of what constitutes "the political", and the public sphere needs to be redefined in view of the phenomena to be observed in social media contexts.

A number of researchers argue that the traditional definition of the political needs to be broadened to include more than rational debate (understood as the contrary to affect and sentiment) (Caldon 2016: 2133). In view of the new forms of mediatised discourses and emergent types of affiliation in social media, some propose integrating non-rational dimensions in contemporary understandings of the political. In her book *Affective Publics*, Papacharissi (2015) argues that the dominating conception of the political is outdated. It should be developed further with the aim of taking into account affective dimensions, such as personal emotions, feelings, storytelling and the like, which are increasingly becoming relevant in political discourse. Beyer (2014) shares this basic view and argues that our understanding of the political in virtual spaces is being transformed due to the ubiquity of digital media in daily life. As the boundaries between online and offline, public and private, become progressively blurred, she argues that anonymous, fragmented and often unfocused online associations in social media can potentially influence the political sphere. Banaji and Buckingham (2013) also attempt to contribute to a redefinition of the political and the concept of citizenship. Similarly to Papacharissi, they view features of popular culture, which are currently not part of traditional political discourse, such as emotions and pleasure, as possible elements of new forms of *cultural citizenship* (Banaji and Buckingham 2013: 5). In this regard, Dahlgren (2013: 2) is more prosaic, but follows similar lines of reasoning when he states that the constituency of politics has become more complex given the many new representations it can take, including personal, single issue, lifestyle, cultural, identity politics and so on.

Taken together, this discussion suggests a critical revision or even replacement of the established model of the public sphere (Loader and Mercea 2011: 758). Instead, conceptions of a networked citizen-centred model, which provides the opportunity to connect private spheres of autonomous identity to a multitude of deliberately chosen political spaces are receiving some attention (Papacharissi 2010; Loader and Mercea 2011: 758). This would entail a departure from ideas of rational deliberation and its understanding of the republican citizen, refocusing on the "*[...] citizen-user as the driver of democratic innovation through the self-actualized networking of citizens engaged in lifestyle and identity politics*" (Loader and Mercea 2011: 758).

Of course, these predominantly theoretical reflections cannot yet deliver answers to the question if and to what extent the claims about the emergence of this type of "personalised politics" is becoming manifest. But the discussion does prompt research to be analytically open to the emerging models of political communication that reach beyond rational deliberative exchanges. These new playful repertoires of using social media could in some ways be regarded as facets of the political. Regardless of its viability, the dangers associated with this deterioration of rational debate, ranging from eroding the capabilities of users to scrutinise the validity of information, solipsistic echo chambers, negative campaigning, populist and authoritarian rhetoric, to extremism and celebrity politics (Loader and Mercea 2011: 761; Gil de Zúñiga et al. 2009), are increasingly becoming manifest in contemporary politics.

2.2.4 Social Media and Their Potential Impacts on Political Participation

In the following, the qualitative effects of the broadened repertoire of communicative actions made available through social media will be discussed with regard to different aspects of political participation. As is well known, a fundamental prerequisite for any form of active political involvement is the access to and reception of politically relevant information. Social media are said to have a high potential to change both the traditional patterns of information flows as well as their production. The current research landscape in this field is highly specialised and, on the whole, tends to be rather inconclusive at this point.

With the advent of social media, the number of discursive online spaces has expanded significantly. While this observation is not disputed in the literature reviewed, the characteristics, meaning and effects of these ever-expanding virtual spaces on political communication are highly controversial (Caldon 2016: 2133). Do these discursive spaces, often labelled as micro- or counter publics, spill over into the real world of politics? While some studies show the emergence of counter publics under certain conditions (e.g. Leung and Lee 2014), the effects for the public sphere are increasingly being discussed (Tripodi 2018; Momeni 2017). Some authors question the political relevance of the communities occupying the social networking sites. Imhof (2015: 18f.) differentiates between predominantly group-oriented, self-referential communication in social media contexts and the principally impersonal communication, which constitutes the public sphere. The online communities are constituted by the reproduction of emotional ties, in-group and out-group differentiation and shared norms (Gebhardt 2010: 327ff.). As the communication patterns observed are predisposed towards the reproduction of shared life-views and moral beliefs, online communities tend to become homogenous. These processes of social closure can be reinforced by the effects of search engines and the like-algorithms of Facebook, which are based on previous online activities, offering users systematically more of the same (Andrejevic 2011; Gerlitz 2011; Hong and Nadler 2015: 104). From this perspective, communication patterns in social media are currently far from establishing a worldwide participatory culture (Imhof 2015: 18).

2.2.4.1 Social Media and Political Communication

Price (2013: 522) notes that, at least in theory, social media provide many additional opportunities to contribute to a better-informed public, thereby increasing the diversity of sources and views. However, Chen (2013) observes that relevant information, which actually triggers political activity is most often provided by existing, well-established groups and organisations. Some literature suggests that through social media sites such as Facebook, users are exposed incidentally to news that they are not actively seeking out. This might have mobilising effects, also because this type of news has been filtered through the users' personal online community networks (Bode 2012; deSilver 2014). Other strands of literature focus on social media's effects on social networks and how this might impact the news exposure of the users (Gil de Zúñiga et al. 2012; Tang and Lee 2013). Some findings in this literature suggest that social media enlarges the social networks of individuals, and this might increase the likelihood of exposure to politically relevant, mobilising information (Boulianne 2015: 525). Others view the role of ties to political or activist organisations as decisive. Findings suggest that people who belong to more organisations are also more likely to engage in political or civic activities (Bode et al. 2014; Tang and Lee 2013). And yet another strand of research emphasises the influential role of peer views within the online network on one's own activities (Vitak et al. 2011).

2.2.4.2 Social Media and the Quality of Deliberation

In addition to the—currently unresolved—question of if and how social media impact mobilisation and participation in terms of quantity, the literature also reflects on the quality of the communicative exchanges in these online environments. On the whole, the literature reviewed tends to share critical perspectives.

Primarily drawing on the work of Gil de Zúñiga et al. (2012), Thimm and Berlinke (2007), Zimmermann (2006), Gerhards and Schäfer (2007) and Imhof (2015: 17) critically question many of the high expectations associated with deliberation in social media contexts. Kies (2010) analyses a large variety of online political forums applying a discourse quality index with a number of deliberative criteria and draws more differentiated conclusions. However, using an adapted version of this index (Kersting 2005) for a comparison of deliberation quality in web forums in 2003 and 2012, Kersting (2017) underlined existing problems with deliberation: the majority being characterised by monologues instead of dialogues, lacking reflexive deliberation and mutual respect of discussion partners, and even showing a decrease of discourse quality over time. Empirical research has shown that political blogs tend to be strongly opinion-based, are weak with regard to the representation of facts and often offer radical positions. This is supported, for instance, by Chen's empirical research (2013: 113ff.), which observes forms of anti-social communication and points to examples of racist, sexist, hate-filled and uncivil communication. With a focus on the quality of dialogue on Twitter, Jericho (2012: 234) drew rather sceptical conclusions about this microblogging platform as a forum of debate. He observes that political tweets are dominated by *twitspits* where political opponents engage in political confrontation but not in real dialogue. Similar findings are reported in Loader and Mercea (2012: 125).

Contrary to many expectations about the potential to infuse more diversity into public debates, political blogs tend to overwhelmingly respond to topics and stories presented by mainstream news media. Along this line of reasoning, some authors also observe the shrinking of the blogosphere, thereby further reducing the potential for more diversity of views, perspectives and opinions. This process is said to be caused by two developments. Since the early 2000s, blogs have been progressively sucked into the so-called "Walled Gardens" (e.g. Paterson 2012) such as Facebook. And particularly political blogs run by ambitious lay journalists are increasingly being linked to and cooperate with large media corporations as part of their social media strategies, creating structures of co-dependency (Davis 2012: 77; Imhof 2015: 16f.). Other authors (Fox and Ramos 2012: 39; Wardle and Derakhsan 2017) contend that the broad range of opportunities to retrieve information through the Internet, and particularly social media, has encouraged content providers to increasingly target information to different, politically narrow audiences, thereby increasing the likelihood of spreading misinformation. However, Redden (2011: 70) argues that the new news sources do counter and challenge much of mainstream media coverage.

2.2.4.3 Political Activism and Social Media

Given the decline in traditional political participation in political parties and established interest groups such as labour unions, social media have often been seen to have the potential to facilitate alternative routes for participation due to their specific characteristics, such as low entry barriers and low costs. In fact, Chen (2013: 137ff.) observes that online-based social movements present online activism to their potential members as an alternative to traditional party membership and forms of political participation. However, these online-based forms of political participation are being debated with regard to their political impact. The literature is sceptical about forms of online activism that do not reach beyond the comfortable media-centred mode of political engagement where political commitment remains largely effortless (Dahlgren 2013: 4). Others also question the depth of *"slacktivism"* or *"clicktivism"*, defined as a *"disconnect between social media's expressive politics and ... the shallowness of these users' political interests and commitments"* (Chen 2013: 77).

2.2.4.4 Political Consumerism

A variant of political participation, which has received increasing attention, is political consumerism (e.g. Baringhorst et al. 2007; Stolle and Micheletti 2013). Gil de Zúñiga et al. (2013) attempt to address the question whether people using social media are more likely to engage in political consumerism compared to those who are not active on social networking sites. While this expectation is by and large supported by the data analysed, the authors raise the interesting question of whether political consumerism is actually political. Given the characteristics of political consumerism as a form of lifestyle politics, Gil de Zúñiga et al. propose to label this type of civic engagement *civic consumerism* (2013: 13). In this view, the characteristics of political consumerism as a lifestyle choice and a form of civic action, which is subject to sharing and peer commentary, might explain the positive relationship between social media use and conscious, ethically motivated consumption.

2.2.4.5 Social Media and Elected Representatives

Social media provide the opportunity for individual politicians and parliamentarians to engage in exchange and dialogue directly with citizens. Being independent from the gate-keeping powers of traditional media, politicians can send their views to anyone who is interested in receiving the messages, and recipients have the choice to respond and comment (Ross and Bürger 2014: 46). A number of studies have examined the social media use of parliamentarians and political parties, leading to rather sobering findings. Jackson and Lilleker (2009) show that most political parties refrain from taking advantage of the interactive features of social media, primarily initiating unidirectional information flows. Other research identifies a tendency on the side of party organisations to keep communication activity under control (Pedersen 2005). With regard to parliamentarians, the analyses of Ross and Bürger (2014) and Williamson (2009) show that most politicians use digital media as a means for information distribution rather than an opportunity to genuinely engage with constituents.

2.2.4.6 Effects on Political Opinion and Behaviour: Inconclusive Results

Much research is conducted on the impact of social media on political opinions and behaviours of citizens. Dahlgren (2013) attempts to understand the role of social media within social contexts, in order to identify what true democratic potential they hold. He warns that weaknesses in democratic systems cannot be solved through social media or media technologies alone, but that this is a job which must lie with citizens. Dahlgren summarises the often-mentioned positive aspects and the hopes for social media as follows: an increase of communication between citizens, cost-effectiveness, room for creative participation, opinion formation, mobilisation and the potential to place a spotlight on political issues, for example, through "going viral", and personal gains such as empowerment. A special emphasis is placed on the value of social media for alternative politics. On the other hand, there are concerns such as the digital divide, the fact that political engagement does not follow purely from Internet and social media access, cyberbullying and harassment, and of course the fear of social media being abused for political surveillance and control, and for deliberate attempts to spread misinformation (Bradshaw and Howard 2017). Dahlgren goes on to remind us that *"political participation is more than merely media access or communicative interaction; these are often necessary, but never sufficient for genuine politics. Politics always involves some degree of contestation—struggle—in the societal world"* (Dahlgren 2013: 3).

Burnett and Bloice (2016) examined Twitter posts during three televised debates about Scottish Independence leading up to the 2014 Scottish Referendum, concluding that posts linking to a variety of resources did have positive effects on unifying perspectives and supporter activism, but did not change political opinions. This makes the impact of social media on the outcome of the 2014 Scottish Referendum questionable. Riezebos et al. (2011) detected no impact of social media on voting behaviour, but changes in political party perception were present, according to their analysis of an online questionnaire during the Dutch national elections in 2010. Hong and Nadler (2015) support findings from Hindmann (2009) that the rate of political mobilisation is not increased through the use of the Internet, stating that online political voices are mostly made up of a small number of large organisations and networks (see also van der Graaf et al. 2016). In the course of a literature review, Dini and Sæbø (2016) make the observation that social media does not take the role of mobilising and creating participation if there is no active community already in place and that challenges such as exclusion, information misuse, deliberate misinformation, security threats, data leaks and privacy issues must be considered when social media is employed.

The question of whether social media leads to online or offline participation has frequently been posed, results being inconclusive and even contradictory. Vissers et al. (2012) point to medium-specific mobilisation effects in the course of an experimental study, meaning that online mobilisation leads to online participation, and offline mobilisation to offline participation, with there being no spillover effects. This result was supported by Vissers and Stolle's (2014) work based on a two-wave panel survey of undergraduate students in Canada in 2014, which claimed that political Facebook participation does promote online participation, but has no effects on offline participation, with the exception of engagement in offline protests. Nam (2012) determines, based on the Citizenship Involvement Democracy survey in the USA, that *"[while] the degree of internet use positively affects the level of activeness in online political activity, internet use intensity has a negative impact on offline activity*" (Nam 2012: 94). Contradicting these results is the conclusion of Theocharis and Lowe (2016) based on their experimental study involving young Greek participants, that the use of Facebook has clear negative impacts on all forms of participation. Gibson and Cantijoch (2013) were interested in the question of whether "[...] *online and offline activities are merging and being performed interchangeably [...] or does the medium matter and the two activities constitute separate and nonrelated spheres of action* [...]" (Gibson and Cantijoch 2013: 714). They conclude with mixed findings regarding this question, with online and offline versions of participatory activities such as petitioning or contacting politicians being interchangeable. Other activities, such as news consumption, appear to be medium-dependent. In addition to this finding, Gibson and Cantijoch (2013: 714) caution that they find there to be an "*underlying multidimensional structure to online participation*", which they deem responsible for the various differing findings in the area of political mobilisation through the Internet, given that the measurement of e-participation requires a higher level of discrimination. Gibson and McAllister (2013) claim that political participation is positively affected by social interactions in the offline world, and that it is therefore of interest to closer examine the effects of different online networks. They used the Australian Election Study, a national self-completed survey conducted after federal elections, from 2007, in order to examine the effects of interactions with *bonding* and *bridging* networks. According to Gibson and McAllister, bonding networks consist of individuals with whom one has an already established relationship in the offline world, while bridging networks are new networks consisting of people who may have little in common in terms of background or culture. Gibson and McAllister could show that there is in fact a difference between these two network types regarding mobilisation of offline participation: "*The findings show that bonding, and not bridging, online social contact predicts offline participation, suggesting that online interactions that do not build on existing offline networks are not as effective in mobilizing 'real world' participation*" (Gibson and McAllister 2013: 21).

Nam (2012) also voices the limited potential of the Internet to increase inclusiveness and, therefore, equality of civic participation in political matters. This is enforced by Cho and Keum (2016), who demonstrate that socio-economic factors play a smaller role for political expression on social networking sites than in political discussions held in the offline realm. Strauß and Nentwich (2013: 5) summarise the main potentials of social network sites as lying in the following areas: "[...] *social learning; new options for participation; strengthening community building; developing social capital; and enhancing political empowerment.*" A further positive effect is documented by Warren et al. (2014) in the course of a survey analysis, concerning trust towards institutions, which increases through the use of social media in the context of civic engagement.

Bicking et al. (2011) present the results of a comparative analysis of MOMENTUM, a support action with the purpose of coordinating e-participation pilot project activity, initiated by the European Commission. They note the lack of a social media strategy in most observed cases, leaving untapped potential in the areas of opinion-mining and bidirectional thought exchange, as well as raising the number of participants and gathering support. It could generally be observed that most of the cases did not successfully achieve any direct policy changes, though policy contributions were made (Bicking et al. 2011).

Local government websites in the USA seem not to have any influence on the participation of citizens in the policymaking process (Garrett and Jensen 2011). However, the design of the website can be an important factor in mobilising citizens (Zheng and Schachter 2016), design of online spaces having an impact on the political participation and deliberation of citizens (Steibel and Estevez 2015). According to Følstad and Lüders (2013), a survey among 90 participants in Norway resulted in 64% stating an online environment for political purposes would result in higher political engagement on their part, fostered by a feeling of having influence, having access to political debate, being regularly updated on events, raising awareness and motivating engagement in the local political sphere. In order for citizens to engage in political debate online, there must be an engaging topic, a certain will to contribute, frustration with a situation and reciprocal learning (Følstad and Lüders 2013). Party websites must offer high-quality information and a space for user interactions in which differing views are tolerated (Følstad et al. 2014). Følstad et al. prioritised informational content above website engagement features for regular users of the website, advising that the information should be complementary to other online content, locally specified and possessing marked perspectives or opinions.

It is not only of interest how the public engages with social media; the social media use of politicians can also provide helpful insights into how the dialogue between citizens and government officials is changing and whether this is leading towards higher levels of e-participation. Stieglitz and Brockmann (2013) examined the smartphone-use of German politicians who they categorised as "heavy smartphone users" through means of a survey and concluded that there is an increasing intensity to be found in the dialogue between politicians and citizens, enabled by social media. Here they recognise potential for increased e-participation. Zheng et al. (2014) also emphasised the role of elected government agents in producing opportunities for e-participation, naming the willingness of government as the key factor. Reddick and Norris (2013) used a national survey of e-participation among US local governments to determine demand to be the driving factor behind political support, with the success of e-participation efforts relying on top-level support, citizen demand and formal planning.

Before concluding this chapter, the contribution of social media to new social and political movements should be acknowledged, such as in the cases of the London and South African demonstrations in 2011 and 2008, the protests in Stuttgart and Istanbul in 2010 and 2013, the 2012 Occupy movements, and the Arab Spring (Norris 2012; Abbott 2012; Herrera 2014). And of course, anti-liberal, non-emancipatory and right-wing populist movements are also successfully taking advantage of the new media's opportunities to influence discourse, organise and mobilise (Dietrich et al. 2017; Müller and Schwarz 2018). Furthermore, social media can be utilised for information dissemination and organisation outside of traditional media, which can be under government control (Wilson and Corey 2012 as quoted in Dunne 2015). Conversely, social media platforms are increasingly being targeted by governments to influence and manipulate public opinion online, in some cases using covert, non-transparent and illegitimate methods (Bradshaw and Howard 2017; Fuchs 2018). Dunne (2015) points to regional differences concerning mobilisation through social media, claiming that certain Western citizens simply do not harbour a strong enough will to increase online or offline direct democracy, due to lack of time or interest, arguing that we would otherwise see more protests of individuals trying to effect change.

2.2.5 Summarising the Perspectives

The discussions and findings in the academic literature dealing with the role social media play in political communication and democratic politics presented in this review by and large reflect a field of academic inquiry, which is still in full motion. Key questions are currently far from being settled—an assessment that comes as no surprise given the relatively recent advent of social media about 10 years ago.

Nonetheless, at a general level, some very tentative conclusions might be drawn from the literature review on the political dimensions of social media. Research tends to agree that social media are playing an increasingly important role in civic and political lives, as these communication opportunities are taken up by social movements, activists, political parties and governments. However, while numerous studies have attempted to provide evidence for tangible political effects of social media use on the levels and quality of political engagement, by and large the transformative power often associated with social media still remains more a potential possibility than a reality confirmed by sound empirical evidence (Williamson et al. 2010; Loader and Mercea 2012; Ross and Bürger 2014: 50; Hong and Nadler 2015; Margetts 2019). Even if finding evidence for these far-reaching expectations about the impact of social media on democracy remain a pressing topic for research, academics and experts in the field should also address the issue of to what extent social media are able to fulfil core functions of public communication such as critique, legitimation and integration (Imhof 2011). In this regard, social media seem not only to challenge established understandings and models of the public sphere, but phenomena such as solipsistic echo chambers, deliberate infusion of misinformation, manipulation and surveillance also seem to threaten the integrity of the public sphere's core functions for democracy. Making sense of malicious distortions of information exchange and debate, as well as of the allegedly increasing role of the private, the personal affective and emotional perspectives in politics, and thinking ahead about ways for democratic institutions to respond to this possible transformation seems expedient.

Finally, in order to avoid the reproduction of old myths about the transformative potential of social media, future research in this dynamic field should also take the broader media ecology into consideration. More careful contextualisations, which reflect the dynamic interrelationships between traditional news media, digital media, and the publics and their undercurrents, will help to avoid the traps of technological determinism.

2.3 Conclusions

E-democracy is now a widely applied term, which describes a broad scope of practices of online engagement of the public in political decision-making and opinion-forming. With regard to theoretical concepts of democracy, e-democracy is usually based on models of participatory and deliberative democracy. Far-reaching, overly enthusiastic expectations of a fundamental transformation of modern democracy through the application of online tools for political participation and public discourse are fading after two decades of experiences with e-democracy, opening space for accounts that are more conceptually and analytically robust and less techno-determinist. There is, however, little doubt that e-democracy will add new modes of communication among citizens and between actors of representative democracy and their constituencies. These changes not only add to the online political processes, but also affect the modes and conditions of offline political processes in many ways. They are dependent on the great variety of e-democracy tools applied, the nature of the political process these are embedded in, and the skills, demands and expectations of those involved in their application.

Research into the impact of social media on democracy remains inconclusive and only allows us to draw some very tentative conclusions on the political dimensions of social media. The literature tends to agree that social media play an increasingly important role in civic and political lives, as these communication opportunities are not only taken up by social movements and activists, but also by governments and government-sponsored groups. However, while numerous studies have attempted to provide evidence for tangible political effects from social media use, by and large the transformative power often associated with social media still remains more a potential possibility than a firmly established reality, particularly with regard to established patterns of political participation. Based on the currently available findings, it can be concluded that social media have ambivalent effects for democratic politics, enabling more inclusive involvement and allowing for the articulation of un(der)represented perspectives, while at the same time providing powerful opportunities for malicious distortions of discourse, misinformation and communicative closure.

While finding coherent empirical evidence for the impact of social media on democracy remains a pressing topic for research, academics and experts in the field should also address the more fundamental issue of the extent to which social media is able to fulfil core functions of public communication, particularly public critique, legitimation and integration. In this regard, social media and the idea of "personalised politics" seem to challenge some of the established understandings and models of the public sphere. Making sense of the allegedly increasing role of personal and emotional perspectives in politics and thinking ahead about ways for democratic institutions to respond to this possible transformation seems more pressing than ever. What is more, phenomena such as solipsistic closure and echo chambers, deliberate misinformation and computational propaganda are threatening the fundamental workings of the public sphere in democratic contexts, increasing the need for effective educational, regulatory and technological responses.

References

Abbott, J. (2012). Social media. In N. Kersting (Ed.), *Electronic democracy* (pp. 77–102). Opladen: Barbara Budrich Publishers.
Adler, A. (2018). *Liquid democracy in Deutschland*. Zur Zukunft digitaler politischer Entscheidungsfindung nach dem Niedergang der Piratenpartei, Bielefeld.
Aichholzer, G., & Strauß, S. (2016). Electronic participation in Europe. In R. Lindner, G. Aichholzer, & L. Hennen (Eds.), *Electronic democracy in Europe. Prospects and challenges of e-publics, e-participation and e-voting* (pp. 55–132). Springer.
Alexa. (2019). *The top 500 sites on the web*. Online: http://www.alexa.com/topsites (06.01.2019).
Andrejevic, M. (2011). Facebook als neue Produktionsweise. In O. Leistert & T. Röhle (Eds.), *Generation facebook* (pp. 31–50). Bielefeld: Über das Leben im Social Net.
Banaji, S., & Buckingham, D. (2013). *The civic web: Young people, the internet, and civic participation*. Cambridge, MA: MIT Press.
Barber, B. J. (1984). *Strong democracy: Participatory politics for a new age*. Berkeley, CA: University of California Press.
Baringhorst, S., Kneip, V., März, A., & Niesyto, J. (Eds.) (2007). *Politik mit dem Einkaufswagen*. Unternehmen und Konsumenten als Bürger in der globalen Mediengesellschaft, Bielefeld.
Becker, T. (1981). Teledemocracy: Bringing power back to the people. *Futurist*, December, 6–9.
Benkler, Y. (2006). *The wealth of networks: How social production transforms markets and freedom*. New Haven, CT: Yale University Press.
Bennett, W. L. (2008). Changing citizenship in the digital age. In W. L. Bennett (Ed.), *Civic life online: Learning how digital media can engage youth* (pp. 1–24). Cambridge, MA: MIT Press.
Beyer, J. L. (2014). *Expect us: Online communities and political mobilization*. Oxford: Oxford University Press.
Bicking, M., Triantafillou, A., Henderson, F., Koussouris, S., & Wimmer, M. A. (2011). Lessons from monitoring and assessing EC-funded eParticipation projects: Citizen engagement and participation impact. *2011 IST-Africa Conference Proceedings, IST 2011*.
Bode, L. (2012). Facebooking it to the polls: A study in online social networking and political behavior. *Journal of Information Technology and Politics, 9*, 352–369.
Bode, L., Vraga, E. K., Borah, P., & Shah, D. V. (2014). A new space for political behavior: Political social networking and its democratic consequences. *Journal of Computer-Mediated Communication, 19*, 414–429.
Boulianne, S. (2015). Social media use and participation: a meta-analysis of current research. *Information Communication and Society, 18*(5), 524–538.
Bradshaw, S. & Howard, P. N. (2017). *Troops, trolls and troublemakers: A global inventory of organized social media manipulation*. Oxford Internet Institute, Working paper no. 2017.12, Oxford.
Bruns, A. (2008). *Gatewatching: Collaborative online news production*. New York: Peter Lang.
Burnett, S., & Bloice, L. (2016). Linking for influence: Twitter linked content in the Scottish Referendum televised debates. *Journal of Information Science, 42*(3), 396–409.

Caldon, P. (2016). Digital publics: Re-defining 'the civic' and re-locating 'the political'. *New Media and Society, 18*(9), 2133–2138.

Carty, V. (2015). *Social movements and new technology*. Boulder, CO: Westview Press.

Chen, P. J. (2013). *Australian politics in a digital age*. Canberra: ANU E Press.

Cho, J., & Keum, H. (2016). Leveling or tilting the playing field: Social networking sites and offline political communication inequality. *Social Science Journal, 53*(2), 236–246.

Coleman, S., & Norris, D. (2005). *A new agenda for e-democracy*. Oxford Internet Institute, Forum Discussion Paper No. 4, January.

Council of Europe. (2009). *Recommendation CM/Rec(2009)1 of the Committee of Ministers to Member States on electronic democracy (e-democracy)*. http://www.coe.int/t/dgap/democracy/Activities/GGIS/CAHDE/2009/RecCM2009_1_and_Accomp_Docs/Recommendation%20CM_Rec_2009_1E_FINAL_PDF.pdf

Dahlgren, P. (2013). *Do social media enhance democratic participation? The importance-and difficulty-of being "realistic"*. Policy Paper 04/2013, Rosa Luxemburg Stiftung, Berlin.

Davis, R. (2012). Interplay: Political blogging and journalism. In R. L. Fox & J. M. Ramos (Eds.), *iPolitics: Citizens, elections, and governing in the new media era*. New York: Cambridge University Press.

della Porta, D., Andretta, M., Mosca, L., & Reiter, H. (2006). *Globalisation from below: Transnational activists and protest networks*. Minnesota, MN: University of Minnesota Press.

deSilver, D. (2014). *Facebook is a news source for many, but incidentally*. Washington, DC: Pwe Research Center.

Dietrich, N., Gersin, E., & Herweg, A. (2017). Analysemöglichkeiten der Online-Kommunikation auf Social Network Sites am Beispiel PEGIDA und Facebook. In W. Frindte & N. Dietrich (Eds.), *Muslime, Flüchtlinge und Pegida* (pp. 235–266). Wiesbaden: Springer VS.

Dini, A. A., & Sæbø, O. (2016). *The current state of social media research for eParticipation in developing countries: A literature review*. Paper presented at the Proceedings of the Annual Hawaii International Conference on System Sciences.

Dunne, K. (2015). ICTs: Convenient, yet subsidiary tools in changing democracy. *International Journal of E-Politics (IJEP), 6*(2), 1–13.

Dutton, H. W. (1999). *Society on the line: Information politics in the digital age*. Oxford: Oxford University Press.

EC – European Commission. (2001). *European Governance*. A White Paper, COM (2001) 428 final, Brussels.

EC – European Commission. (2010). *The European eGovernment Action Plan 2010-2015*. Harnessing ICT to promote smart, sustainable and innovative government. SEC(2010)1539 final, Brussels.

Farrell, H. (2014). New problems, new publics? Dewey and new media. *Policy and Internet, 6*(2), 176–191.

Følstad, A., & Lüders, M. (2013). Online political debate: Motivating factors and impact on political engagement. In M. A. Wimmer, E. Tambouris, & A. Macintosh (Eds.), *Electronic participation, Epart 2013* (Vol. 8075, pp. 122–133).

Følstad, A., Johannessen, M. R., & Luders, M. (2014). The role of a political party website: Lessons learnt from the user perspective. In E. Tambouris, A. Macintosh, & F. Bannister (Eds.), *Electronic participation, Epart 2014* (Vol. 8654, pp. 52–63).

Fox, R. L., & Ramos, J. M. (Eds.). (2012). *iPolitics: Citizens, elections, and governing in the new media era*. New York: Cambridge University Press.

Fuchs, C. (2018). *Digital demagogue: Authoritarian capitalism in the age of Trump and Twitter*. London: Pluto.

Garrett, R. K., & Jensen, M. J. (2011). E-DEMOCRACY WRIT SMALL: The impact of the Internet on citizen access to local elected officials. *Information Communication and Society, 14*(2), 177–197.

Gebhardt, W. (2010). "We are different!" Zur Soziologie jugendlicher Vergemeinschaftung. In A. Honer, M. Meuser, M. Pfadenhauer, & R. Hitzler (Eds.), *Fragile Sozialität: Inszenierungen, Sinnwelten, Existenzbastler* (pp. 327–339). Wiesbaden: VS Verlag für Sozialwissenschaften.

Gerhards, J., & Schäfer, M. (2007). Demokratische Internetöffentlichkeit? Ein Vergleich der öffentlichen Kommunikation im Internet und in den Printmedien am Beispiel der Humangenomforschung. *Publizistik, 52*(2), 210–228.

Gerlitz, C. (2011). Die like economy. Digitaler Raum, Daten und wertschöpfung. In O. Leistert & T. Röhle (Eds.), *Generation Facebook* (pp. 101–122). Bielefeld: Über das Leben im Social Net.

Gibson, R. (2014). Introduction. In: B. Grofman, A. Trechsel, & M. Franklin (Eds.), *The internet and democracy in global perspective. Voters, candidates, parties, and social movements introduction* (Studies in public choice, Vol. 31, pp. 1–5), Cham.

Gibson, R., & Cantijoch, M. (2013). Conceptualizing and measuring participation in the age of the internet: Is online political engagement really different to offline? *Journal of Politics, 75*(3), 701–716.

Gibson, R. K., & McAllister, I. (2013). Online social ties and political engagement. *Journal of Information Technology and Politics, 10*(1), 21–34.

Gil de Zúñiga, H., Puig-I-Abril, E., & Rojas, H. (2009). Weblogs, traditional sources online and political participation: An assessment of how the Internet is changing the political environment. *New Media and Society, 11*(4), 553–574.

Gil de Zúñiga, H., Jung, N., & Valenzuela, S. (2012). Social media use for news and individuals' social capital, civic engagement and political participation. *Journal of Computer-Mediated Communication, 17*, 319–336.

Gil de Zúñiga, H. G., Copeland, L., & Bimber, B. (2013). Political consumerism: Civic engagement and the social media connection. *New Media and Society, 16*(3), 488–506.

González-Bailón, S., Borge-Holthoefer, J., & Moreno, Y. (2013). Broadcasters and hidden influentials in online protest diffusion. *American Behavioral Scientist, 57*(7), 943–965.

Grofman, B., Trechsel, A., & Franklin, M. (Eds.) (2014). *The internet and democracy in global perspective. Voters, candidates, parties, and social movements introduction* (Studies in Public Choice, Vol. 31), Cham.

Habermas, J. (1992). Drei normative Modelle der Demokratie: Zum Begriff deliberativer Politik. In H. Münkler (Ed.), *Die Chancen der Freiheit. Grundprobleme der Demokratie* (pp. 11–24). München: Piper.

Hacker, K. L., & van Dijk, J. (Eds.). (2000a). *Digital democracy: Issues of theory and practice*. Sage: London.

Hacker, K. L., & van Dijk, J. (2000b). What is digital democracy? In K. L. Hacker & J. van Dijk (Eds.), *Digital democracy. Issues of theory and practice* (pp. 1–9). London: Sage.

Hagen, M. (1997). *Elektronische Demokratie. Computernetzwerke und politische Theorie in den USA*. Hamburg: LIT Verlag.

Hague, B. N., & Loader, B. D. (Eds.). (1999). *Digital democracy: Discourse and decision making in the information age*. Routledge: London.

Held, D. (2006). *Models of democracy*. Cambridge: Polity.

Herrera, L. (2014). *Revolution in the age of social media: The Egyptian popular insurrection and the Internet*. London: Verso.

Hindmann, M. (2009). *The myth of digital democracy*. Princeton: Princeton University Press.

Hoff, J., & Scheele, C. E. (2014). Theoretical approaches to digital services and digital democracy: The merits of the contextual new medium theory model. *Policy and Internet, 6*(3), 241–267.

Hong, S., & Nadler, D. (2015). The unheavenly chorus: Political voices of organized interests on social media. *Policy and Internet, 8*(1), 91–106.

Imhof, K. (2011). *Die Krise der Öffentlichkeit. Kommunikation und Medien als Faktoren des sozialen Wandels*, Frankfurt/Main.

Imhof, K. (2015). Demokratisierung durch social media? In K. Imhof, R. DeBlum, H. Bonfadelli, O. Jarren, & V. Wyss (Eds.), *Mediensymposium 2012* (pp. 15–26). Wiesbaden.

Imhof, K., DeBlum, R., Bonfadelli, H., Jarren, O., & Wyss, V. (eds.) (2015). *Demokratisierung durch Social Media?* Mediensymposium 2012. Wiesbaden.
Jackson, N. A., & Lilleker, D. G. (2009). Building an architecture of participation? Political parties and Web 2.0 in Britain. *Journal of Information Technology and Politics, 6*(3–4), 232–250.
Jenkins, H. (2006). *Convergence culture. Where old and new media collide.* New York: New York University Press.
Jericho, G. (2012). *The rise of the fifth estate: Social media and blogging in Australian politics.* Melbourne: Scribe Publications.
Jessop, B. (2003). Governance and meta-governance: On reflexivity, requisite variety and requisite irony. In H. P. Bang (Ed.), *Governance as social and political communication* (pp. 106–116). Manchester: Manchester University Press.
Johnson, S. B. (2012). *Future perfect: The case for progress in a networked age.* New York, NY: Penguin Books.
Kersting, N. (2005): *The quality of political discourse: Can E-discussion be Deliberative?* Conference paper. Annual Conference of the British Political Studies Association, Leeds, England, 5–7 April.
Kersting, N. (2013). Online participation: from 'invited' to 'invented' spaces. *International Journal of Electronic Governance, 6*(4), 270–280.
Kersting, N. (2017). Online-Partizipation und Medienkompetenz: Kann man Netiquette lernen? In H. Gapski, M. Oberle, & W. Staufer (Eds.), *Medienkompetenz. Herausforderung für Politik, politische Bildung und Medienbildung* (pp. 63–72). Bonn: Bundeszentrale für politische Bildung.
Khamis, S. (2011). The transformative Egyptian media landscape: changes, challenges and comparative perspectives. *International Journal of Communication, 5*, 1159–1177.
Khondker, H. (2011). The role of the new media in the Arab Spring. *Globalization, 8*(5), 675–679.
Kies, R. (2010). *Promises and limits of web-deliberation.* New York: Palgrave Macmillan.
Kohler-Koch, B., & Quittkat, C. (Eds.). (2013). *De-mystification of participatory democracy.* Oxford: EU Governance and Civil Society.
Lembcke, O., Ritzi, C., & Schaal, G. (2012). Zwischen Konkurrenz und Konvergenz. Eine Einführung in die normative Demokratietheorie. In O. Lembcke, C. Ritzi, & G. Schaal (Eds.), *Zeitgenössische Demokratietheorie. Band* (Vol. 1, pp. 9–32). Wiesbaden: Normative Demokratietheorien.
Leung, K. K., & Lee, F. (2014). Cultivating an active online counterpublic: Examining usage and political impact of internet alternative media. *International Journal of Press/Politics, 19*(3), 340–359.
Lindner, R. (2007). *Politischer Wandel durch digitale Netzwerkkommunikation? Strategische Anwendung neuer Kommunikationstechnologien durch kanadische Parteien und Interessengruppen,* Wiesbaden.
Lindner, R., Beckert, B., Aichholzer, G., Strauß, S., & Hennen, L. (2010). *E-democracy in Europe – prospects of internet-based political participation.* Interim Report – Phase I (European Parliament, Science and Technology Options Assessment STOA), Brussels/Strasbourg.
Lindner, R., Aichholzer, G., & Hennen, L. (2016a). Electronic democracy in Europe: An introduction. In R. Lindner, G. Aichholzer, & L. Hennen (Eds.), *Electronic democracy in Europe. Prospects and challenges of e-publics, e-participation and e-voting* (pp. 1–17). Cham: Springer.
Lindner, R., Aichholzer, G., & Hennen, L. (Eds.). (2016b). *Electronic democracy in Europe. Prospects and challenges of e-publics, e-participation and e-voting.* Cham: Springer.
Loader, B. D., & Mercea, D. (2011). Introduction. Networking democracy? Social media innovations and participatory politics. *Information Communication and Society, 14*(6), 757–769.
Loader, B. D., & Mercea, D. (2012). *Social media and democracy: Innovations in participatory politics.* Abingdon: Routledge.
Macková, A. (2014). Review: Dahlgren, Peter: The political web: Media, participation and alternative democracy (2013). *Czech Journal of Political Science, 2*, 156–158.

Margetts, H. (2019). Rethinking democracy with social media. *The Political Quarterly, 90*(S1), 107–123.
Margetts, H., John, P., Hale, S., & Yasseri, T. (2015). *Political turbulaence: How social media shape collective action.* Princeton: Princeton University Press.
McLuhan, M. (1964). *Understanding media: The extensions of man.* New York, NY: Mentor Book.
Momeni, M. (2017). Social media and political participation. *New Media and Society, 19*(12), 2094–2100.
Müller, K., & Schwarz, C. (2018). *Fanning the Flames of Hate: Social Media and Hate Crime (November 30, 2018).* Available at SSRN: https://doi.org/10.2139/ssrn.3082972
Nam, T. (2012). Dual effects of the internet on political activism: Reinforcing and mobilizing. *Government Information Quarterly, 29*(1), 90–97.
Norris, P. (2012). Political mobilization and social networks. The example of the Arab spring. In N. Kersting (Ed.), *Electronic Democracy* (pp. 53–76). Opladen: Verlag Barbara Budrich.
Noveck, B. S. (2009). *Wiki government: How technology can make government better, democracy stronger, and citizens more powerful.* Washington, DC: Brookings Institution Press.
Oblak Črnič, T. (2012). Idea(l)s on e-democracy and direct online citizenship. *Southeastern Europe, 36*(3), 398–420.
Päivärinta, T., & Øystein, S. (2006). Models of E-democracy. *Communications of the Association for Information Systems, 17*(Article 37), 818–840.
Papacharissi, Z. (2010). *A private sphere: Democracy in a digital age.* Cambridge: Polity Press.
Papacharissi, Z. (2015). *Affective publics: Sentiment, technology, and politics.* Oxford: Oxford University Press.
Pariser, E. (2011). *The Filter Bubble. What the Internet is hiding from you.* London.
Paterson, N. (2012). Walled gardens: The new shape of the public internet. *iConference '12. Proceedings of the 2012 iConference*, New York, pp. 97–104.
Pedersen, K. (2005). New Zealand parties in cyberspace. *Political Science, 57*(2), 107–116.
Pichler, J. W. (2011). The citizens' participatory democracy's holistic architecture beyond the ECI – from articles 10.3 to 11.1 to 11.2 to 11.3 to 11.4 TEU to Art. 17 TFEU and Art. 24 TFEU. In J. W. Pichler, & B. Kaufmann (Eds.), *Modern Transnational Democracy. How the 2012 launch of the European Citizen's Initiative can change the world* (pp. 21–26). Schriften zur Rechtspolitik, Bd. 33. Wien-Graz: Neuer Wissenschaftlicher Verlag.
Postill, J. (2018). Populism and social media: A global perspective. *Media, Culture and Society, 40* (5), 754–765.
Price, E. (2013). Social media and democracy. *Australian Journal of Political Science, 48*(4), 519–527.
Redden, J. (2011). Poverty in the news. A framing analysis of coverage in Canada and the UK. *Information Communication and Society, 14*(6), 820–849.
Reddick, C., & Norris, D. F. (2013). E-participation in local governments: An examination of political-managerial support and impacts. *Transforming Government: People, Process and Policy, 7*(4), 453–476.
Reichert, R. (2013). *Die Macht der Vielen. Über den neuen Kult der digitalen Vernetzung*, Bielefeld.
Rheingold, H. (1993). *The virtual community: Homesteading on the electronic frontier.* Reading, MA: Addison-Wesley.
Riezebos, P., De Vries, S. A., De Vries, P. W., & De Zeeuw, E. (2011). *The effects of social media on political party perception and voting behavior.* Paper presented at the Proceedings of the IADIS International Conference ICT, Society and Human Beings 2011, Proceedings of the IADIS International Conference e-Democracy, Equity and Social Justice 2011, Part of the IADIS, MCCSIS 2011.
Ross, K., & Bürger, T. (2014). Face-to-face(book) social media, political campaigning and the unbearable lightness of being there. *Political Science, 66*(1), 46–62.

Sandoval-Almazan, R., & Gil-Garcia, J. R. (2014). Towards cyberactivism 2.0? Understanding the use of social media and other information technologies for political activism and social movements. *Government Information Quarterly, 31*(3), 365–378.
Santos, H. R., & Tonelli, D. F. (2014). *Possibilities and limits of E-participation: A systematic review of E-democracy*. XXXVIII Encontro de ANPAD, Rio de Janeiro, 13–17 September.
Saurugger, S. (2010). The social construction of the participatory turn: The emergence of a norm in the European Union. *European Journal of Political Research, 49*(4), 471–495.
Schaal, G. S. (2016). E-Democracy. In O. W. Lembcke, C. Ritzi, & G. S. Schaal (Eds.), *Zeitgenössische Demokratietheorie. Band 2: Empirische Demokratietheorien* (pp. 279–305). Wiesbaden: Springer VS.
Scharpf, F. W. (1999). *Regieren in Europa: effektiv und demokratisch?* Frankfurt a.M.: Campus.
Schill, D. & Hendricks, J. A. (Eds.) (2018). *The presidency and social media: Discourse, disruption, and digital democracy in the 2016 presidential election*, New York.
Schmidt, M. G. (2008). *Demokratietheorien*. Wiesbaden: Eine Einführung.
Schultze, R.-O. (2004). Deliberative Demokratie. In D. Nohlen, & R.-O. Schultze (Eds.) *Lexikon der Politikwissenschaft. Theorien, Methoden, Begriffe* (Vol. 1, pp. 121–122). München.
Skoric, M. M., Zhu, Q., Goh, D., & Pang, N. (2016). Social media and citizen engagement: A meta-analytic review. *New Media and Society, 18*(9), 1817–1839.
Smith, G., & Dalakiouridou, E. (2009). Contextualising public (e)Participation in the governance of the European Union. *European Journal of ePractice, 7*, 4–14.
Steibel, F., & Estevez, E. (2015). *Designing web 2.0 tools for online public consultation Impact of Information Society Research in the Global South*, pp. 243–263.
Stieglitz, S., & Brockmann, T. (2013). *The impact of smartphones on e-participation*. Paper presented at the Proceedings of the Annual Hawaii International Conference on System Sciences.
Stolle, D., & Micheletti, M. (2013). *Political consumerism: Global responsibility in action*. Cambridge: Cambridge University Press.
Strauß, S., & Nentwich, M. (2013). Social network sites: Potentials, impacts and major privacy challenges. *STOA Cloud Computing Deliverable* 4. Brussels
Tang, G., & Lee, F. L. F. (2013). Facebook use and political participation: The impact of exposure to shared political information, connections with public political actors, and network structural heterogeneity. *Social Science Computer Review, 31*(6), 763–773.
Theocharis, Y., & Lowe, W. (2016). Does Facebook increase political participation? Evidence from a field experiment. *Information Communication and Society, 19*(10), 1465–1486.
Thimm, C., & Berlinke, S. (2007). Mehr Öffentlichkeit für unterdrückte Themen? Chancen und Grenzen von Weblogs. In H. Pöttker & C. Schulzki-Haddouti (Eds.), *Vergessen? Verschwiegen? Verdrängt?* (Vol. 10, pp. 81–101). Wiesbaden: Jahre „Initiative Nachrichtenaufklärung.
Tripodi, F. B. (2018). Radicalism, authoritarianism, and the role of new media. *New Media and Society*. Available at https://doi.org/10.1177/1461444818816085 (06.01.2019).
van der Graaf, A., Otjes, S., et al. (2016). Weapon of the weak? The social media landscape of interest groups. *European Journal of Communication, 31*(2), 120–135.
van Dijk, J. (1999). *The network society, social aspects of new media*. London: Sage.
van Dijk, J. (2012). Digital democracy: Vision and reality. In I. Snellen, M. Thaens, & W. van de Donk (Eds.), *Public administration in the information age: Revisited* (pp. 49–61). Amsterdam: IOS-Press.
Vedel, T. (2006). The idea of electronic democracy: Origins, visions and questions. *Parliamentary Affairs, 59*(2), 226–235.
Vissers, S., & Stolle, D. (2014). Spill-over effects between facebook and on/offline political participation? Evidence from a two-wave panel study. *Journal of Information Technology and Politics, 11*(3), 259–275.

Vissers, S., Hooghe, M., Stolle, D., & Mahéo, V. A. (2012). The impact of mobilization media on off-line and online participation: Are mobilization effects medium-specific? *Social Science Computer Review, 30*(2), 152–169.

Vitak, J., Zube, P., Smock, A., Carr, C. T., Ellison, N., & Lampe, C. (2011). It's complicated: Facebook users' political participation in the 2008 election. *Cyberpsychology, Behavior, and Social Networking, 14*(3), 107–114.

von Behr, I., Reding, A., Edwards, C., & Gribbon, L. (2013). *Radicalisation in the digital era. The use of the internet in 15 cases of terrorism and extremism*, RAND Europe.

Voss, K. (Ed.) (2014). *Internet und Partizipation. Bottom-up oder Top-down? Politische Beteiligungsmöglichkeiten im Internet*, Wiesbaden.

Vowe, G. (2014). Digital Citizens und Schweigende Mehrheit: Wie verändert sich die politische Beteiligung der Bürger durch das Internet? In K. Voss (Ed.) *Internet und Partizipation. Bottom-up der Top-down? Politische Beteiligungsmöglichkeiten im Internet* (pp. 25–52), Wiesbaden.

Wardle, C., & Derakhsan, H. (2017). *Information disorder: Toward an interdisciplinary framework for research and policy making*. Council of Europe Report DGI (2017)09, Strasbourg.

Warren, A. M., Sulaiman, A., & Jaafar, N. I. (2014). Social media effects on fostering online civic engagement and building citizen trust and trust in institutions. *Government Information Quarterly, 31*(2), 291–301.

Wehling, P. (2012). From invited to uninvited participation (and back?): Rethinking civil society engagement in technology assessment and development. *Poiesis and Praxis, 9*(1), 43–60.

Williamson, A. (2009). The effect of digital media on MPs' communication with constituents. *Parliamentary Affairs, 62*(3), 525.

Williamson, A., Miller, L., & Fallon, F. (2010). *Behind the digital campaign: An exploration of the use, impact and regulation of digital campaigning*, London.

Wilson, M. I., & Corey, K. E. (2012). The role of ICT in Arab spring movements. *Netcom. Réseaux, Communication et Territoires, 26*(3/4), 343–356.

Zheng, Y., & Schachter, H. L. (2016). Explaining citizens' E-participation use: The role of perceived advantages. *Public Organization Review*, 1–20.

Zheng, Y. P., Schachter, H. L., & Holzer, M. (2014). The impact of government form on e-participation: A study of New Jersey municipalities. *Government Information Quarterly, 31*(4), 653–659.

Zimmermann, A. (2006). *Demokratisierung und Europäisierung online? Massenmediale politische Öffentlichkeiten im Internet*, Berlin. Available at: http://www.diss.fu-berlin.de/diss/servlets/MCRFileNodeServlet/FUDISS_derivate_000000003532/00_Titel_Inhalt.pdf?hosts (06.01.2019)

Open Access This chapter is licensed under the terms of the Creative Commons Attribution 4.0 International License (http://creativecommons.org/licenses/by/4.0/), which permits use, sharing, adaptation, distribution and reproduction in any medium or format, as long as you give appropriate credit to the original author(s) and the source, provide a link to the Creative Commons licence and indicate if changes were made.

The images or other third party material in this chapter are included in the chapter's Creative Commons licence, unless indicated otherwise in a credit line to the material. If material is not included in the chapter's Creative Commons licence and your intended use is not permitted by statutory regulation or exceeds the permitted use, you will need to obtain permission directly from the copyright holder.

Chapter 3
E-Democracy and the European Public Sphere

Leonhard Hennen

Abstract The chapter starts with an outline of outstanding recent contributions to the discussion of the EU democratic deficit and the so-called "no demos" problem and the debate about European citizenship and European identity—mainly in the light of insights from the EU crisis. This is followed by reflections on the recent discussion on the state of the mass media-based European public sphere. Finally, the author discusses the state of research on the Internet's capacity to support the emergence of a (renewed) public sphere, with a focus on options for political actors to use the Internet for communication and campaigning, on the related establishment of segmented issue-related publics as well as on social media and its two-faced character as an enabler as well as a distorting factor of the public sphere. The author is sceptic about the capacities of Internet-based political communication to develop into a supranational (European) public sphere. It rather establishes a network of a multitude of discursive processes aimed at opinion formation at various levels and on various issues. The potential of online communication to increase the responsiveness of political institutions so far is set into practice insufficiently. Online media are increasingly used in a vertical and scarcely in a horizontal or interactive manner of communication.

3.1 Introduction

The motives and driving forces of e-democracy are manifold. However, at the centre of all the efforts of (not only but in particular) the European Union (EU) to apply e-democracy and e-participation tools is the particular problem that the EU (and other transnational political bodies) has to directly refer and relate to a specific constituency, causing problems of legitimising its policy. The so-called "democratic deficit" of the EU institutions, caused by its indirect legitimisation by the European

---

L. Hennen (✉)
Institute of Technology Assessment and Systems Analysis, Karlsruhe Institute of Technology, Karlsruhe, Germany
e-mail: leonhard.hennen@kit.edu

© The Author(s) 2020
L. Hennen et al. (eds.), *European E-Democracy in Practice*, Studies in Digital Politics and Governance, https://doi.org/10.1007/978-3-030-27184-8_3

constituency, is closely connected to the problem of European citizenship. Besides the objective formal rights of citizens (as enacted in the Treaty of the European Union), democratic legitimisation needs, as its backbone, the joint commitment and feeling of belonging of citizens to a community. This cultural fundament historically emerged or co-developed with the nation state, so that national democratic systems can rely to some degree on a general overarching solidarity of citizens that allows for conflict and dissent on particular political issues, and the acceptance of majority decisions by those members of the constituency that disagree. To what extent the European Union can rely on a European "demos" in this regard is a matter of contention. The same applies for the European public sphere as a space of societal debate and political exchange, which at the same time controls the European institutions' policies and informs them about and feeds them with society's expectations, demands and interests. Public opinion forming and exchange about European politics almost exclusively takes place in nationally organised mass media publics, and in this respect there obviously is no specific overarching trans-European public sphere. Trans-European media (TV or press) have a marginal relevance, and national mass media—due to, among other things, language problems—offer no or only weak options for trans- or inter-European exchange across borders (Lindner et al. 2016). This problem has been the core motivation for all attempts of the European Commission (EC) throughout its history to explore and invest in new options for political communication via means of new media and especially the Internet.

In a tour d'horizon of the history of the European Commission's communication strategies, Lodge and Sarikakis (2013) regard this as a long and winding road of attempts to establish a European public sphere, which have often been confused with goals such as mobilising electoral support, or strategies of positioning the EU in national media. Later, with the "Plan D for Democracy, Dialogue and Debate" (see Lindner et al. 2016), the strategies for mediating a European public sphere adopted the goal of including the European citizen directly in political discourse by means of (online) public consultation, and more recently, by establishing the European Citizen Initiative, by means of which citizens can invite the EC to put forward proposals on EU policy issues supported by a sufficient quorum of citizens from all over Europe. The relevance of e-participation tools has also been highlighted in the EC's action plan on e-governance 2010–2015 (EC 2010) in order to "... *improve the ability of people to have their voice heard and make suggestions for policy actions in the Member States and the European Union as a whole*" (EC 2010: 8). The undeniable fact that nowadays political communication is to a great extent taking place via Internet websites, blogs and in social media puts to the fore speculations and hopes that the lack of a mass media in the European public sphere will find a remedy in the emergence of a "networked" European public sphere. The relevance of expectations and hopes that the Internet has the power to at least support public debate on European issues, in a way that also helps to foster a European identity among European citizens, is underlined by the fact that it is believed by many that the EU's democratic deficit will not find "redress" as long as no European-wide public sphere emerges (Hoffmann and Monaghan 2011).

3.2 The Democratic Deficit of the European Union

The focus of the following section will be the problem of the European public sphere and the role of new media and Internet communication in contributing to making a European public sphere emerge, or working as a proxy for a so far missing mass-mediated European public sphere. The body of literature on the European democratic deficit, on the state of a European public sphere, and about the option for an "e-Public" in Europe has grown in recent years. The discussion of this body of research and scholarly debate will necessarily have to find a focus. We mainly draw here on literature dealing explicitly with the European context (we refer to the more general literature on problems of transnational publics in general where necessary). It cannot come as a surprise that the issues of the European democratic deficit, of European identity and citizenship as well as of the European public sphere come into specific perspective with regard to the recent symptoms of a crisis of the EU. The consequences of the legitimation or democratic deficit of EU politics has been drastically revealed by increasing EU-scepticism during the recent years of financial and sovereign debt crisis, followed by fierce recession in some of the weaker economies of Member States, the discussion about the bailout of Greece and in the British referendum showing a small majority of voters opting for the "Brexit". Thus, the effect and reflection of these recent developments in scholarly debates and research will be the focus of this section. The section starts with an outline of outstanding recent contributions to the discussion of the EU democratic deficit and the so-called "no demos" problem and the debate about European citizenship and European identity—mainly in the light of insights from the EU crisis. This will be followed by an outline of the recent discussion on the state of the mass media-based European public sphere, for which the recent EU crisis also is of some relevance. Finally, the chapter will discuss the state of research on the Internet's capacity to support the emergence of a (renewed) public sphere. Here we focus on options for political actors to use the Internet for communication and campaigning and the related establishment of segmented issue-related publics, as well as on social media and its two-faced character as an enabler as well as a distorting factor of the public sphere.

3.2.1 Legitimisation of EU Politics in Times of Crisis

Even with direct parliamentary European elections and after fostering the initiative and controlling rights of the European Parliament, the EU is still regarded by many—including European policymakers—to suffer from what has been coined a "democratic deficit" (Grimm 1995). This is due to the fact that the EC, with its growing competences as a European government, has no direct liability to European citizens, but is enacted and controlled by a multilevel system of policymaking, as a rather indirect mode of democracy. At the same time, the EU acts as a body representing European citizens, and functions as "... *a uniquely large and complex body of specialized decision-making, often operating outside the control of formalized and territorially bound systems of representative democracy*" (Michailidou and Trenz 2013: 260).

In a summary of the democratic deficit discussion and with a view to the current EU crisis and widespread criticism of the EU institutions' crisis management, Habermas (2015: 547) refers to the term by noting an "increasing distance separating the decision-making processes of EU-authorities from the political will formation of European citizens in their respective national arenas". Thus, the "democratic deficit" of the EU institutions continues to be a central feature of discussions about the future and the further development of the European Union. It becomes more relevant with the obvious problems of how to arrive at an integrated widely accepted European solution with regard to problems such as the financial crisis or the EU refugee policy. The central question is then, to what extent can the European institutions evolve into a European government with extended responsibilities (particularly with regard to social welfare and transfer politics), and how can this European government be democratically legitimised? Or is it unrealistic to expect this because the given diversity of Europe in terms of political culture, economic power and development of social welfare cannot simply be overcome by democratic structural reforms (e.g. strengthening the European Parliament and a European government elected by the Parliament)?

In a recent seminal dispute between public intellectuals about the future of Europe, both positions are prominent: On the one hand, it is held that there is a need to expand EU competences and that this has to (and can) be done by democratising the EU political system, in order to overcome the democratic deficit as well as the symptoms of the EU crisis (Habermas 2014a, b, 2015; Offe 2013a, b). On the other hand, there is the notion that it is the crisis itself which makes it obvious that further integration of Europe, as well as a way out of the legitimisation crisis by giving more competences to Brussels, is not an option (Scharpf 2014, 2015; Streeck 2013, 2015). Both positions hold that EU politics, as executed by the European Commission and the European Council, lacks democratic legitimation and responsiveness to the European citizenry. However, while from the one perspective (Scharpf, Streeck) this leads to the demand of restricting the competences of the EU to the advantages of national governments, keeping the EU in the status of a "regulatory state" (Majone 1996; see Lindner et al. 2016), from the other perspective (Habermas, Offe) this leads to demands of expanding the competences of the Union at the costs of national governments and at the same time strengthening the democratic legitimation of the European institutions by making them subject to direct elections and control by the European citizenry.

Especially, the Euro crisis has led to vivid debates about the legitimacy of the EU institutions' policy, the dominance of the European Central Bank (ECB) over the Parliament and the relation between national and European sovereigns, in the context of a discussion about EU fiscal policy, which cannot be discussed in detail here (see contributions in de Witte et al. 2013; see also Streeck 2015). It is, however, striking with regard to the Euro crisis that for both positions held with regard to the right fiscal policy, the democratic deficit "strikes back". Those who support the austerity and neoliberal programme of forcing Greece into a process of lowering the level of social welfare are confronted with the accusation that technocratic institutions are overruling democratically legitimised governments in Member States without themselves being backed up by democratic legitimisation. For those in favour of reacting to the crisis by installing a European fiscal and social policy (including a fiscal union), backing by a transnational solidarity consensus is needed, but is not in sight, given the apparently even deeper separation of the EU citizenry and the public sphere by predominant national interests.

Fritz W. Scharpf's (1999) influential distinction between input and output legitimacy helps to understand the particular relevance of the democratic deficit in times of crisis. Due to their transnational character, the EU institutions' legitimisation cannot be rooted in strong channels of information from citizens to the EC (input legitimacy) and thus must rely on legitimising its policies by the quality of its output, i.e. its decisions and regulations being in the best interests of, and thus supported by, the citizenry. The fact that in the latter respect the means of the EU institutions are also restricted has a special bearing in times of crisis. The missing input legitimacy becomes all the more problematic the weaker output legitimacy becomes, with apparent difficulties in establishing a consensus on a European way out of the fiscal crisis, or a joint European policy to solve the refugee problem. In a situation where strong decisions have to be taken at the EU level (beyond national interests), input legitimacy is urgently needed. For this reason, some regard a rearrangement of the EU institutional setting to be necessary. In order to (re)establish the bridge between the European citizenry and the European political elites, a strong European Parliament is needed. This implies a European electoral contestation between European (not nationally defined) political parties, on the basis of which the European Commission would be transformed into a government which is accountable to the Parliament representing the European citizenry. Offe (2013a), regarding the growing competence of institutions like the ECB, considers it to be detrimental to the project of European integration that those institutions which are *"farthest remote from democratic accountability"* have the *"greatest impact on daily life of people"*. He regards this to have developed into a *"deep divorce between politics and policy"* at the European level. Politics is based on often populist national mass politics with limited implications for the lives of people, whereas policymaking becomes an elitist matter that *"has no roots in, no links to nor legitimation through politics"* (Offe 2013a: 610). Also, in Habermas' view the democratic deficit has deepened in the course of establishing the Fiscal Compact and the European Stability Mechanism, because the European Parliament alone did not benefit from the increase of competences of the EU institutions (Habermas 2015: 551).

As a way out of the democratic deficit as well as of the crisis of EU integration, Habermas (2015)—despite the current climate against it—considers far-reaching institutional reform to be necessary. Due to the transnational character of the European Union, the democratic legitimisation of the institutions has to be backed up by a double "sovereign", represented in two chambers: on the one side the Parliament (citizenry) and on the other side the European Council, which he would like to see as the second legislative "leg" alongside the Parliament, representing as a second sovereign the European Member States and their peoples ("House of States"). He regards this to be the way to take account of both the transnational character of the European Union and European citizens' interests in having their ways of living and wealth protected by their national governments. This is in line with the conceptualisation of "transnational" democracy in Articles 9–12 of the Lisbon Treaty (Bogdandy 2012). The concept of "people" is reserved for the nation state, whereas individual citizenship (with individual political rights) is seen as the foundation of democratic legitimacy of the European Union.

On the other hand, it is argued that the conditions for expanding the competences of the European Parliament and deepening integration are not given. The crisis, requiring strong decisions on redistribution of resources, which have to be taken according to the majority rule, reveals that European solidarity is weak. The crisis has obviously brought about a reorientation towards national interests. As Offe (2013b: 75) puts it: the bank crisis has been transformed into a crisis of state finances (via the obligations that have been taken over by national governments to save the banks), which has turned out to cause a crisis of European integration, where rich countries force poorer countries into an austerity policy in order to re-establish trust in the financial industry. This has widely led to "*a renationalization of solidarity horizons*" in the European Union (*Renationalisierung der Solidaritätshorizonte*). Thus, what is needed for institutional reform and a further integration of the EU is lacking more now than ever before (Scharpf 2014; Streeck 2015). More generally, it is believed that the heterogeneity of Europe with regard to local, regional and national ways of living and economies only allows for a democratic European constitution that acknowledges these differences by way of far-reaching autonomy rights, which, with regard to financial constitutional questions, implies low mutual obligations of financial solidarity among partners (Streeck 2013).

Thus, beyond any debates of the actual problems of European policymaking, the discussion points to the more fundamental problems of European citizenship and the European public sphere. It can be argued that especially in times of crisis, it would be necessary to legitimise far-reaching decisions that will deeply influence living conditions in the European Member States through a vivid process of deliberation about pro and cons, needs, demands and duties. This, however, appears to have even less chance of being fostered, precisely due to the crisis mechanism that leads to focusing on national interests (Scharpf 2014; Streeck 2015).

Is there enough homogeneity and a European citizenship that can motivate European integration, and is there a European public sphere that can provide the fundaments for joint democratically legitimised European political action? In the following, we will first discuss the question of the European "demos" and then turn to actual research on the state of the European Public sphere.

3.2.2 "No Demos"? European Identity and Citizenship

It has always been a major pillar of the legitimisation of the European integration project that it will bring about increasing prosperity and general welfare through stimulating economic growth. Thus, it cannot come as a surprise that in an economic situation causing obvious difficulties in achieving consensus about common solutions at the European level, citizens expect their national governments to look at national economies first and protect them against a loss in welfare. Accordingly, based on Eurobarometer data, a study of the average European's identification with Europe as a part of their identity as citizens showed that "a sense of being European" dropped significantly in many European countries during the financial crisis in the period of 2005–2010. The general decrease in identification with Europe was strongest in those countries which suffered most in terms of decrease of per capita GDP or increase in unemployment as a result of the recession caused by the financial crisis, namely, the Baltic states, Great Britain, Italy, Ireland, France and Greece (Polyakova and Fligstein 2016).

It is this observation of weak European solidarity and the predominance of national perspectives that feeds the so-called "no demos" discussion among scholars of European politics. The debate dates back to the 1990s and starts from the notion that in order to work, democracy needs to be rooted in a "demos", a political (as opposed to an ethnic) community which is rooted in "a strong sense of community and loyalty among a political group"—this being, as it were, the socio-cultural prerequisite of democracy (Risse 2014: 1207). The assumption that a "demos" of this kind does not exist at the European level, but only at the national level, and that the different "demoi" of the Member States do not form a meta-national demos, implies that democracy at the transnational level cannot (and must not) be based on input legitimacy, but mainly on the quality of the output of the political system. Authors such as Scharpf (see above) hold that due to the heterogeneity (cultural as well as economic) of living conditions in the Member States, there is no basic consensus—or subjectively felt citizenship—which could function as a cultural backbone holding the community together against conflictive majority decisions in the (reformed) European Union. The acknowledgement of majority decisions that might be against their own interests (at least until the next elections) can only be expected on the grounds of an implicit cultural consensus based on shared citizenship.

In other words, no pre-political community exists for integration at the European level that is comparable to integration at the level of the nation state. Europe is not a nation state but can be thought of as a "mixed commonwealth", in which national and supranational identities coexist with each other. Europe "... *possesses aspects of a nation, but it is a rather watered-down version of it [...]. It relies on a body of treaties that provides a framework of 'constitutionality' but without a constitution. It offers membership, but subordinated to the stronger Member State form. Its members are related, but with a link much weaker than that of ordinary polities. Such a link is based on some commonalities—which ground a very vague shared political identity among its members, but not comparable with political identities at nation state level*" (Lobeira 2012: 516).

This type of observation is not contested by those who are optimistic about the possibility of European citizenship; however, they hold that it neglects the specific character of transnational compared to national citizenship (Habermas 2015). Instead, it is argued that European democracy is not in need of a "demos" in terms of a cultural (national) community, but that European citizens' commitment to the fundaments of the European political constitution is sufficient to establish a new form of "citizenship". This "constitutional patriotism", together with a well-functioning European democracy, would be sufficient as a solidarity fundament for the European Union (see also Lindner et al. 2016).

With the current conflicting mode of policymaking in the EU, this position is confronted with new scepticism. A prominent observer from abroad, the US philosopher and communitarian thinker Amitai Etzioni (2013), considers neither the democratic deficit nor a weakness of the European political system to be Europe's current main problem. From his perspective, what proves to be crucial in this crisis is what he calls the "communitarian deficit", i.e. the lack of a post-national sense of community or European citizenship: *"The insufficient sharing of values and bonds— not the poor representative mechanisms—is a major cause of alienation from Brussels' and limits the normative commitment to make sacrifices for the common good*" (Etzioni 2013: 312). He holds that there needs to be more than constitutional patriotism to establish enough solidarity to solve the problems of economic disparities among the European Member States: *"Membership in a more interdependent EU involves not just rights but burdensome duties (such as bailing out the Greeks) that will only be voluntarily met if citizens feel the value of communal obligation to those beyond their national borders*" (Etzioni 2013: 315).

Contrary to this communitarian view, it is believed that European citizenship cannot be understood according to national citizenship coupled with cultural identity as it emerged with the constitution of the nation state in early modernity. Transnational identity or citizenship and the related sense of belonging "*... involves starting from a different standpoint, one that sees belonging as an identity 'in the making' and that imagines it to be 'deterritorialised' and set in a transnational dimension*" (Scalise 2014: 52). Indeed, there are at least weak indications from some qualitative research that a "mixed identity" can be found in Europe. Based on interviews with a group of 40 people from a local community in Italy, Scalise (2014) undertook to reconstruct the narratives about Europe that emerge and are shared among "average" European citizens, and highlights this specific type of identity and citizenship in the following way: *"Different narratives of Europe are shared among Europeans: stories related to the cultural and historical roots of the continent, institutional and 'official' narratives of the EU, biographical stories weaved together with collective memories. Multi-level stories, a mixture of values and references coming from the local and national heritage and linked to the European post-national plot. In the broad range of the narratives which have emerged, the influence of the local context, where the stories originate, can always be identified. The stories of Europe are embedded in the regional territories. [...] There is a dynamic relation between* *the local, national, supranational and transnational dimensions. These levels interact in the European identity construction process*" (Scalise 2014: 59).

To what extent this can be regarded as an indication of a general European identity is of course an open question and has to be confirmed by much broader research approaches. Beyond this, however, proponents of a further integration of the EU base their cautionary optimism with regard to the "Europeanisation of European citizens" in the further development of the discourse about Europe and, thus, in the further development of the European public sphere (see the next section). From this perspective the development of European identity and solidarity depends on the chances and opportunities to discuss and define what is in the common European interest via a common European political discourse. For this—and the democratic deficit comes into perspective again—it is necessary for the European Parliament to function as a European public space, which foremost implies that societal interests and political debate on the "common good" are not organised alongside national party lines but are fostered by European (transnational) party groups (Habermas 2014a: 94). A European party system is a precondition for overcoming the national restriction of perspectives and would prepare the ground for a will formation at the European level, i.e. in the light of shared (and not nationally divided) normative principles of social justice, and with regard to shared assessments of the problems at stake and the way out (Offe 2013a: 606 f.). The constitution of the EU generally has the effect that European citizens in their national contexts are not confronted with alternatives of European policies to be discussed publicly, but are just affected by the results of EU policies decided on by the EC and the Council of Ministers. From this perspective, identity is not culturally given (as supposed by a communitarian perspective; see Etzioni, above), but evolves in a political process. In this way, citizenship must (and can) emerge out of debates and conflicts about the public good—as was the case for national identities in the conflictual emergence of the nation state (Habermas 2015). Thus, it is important to what extent the EU polity allows for a vivid political discourse among citizens. From this perspective, it clearly makes a difference whether the citizenry is consulted by means of e-participation methods (see below), or to what extent institutional innovations, like the European Citizen Initiative, add to the set of citizens' rights by giving citizens a voice in lawmaking (Ene and Micu 2013).

3.2.3 Politicisation of Europe and European Citizenship

In this respect the contestation of European issues in the context of the fiscal or refugee crisis is regarded by many as not necessarily an indication of disintegration, but as an indication of the Europeanisation of politics. Scholars of European politics thus speak of a "politicisation of the European integration" with positive connotations, meaning that there is an observable tendency to publicly address the issues and problems of European multi-level democracy (Wendler 2012; de Wilde and Zürn 2012; Hooghe and Marks 2008). The contestation of European integration has for around a decade been observed to be based in conflicts around cultural identity (Hooghe and Marks 2008; Kriesi et al. 2007), in the lack of compatibility between national and supranational institutions (Schmidt 2008) and in resource and distribution conflicts in the context of regulation of the European market (Hix 2009; Majone 2002). The so-called "permissive consensus", characterised by wide implicit EU-scepticism, but where citizens do not engage with EU issues and leave the playing field to political elite with the effect of the de-thematisation of Europe in national public spheres, has come to an end. Underlying conflicts have now come to the fore and made Europe a public issue (Hooghe and Marks 2008).

Politicisation of European integration is then regarded as being driven by an expanding public discourse that provides for transparency of decision-making, includes civil society and provides for critical feedback to decision-makers, thus having a "democratising function". The contestation of Europe in the actual crisis is also regarded as being a sign of a functioning Europeanised public sphere with a potential for democratic reform of the European polity (Statham and Trenz 2012, 2015). However, insofar as this reform does not take place, the weakness of the EU institutional system will be further exposed in the public sphere, which will foster scepticism even further (ibid.)

Despite the obvious fact that politicisation of the issue of European integration in the Euro crisis is accompanied by national interests and the dominance of national stereotypes in national public debates, many observers (Risse 2015c; Hutter and Grande 2012; Rauh 2013) hold that politicisation, when coupled with an opening of national public spheres in terms of Europeanisation (see below), can be regarded as an indicator of increased awareness of the relevance of Europe for Europeans. It depends on the framing of EU issues whether or not the growing politicisation of EU affairs increases the sense of community in Europe. In this respect, it is also held that politicisation of European integration is clearly induced by the growing authority of the European institutions since the 1980s. It is therefore believed that it is decisive to actively address and deal with the problem of the growing authority of the EU institutions and the need to back this up by fostering their democratic legitimacy (de Wilde and Zürn 2012).

An overview of recent research about European identity even concludes that there are indications for a gradually growing identification of citizens with Europe as well as the Europeanisation of national public debates. In a 2013 Eurobarometer poll, 59% of polled citizens showed some degree of identification with the EU while only 38% identified exclusively with the nation state. No significant divisions could be found in creditor and debtor countries of the Eurozone in this respect (Risse 2014: 1208 f.). There are also indications that identification with Europe does not mainly come as a symbolic attitude. According to Kuhn and Stoekel (2014), polling data shows that the more people identify with Europe the more they are also prepared to support policies of economic governance with re-distributional effects to overcome the Euro crisis. Thus, the crisis and related conflicts do not necessarily lead to reduced solidarity. Risse (2014: 1210) summarises that available opinion poll data challenges the "no demos" thesis, leading to an optimistic notion that "... *the European polity is more mature than many scholars assume. A sense of community does exist among Europeans and this community might even be prepared to accept redistributive consequences*". In the same vein, based on opinion polls and long-term panel research with citizens from six European countries, Harrison and Bruter (2014) conclude that there is evidence that the politicisation of European issues can be seen as a cause as well as a result of the emergence of a European identity. This implies that the more people appropriate themselves to the European polity, "*the more politicized is their perception of their—thereby appropriated—system*" (Harrison and Bruter 2014: 166).

However, these optimistic conclusions are not uncontested, and with a look at nationalist and populist EU-scepticism all around Europe, not least after the Brexit vote, it can reasonably be argued that neither politicisation nor an increase in Europeanisation of media reporting in the current crisis (if observable) will have positive effects on identities. The crisis clearly brings new forces and actors to the fore that are not supportive of European integration and offer views that focus on national interests and thus help to strengthen national identities (Checkel 2015; Checkel and Katzenstein 2009). Based on a media analysis in six European countries up to 2012 (thus including the Euro crisis), Grande and Kriesi (2015) report a substantial increase in politicisation as well as Europeanisation of public discourses, but are sceptical with regard to the effects of this on the identification of citizens with Europe. They hold that since negative framing of the European integration goes across the left–right party political cleavage, politicisation under the given political structures will contribute to more EU-scepticism.

There is, however, consensus—also among observers with a more pessimistic view on the current state of European solidarity and citizenship—that the European public sphere has a strong bearing on the development of a European identity: "*It is in public debate that collective identities are constructed and reconstructed and publicly displayed thereby creating political communities*" (Pfetsch and Heft 2015: 30). It is therefore decisive to understand to what extent a public sphere in Europe exists.

3.3 A European Public Sphere?

The public sphere can be understood as a space of political communication among members of a territorially defined entity with a normative, legitimising function for a particular political institution (see Lindner et al. 2016). Historically, the development of a political public sphere is connected with the emergence of the nation state, so that until the 1980s, speaking of a public sphere implied speaking of national public spheres. However, with the globalisation of politics, policymaking is to a growing extent related to transnational problems and problem-solving and, consequently, the space of political communication is one that transcends national borders. Europe is without doubt an example of transnational policymaking (Hepp et al. 2012: 22 ff.). However, it is the subject of debate to what extent transnational policymaking is accompanied and thus legitimised by a functioning transnational European space of political communication.

3.3.1 National Public Spheres "Europeanised"?

According to a recent review of scholarly discussion on the European public sphere, the following can be regarded as being consensus among researchers: *"The concept of a utopian European public sphere, defined as a singular supranational space that echoes the national public sphere, is nowadays rejected in the literature under the evidence of a missing common European identity, the lack of significant purely European media, and communication difficulties, namely language differences"* (Monza and Anduiza 2016: 503).

The European public sphere is almost exclusively conceptualised as the Europeanisation of national public spheres. Europeanisation is then observable by a change of national public spheres in three respects: (1) European issues, policies and actors are visible in the "national" public spheres, i.e. in mass media coverage of political issues, (2) there is reference in national media not only to EU policymaking actors (vertical) but also to actors from other European Member States (horizontal) and (3) the same issues are addressed in the different national public spheres and similar frames of reference or claims and arguments are put forward. In all these respects, there is apparently a consensus in research that a Europeanisation of public spheres has taken place. Mass media studies have shown that over the past 15 years, national publics have become more European in terms of the visibility and salience of EU issues and actors, the presence of other Europeans in national public spheres, as well as with regard to the similarity of interpretative frames of reference or claims across borders, without the existence of European-wide media (Koopmanns and Zimmermann 2010; Hepp et al. 2012; Sicakkan 2013; Risse 2014, contributions in Risse 2015a). It can be said that positions claiming that the emergence of a European public sphere is impossible, due to structural or mainly language barriers (e.g. Grimm 1995), are almost no longer visible (Risse 2015b: 3). Meanwhile, the Europeanisation of national public spheres has also been found by many issue-specific media studies, such as in the discourse on the EU Diversity directive in France (Dressler et al. 2012), the media coverage of the EU's growth and job strategy (de la Porte and van Dalen 2016), media coverage of the discussion about a common EU foreign and security policy (Kandyla and de Vreese 2011) or by analysis of references to the "European citizen" in national media (Walter 2015). Additionally, a methodological approach which differs from the usual news content analysis supports the notion of horizontal integration of the mediated European public sphere. Data provided by Veltri (2012) via a network analysis of information flow between Central European high-quality newspapers (UK, Germany, Spain, France) indicate that from 2000 to 2009 the information flow became less dense among the newspapers analysed, but that a more balanced network of information flows among European newspapers took shape that can be interpreted as a signal of a qualitative transformation of the European communicative exchange in the direction of horizontal integration. Beyond these general findings, in recent years research on the European public sphere has brought about results that help to understand in what respects we can speak of Europeanisation and also what its limits are. Despite growing interest in Internet-based public communication and the role of social media (see below), the vast majority of empirical work regarding the European public sphere is still on the coverage of European issues, actors and institutions in (national) mass media (mainly press). The vast amount of studies published in recent years cannot be covered in detail in this chapter. In the following, we briefly sketch the most interesting findings.

3.3.1.1 Dominance of EU Executive Institutions at the Costs of the European Parliament

As regards the visibility of European actors, it appears that the European Parliament lags behind other European institutions in being referred to in national mass media reporting, and that national actors gained visibility due to the role of the European institutions in the financial crisis. Koopmanns (2015) explores the degree of Europeanisation on the basis of newspaper reports in six European countries from 1990 to 2002, and newspaper reporting on the financial crisis from 2010 to 2012 in Germany. He found that for the debate on monetary politics the visibility and roles of actors from the EU central institutions (vertical Europeanisation) as well of those from other European countries (horizontal Europeanisation) in the newspapers' coverage of European issues was comparable to the roles of national central and regional actors in reports about national politics. However, the European level was *"more present as a target than as a speaker of claims in their own right"*. Nevertheless, he concludes that *"with one third of claims coming from [...] European-level actors (mainly the European Central Bank), they make a substantial contribution to opinion formation"* (Koopmanns 2015: 81). For Germany, he found that in the years of the financial crisis, 2010–2012, the discursive influence in media reports in Germany *"was almost equally balanced among domestic, transnational, and European-level actors"*, whereas during the introduction of the Euro (2000–2002), there was a strong dominance by the European institutions. Koopmanns concludes that Europeanised political communications *"stand the comparison to the yardstick of national public debates"* (Koopmanns 2015: 82). From the German case he concludes that the fact that national parliaments and other national political actors regained influence in media reports on European financial issues can be read as a welcome signal for the democratisation of European politics, whereas the significant losses of discursive influence of all European institutions (except the ECB) indicate the emergence of a more "intergovernmental" and "domesticated" Europe at the cost of a supranational European polity (Koopmanns 2015: 82).

3.3.1.2 EU-Scepticism as an Indication of Europeanisation of Public Spheres

Not surprisingly the growing EU-scepticism in recent years is reflected in the media coverage of European issues. However, this can also be seen as an indication of the Europeanisation of the public sphere. A study of mass media reporting in *The Guardian*, *Le Monde*, *El País*, *La Stampa* and *Süddeutsche Zeitung* on the European Parliament elections in 2014 revealed a significant Europeanisation of reporting in terms of the visibility of the EU campaign in the media analysed, as well as the visibility of the EU institutions and actors (Belluati 2016). Despite national particularities the study also found converging narratives on the elections and on European integration. Paradoxically, the significant role of EU-scepticism in the election campaign (such as UKIP in Great Britain, FN in France, AfD in Germany or the Five Star Movement in Italy) led to a politicisation of the issue of European integration that can be read as a "Europeanisation" of public debates, without necessarily supporting a Eurosceptic tendency in the media reporting. The study holds that the broad coverage of the EU election campaign, apart from the Euroscepticism issue, was due to the fact that *"the electorate has gained a more direct voice in the selection of the President of the European Commission"*, and EP parties *"for the first time have selected candidates for this position, hence structuring the electoral campaign and giving visibility to such candidates..."* (Belluati 2016: 131). This finding could possibly support the argument for the salience of a European party system for the emergence of European will formation beyond national borders, as discussed above.

A broad empirical study (www.Eurosphere.org) conceptualised the European public sphere as a "conflictive space" by which the *"vertical, pro-European, elite dominated trans-European public sphere"*, which is constituted by the EU institutions' policies of European integration, comes into a relationship of conflict and contestation with existing national and regional public spaces. The study's results suggest that this mode of Europeanisation of the public sphere is an existing reality (Sicakkan 2013: 2). The study comprised interviews and media analysis of the EU's integration policies in 16 European countries and found that EU policies managed to link national constituencies with the EU to a clearly discernible extent. This vertical European public sphere, however, is dominated by an elitist and expert discourse of democratisation, inclusion and Europeanisation. However, the "populist" reaction against this discourse has transformed national publics into *"horizontal trans-European publics"* (Sicakkan 2013: 68). Thus, the criticism of Europeanisation itself—as it were—is "Europeanised".

3.3.1.3 Dominance of Political Elites, Lack of Visibility of Civil Society Actors

The notion of a dominant role for political elites and the EU administration in Europeanised public spheres is supported by the findings of Koopmanns and Statham (2010). Studying media coverage of European political issues in the period 2001–2004, they found support for the notion that a European public sphere exists in terms of the visibility of EU politics in national media. But it is mainly the political elites that are represented, whereas civil society remains underrepresented as political actors on EU issues. For the period covered by the study, they found that this was connected with an overly supportive voice for European integration—remarkably with the exception of the British media coverage of the European institutions and issues. Thus, they found a lack of contestation regarding EU issues (reflecting what has been called the "permissive consensus"; see above). Studies covering the period of the politicisation of Europe reflect the move away from the "permissive consensus" of recent years (see below).

3.3.1.4 National Frames of Reference and Cultural Differences Remain Relevant

One of the most salient results is that Europeanisation does not exclude and diminish the role of national differences. It is obvious that with the lack of a common European language or European media, political discourse on Europe still, and despite Europeanisation, "...comes largely by way of national political actors speaking to national publics in national languages reported by national media and considered by national opinion" (Schmidt 2013: 13). To add to this picture, only a small minority of educated EU citizens observe foreign media (Gerhards and Hans 2014, based on Eurobarometer surveys 2007: 2010). It also must be acknowledged that generally EU issues still often rank behind national issues. A study of the media coverage of the 2004 and 2009 European elections in the Czech Republic and Slovakia (Kovář and Kovář 2013) found that—in line with the low voter turnout and the "second order elections" thesis (that EP elections are politically less relevant than national ones)—media only marginally cover EP elections and notably less than national "first-order" elections. Additionally, coverage of EP elections is dominated by domestic EU political actors, whereas visibility of EU actors was low. Both applied especially to private TV stations, and to a lesser degree for quality newspapers.

In those countries with (according to opinion polls, Eurobarometer) a more positive attitude to the European Union, media coverage of EU issues is also more intense than in countries with lower support for the EU, as was found in a study on press coverage of the European Parliament in six EU countries between 2005 and 2007 (Gattermann 2013). Beyond these differences in the level of Europeanisation, national discourses often differ significantly, and the way European issues are communicated by mass media is still to a great extent based on national identities, which, e.g. is in turn reflected by a more sceptical and detached attitude towards European integration in Britain as compared to a more positive one in Germany, as is shown by Novy (2013). Hepp et al. (2012) analysed the development of references to Europe and European policymaking in the content of quality and boulevard press in six European countries, using media samples from the period of 1982–2008. They clearly confirm the otherwise supported finding that national public spheres have over the period of 26 years been increasingly transnationalised, i.e. Europeanised, in terms of referring to European policy issues and discussing this with a view to other public spheres in other EU Member States. Beyond this, Hepp et al.—via interviews with journalists and observation of journalism practice in the countries included in the study—found segmentation at the national level of an existing European public sphere by different national discourse cultures which affect the practice of journalism. This, e.g. shows up in different references to transnational (European) issues: Whereas, e.g. in Denmark and the UK, reference to European issues is made in a more distanced way, segregating these issues from the national context, in Germany, France and Austria, such reference is made by relating it to the national context, regarding the national as part of the transnational, European context. Despite such effects of national discourse cultures, Hepp et al. conclude that in all countries involved (except for Britain) reference to Europe is a routine part of journalism in Europe and that it is a general practice to "construct" national identity in the context of other European nations, so that somewhat paradoxically "... *the stability of national political discourse cultures are an aspect of the 'substructure' of a transnational European public sphere*" (Hepp et al. 2012: 209, own translation).

Scarce studies dedicated to media analysis in new Member States often show more negative results as regards the Europeanisation of public spheres. This sceptical perspective is supported by an analysis of the role of EU issues during the Czech national parliament election campaigns in 2002, 2006 and 2010 (Urbanikova and Volek 2014). The authors conclude from the low number and the content of articles that referred to the EU that in the Czech press the EU agenda was increasingly less visible over the period observed. Moreover, they discovered that it was increasingly negatively framed. The study also found that the EU agenda was mainly discussed with regard to economic and monetary issues, indicating that the EU agenda "*is increasingly reduced to an economic agenda*" (Urbanikova and Volek 2014: 468), obviously indicating the growing importance of the fiscal and monetary debate (not only in the Euro Zone), at least since 2009. Differences in national framing among Member States have to be taken into account, and media coverage of EU issues is more frequent in old Member States than in new ones. The attitudes of actors prominent in media reports also tend to be more negative towards European integration in the new rather than in the old Member States—as is supported by data from the Eurosphere project (eurosphere.eu) on media coverage of the issues of the "Reform Treaty" and the "EU Constitution" in 2008 (Zografova et al. 2012).

3.3.2 Politicisation of the European Public Sphere

As with the debate about European identity, the notion of a "politicisation" of Europe and the future of European integration is prominent in discussions and research on the European public sphere. Despite the strong current of EU-scepticism that comes with it, politicisation is believed by many to indicate a vitalisation of the European public sphere (Statham and Trenz 2015). *"Politics is back"*, as a volume with contributions on the latest state of debate about the European public sphere puts it (Risse 2015a). Europe—its future, its mode of policymaking and its democratic legitimacy—is an issue of vivid public debate more than ever before. A few empirical studies are available on the effects of the crisis and the subsequent politicisation of European integration on the "European public spheres". Their results show a growing dominance of national perspectives and interest in public discourse on the EU, but do not necessarily dismiss the notion of a European public sphere.

Findings of a large-scale media content analysis of newspaper and television news in the EU-15 (1999), EU-25 (2004) and EU-27 (2009) in relation to European Parliament elections show that media coverage of EU issues is dependent on the elites' or parties' positions in the respective countries (Boomgaarden et al. 2013). The more disputes among elites and national parties about European issues, the more Europe becomes visible in the national media—which, however, implies a strong position of EU-critical positions. It could be shown that "...*increases in EU news visibility were strongest in a situation in which there was both increasing negativity about the EU in a country's party system and increasing party disagreement about the EU*" (Boomgaarden et al. 2013: 621). The authors conclude that "... *ironically, euro-scepticism, in the form of elite polarisation, is one of the best chances for improving EU democracy by sparking news coverage of EU affairs*" (Boomgaarden et al. 2013: 625).

A study (Monza and Anduiza 2016) focusing on exploring the visibility of the EU and European subjects in national media during the financial and Euro crisis started from the plausible hypothesis that with the strong consequences of EU policies, the salience of EU issues in the news should have been increased, especially in those countries that are subject to the EU austerity policy. The study—based on a set of articles with reference to the crisis, recession or austerity from leading newspapers in Germany, Greece, Italy, Spain, Poland, Sweden, Switzerland and the UK in the period of 2008–2014—found that the visibility of European actors (in terms of claims made related to the crisis as reported in the media as well as the addressees of claims) was surprisingly low when compared to national actors, indicating that the national perspective and national policymakers were dominant in the crisis discourse. The visibility of EU actors was highest in Germany (11% of the sample) and Greece (11%), and lowest in the UK (4%) and Switzerland (1%). Differences in the visibility of EU actors and issues were not correlated with the countries' degree of negative effect from the recession. The relative prominence of European issues and actors in Germany and Greece can be explained by the German government's leading role in debates on the Greek bailout and by Greece being the main addressee of the European institutions' austerity policy.

An analysis of news coverage of the Euro crisis (2010–2013) and the 2009 parliamentary elections in online media news platforms, held by leading national newspapers or TV channels in 13 European countries (Michailidou 2015), found that in all countries covered by the study the EU was uniformly contested and criticised from the perspective of national politics, which in all cases were the key defining frame of media reporting. The results of the content analysis suggest that there is indeed a European-wide pattern of discussing the financial crisis and the role of EU politics, mainly made up by EU contestation, which refers to the issue of (lacking) democratic legitimation of EU politics, but mainly in a diffuse or emotional manner. Interestingly, especially concerning the online comments on EU news posted by readers, the study showed that, "...*democracy is the most frequently used category to contextualise or justify not only Eurosceptic comments but evaluations of the EU polity across the entire 'affirmative European to anti-European' spectrum. What unites the user community is its anti-elitism and self-understanding of constituting the people's voice that mobilizes in defence of the representative system of democracy or more frequently against the corrupt, decaying version*" (Michailidou 2015: 332). What appears to be interesting about this finding is that the crisis apparently brought the issue of democracy into the centre of the debate, thus stressing the relevance of the "EU democratic deficit" issue for the European public sphere in times of crisis.

In the politicised and Europeanised national public spheres, the national perspective in times of crisis appears to be dominant, but a study on the few broadcasting formats at the transnational European level found the framing of European issues in terms of European solidarity to be dominant (Williams and Toula 2017). In an analysis of the debate programme "Talking Europe", which is produced with the sponsorship of the European Parliament and the Commission and has been broadcast on "France 24" since early 2009, it was found "... *that the solidarity frame is used to define problems and causes of issues and events as attributable to a lack of solidarity between EU members and also to present the solution of increasing solidarity as a means to enhance policy and practice. Moral judgments are introduced to cast blame on those actors who do not demonstrate solidarity. Problems framed in terms of solidarity deficits are then remedied through three-pronged solutions of integration, harmonization, and calls for greater solidarity*" (Williams and Toula 2017: 8). The analysis focused on episodes dealing with the Eurozone crisis between January and November 2011.

All in all, empirical research on the effects of the crisis on the Europeanisation of national media publics appears to show mixed results. "Politicisation" is an indicator of European issues coming to the fore of national agendas, but this, of course, does not necessarily lead to issues being framed as questions of common European concern requiring European solutions. It depends on discursive structures and dynamics of whether politicised debates about Europe foster European common thinking and identities or renationalisation. Politicisation must come with Europeanisation: With a view to Brexit, it is interesting to note that research has shown that in the British public sphere Europe is highly politicised but Europeanised to a much lower degree (with respect to frames and visibility of European actors, Koopmanns and Statham 2010; see also Koopmanns 2015). It thus appears to be important whether or not pro-European elites use the politicisation of Europe for rethinking the democratic structures of the EU and/or actively engage in a discussion about options to address the democratic deficit (Risse 2015c). The fact that issues of European integration, European democracy as well as modes of European governance are found to be increasingly contested in the European public spheres does not necessarily imply dysfunctional workings of European political communication. Contestation and conflict are as much a necessary function of the public sphere as striving for consensus and compromise, or aggregation of political will. It can even be said that if empirical studies should find a lack of disagreement on central constitutional issues—as are at stake in debates on the legitimacy of EU policy interventions in times of crisis—this might not be taken as an indication that "*desired consensus processes has run its course in the European public spheres*". It could also be seen as an indication that public arenas are not yet "*fully developed and utilized in a truly democratic manner*" (Føllesdal 2015: 254). In other words, as is held by a broad scope of scholars of European studies, the contestation of Europe as a democratic project is as much an indication of a failure of the European public sphere as the long period of the so-called "permissive consensus"—with a low level of discussion about European integration—was an indication of its functioning.

3.3.3 Deficits of Research

The discussion of media analysis of the European public sphere has brought up some shortcomings and deficits of research that should be taken account of when interpreting research results. Especially with regard to the increasing EU criticism in some new Member States, it has to be kept in mind that research has so far mainly focused on the old EU15, and there is not much data about the development of the public sphere in new Member States (especially in those countries currently being front runners of EU-scepticism). Data showing a widely Europeanised public sphere is mainly from central and western European Member States (with the exception of the UK). On the one hand, research would expect that "in the course of time differences in the Europeanisation of old and new Member States seem to vanish", since they observe a "pattern of catch-up Europeanisation" (Kleinen von Königslow and Möller 2009: 101, cit. Pfetsch and Heft 2015: 45). Others hold a more pessimistic view with regard to this "modernisation story" and point to the different historical backgrounds of new Member States in Central and Eastern Europe, as well as cultural aspects like a strong and orthodox religious current in some countries that might persist (Checkel 2015: 236 f.).

Since media analysis is mainly done by using data from quality newspapers, which are read mainly by elites, the finding of a step-by-step Europeanisation found here might not apply for TV or other newspapers, which are the reference for the average public (Koopmanns 2015). It has also been stressed that we have to take into account that the focus of research on elite mass media communication neglects the relevance of new Internet-based communication networks mainly applied by social movements, which can be regarded as a Europeanisation of public spheres "from below" (Bennett et al. 2015). The focus of research on mass media might on the one hand overstate Europeanisation, but on the other might underestimate the diversity of publics and their segmentation, the latter coming into focus in research on political communication via the Internet.

3.4 The Internet and the Public Sphere

The idea of the Internet as a "virtual" or a "networked" public sphere—as articulated by Castels (2008)— starts from the notion that due to the option of interactive communication which is unrestricted with regard to time and space, the web is enabling a new and enhanced public sphere that transcends national boundaries. For example, it provides new options for civil society actors to make their demands visible and reinforces communication between constituencies and their political representatives. Recent years have brought about more detailed empirical analysis of the Internet's relevance for political communication, thus complementing the previously mass media focused research on the public sphere. With a view to the widespread use of political blogs and social media by political actors of all kinds, there can be no doubt that the web has developed into a new space of political exchange alongside the mass media. Political actors can address their communities and followers directly and forward their comments and news via Internet platforms and social media (and vice versa). Mass media has built up web-based news platforms and uses the web as a source for news production. However, research and scholarly debate on the virtual public sphere—an overview of which is given in the following pages—do not give uncontested evidence for a new or revitalised public sphere being realised by the options of political Internet communication. Whereas the new means of communication among citizens as well as between policymakers and their constituencies have been seen initially mainly as drivers towards a more vivid public sphere of open debate, meanwhile the negative, as it were, "anti-deliberative" aspects of social media have come to the fore.

3.4.1 The Democratic Potential of the Internet as a Public Sphere

Bohman (2004; see also Lindner et al. 2016) regarded the Internet as opening up a new mode of transnational political publics, due to the possibility of allowing for communication across the restrictions of time and space and also national and linguistic boundaries. He thus expressed some optimism that, while we find a decline of national public spheres with passive audiences and disenchantment with politics, the Internet could support the emergence of a transnational public sphere that is more inclusive and deliberative and is rooted in a transnational civil society. But such far-reaching expectations are now rarely put forward.

There is, without doubt, a growing importance and public visibility of so-called "dot.com" protest platforms and social media-based exchange across national borders on humanitarian or environmental issues, which is held to show features of an emerging global civil society. Local protest movements can have outreach to the world, make their demands known and gather support globally—e.g. the movement of the outraged in Spain and Greece. The "Occupy Wall Street" movement managed to engage on a global level via social media. World economic summits and climate change summits are regularly accompanied by online mediated activities of NGOs. Thus, globalisation at the economic and governmental levels can be regarded as being complemented by an Internet-supported global civil society organising counter- or protest discourses (e.g. Frangonikolopoulos 2012). Bohman (2004; see Lindner et al. 2016) conceptualised this Internet-based transnational public sphere as consisting of multiple issue-related publics, thus creating a public of publics with a distributed rather than a centralised structure. Additionally, currently observers who are more sceptical with regard to the emergence of a transnational public sphere underline the capacity of Internet communication to induce global political communication in an "... *indirect and networked sense—not as a supra-national sphere, but as a multitude of mediated and unmediated discursive processes aimed at opinion formation at various levels, interconnected directly and indirectly*" (Rasmussen 2013: 103). If this is a correct description of the Internet's structure as a public sphere, then the decisive question is to what extent these multiple publics are related to or cut off from one another. Smith (2015) regards the ease of creating new websites or digital platforms (by everybody and for any purpose) as a political "double-edged sword", as it makes it "*both easier to create common realms open to all and to leave the common world and create one's own little realm where no opposing viewpoints can be heard*" (Smith 2015: 256). Thus, the Internet has the potential for both creating new public spaces and weakening the general public sphere.

A fundamental critique of the discourse on the virtual public sphere looks at the economic fundaments of social media and peer-to-peer networks. From this perspective the democratic potential of the Internet's ability to allow for self-production of content, independent of the restrictions of the mass media, is called into question. The explosion of self-production and exchange of content is regarded as fundamentally based on a growing economy of transmission and exchange of data by providers such as Google or Facebook. With a view inspired by Michel Foucault's analysis of governmentality, Goldberg (2010) concludes the following in his criticism of the scholarly discourse on the "virtual public sphere": "*On the internet there is no 'debating and deliberating' that is not also 'buying and selling'[...]; participation is a commercial act. Every instance of participation involves a transfer of data which has been economized, driving the profitability and viability of the networking industry and of internet based companies like Google that cover infrastructure costs through innovative advertising, 'freemium' business models, and other methods*" (Goldberg 2010: 749).

Jürgen Habermas, one of the most important thinkers of the model of deliberative democracy, appears to be rather sceptical as regards the potential of the Internet to foster a modernised, renewed democratic sphere of public discourse when postulating the decisive and indispensable function of a lively public sphere for modern democracy. When asked in an interview in 2014, "Is internet beneficial or unbeneficial for democracy?", his answer was "neither one nor the other" (Habermas 2014b). He substantiates this notion by referring to what in his view was and is the central function of the public sphere for democracy, which allows for the simultaneous attention of an undefined number of people to be paid to public problems. Despite increased transparency and access to information for everybody as well as the option to make every reader an author of statements on the web, the web in Habermas' view does not help to *concentrate* the attention of an anonymous public on a few *political important questions*. By opening up a vast scope of single-issue spaces, the web rather "*distracts and dispels*". The web thus is a *mare magnum* of digital noises containing billions of communities as *dispersed archipelagos* and is not able to bring about a space of common (public) interests. In order to bring about *concentration*, the *skills of good old journalism* are still needed (all quotations from Habermas 2014b).

The conclusion by West (2013, following Dahlgren 2005) that the Internet may be best understood as an agent of mobilisation of sub-publics with regard to all kinds of issues as an "extension" for the mass media public sphere appears to catch a seminal feature of Internet political communication, but also underlines the restrictions of its democratic potential: "*The ability of the internet to quickly rally people, as in the 2011 'Occupy' movements, is difficult to contest. But, as subsequent events has (sic) shown, the ability of the new electronic media to transform those movements into lasting social change, or to use the new media as a public sphere whose discourse must be reckoned with, is not yet evident*" (West 2013). In this respect the conclusion we drew a couple of years ago (Lindner et al. 2016) that the Internet is at best an emerging public sphere would still hold. However, substantial differentiation with regard to different modes and formats of political Internet communication is visible in the scholarly debates and empirical research in publications of the past few years.

3.4.2 A New Landscape of Political Communication: A Public Sphere from Below?

The widespread use of new modes of political communication via the Internet indicates that Internet communication is indeed about to modify the public sphere from one mediated by mass media (and mass communication) to one mediated by a multitude of networks based on the interpersonal exchange and interactivity allowed by the Internet. From this point of view, the public sphere then exists of a network with nodes being made up by web-based spaces of political discussion, organised on websites or social media sites held by individuals, social interest groups, governmental authorities or political parties. Ideally, these different nodes are connected to one another so that the different issue-related or socially organised political communication spaces are not completely isolated but form some sort of new networked public sphere. As far as such networks also reach across national borders, one might speak of *transnational public spheres* emerging *from below,* rather than *from above* through the mega television networks offered to world audiences (Munteanu and Staiculescu 2015).

Transnational issue advocacy networks of Civil Society Organisations (CSOs) mainly mediated via social media (Twitter, Facebook, YouTube) and NGO websites are held to have the capacity *"to engage large publics directly"* and bring them into contact with government institutions, enabling people to coordinate action across national boundaries (Bennett 2012: 6). In the social science literature on the political relevance of social media, there are both expectations that social media have the potential to empower underrepresented interests, as well as more sober assessments which doubt that social media will help to reduce inequalities in the political sphere. Despite these far-reaching and contradictory expectations, a recent analysis of literature on interest groups' use of social media concludes that *"systematic, quantitative literature of social media use of interest groups is scarce"* (van der Graaf et al. 2016: 121).

The new modes of communication via the Internet have obviously modified formats of mass communication. Nowadays, there is probably almost no mass media which do not host an Internet-based news site besides their print or broadcasting versions. These news sites regularly have comment sections, which offer the opportunity for online readers to comment on and discuss the news articles offered at the site. Thus, previously passive readers have the option to publicly express their political thoughts and ideas. A media content analysis including a study of reader's comments via online news sites, published in 2015, found that at the beginning of the period of research in 2009 social media was not very well integrated in online news sites. Since then, all news sites have incorporated social media "sharing" functions, and in the EU "... *readers' participation through Web 2.0 functions has thus dramatically increased*". This was found to apply particularly "... *in Southern Member States where internet availability and use was previously lagging behind the North-Western countries*" (Michailidou 2015: 331).

Social media currently also function as a news source for mass media. Facebook and Twitter posts trigger mass media reports. Especially, online portals of mass media not only have their own Twitter or Facebook accounts but allow readers to forward news from online news portals. Mass media also regularly include social media posts in their news and reports about political issues. In this respect, there are channels that allow content from segmented and issue- or community-specific publics organised via social media to find its way into the general political public sphere.

Social media are increasingly used by interest groups and play an important role in political campaigning and organisation, and the coordination of political activities, since they are supportive of building communities around certain issues and interests by direct communication with supporters. There is no doubt about the growing importance of social media for political communication (Chalmers and Shotton 2013; Obar et al. 2012). Social media, or formats like political blogs, have changed the public sphere, not only by adding something to old forms of mass media public spheres but also by partially substituting them. Expectations from 10 years ago that political blogging would substitute traditional journalism still appear to be exaggerated. But notions predicting that web communication would not affect mass media journalism at all have proved to be dewy-eyed. Today, new mixed models of journalism are observed where leading newspapers incorporate *"blogs, columns and news stories and where writers may be bloggers one day and reporters the next"* (Zuckerman 2014: 158 for an analysis of digital journalism; see also Peters and Witschge 2015). The enormous popularity of comment sections has recently attracted intense interest among communication scholars (for an overview see Toepfl and Piwoni 2015). Surveys show an increased spread of comment sections on online news sites, and research indicates that user-generated content on comment sites influences readers' perceptions of public opinion and can change the reader's personal opinion.

Internet activism as a new form of protest is gaining influence in the public sphere. There is little doubt among researchers that meanwhile it is obvious that it is *"the norm, not the exception, for political and activist campaigns to rely on social media, crowdfunding and other digital techniques as well as advertising, lobbying and conventional fundraising"* (Zuckerman 2014: 158). Online communication is used by political actors and activists in many ways: for spreading information and news online, for e-mobilisation (using online tools to facilitate offline protests), for online participation (e.g. online petitions) and for organising movement efforts online, so that there are discussions of whether pure online activism might reduce the relevance of (offline) NGOs (Earl 2015). Thus, social media and online debates are regarded as having the potential to function as *counter-publics* to the established and published discourse (originally Fraser 1992; see Dahlberg 2011). Especially in developing countries, which often lack media channels for underprivileged groups, social media is seen as a means to empower the poor and increase the possibilities for them to influence or petition the government (e.g. Hoskins 2013). Impressive social movements and uprisings in recent years have shown that the Internet, and especially communication via social media, has been widely supportive of networking and the public campaigning of social movements. The attention to completely new forms of bottom-up spontaneous political activism fostered by the political use of social media was especially triggered by the revolutionary movements in North-African countries (the so-called Arab Spring) that led (albeit mostly temporarily)—to fostering democratic structures of public debate and governance in previously autocratic regimes (see contributions in Kumar and Svensson 2015; Özcan 2014). This perspective has not only been tempered by the observable autocratic or oligarchical backlash in most of the Spring-countries, but also by analysis that shows that years of offline planning, negotiation and organisation made the Arab Spring possible, suggesting that social media was nothing but a supportive tool that has been used for campaigning and organising counter-publics (Lim 2012; Bennett and Segerberg 2012).

The potential of social media to establish "counter-publics" is undoubtable, but this potential also has its downside, with effects which are detrimental to a democratic public sphere. Following the public sphere concept of John Dewey (2012: 1927), that publics emerge as soon as knowledge about a public problem evolves, it appears to be plausible that such knowledge is now more easily spread and thus potentially combines formerly unconnected individuals into concerned publics (see Farrell 2014) by organising all kinds of Internet fora, social media, etc. on any political question. It is, however, evident that new modes of political Internet communication not only have the capacity to support the emergence of counter-publics and the empowerment of civil society groups, but are also effective tools for campaigning by established political actors, institutions and groups. It was quite clear, before Donald Trump as US President made Twitter his preferred media of political communication, which has dominated mass media coverage of the elections in many ways (Enli 2017), that political Internet communication can also be regarded as a battlefield, with all kinds of manipulative strategies and tools applied to steer public opinion (Bradshaw and Howard 2017). The use of social media in electoral campaigning in Western democracies, often referred to as improving the options for civil society to connect to political representatives, is—as has been shown by analysis of the use of social media in US electoral campaigns (Kreiss 2012, also Towner and Dulio 2012)—far from being self-organised bottom-up support for candidates, but is *"meticulously planned, tested, and crafted by highly bureaucratic, hierarchical institutions"* (Wells 2014).

It is also noteworthy that the option for organised as well as individual actors to introduce their political thoughts or preferences into the public sphere and establish counter-publics is not bound to anti-establishment or grass-root world views. A study of the online news site of opinion-leading German newspapers, published in the aftermath of the 2013 national elections (Toepfl and Piwoni 2015), analysed journalistic articles as well as user comments regarding the new German Anti-Euro party "AfD" and found clear indications that while the news sections of the sites (journalists' content) unanimously painted a dismissive picture of the new party, the comment sections were mainly used to challenge this mainstream consensus. The authors conclude that in the comment sections, "... *a powerful counter (sub) public sphere had emerged. Remarkably, approximately 75% of comments supported a new party that just days before only 4.7% of the electorate had voted for. In essence, these findings thus showcased how an emergent collective of counter public-minded individuals were exploiting the comment sections of Germany's opinion-leading news websites in order to create a highly visible—and therefore enormously powerful - counter-public sphere*" (Toepfl and Piwoni 2015: 482).

All in all, the landscape of political communication has changed, which has in many ways empowered civil society to get access to the public sphere. However, this may not challenge existing structures and hierarchies as much as expected by e-democracy enthusiasts. As referred to above, Koopmanns and Statham (2010; see also Koopmanns 2015) found claims of CSOs being underrepresented in media reporting on European political issues when compared to institutional actors, based on a sample of quality journals in six EU Member States. This was especially the case for media reports on European issues. Interestingly, an analysis of websites conducted within the framework of the same study did not find a more balanced representation of institutional and civil societal actors (Koopmanns and Zimmermann 2010), leading to the conclusion that the Internet replicated power hierarchies that affected actors' abilities to reach audiences. Without overstating this (and other) single findings, since the overall state of research on the empowering force of the Internet is still insufficiently developed, it can be summarised that there is an online space for political communication with many new features and options that go beyond or bypass mass media channels. It is, however, subject to debate as to what extent these features have the potential and are set into practice to democratise political communication and public discourse. It is quite clear that despite the democratic potential of many of its features, "...*the internet and related technologies are increasingly identified as posing threats to democratic structures and participation in politics and society*" (Dutton 2018: 4). Features that add to this picture are the misuse of personal data for political advertising, by personal profiling and micro-targeting (Kind and Weide 2017; Dubois 2017), as in the case of Facebook, where user data was obtained by the political consulting company Cambridge Analytica for personal profiling and selective political campaigning. Manipulative strategies are supported by the application of algorithms (social bots) to automatically spread messages in social media communities which are presented as having been posted by users, and thus falsely produce the perception that the message spread is shared by a vast majority of (fake) community members (Wardle and Derakshan 2017). A basic feature of political Internet communication that is massively opposed to any notion of a public sphere as a shared space of rational discourse is the tribal structure of social media communication. Any content is shared and distributed mainly among communities of like-minded people, who join the same filter bubble (Pariser 2011) of content. Anything that is posted by members of these bubbles (or by a bot pretending the content has been posted by many members) has a pre-established reliability bonus since it confirms the worldviews and identities held by members and is (factually or apparently) distributed by people "like us" in whom we can trust. Social media in this respect can be regarded as being tailor-made for spreading news and preventing it from being counter-checked by other sources. News is travelling within or in between peer-to-peer networks and not via media, which are able to create a public space in which content might be checked by gatekeepers and, can be, respectively, criticised in a public (i.e. open to everybody) manner. One effect of this, beyond any single attempts at disinformation or manipulation, might be to render a rational debate impossible, because citizens enclosed in their specific filter bubble do not see any possibility—beyond their peer community—to tell wrong from right, deceit from the truth or rational reasoning from emotional affect.

3.4.3 Deliberative Quality of Online Political Communication

Despite the negative effects mentioned above, it still is the interactive quality of Internet communication that is the anchor of accounts that the virtual public sphere has the potential to foster the deliberative quality of public discourse, compared to mass media publics. Deliberative quality implies an open exchange among a broad spectrum of perspectives and views, without restrictions as regards access to the discourse, the right to speak, and the willingness to listen and rationally react to opposing perspectives. With regard to this, political social media sites and political blogs come into perspective. In a review of research on online deliberation, Freelon (2015) sees two perspectives being dominant in research. One research thread studies the deliberative content of online political communication, asking to what extent online political communication meets normative criteria such as civility, reciprocity and reason-giving. The other thread focuses on "selective exposure", based on the assumption that *"exposure to a diverse array of information sources is good for democracy, while the exclusive consumption of opinion reinforcing content is problematic"* (Freelon 2015: 774). Many studies focus on specific case studies of Internet fora, blogs and others. According to Freelon, there is consensus that online political discussions mostly do not meet the quality criteria of deliberative content. As regards the "selective exposure" perspective, Freelon sees mixed results. Some studies support the notion that online debates reinforce the exclusive consumption of opinion-reinforcing content, while other studies cannot support the selective exposure thesis (Freelon 2015: 773 ff.). Liu and Weber (2014) come to similar conclusions for research on social media. Due to the enormous amount of literature available, it is impossible to undertake a systematic tour d'horizon through available research at this point. In the following, a few examples from recent studies are given to illustrate the "quality of content" as well as the "selective exposure" perspective.

Generally, the political "blogosphere", which began in the late 2000s, gave rise to far-reaching expectations of the positive effects on democracy in terms of bringing about a new space for open and rational exchange across political affiliations. Seen from the perspective of established politics, the blogosphere should bring about a new space to learn about public worries, expectations and needs, thus supporting the functionality of the public sphere for the responsiveness of the political system. However, blogs often show features of political exchange among elites and/or well-educated publics, and rather than opening up spaces for deliberation across political communities or perspectives, they often appear to foster communication only among like-minded communities. As regards the quality of content, new social media and the so-called "blogosphere" have been diagnosed to show strong discrepancies along the lines of established politics and more informal use by citizens. While online media are often used by policymakers in a vertical manner of communication and *"replicate the worst aspects of the established political communication system, with politicians running blogs that look like old-fashioned newsletters"*, citizens' initiatives use blogs and social media more as a means of horizontal communication among peers (Coleman and Blumler 2012: 146).

Empirical studies, mainly based on an analysis of hyperlinks between different political blogs, show contradictory results: There are indications that blogs have a potential to foster deliberation in terms of exchange on political issues across political affiliations, as well as examples of blogs that function as spaces for in-group self-assurance (see research overview in Silva 2014). A study of the leading political blogs in Romania (2013, 2014) found that other than the mass media commitment to neutrality, users of political blogs clearly tend to choose blogs that support their political thinking and position (Munteanu and Staiculescu 2015). A network analysis of 20 of the most popular political blogs in Portugal (Silva 2014: 200) during national election campaigns could not find support for the thesis that blogs tend to polarise political positions "*... blogs managed by citizens interested in politics do engage in conservations and debates regardless of the ideology. We find right and left wing blogs linking to each other, thus indicating that they share issues and themes of debate, interests, and arguments*". Negative reactions among participants "*... that intend to mock or show contempt, insult and hamper dissident voices*" were found to be of minor relevance.

The example of the Norwegian Labour Party's (MyLabourParty) websites, with blog-like articles and comments, shows that the extent to which online blogs or social media sites allow for open debates and political communication depends on their design and purpose. For inner party communication, blogs are used for distributing news among party members and supporters, while others are meant to reach out to a wider public. Analysing different online offerings from the Norwegian Labour Party (Johannessen and Følstad 2014), it was found that blogs whose contributors are mainly or only party members tend to be restricted in triggering debates when compared to sites that are also open to opposing political opinions. It has been shown by a broad network analysis of the online discussion forum of the Italian Five Star Movement that online discussion platforms provided by political parties and groups are not necessarily platforms for mutual self-assurance. The Five Star Movement owes its foundation to the exceptional success of a political blog run by its founder, Beppe Grillo, in 2009. The widely used online forum of the movement, according to Bailo (2015), did not show significant tendencies of fragmentation of the online community using the forum. Many users engaged in discussions on different topics, thus the debate was not structured in accordance with specific interests or values held. The author concludes that people "*are more interested in engaging rather than convincing each other*" and they come to the forum "*mainly to socialise their ideas and be exposed to other's thoughts on issues they are interested in*" (Bailo 2015: 564).

As regards the quality of communication, the anonymity that is allowed for in Internet chats, fora or social media has always been held to be conducive to allow for a situation that comes close to the ideal of deliberative exchange of arguments implied in Habermasian discourse theory, because anonymity allows us to disregard hierarchical factors such as social status. It is, however, mainly the anonymity of communication that often gives way to idiosyncratic and untrustworthy talk, to bullying or the erratic dismissal of the arguments of other users. While anonymity can strengthen the focus of participants on the argument rather than the person, and thus increase deliberative quality, at the same time it implies a lack of social control that can lead to emotional and erratic behaviour, as has been found, e.g. by analysis of Twitter discussions on new abortion legislation in the UK by Jackson and Valentine (2014). This—with regard to a rational exchange of arguments as the core of a deliberative public sphere—destructive feature of Internet communication, especially of social media, is represented by the "troll". The intervention of the troll in social media communication, or in the comment sections of mass media, by posting statements meant to destroy the mood of serious exchange of arguments by insulting and bullying participants, discrediting their credibility and spreading doubtful "news", is a ubiquitous phenomenon. The role of the troll—originally an obscure niche existence—can even be said to have made it into mainstream political communication (Hannan 2018). Not only does the "puer robustus", like US President Trump, stand for this but also the aggressive style of political communication introduced by many populist, right-wing movements in Europe. "Twitter wars" are meanwhile featured in quality mass media. Hannan (2018), in an instructive and pessimistic analysis, develops an account of trolling as the political mode of communication inscribed in the social media technology itself, undermining the value of "truth": *"Disagreements on social media reveal a curious epistemology embedded within their design. Popularity now competes with logic and evidence as an arbiter of truth. [...] Lengthy detailed disquisitions do not fare well against short, biting sarcasm. They also do not fare well against comments that, however inane, rack up a far greater number of likes. In the mental universe of social media, truth is a popularity contest"* (Hannan 2018: 33).

Looking at empirical studies of communicative practice in political fora and other spaces, the seriousness of the above sketched analysis revealing the anti-democratic aspect of Internet communication cannot really be questioned, but such studies can support the notion that there is another, democratic potential that can be realised given the right frame of conditions. This deliberative quality was found to be dependent on factors of political culture. A study using 15,000 comments from five national newspaper online sites conducted by Ruiz et al. (2011) found two models of audience participation in online fora of newspapers: in the first, "communities of debate" are formed based on mostly respectful discussions between diverse points of view. This model—more in line with deliberative norms—was found in Anglo-American newspapers (*The Guardian* and *The New York Times*). The second model of "homogenous communities" is characterised by expressing feelings about current events and has fewer features of an argumentative debate, less respect between participants and less pluralism, and was found in European newspapers (*El País*, *Le Monde* and *La Republica*). The authors regard this difference to be an effect of different cultures of journalism based on the political cultures of the respective countries. While a culture of "internal pluralism" is dominant in the Anglo-American case, with newspapers not being aligned with a particular political position, a culture of "polarised pluralism" is dominant in the European case, where *"participants are mostly aligned with the ideological perspective of the newsroom: Citizens participate in the spaces provided by their news website of choice, mostly finding similar positions to theirs and editorial content that fosters political polarization"* (Ruiz et al. 2011: 483).

Freelon (2015) has conducted a comparison across two technical platforms: Twitter hashtags and online newspapers comment sections. One of his central conclusions is that issue hashtags on Twitter made it more likely that discussions were of a more "communitarian"—meaning in-group and self-assurance—character, whereas comment sections on online news (which are more open to and are accessible by broader mass publics) were more likely to generate discourse with deliberative features such as openness to and exchange among a diverse and contradicting scope of arguments and statements. Research regarding the question of to what extent blogs, Internet fora and political social network sites can contribute to or foster features of an ideal public sphere (in terms of equality, inclusiveness and rationality of discourse) generally show mixed results.

It is well known that new populist movements rely very much on social media to organise and mobilise their members and followers (e.g. Januschek and Reisigl 2014). There are indications that social media fosters a "closed shop" in which those who are already convinced mutually reconfirm their ideology and their prejudices, rather than providing for a democratic and open rational exchange of arguments. Generally, this thesis is connected to the notion that while mass media normally provide for a mixed or balanced view of differing standpoints on political issues, the Internet (due to its ability to organise certain communities) is suspected *"that recruitment, radicalization, and incitement are facilitated"* via its tendency *"to foster echo chambers where people are denied feedback contrary to their own views, which are therefore reinforced"* (O'Hara and Stevens 2015). While O'Hara and Stevens reject this thesis as portraying a general feature of political Internet communication, there are indications that it holds true for the use of social media and website communication by extremist and populist movements (Warner and Neville-Shepard 2014).

In a broad review of research and scholarly discussion on the changes in news supply and consumption on the Internet, Tewksbury and Rittenberg (2012) found some evidence for fragmentation and polarisation of audiences alongside political predispositions, due to the multitude of specialised news sites. However, they argue that the fact that there is a multitude of specialised news sites and that some people restrict their information consumption to a certain set of news sites does not necessarily imply that they do not share common public knowledge as well as public agendas: *"Fragmentation and polarization are ideas, still, more than observable realities. There is ample evidence that many people are specialising their news consumptions in ways that might lead to either or both outcomes. There is less evidence that knowledge and opinion are fragmenting and/or polarizing. Most of the uncertainty about the operation of these phenomena stems from a lack of research; it rarely lies with disconfirming studies"* (Tewksbury and Rittenberg 2012: 143). On the other hand, they found evidence that the Internet offers more user control with regard to choice of content as well as with regard to contribution to news production, which can be regarded as "information democratization". But also in this regard, it is not yet clear to what extent the potential will become a reality. Counter tendencies of fragmentation and the dominance of strong media companies on the web, as well as regulation on the content of the Internet are regarded as interfering with the democratic empowerment of the audience (Tewksbury and Rittenberg 2012: 144 ff.).

Political communication via social media extends the opportunities for individuals to post their own thoughts about any kind of public event and share it with friends or peer groups. In a more optimistic view, this is regarded as being in line with a general change of civic identities that has been observed for decades and represents a shift away from materialist to post-materialist and individualist values. More individualistic expression of self and weakening ties to formal organisations (parties, unions), and collectives (class) is regarded as being expressed as well as pushed by the use of social media. Individual choices made possible by the Internet allow connection to all kinds of cultures, social groups and preferences, and this comes at the cost of adherence to widely shared ideologies or bigger (public) formal organisations such as political parties (see, e.g. Wells 2014; Bennett and Segerberg 2012).

On the other hand, a clear danger when restricting oneself to these formats of political information and communication is the segmentation into peer groups or issue-related publics. In addition, one runs the danger of the complete loss of connection to any broader sphere of exchange among competing perspectives on contested issues of public (in the meaning of national or transnational) interest—which in the worst case would lead to idiosyncratic discussions and worldviews. As Zuckerman (2014: 165) puts it: *"Social media allows the friends you follow online to participate in setting your political agenda, adding dots to the canvas that are in your immediate line of sight. We likely need a new class of tools and practices too help us step back and see our interests and perspectives in a broader context."*

3.4.4 The Internet and the European Public Sphere

The visibility of European issues in mass media has always been part of the focus of empirical research on the European public sphere. However, research on the relevance of political communication on the Internet for building a European public sphere or supporting the Europeanisation of national public spheres is scarce. What comes into focus first is the use of web-based communication by the European Commission. It is only recently that "issue publics", organised via the web by civil society actors, has come into the focus of research with regard to their potential to "Europeanise" the public sphere. This also applies for the use of social media by Eurosceptic movements and political parties. The latter, as has been shown above, can be said to form real "echo-chambers" of "EU bashing".

Following a programmatic turn to new and open forms of governance laid out in the White Paper on Governance (EC 2001), following the Irish "No" to the treaty of Nice (2001), the EC began to actively fund and set up citizen participation and public consultation activities through its "Plan D for Democracy Dialogue and Debate" (EC 2005) in 2005, as a response to the rejection of the constitutional treaty in the

French and Dutch referenda. This was explicitly meant to strengthen the development of the European public sphere, also via means of e-participation (see Yang 2013; see also Lindner et al. 2016). Part of this strategy was to connect the process of EU policy formulation and legislation to the European constituency by inviting civil society actors and interest groups to participate in online consultations on issues under EU regulation via the EC's web portal, "Your voice in Europe". Another outcome was the set-up of citizen consultations and online fora. In the following, a brief overview of new research available on the citizen consultations and the online consultations of the EC is given.[1]

Summarising research on the European Commission's online consultations, "Your voice in Europe", Dieker and Galan (2014) conclude that although many consultations are "open", allowing any group to participate, the consultations—in terms of the effects at the European public sphere—at best contribute to establishing segmented and mainly expert public spheres. The consultations normally do not attract interest from groups beyond those interest groups already represented in Brussels. Due to the fact that participation in online consultations is resource-consuming, it is mostly professional and well-organised groups that participate. According to a study from 2011, business associations make up 39% of all participants in online consultations (Quittkat 2011, acc. to Dieker and Galan 2014). As regards the potential to contribute to a more inclusive mode of policymaking and to a European will-formation in the sense of (segmented) public spheres, the consultations are perceived to suffer from shortcomings. The consultation process lacks transparency with regard to clear information about the criteria for weighting contributions and deciding on whether they are taken into consideration or not. Contributions are not made accessible to participants and no exchange among participants about contributions is possible. The purpose of the consultations is to search for input to the policymaking process rather than public deliberation with or among the groups contributing. However, the function of transmitting demands and interests from civil society to the European institutions is regarded as being restricted, since agenda-setting lies solely with the European Commission, which decides about the issues that are made open for online consultation. Since online consultations take place in highly segmented public spheres with mainly expert and stakeholder communities participating, consultations are regarded as having a highly professional character which does not allow them to take up a Europeanising function in terms of active European citizenship (Dieker and Galan 2014, 245).

Between 2001 and 2010, 23 transnational citizen consultation projects supported by the European Commission have been conducted, involving participants from a minimum of three European countries. They included face-to-face meetings as well as online discussions on specific issues, including the social and political implications of brain research as well as more general issues such as the European

---

[1]For more information on the EU's online activities see Lindner et al. (2016) as well as Chap. 4 of this report. For the "European Citizen Consultations", the "Futurium platform" and the web portal "Your voice in Europe", see the case studies carried out as part of this report in Chap. 9.

constitution and the future of Europe (Yang 2013: 25 f.). The six transnational "Deliberative Citizens Involvement Projects" (DCIP) covered by the Plan D programme involved approximately 40,000 people. The online project "Speak up Europe" alone involved 300,000 users in discussions on European politics (Yang 2013: 27). An evaluation of these DCIPs with regard to their deliberative quality as well as impact has been undertaken by contributions in Kies and Nanz (2013a). The case studies presented support the notion that DCIPs have a "...*potential to ameliorate the legitimacy of the EU and to promote a more substantial EU citizenship*" (Kies and Nanz 2013b: 10). The interactive aspect of deliberation is held to be a feature that can support the experience of European citizenship. However, this study also holds formats applied by the EU to function in a suboptimal way, such as "Your voice in Europe", which allow citizens to send comments to policymakers, since they provide no space for deliberation and interaction among citizens on the issues addressed (Smith 2013: 209). In the EC's approaches to citizen participation, the study found a tendency—mainly due to the lack of common language—to reduce the role of citizens to posting statements or commenting on statements by policymakers, rather than engaging in a European citizens' debate and jointly working out policy options to be forwarded to policymakers. Most disappointing, according to the authors, was the lack of any follow-up activities or visible impact of the deliberative experiments on policymaking (Smith 2013: 215; Kies et al. 2013: 74 f.). Friedrich (2013: 44 ff.), discussing EU governance innovations, attests a strong bias to expert involvement. The approaches for dialogue with CSOs failed to realise their potential to strengthen the ties between EU authorities and European civil society or to support the construction of a European demos, due to a lack of commitment and "discretionary" patterns of participation. It is concluded that as long as a regulated integration of DCIPs in EU policymaking processes is not provided for and as long as DCIPs are mainly held on broad topics such as the social and economic future of Europe rather than on concrete challenges and the problems of decision-making, there is a danger that they are increasingly perceived as being more of a promotional instrument than serious attempts to engage the European citizenry in EU policymaking (Kies and Nanz 2013b: 11 f.). According to this analysis the potential of public consultations at the EU level to contribute to a lively European space of debate about EU policy, which could contribute to a European public sphere, appears to be restricted at this point.

The roles of segmented publics which are emerging around European issues, be it via initiatives taken by the EU institutions or bottom-up by interest groups across the borders of Member States, are regarded to have the potential to serve as nodes for a European networked public sphere alongside mass media publics (see Lindner et al. 2016). Kriesi et al. (2010: 225) argue that due to their frequent cross-national character, interest groups, and business and professional organisations (rather than political parties) can be regarded as a "Europeanized type of political actor". But such organisations engaged in consultations with decision-makers can hardly be regarded to be functioning as nodes of a political public sphere. Issue publics that are exclusively "*based on the horizontal intermediation between bureaucrats, experts and organized interests fall way short of complying with democratic provisions of openness and equal access*" (Eriksen 2005, cit. Pfetsch and Heft 2015: 33; see also Eriksen 2007 and Lindner et al. 2016), for which online consultations (see above) provide an example. However, as far as such issue publics involve a broad range of actors, or are organised bottom-up by civil society actors, they are held to be more inclusive (in terms of reaching the average European citizen) than mass media debates on European integration issues, that are often driven mainly by elites, with the general public in the position of an observer in the gallery (Pfetsch and Heft 2015).

An analysis of the capacities of Internet-based issue publics created by networks of civil society active in Fair Trade and Climate Change campaigning (Bennett et al. 2015), however, found sobering results regarding the capacity of such networks to support the Europeanisation of publics. European-level networks for the issues of Climate Change and Fair Trade identified by the study have been found to be weak (compared to the connectivity of nationally based networks). The study found a certain amount of "Europeanisation" as far as nation-based networks move into networks active at the European level. But national networks mainly remain separate from each other and from those networks organised around issue-related EU platforms. It was also found that EU-platform-related issue networks of NGOs were able to engage citizens with the issues at stake to a much lesser extent than their national counterparts. The authors regard their findings as supporting the notion that "...*civil society organisations in the Brussels area often serve as substitutes for the voices of European citizens, creating a civil order without credible levels of public engagement, and thereby deepening the EU's democratic deficit*" (Bennett et al. 2015: 135). Thus, it appears that the problem of segmentation in the sense of restriction of publics to "epistemic communities" and experts (as addressed with regard to European sub-publics organised around European issues and particular EU regulatory activities, Eriksen 2007; see Lindner et al. 2016) is not easily ruled out by Internet-based networks organised by NGOs.

First results on the use of social media by interest groups active in EU lobbying are available from a large European-funded project on the activity of EU lobbying groups (www.intereuro.eu). Van der Graaf et al. (2016) revealed, based on a data set of groups active in EU lobbying provided by this project, that when regarding the scope and volume of social media use there is little evidence that social media use was able to change inequalities in power and social representation at the EU level. The study comprised around 500 interest groups with reported activity at the EU level. "Range" was measured by the presence of interest groups on 11 selected social media platforms, and "Volume" was measured by the activity of groups on Twitter and Facebook. As regards the volume of social media use, small interest groups (citizens, workers unions) prevail over internationally organised groups, as well as big companies. However, when it comes to "range", large organisations and firms with big resources prevail. Thus, at least with regard to interest groups at the EU level, social media appear not to provide for a level playing field for democratic will formation. The authors conclude with regard to the "democratic effects" of the "online world of interest representation": "*Rather than representing a new playing field where pre-existing resource differences between groups play less of a role, our analysis underlines the importance of resources both when we consider the range and volume of social media use*" (van der Graaf et al. 2016: 122).

When analysing online comments of readers in political blogs, news platforms and transnational websites in 12 European countries during the 2009 EP election campaigns, de Wilde et al. (2014) found patterns of communication similar to those in mass media communication in the blogosphere with regard to European issues. The study found that diffuse Eurosceptic evaluations dominate public debates across Member States. The majority of evaluations made, particularly those by citizens leaving comments online, were Eurosceptic, constituting a gap between them and political elites who intervened with EU-affirmative statements. More complex evaluations of EU politics on the side of citizens were missing. These diffuse negative statements however were mainly about actual politics (complaining about the democratic deficit) than against EU integration as such. All in all, the authors conclude that there is "*little evidence of the potential for legitimation through politicization in online public spheres*" (de Wilde et al. 2014: 779). However, the study could not support the often-purported notion of a fragmentation of audiences in online discourse: debates intensified with politicisation of the European integration issue, but pro and con arguments were related to each other. Less "ambivalent" findings as regards the fragmentation of publics can be expected to apply for social media communication in Eurosceptic and right-wing groups. The negative aspects of social media communication as addressed in the previous section are no doubt relevant for any attempt to appraise the Internet's possible effects on the European public sphere. As the prominent case of the activities of Cambridge Analytica (not only in the US elections) show: micro-targeting obviously played a role in the British referendum to leave the European Union. And social media is the central means of right-wing populist movements across the Union to set up information echo-chambers for their followers in order to provide information to counteract the so-called mainstream media that are defamed as providing fake news. As not only the case of Brexit shows, social media meanwhile is a means for politicians as well as grass-roots campaigners to reach audiences directly and bypass the filters of mass media journalism, to an extent that is about to dominate election campaigns (Enli 2017; Mair et al. 2017; Toepfl and Piwoni 2015). An analysis of Twitter communication during the Brexit referendum campaign found that Twitter users supporting the Leave campaign were more active (they tweeted more frequently) than Remain users and showed a strong tendency to interact only with like-minded persons (Hänska and Bauchowitz 2017). Setting aside the unanswerable question of whether or not social media campaigning and communication did decide the British referendum on EU membership, social media are without doubt the media of choice for activist groups and individuals challenging the mainstream, and not surprisingly, this counts not only for democratic civil society organisations but also for populist movements and campaigns.

In view of the phenomenon of the organised spreading of dis-information via social media by using so-called social bots or by other means of campaigning, and also with a view to the Cambridge Analytica case, the European Commission has set up a High Level Expert Group on online dis-information to make suggestions on how to steer against these "post-truth" currents and provide for quality safeguarding in Internet communication. The measures suggested range from increasing the transparency of Internet platforms' use of data for advertising purposes, to establishing independent fact checkers in news media and safeguarding the diversity of the European news media ecosystem. The observation the Expert Group starts from, is to state the obvious downside to the structure of Internet communication that originally gave rise to hopes for a more vivid public sphere: *"an increasingly digital environment gives European citizens many new ways of expressing themselves and of finding and accessing diverse information and views. It also enables an increase in the volume of various kinds of disinformation in circulation"* (High Level Expert Group 2018: 10).

3.5 Conclusion

3.5.1 The EU Democratic Deficit in Times of Crisis

It is quite clear that scholarly debate as well as research on the European public sphere and on European citizenship and identification with Europe as a political community has intensified over the past years, due to the symptoms of an actual crisis of the EU institutions and the idea of European integration. It is still believed by many that the perceived democratic deficit of the European Union indicates the need for fostering a European public sphere as a space of debate across public spheres which are established at (and restricted to) national Member States. Moreover, there is a consensus that the new modes of political communication via the Internet have to play a role in that respect. However, far-reaching expectations and optimism envisaging the Internet as a panacea to political disenchantment and as a way to establish new transnational spaces of European bottom-up political communication are scarce compared to a decade ago.

As regards the state of the European political system, it is argued on the one hand that precisely in times of crisis, it is necessary to legitimise far-reaching decisions that will deeply influence living conditions in the European Member States. These decisions are to be reached through a vivid process of deliberation about pro and cons, about needs, demands and duties. On the other hand, there is pessimism whether—in the actual crisis that leads to focusing on national interests—there is enough homogeneity in the Union and strong identification with the EU as a transnational political entity. It is the observation of weak European solidarity and predominance of national perspectives that actually feeds the so-called "no demos" discussion among scholars of European politics. The point of dissent here is whether Europe is in need of the development of a transnational cultural identity (which is held by many to be exclusively bound to the national state) or whether a political identity—i.e. the European citizens' commitment to the fundaments of the European political constitution—is sufficient to establish a new form of "European citizenship". Proponents of a further integration of the EU base their cautionary optimism with regard to the "Europeanisation of European citizens" in the further development of the discourse about Europe and thus in the further development of the European public sphere. In this respect, the development of European identity and solidarity depends on the chances and opportunities to discuss and define what is in the common European interest via a common European political discourse. This would include fostering the role of the European Parliament and a European cross-national party system.

In this respect, what has been coined the "politicisation of Europe" in the actual crisis is—despite the undeniable symptoms of a renationalisation of political discourse and EU-scepticism—regarded as offering the opportunity to strengthen European identity. Since citizenship evolves in a political process of debate and emerges precisely outside of debates and conflicts about the public good, the current conflicts about EU policies and democratic legitimisation are regarded as a result of stronger engagement of citizens with the idea of Europe. On the other hand, it is evident that the crisis brings new forces and actors to the foreground that are not supportive of European integration and offer views that focus on national interests and thus help to strengthen national identities. There is, however, consensus that the European public sphere has a strong bearing on the development of a European identity as a space of debate where collective identities are constructed, and political communities are created.

3.5.2 The Internet and the European Public Sphere

With regard to the state of research on the European public sphere it has been critically stressed that so far, the focus of research has been on elite mass media communication and that research has neglected the relevance of new Internet-based communication networks mainly applied by civil society actors. In this respect some change can be observed, as there is a growing interest in Internet-based political communication and its potential for establishing new public spheres. However, a decade ago optimism was widespread that, while we find a decline of national public spheres with passive audiences and disenchantment with politics, the Internet could support the emergence of a trans-national public sphere that is more inclusive, deliberative and rooted in a transnational civil society. Such far-reaching expectations are scarcely put forward nowadays. Political communication via social media is currently in the focus of research, but it is difficult to draw clear conclusions with regard to their role in supporting the emergence of a vivid political public sphere:

- Internet-based political communication is not likely to develop into a supranational public sphere, but rather establishes a network of a multitude of mediated and unmediated discursive processes aimed at opinion formation at various levels and on various issues.

- It is a matter of contestation whether this multitude is able to bring about a space of common (public) interests, or whether these dispersed spaces restrict political communication to issue related or ideologically closed communities.
- Indications and arguments for both can be found: that social media can empower underrepresented interests as well as that there are reasons to doubt that social media would help to reduce inequalities in the political sphere.
- Online political communication has a potential to increase responsiveness of, and exchange with, political representatives and their constituencies. However, so far this potential is set into practice insufficiently. Online media are increasingly used by political institutions in a vertical and scarcely in a horizontal or interactive manner of communication.

Since the overall state of research on the empowering force of the Internet is still insufficiently developed, the actual potential for the Internet to bring about a new "public sphere" is impossible to assess. It can be summarised that there is an online space for political communication with many new features and options that go beyond or bypass mass media channels. It is, however, the subject of debate as to what extent these features have the potential to democratise political communication and public discourse.

It is held by many researchers that, in principle, the use of interactive tools of e-participation at the European level can contribute to fostering the legitimacy of the EU and to promote a more substantial EU citizenship. However, it is observed that the role of citizens is often reduced to just posting statements or commenting on statements by policymakers rather than engaging in a European citizens' debate and jointly working out policy options to be forwarded to policymakers. Also, the notion put forward in our report to the European Parliament a decade ago (Lindner et al. 2016), that public spaces established by consultation processes offered by the European institutions are often restricted to expert communities and at best help to establish segmented issue-related elite publics on the European level, as confirmed by recent research, is just about to emerge. First results of the research on the use of social media and Internet sites by civil society organisations active on the European level indicate that the restriction of publics at the European level to "epistemic communities" and experts is not easily ruled out by Internet-based networks organised by NGOs. Moreover, political communication via social media plays a destructive role by supporting filter bubbles and dis-information. This is widely used by anti-European populist movements all over Europe with, as is suggested by research on the role of Internet communication in the British EU referendum on the EU membership, significant detrimental effects to public deliberation.

References

Bailo, F. (2015). Mapping online political talks through network analysis: A case study of the website of Italy's Five Star Movement. *Policy Studies, 36*(6), 550–572.

Belluati, M. (2016). Signs of Europeanization?: The 2014 EP election in European newspapers. *Rivistaltaliana di ScienzaPolitica, 46*(2), 131–150.

Bennett, L. (2012). Grounding the European public sphere. Looking beyond the mass media to digitally mediated issue publics. *KFG Working Paper Series*, No. 43, Freie Universität Berlin.

Bennett, W. L., & Segerberg, A. (2012). The logic of connective action. Digital media and the personalization of contentious politics. *Information Communication and Society, 15*(5), 739–768.

Bennett, W. L., Lang, S., & Segerberg, A. (2015). European issue publics online: The case of climate change and fair trade. In T. Risse (Ed.), *European public spheres: Politics is back* (pp. 108–140). Cambridge: Cambridge University Press.

Bohman, J. (2004). Expanding dialogue: The Internet, the public sphere and prospects for transnational democracy. *Sociological Review, 52*(s1), 131–155.

Boomgaarden, H. G., De Vreese, C. H., et al. (2013). Across time and space: Explaining variation in news coverage of the European Union. *European Journal of Political Research, 52*(5), 608–629.

Bradshaw, S., & Howard, Ph. N. (2017). *Troops, trolls and troublemakers: A global inventory of organized social media manipulation*. Computational Propaganda Research project. Working Paper No. 2017.12, University of Oxford.

Castels, M. (2008). The new public sphere: Global civil society, communication networks, and global governance. *The Annals of the American Academy of Political and Social Science, 616*(1), 78–93.

Chalmers, A., & Shotton, P. (2013). *Advocacy and social media: Explaining when and why interest organizations use social media tactics*. Paper presented at the ECPR general conference, 4–7 September 2013, Bordeaux.

Checkel, J. (2015). Identity, Europe, and the world beyond public spheres. In T. Risse (Ed.), *European public spheres: Politics is back* (pp. 227–246). Cambridge: Cambridge University Press.

Checkel, J., & Katzenstein, P. J. (2009). The politicisation of European identities. In J. Checkel & P. J. Katzenstein (Eds.), *European identities* (pp. 1–25). Cambridge: Cambridge University Press.

Coleman, S., & Blumler, J. C. (2012). The internet and citizenship: Democratic opportunity or more of the same. In: *The Sage handbook of political communication*. London: Sage, pp. 141–153.

Dahlberg, L. (2011). Re-constructing digital democracy: An outline of four "positions". *New Media and Society, 13*, 855–872.

Dahlgren, P. (2005). The internet, public spheres, and political communication: Dispersion and deliberation. *Political Communication, 22*(2), 147–162.

de la Porte, C., & van Dalen, A. (2016). Europeanization of national public spheres? Cross-national media debates about the European Union's socio-economic strategy. *European Politics and Society, 17*(3), 1–15.

de Wilde, P., & Zürn, M. (2012). Can the politicisation of European integration be reversed? *Journal of Common Market Studies, 50*(S1), 137–153.

de Witte, B., Héritier, A., & Trechsel, A. H. (2013). *The Euro crisis and the state of European democracy*. Firenze: European University Institute.

de Wilde, P., Michailidou, A., & Trenz, H. J. (2014). Converging on euroscepticism. Online polity contestation during European Parliament elections. *European Journal of Political Research, 53*(4), 766–783.

Dewey, J. (2012). *The public and its problems*. Athens, OH: Ohio University Press. (originally published 1927).

Dieker, J., & Galan, M. (2014). Creating a public sphere in Cyberspace: The case of the EU. In E. G. Carayannis, D. F. J. Campbell, & M. P. Efthymiopoulos (Eds.), *Cyberdevelopment, cyberdemocracy and cyber-defense: Challenges, opportunities and implications for theory, policy and practice* (pp. 231–258). Springer: New York, NY.

Dressler, W., Sicakkan, H. G., et al. (2012). The French Republican model, the European Diversity Perspective and the European Public Sphere. *Social Science Information Sur Les Sciences Sociales, 51*(3), 418–447.

Dubois, F. (2017). Is political micro-targeting hijacking European democracy? Interview with Tom Dobber and Natalie Helberger. *Internet Policy Review.*

Dutton, W. H. (2018). Networked publics: Multi-disciplinary perspectives on big policy issues. *Internet Policy review, 7,* 1–15.

Earl, J. (2015). The future of social movement organizations: The waning dominance of SMOs online. *American Behavioural Scientist, 59*(1), 35–52.

EC – European Commission. (2001). *European Governance.* A White Paper, COM (2001) 428 final, Brussels.

EC – European Commission. (2005). *The Commission's contribution to the period of reflection and beyond: Plan-D for Democracy, Dialogue and Debate.* Communication from the Commission to the Council, The European Parliament, the European Economic and Social Committee and the Committee of the Regions, COM (2005) 494 final, Brussels.

EC – European Commission.(2010). *Communication from the Commission to the European Parliament, the Council, the European Economic and Social Committee and the Committee of the Regions.* The European eGovernment Action Plan 2011–2015 Harnessing ICT to promote smart, sustainable and innovative Government. Accessed 06.02.2019, from https://eur-lex.europa.eu/LexUriServ/LexUriServ.do?uri=COM:2010:0743:FIN:EN:PDF

Ene, C., & Micu, A. (2013). European Union citizenship from 1993 to 2013 and after. *European Journal of Science and Theology, 9,* 55–64.

Enli, G. (2017). Twitter as arena for the authentic outsider: Exploring the social media campaigns of Trump and Clinton in the 2016 US presidential election. *European Journal of Communication, 32,* 50–61.

Eriksen, E. O. (2005). An emerging public sphere. *European Journal of Public Theory, 8*(3), 341–361.

Eriksen, E. O. (2007). Conceptualising European public spheres: General, segmented and strong publics. In J. E. Fossum & P. Schlesinger (Eds.), *The European Union and the public sphere* (pp. 23–43). London: Routledge.

Etzioni, A. (2013). The EU: The communitarian deficit. *European Societies, 15*(3), 312–330.

Farrell, H. (2014). New problems, new publics? Dewey and new media. *Policy and Internet, 6*(2), 176–191.

Føllesdal, A. (2015). Democracy, identity, and European public spheres. In T. Risse (Ed.), *European public spheres: Politics is back* (pp. 247–262). Cambridge: Cambridge University Press.

Frangonikolopoulos, C. A. (2012). Global civil society and deliberation in the digital age. *International Journal of Electronic Governance, 5*(1), 11–23.

Fraser, N. (1992). Rethinking the public sphere: A contribution to the critique of actually existing democracy. In C. Calhoun (Ed.), *Habermas and the public sphere* (pp. 109–142). Cambridge, MA: MIT Press.

Freelon, D. (2015). Discourse architecture, ideology, and democratic norms in online political discussion. *New Media and Society, 17*(5), 772–791.

Friedrich, D. (2013). European governance and the deliberative challenge. In R. Kies & P. Nanz (Eds.), *Is Europe listening to us? Success and failure of EU citizen consultations* (pp. 35–56). Ashgate: Farnham.

Gattermann, K. (2013). News about the European Parliament: Patterns and external drivers of broadsheet coverage. *European Union Politics, 14*(3), 436–457.

Gerhards, J., & Hans, S. (2014). Explaining citizens' participation in a transnational European public sphere. *Comparative Sociology, 13*(6), 667–691.

Goldberg, G. (2010). Rethinking the public/virtual sphere: The problem with participation. *New Media and Society, 13*(5), 739–754.

Grande, E., & Kriesi, H. (2015). The restructuring of political conflict in Europe and the politicization of European integration. In T. Risse (Ed.), *European public spheres: Politics is back* (pp. 190–226). Cambridge: Cambridge University Press.

Grimm, D. (1995). Does Europe need a constitution? *European Law Journal, 1*(3), 282–302.

Habermas, J. (2014a). Für ein starkes Europa – Aber was heißt das? *Blätter für deutsche und internationale Politik, 59*(3), 85–94.
Habermas, J. (2014b). *Internet and public sphere – What the web can't do*. Interview with Markus Schwering. Resetdoc.org [accessed 27 July 2016], (originally published in German under the title "ImSog der Gedanken", Frankfurter Rundschau 14/15 June 2014).
Habermas, J. (2015). Democracy in Europe: Why the development of the EU into a transnational democracy is necessary and how it is possible. *European Law Journal, 21*(4), 546–557.
Hannan, J. (2018). Trolling ourselves to death? Social media and post-truth politics. *European Journal of Communication, 33*, 214–226.
Hänska, M., & Bauchowitz, S. (2017). Tweeting for Brexit: How social media shaped the Referendum campaign. In J. Mair, T. Clark, N. Fowler, R. Snoddy, & R. Tait (Eds.), *Brexit Trump and the media* (pp. 27–31). Bury St. Edmunds: Abramis.
Harrison, S., & Bruter, M. (2014). Media and identity: The paradox of legitimacy and the making of European citizens. In T. Risse (Ed.), *European public spheres: Politics is back* (pp. 165–189). Cambridge: Cambridge University Press.
Hepp, A., Brüggemann, M., Kleinen-von Königslöw, K., Lingenberg, S., & Möller, J. (2012). *PolitischeDiskurskulturen in Europa: Die MehrfachsegmentierungeuropäischerÖffentlichkeit*. Wiesbaden: VS Springer.
High Level Expert Group on Fake-News and Online Disinformation. (2018). *A multi dimensional approach to disinformation*. European Commission, Brussels 2018.
Hix, S. (2009). *What's wrong with the European Union and how to fix it*. Cambridge: Polity Press.
Hoffmann, L., & Monaghan, E. (2011). Public debate on the future of the European Union: A viable legitimising strategy? *Politics, 31*(3), 140–147.
Hooghe, L., & Marks, G. (2008). A postfunctionalist theory of European integration: From permissive consensus to constraining dissensus. *British Journal of Political Science, 39*(1), 1–23.
Hoskins, G. T. (2013). Meet the habermasses: Charting the emergence of a social media-enabled public sphere in new democracies. *International Journal of Technology, Knowledge and Society, 9*(4), 25–39.
Hutter, S., & Grande, E. (2012). *Politicizing Europe in the national Electoral Arena. A Comparative Analysis of Five European Countries, 1970 to 2010*. Paper presented at the PoIEU Project Meeting, Florence.
Jackson, L., & Valentine, G. (2014). Emotion and politics in a mediated public sphere: Questioning democracy, responsibility and ethics in a computer mediated world. *Geoforum, 52*, 193–202.
Januschek, F., & Reisigl, M. (2014). Populismus in der digitalen Mediendemokratie. *OBST, 86*, 7–17.
Johannessen, M. R., & Følstad, A. (2014). Political social media sites as public sphere: A case study of the Norwegian labour party. *Communications of the Association for Information Systems, 34*(1), 1067–1096.
Kandyla, A.-A., & de Vreese, C. (2011). News media representations of a common EU foreign and security policy. A cross-national content analysis of CFSP coverage in national quality newspapers. *Comparative European Politics, 9*(1), 52–75.
Kies, R., & Nanz, P. (Eds.). (2013a). *Is Europe listening to us? Success and failure of EU citizen consultations*. Ashgate: Farnham.
Kies, R., & Nanz, P. (2013b). Introduction. In R. Kies & P. Nanz (Eds.), *Is Europe listening to us? Success and failure of EU citizen consultations* (pp. 1–16). Ashgate: Farnham.
Kies, R., Leyenaar, M., & Niemöller, K. (2013). European Citizen's consultation: A large consultation on a vague topic. In R. Kies & P. Nanz (Eds.), *Is Europe listening to us? Success and failure of EU citizen consultations* (pp. 59–78). Ashgate: Farnham.
Kind, S., & Weide, S. (2017). *Microtargeting: PsychmetrischeAnalysemittels Big Data*. Berlin: Büro für technikfolgenabschätzung beim Deustchen Bundestag.
Kleinen von Königslow, K., & Möller, J. (2009). Nationalisierte Europäisierung: Die Entwicklung der polnischen Medienöffentlichkeitnach 1989. *JahrbuchNordostArchiv, 18*, 101–139.

Koopmanns, R. (2015). How advanced is the Europeanisation of public spheres? Comparing German and European structures of political communication. In T. Risse (Ed.), *European public spheres: Politics is back* (pp. 53–83). Cambridge: Cambridge University Press.

Koopmanns, R., & Statham, P. (Eds.). (2010). *The making of the European public sphere. Media discourse and political contentions*. New York, NY: Cambridge University Press.

Koopmanns, R., & Zimmermann, A. (2010). Transnational political communication on the Internet. Search engine results and hyperlink networks. In R. Koopmanns & P. Statham (Eds.), *The making of the European public sphere. Media discourse and political contentions* (pp. 171–194). New York, NY: Cambridge University Press.

Kovář, J., & Kovář, K. (2013). Towards the European(-ised) public sphere: The case of EP elections in the Czech Republic and Slovakia. *Journal of Contemporary European Research, 9*(5), 693–722.

Kreiss, D. (2012). *Taking our country back. The crafting of networked politics from Howard Dean to Barack Obama*. New York, NY: Oxford University Press.

Kriesi, H., Grande, E., Lachat, R., Dolezal, M., Boernschier, S., & Frey, T. (2007). *Westeuropean politics in the age of globalisation*. Cambridge: Cambridge University Press.

Kriesi, H., Trsch, A., & Jochum, M. (2010). Going public in the European Union: Action repertoires of collective political actors. In R. Koopmanns & P. Statham (Eds.), *The making of the European public sphere. Media discourse and political contentions* (pp. 223–244). New York, NY, Cambridge University Press.

Kuhn, T., & Stoekel, F. (2014). When European integration becomes costly: The Euro crisis as a test of public support for European economic governance. *Journal of European Public Policy, 21*(4), 624–641.

Kumar, V., & Svensson, J. (2015). *Promoting social change through. Information Technology*. Hershey, PA: IGI Global.

Lim, M. (2012). Clicks, cabs and coffee houses: Social media and oppositional movements in Egypt 2004-2011. *Journal of Communication, 62*(2), 231–248.

Lindner, R., Aichholzer, G., & Hennen, L. (Eds.). (2016). *Electronic democracy in Europe. Prospects and challenges of e-publics, e-participation and e-voting*. Cham: Springer.

Liu, Z., & Weber, I. (2014). Is Twitter a public sphere for online conflicts. A cross-ideological and cross-hierarchical look. In: L. M. Aiello, & D. McFarland (Eds.), *Social informatics* (pp. 336–347), LNCS 8851.

Lobeira, P. C. (2012). EU citizenship and political identity: The demos and telos problems. *European Law Journal, 18*(4), 504–517.

Lodge, J., & Sarikakis, K. (2013). Citizens in 'an ever-closer union'? The long path to a public sphere in the EU. *International Journal of Media and Cultural Politics, 9*(2), 165–181.

Mair, J., Clark, T., Fowler, N., Snoddy, R., & Tait, R. (Eds.). (2017). *Brexit, Trump and the Media*. Bury St. Edmunds: Abramis.

Majone, G. (1996). *Regulating Europe*. London: Routledge.

Majone, G. (2002). The European Commission: The limits of centralization and the perils of parliamentarisation. *Governance, 15*(3), 375–392.

Michailidou, A. (2015). The role of the public in shaping EU contestation: Euroscepticism and online news media. *International Political Science Review, 36*(3), 324–336.

Michailidou, A., & Trenz, H. J. (2013). Mediatized representative politics in the European Union: Towards audience democracy? *Journal of European Public Policy, 20*(2), 260–277.

Monza, S., & Anduiza, E. (2016). The visibility of the EU in the national public spheres in times of crisis and austerity. *Politics and Policy, 44*(3), 499–524.

Munteanu, A. M., & Staiculescu, A. R. (2015). Democracy facing complexity. The network form of the public sphere. *Mediterranean Journal of Social Sciences, 6*, 45–54.

Novy, L. (2013). *Britain and Germany imagining the future of Europe. National identity, mass media and the public sphere*. Basingstoke: Palgrave/Macmillan.

O'Hara, K., & Stevens, D. (2015). Echo chambers and online radicalism: Assessing the internet's complicity in violent extremism. *Policy and Interne, 7*(4), 401–422.

Obar, J. A., Zube, P., & Lampe, C. (2012). Advocacy 2.0: An analysis of how advocacy groups in the United States perceive and use social media as tools for facilitating civic engagement and collective action. *Journal of Information Policy, 2*, 1–25.

Offe, C. (2013a). Europe entrapped. Does the EU have the political capacity to overcome its current crisis? *European Law Journal, 19*(5), 595–611.

Offe, C. (2013b). Europa in der Falle. *Blätter für deutsche und internationale Politik, 1*, 67–80.

Özcan, T. (2014). Democratisation in the Middle East and North Africa: Tunisia, Egypt, and Turkey. In E. G. Carayannis, D. F. J. Campbell, & M. P. Efthymiopoulos (Eds.), *Cyber-development, cyber-democracy and cyber-defense. Challenges, opportunities and implications for theory, policy and practice* (pp. 175–195). New York: Springer.

Pariser, E. (2011). *The filter bubble: How the new personalized web is changing what we read and how we think*. London: Penguin Books.

Peters, C., & Witschge, T. (2015). From grand narratives of democracy to small expectations of participation: Audiences, citizenship, and interactive tools in digital journalism. *Journalism Practice, 9*(1), 19–34.

Pfetsch, B., & Heft, A. (2015). Theorising communication flows within a European public sphere. In T. Risse (Ed.), *European public spheres: Politics is back* (pp. 29–53). Cambridge: Cambridge University Press.

Polyakova, A., & Fligstein, N. (2016). Is European integration causing Europe to become more nationalist? Evidence from the 2007–9 financial crisis. *Journal of European Public Policy, 23*(1), 60–83.

Quittkat, C. (2011). The European commission's online consultations: A success story? *Journal of Common Market Studies, 49*(3), 653–674.

Rasmussen, T. (2013). Internet-based media, Europe and the political public sphere. *Media, Culture and Society, 35*(1), 97–104.

Rauh, C. (2013). *A widening audience. Ever more interested and active? The public politicisation of European integration in EU6, 1990-2011*. Wissenschaftszentrum Berlin fürSozialforschung, Berlin

Risse, T. (2014). No demos? Identities and public spheres in the euro crisis. *Journal of Common Market Studies, 52*(6), 1207–1215.

Risse, T. (Ed.). (2015a). *European public spheres: Politics is back*. Cambridge: Cambridge University Press.

Risse, T. (2015b). Introduction. In T. Risse (Ed.), *European public spheres: Politics is back* (pp. 1–25). Cambridge: Cambridge University Press.

Risse, T. (2015c). European public spheres, the politicization of EU affairs and its consequences. In T. Risse (Ed.), *European public spheres: Politics is back* (pp. 141–146). Cambridge: Cambridge University Press.

Ruiz, C., Domingo, D., Micó, J. L., Díaz-Noci, J., Meso, K., & Masip, P. (2011). Public sphere 2.0? The democratic qualities of citizen debates in online newspapers. *The International Journal of Press-Politics, 16*, 463–487.

Scalise, G. (2014). European identity construction in the public sphere: A case study on the narratives of Europe. *International Journal of Cross-Cultural Studies and Environmental Communication, 2*, 51–62.

Scharpf, F. W. (1999). *Regieren in Europa: effektiv und demokratisch?* Frankfurt a.M.: Campus.

Scharpf, F. W. (2014). Das Dilemma der supranationalen Demokratie in Europa. *Leviathan, 43*(1), 11–28.

Scharpf, F. W. (2015). Deliberative Demokratie in der Mehrebenenpolitik – eine zweite Replik. *Leviathan, 43*(2), 155–165.

Schmidt, M. G. (2008). *Demokratietheorien*. Wiesbaden: Eine Einführung.
Schmidt, V. A. (2013). Legitimacy in the European union revisited: Input, output and throughput. *Political Studies, 61*(1), 2–22.
Sicakkan, H. G. (2013). *Eurosphere. Diversity and the European Public Sphere: Towards a Citizen's Europe*. The Eurosphere Project. Final comparative study. University of Bergen (eurosphere.org)
Silva, E. C. (2014). A deliberative public sphere? Picturing Portuguese political blogs. *Observatorio (OBS), 8*(4), 187–204.
Smith, G. (2013). Designing democratic innovations at the European level: Lessons from the experiments. In R. Kies & P. Nanz (Eds.), *Is Europe listening to us? Success and failure of EU citizen consultations* (pp. 201–216). Ashgate: Farnham.
Smith, T. (2015). The possibility of an online political realm. *New Political Science, 37*(2), 241–258.
Statham, P., & Trenz, H. J. (2012). *The politicization of the European Union: From constitutional dreams to Euro-Zone crisis nightmares*. ARENA, University of Oslo.
Statham, P., & Trenz, H. J. (2015). Understanding the mechanisms of EU politicization: Lessons from the Eurozone crisis. *Comparative European Politics, 13*(3), 287–306.
Streeck, W. (2013). Was nun, Europa? Kapitalismusohne Demokratieoder Demokratieohne Kapitalismus. *Blätter für deutsche und internationale Politik, 58*(4), 57–68.
Streeck, W. (2015). Why the Euro divides Europe. *New Left Review, 95*, 5–26.
Tewksbury, D., & Rittenberg, J. (2012). *News on the Internet: Information and citizenship in the 21st century*. New York: Oxford University Press.
Toepfl, F., & Piwoni, E. (2015). Public spheres in Interaction: Comment sections of news websites as counterpublic spaces. *Journal of Communication, 65*(3), 465–488.
Towner, T. L., & Dulio, D. A. (2012). New media and political marketing in the United States: 2012 and beyond. *Journal of Political Marketing, 11*, 95–119.
Urbanikova, M., & Volek, J. (2014). Between Europeanization and De-Europeanization: A comparative content analysis of the pre-election presentation of the EU Agenda in the Czech Quality Press. *Communications-European Journal of Communication Research, 39*(4), 457–481.
van der Graaf, A., Otjes, S., et al. (2016). Weapon of the weak? The social media landscape of interest groups. *European Journal of Communication, 31*(2), 120–135.
Veltri, G. A. (2012). Information flows and centrality among elite European newspapers. *European Journal of Communication, 27*(4), 354–375.
von Bogdandy, A. (2012). The European lesson for international democracy: The significance of articles 9-12 EU Treaty for international organizations. *The European Journal of International Law, 23*(2), 315–334.
Walter, S. (2015). *European Political Science Review*/FirstView Article/June 2016, 1–21, Published online: 16 November 2015.
Wardle, C., & Derakshan, H. (2017). *Information disorder: Towards an interdisciplinary framework for research and policy making*. Strasbourg: Council of Europe. www.coe.int.
Warner, B. R., & Neville-Shepard, R. (2014). Echoes of a conspiracy: Birthers, truthers, and the cultivation of extremism. *Communication Quarterly, 61*(1), 1–17.
Wells, C. (2014). Civic identity and the question of organisation in contemporary civic engagement. *Policy and Internet, 6*(2), 209–216.
Wendler, F. (2012). Die Politisierung von Rechtfertigungen der Europäischen Union. In: A. Geis, F. Nullmeire, & C. Daase (Hrsg.), Der Aufstieg der Legitimitätspolitik. *Leviathan*. Sonderband 27 (pp. 190–207). Baden-Baden.
West, M. D. (2013). Is the internet an emergent public sphere? *Journal of Mass Media Ethics, 28*(3), 155–159.
Williams, A. E., & Toula, C. M. (2017). Solidarity framing at the union of national and transnational public spheres. *Journalism Studies, 18*(12), 1576–1592.

Yang, M. (2013). Europe's new communication policy and the introduction of transnational deliberative citizen's involvement projects. In R. Kies & P. Nanz (Eds.), *Is Europe listening to us? Success and failure of EU citizen consultations* (pp. 17–34). Ashgate: Farnham.

Zografova, Y., Bakalova, D., & Mizova, B. (2012). Media reporting patterns in Europe. *Javnost–The Public, 19*(1), 67–84.

Zuckerman, E. (2014). New media, new civics? *Policy and Internet, 6*(2), 151–168.

Open Access This chapter is licensed under the terms of the Creative Commons Attribution 4.0 International License (http://creativecommons.org/licenses/by/4.0/), which permits use, sharing, adaptation, distribution and reproduction in any medium or format, as long as you give appropriate credit to the original author(s) and the source, provide a link to the Creative Commons licence and indicate if changes were made.

The images or other third party material in this chapter are included in the chapter's Creative Commons licence, unless indicated otherwise in a credit line to the material. If material is not included in the chapter's Creative Commons licence and your intended use is not permitted by statutory regulation or exceeds the permitted use, you will need to obtain permission directly from the copyright holder.

Chapter 4
Experience with Digital Tools in Different Types of e-Participation

Georg Aichholzer and Gloria Rose

Abstract The chapter offers a systematic overview of the use of digital tools for various forms of political participation and the experiences made so far, based on an extensive literature review. Discerning three key functions of e-participation—monitoring, agenda-setting and input to decision-making—the authors review a variety of formally institutionalised mechanisms as well as informal expressions of civic engagement, including social media. The examination of digital tool use for monitoring purposes extends from electronic information access and exchange to e-deliberation, while the role for agenda-setting mainly includes uses for e-petitions and e-campaigning, showing a mixed picture of democratic impacts. The review of e-participation providing input for decision-making focusses on e-consultations, e-participative budgeting and e-voting, identifying several persisting problems with the latter instrument. A special section examines e-participation at EU-level, from deliberative citizens' involvement projects and e-consultation to the European Citizens' Initiative (ECI) and e-petitions to the European Parliament. Findings show that digital tools enhance direct and participative democracy in many respects; however, exaggerated expectations of new democratic potentials remain unfulfilled: deliberative participative designs lack any impact on decision-making, and the ECI still is rather an instrument for civil society mobilisation than citizen empowerment.

4.1 Three Basic Functions of e-Participation

Understanding "e-participation" as the use of digital tools for political participation in the wider sense includes a wide variety of formally institutionalised mechanisms, as well as informal expressions of civic engagement. According to their predominant function in the policy cycle, we can discern three basic functions of participation (we prefer this typology because of the focus on level of impacts):

G. Aichholzer (✉) · G. Rose
Institute of Technology Assessment, Austrian Academy of Sciences, Vienna, Austria
e-mail: aich@oeaw.ac.at; gloria.rose@oeaw.ac.at

© The Author(s) 2020
L. Hennen et al. (eds.), *European E-Democracy in Practice*, Studies in Digital Politics and Governance, https://doi.org/10.1007/978-3-030-27184-8_4

1. *Monitoring*: A basic category of participatory activities comprises monitoring and control of political processes, actors and decisions via access to relevant digital information (e-information), online deliberation and discussion (e-deliberation). Information is of course also relevant to all other functions of participation, however, a condition sine qua non for enabling monitoring and control.
2. *Agenda setting*: A second category may also start with accessing politically relevant information and discussing political issues but extends to activities such as mobilising support for political projects (e-campaigning) and submitting formal requests to government institutions (e-petitions).
3. *Decision-making*: Finally, providing cognitive or evaluative input to political decisions (e-consultation), setting priorities for or determining budget expenditure (e-participatory budgeting) and casting votes on political alternatives (e-voting) comprise a third type of e-participation.

Before we focus on these three basic functional categories and relevant sub-types of e-participatory activities within each, we will start this section with some overall assessments on the use and effects of digital tools for democratic processes.

Despite the long history of digital or e-democracy, the implementation of digital tools for political participation on a broader scale has come at a much slower pace than the expansion of e-government, i.e. electronic services in the public sector. Mahrer and Krimmer (2005: 38 ff.) speculate about fear of change and latent as well as overt opposition amongst politicians in legislative government branches as inhibiting forces, based on a study in Austria: "[...] the very same parliamentarians who would be responsible for introducing new forms of citizens' participation for political decision-making are explicitly and implicitly opposing these reforms". Various earlier assessments of experiences with e-democracy provide a reference for an update with the most recent evidence.

Striking a balance after 25 years of e-democracy, van Dijk concluded that the primary achievement of digital democracy was a significant improvement in access to and exchange of politically relevant information. However, most disappointing from the perspective of direct democracy, "no perceivable effect of these debates on decision-making of institutional politics" was detected (van Dijk 2012: 53 ff.). The general conclusion then was that e-participation is largely confined to the initial and the final stages of the policy cycle (agenda setting, policy preparation, policy evaluation), and that it rarely allows for entries into the core stages of decision-making and policy execution. It was also found that bottom-up initiated e-participation was more successful than top-down initiatives and that the required set of digital skills was one of the greatest barriers to an effective enhancement of participation. In addition, Lindner (2012) finds the balance of empirical research on the use of e-participation sobering and could determine no evidence of increased and more inclusive participation to date. Though he acknowledges increased information transparency, the Internet's function to support critical monitoring and control and the extension of communication of political institutions with citizens, he deems the e-petitioning, e-consultation and online discussion platforms offered as being rather marginal in terms of power. Santos and Tonelli's conclusions (2014) largely tend to echo the general thrust of these findings.

A meta-analysis of e-participation research by Medaglia (2011), covering 123 articles from April 2006 to March 2011, determined that the field was very dynamic in those years. One of the most noticeable developments was a shift from research on activities towards impacts and evaluations. No great attention was paid to the areas of e-activism, e-campaigning and e-petitioning during this time. E-voting, however, was experiencing increasing interest, though publications in this area tend to be about design proposals. Medaglia emphasises a "need to move beyond a technological perspective, encouraging the ongoing shift of research focus from government to citizens and other stakeholders" (Medaglia 2012: 346; see also Medaglia 2011: 99).

Panopoulou et al. (2014) attempted to determine what the success factors for e-participatory projects are. Having reviewed literature on e-government and e-participation success, Panopoulou and her colleagues went on to conduct a survey of practitioners across Europe. Success factors which were brought up by all three sources, namely, the e-government and e-participation literature as well as the surveyed practitioners, were as follows: management and planning, security and privacy, sustainability, addressing the digital divide and inclusivity, meeting user needs and expectations, government or management support, technological advances and good practice, a promotion plan and value for citizens as well as for the government or organisations. From the practitioners' perspective value for citizens, user needs and expectations, promotion plan, support from government/management, management and planning and attention to digital divide issues are of highest priority (Panopoulou et al. 2014: 203). Based on the results of the literature and practitioner surveys, the researchers propose an e-participation success factor model including specific activities associated with the identified success factors (see Panopoulou et al. 2014: 204–205).

On the question of effects of e-participation, Font et al. (2016) took a closer look at what proposals resulting from participatory processes in Spain ended up being implemented, by studying 611 proposals from 39 different processes. The results are rather positive regarding implementation, with the team categorising a third of the proposals as having been fully implemented, another third partially implemented (e.g. with amendments) and a third not being implemented at all. Their assessment of accountability, however, concluded that in most cases there are no explanations given as to why certain amendments were made to the proposals or why proposals were not implemented, an area which could certainly use improvement. Font et al. (2016) determined that a participatory mechanism has a strong influence on the successful implementation of proposals, finding that "[...] the odds that a proposal emerging from a participatory budget or other permanent mechanisms (e.g. citizen councils) is fully implemented double those of proposals coming out from a case of strategic planning or other temporary processes" (Font et al. 2016: 18). The team also notes that the processes which were categorised as fully implemented had short proposal lists.

A crucial, largely latent but decisive factor influencing the use of digital tools for political participation is trust. Scherer and Wimmer (2014) conducted a literature review of trust in e-participation, referencing Im et al. (2014) as having found a negative relationship between general Internet use and trust in government, but voicing hope in the possibility that e-government may mitigate these effects. Grimmelikhuijsen and Meijer (2014) are quoted as saying they did not determine there to be a positive relationship between transparency and perceived trustworthiness. Within the literature review, Kim and Lee (2012) are noted as discovering an increase of trust in local government as a result of positive experiences regarding government responsiveness quality and e-participation application usefulness. Another interesting insight by Wang and Wan Wart (2007) is brought up within the review, namely, stating that participation events resulting merely in consensus building will not increase public trust, but situations in which services the public wants can be achieved, public trust can be increased (Wang and Wan Wart 2007: 276 as quoted by Scherer and Wimmer 2014: 63). Services which are of specific interest to citizens and therefore enjoy much citizen involvement are zoning and planning, parks and recreation as well as policing and public safety (Wang and Wan Wart 2007: 273).

The next subchapters will present the main results and insights gathered from the literature, structured into the three basic categories of monitoring, agenda setting and decision-making as well-related types of participatory activities (e-information, e-deliberation, e-petitions, e-campaigning, e-consultation, e-budgeting and e-voting), followed by a separate subchapter on experiences with the main participatory instruments in use at EU level.

4.2 Monitoring

4.2.1 E-information

Barber's seminal contribution to the idea of participatory democracy regarded "equalizing access to information" (1984: 276) as one of the greatest potentials of interactive technologies and proper information as a principal precondition for political judgement and active participation as a responsible citizen. Indeed, according to van Dijk's (2012) assessment, the greatest achievement was much better access to political and government information, meaning provision, retrieval and exchange between governments and citizens, but also public administrations, representatives and political and community organizations. Professional information brokers, journalists and sufficiently educated citizens have profited most from the content available on governmental and NGO websites and portals, public information systems, campaign sites of parties and candidates, weblogs, voter guides, online newspapers, journals and web-TV channels (van Dijk 2012: 53 ff.).

Access to e-information holds special relevance for the monitoring citizen. Monitoring by citizens is envisioned to be a way of ensuring state accountability and is the prerequisite for citizens to contest or question political decisions made. TheyWorkForYou.com is an example of parliamentary monitoring employed in the UK, meant to provide access to neutral and nonpartisan information on activities of Members of Parliament (MPs) (Escher 2011). A similar tool is provided by the platform abgeordnetenwatch.de in Germany. According to Rumbul (2014), however, monitoring the amount of times MPs spoke in the chamber led to an increase of statements from MPs which contained little relevant content. Such cases reveal significant gaps in current monitoring tools.

The importance of a quantum leap in improved access to information cannot hide the deficit regarding opportunities for democratic participation in more influential forms at different levels of government. For example, at national level such as in Portugal where e-participation initiatives are sparse, with the function of most initiatives at the local level being to inform, as the government primarily supports e-informing rather than e-consulting and e-collaborative efforts (Fedotova et al. 2012). This lack of effective e-participation is not restricted to Portugal, however, with Boussaguet (2016) making similar claims about participatory mechanisms at the EU level, criticising the lack of use of participatory experiments or tools and the failure to include "ordinary" citizens.

4.2.2 E-deliberation

Deliberation, understood as careful reflection and exchange of arguments on a specific issue to arrive at considered judgement, is a basic element behind the idea of deliberative democracy. A deliberative process thus involves both an individual and collective activity. Its democratic relevance is not only to improve the quality of public decisions but also to participate in reaching decisions about what actions to take. "It orients toward understanding, thoughtful reflection, mutual respect, and much more, but it points toward a final decision-making stage" (Gastil 2013: 218). Before diving into the subject of e-deliberation, it is perhaps appropriate to repeat the words of Coleman and Moss (2012), that "[...] there exists no scholarly consensus about what even the most basic characteristics of deliberation are, and scholars are leading players in the effort to construct a meaning that is sufficiently compelling to relate the notion of deliberative citizenship to the empirical world around them" (Coleman and Moss 2012: 5). This lack of consensus must be kept in mind when examining research results.

In order for deliberative civic engagement processes to be successful, one needs the engagement of public officials and politicians (Barrett et al. 2012). Structural components identified by Knobloch et al. (2013) as cultivating successful offline deliberation are deliberative skills training and a mix of discussion formats and extended question–answer sessions. When regarding offline deliberative civic engagement processes, Weiksner et al. (2012: 3) observe that they can lead to short, medium as well as long-term policy impacts. Deliberative formats enjoy high citizen interest, can be cost-effective and superior to conventional processes concerning the inclusion of various viewpoints and coping with prejudices (Collingwood and Reedy 2012). Deliberative civic engagement can also prove helpful in situations where the citizenship is deeply divided, such as intercultural conflicts, though Siu and Stanisevski (2012) caution about its limitations and feasibility on a case-to-case basis. Contributions can also be made to community capacity (Kinney 2012; Weiksner et al. 2012). Knobloch and Gastil (2015) examined highly structured deliberative events (the Australian Citizens' Parliament and the Oregon Citizens' Initiative Review) and found civic transformation and increases in deliberative and internal efficacy as well as communicative and community-based engagement, with feelings of empowerment regarding politics and public life. In general, deliberative civic engagement seems to be of a more temporary nature, being employed for singular issues and spanning only a short amount of time, embeddedness in political decision-making and problem-solving routines being the exception rather than the rule (Leighninger 2012).

Common criticisms of deliberative systems include the prevalence of idealism, low motivation and aptitude as well as narrow-mindedness of citizens, the prioritising of purely reason-based argumentation, a lack of heterogeneous representation and a lack of impact on policymaking (Collingwood and Reedy 2012; Weiksner et al. 2012).

When comparing offline and online deliberation, Davies and Chandler (2013) find that voice deliberation in real-time is more effective than deliberations concluded through text, in particular regarding mutual understanding and opinion forming. On the other hand, they also find benefits of anonymity concerning the willingness to participate, but at the cost of satisfaction for the participants. Online discussions with deliberative design show increased positive individual-level outcomes compared to non-deliberatively designed online discussions, with these effects being most prominent in anonymous conditions: "[...] deliberative design positively affected participants' opinions and values, coherence, efficacy, and trust for institutions, but not generalized trust or readiness for political action" (Strandberg 2015: 466–468). The above-mentioned problems of deliberative systems concerning lack of heterogeneous representation are particularly pronounced in online deliberation, with a tendency to over-represent white males who are young and educated, as was found to be the case by Baek et al. (2012) in a comparison with face-to-face deliberations in the USA. On the related subject of unrepresentativeness, Davis observes the following: "Online discussants vary significantly from the general public demographically and in terms of media usage, political interest, political attitudes, and behavior" (Davis 2005: 124). It is due to this, that the public opinion is distorted in online spaces. Online discussions are nonetheless being used to draw conclusions about public mood, with reactions to events trickling in minutes after occurring.

It is, however, also possible for many alternative viewpoints to be included in deliberative processes, despite not achieving high representativeness. This was observed for a case study in Finland investigating a special format of online deliberation, so-called "crowdsourced deliberation", "[...] an open, asynchronous, depersonalized and distributed kind of online deliberation among self-selected participants in the context of an attempt by government or another organization to open up the policymaking or lawmaking process" (Aitamurto and Landemore 2016: 1). The process of the investigated case study had the character of democratic deliberation and covered many varying viewpoints, despite statistical representativeness not being given, showing that "lack of statistical representativeness thus does not necessarily mean poverty of views, information and arguments and low-quality deliberation" (Aitamurto and Landemore 2016: 2). Cho and Keum (2016) observed that political expression is also more independent of socioeconomic status on social networking sites than in offline political discussions, based on the findings of a national survey in the USA from 2012, whereby the individuals who use social networking sites for political purposes are also generally less affected by their social economic status, also regarding their offline discussions.

Another issue commonly raised with online deliberation concerns the quality of the discussions. Kersting (2013: 270) criticises the quality of online deliberative instruments as "[...] more oriented towards the construction of identity and community bulding than towards political dialogue and deliberation". He also finds that web forums "[...] are not argumentatively-respectful and consensus-oriented, but are often pure monologues and frequently aggressive" (Kersting 2005 as quoted in Kersting 2013: 277). His conclusion is a very critical view on online third spaces, mentioning lack of openness and exclusion as additional attributes next to self-affirmation and in-group bonding, but sees a future in combining online and offline instruments. Online forums were also investigated by Loveland and Popescu (2011), who regarded the posts of five regional web forums hosted by a US newspaper. They were unconvinced of the quality of debates, noting that discussions remained for a large part unfinished and were of an episodic nature. Davis (2005) makes similar observations in his publication "Politics Online", concluding that online political discussions do not reflect opinions of the public, due to several reasons, above all obstacles in the environment for participation and the lack of representativeness. The problems of the environment are caused primarily by the lack of moderation and the lack of accountability. Social rules can be broken without consequences, oftentimes leading to chaos, hostile interactions and absence of rational argumentation. Another obstacle is audience fragmentation, typical for online environments due to specialised forums and groups. This leads to political talk being conducted within "own discussion ghettoes". "The individual poster seems less interested in engagement than in pronouncement. Opinions are set. The goal clearly is expression and reinforcement, not interaction and exchange" (Davis 2005: 123). Respectful conversations can, however, be ensured through a moderator, as was shown in the case of the Oregon Citizens' Initiative Review by Knobloch et al. (2013). Lampe et al. (2014) as well as Davies and Chandler (2013), Coleman and Moss (2012) and Weiksner et al. (2012) voice their support for a moderation system and structure to accompany online deliberations to ensure the quality of online discourse, which Lampe et al. estimate would even be possible for large-scale online political discussion spaces. For online environments, it is important to ensure that the online communicative environment matches the deliberative task at hand and is engaging and rich in media (Davies and Chandler 2013).

Despite the described shortfalls of discussion forums which can often be observed concerning quality and the culture of discourse, positive examples can also be found. According to the results of an analysis of three UK-based discussion forums from 2010 to 2014, Graham et al. (2016) claim that political actions can in some instances be cultivated in third spaces, such as online lifestyle community spaces. In order for political action to follow up on online discussions, the following factors are identified: a helpful and supportive culture or structure, framing topics in a personal manner or in connection to everyday life and communicating in an interactive and reciprocal community or platform. An investigation of online lifestyle community spaces highlights "[...] the importance of political talk for triggering both manifest and latent political participation" (Graham et al. 2016: 1383). Dunne (2015) examined 138 online forums dedicated to local politics regarding their impact and found none on direct democracy, as none of these forums provided any voting mechanism.

Mechant et al. (2012) report idea-generation and -evaluation strategies successfully working for two case studies of smart city applications in Belgium, applauding methods such as brainstorming sessions, online expert and end-user surveys and online crowdsourcing. Strandberg and Grönlund (2012), however, note few noticeable changes from a pilot citizen deliberation experiment carried out in Finland, mentioning knowledge gains and opinion changes but few other effects in the areas of political efficacy or interpersonal trust. Based on an examination of the Comparative National Elections Project (CNEP), a cross-national data set of 29 postelection national surveys, Torcal and Maldonado (2014) conclude that an interest in politics is not necessarily encouraged by political deliberation, but that effects such as political disengagement can also be entailed. While plural media information has a positive impact on political interest and political engagement, it is the exposure to personal discussions which carries the potential of detrimental effects. Interest and engagement are lowered when individuals are confronted with differing opinions on political subjects (see also Lu et al. 2016 as well as Guidetti et al. 2016).

An exploratory case study was done by Chadwick (2011) on the failure of an online citizen engagement initiative in "TechCounty". The case is particularly interesting because the conditions seemed ideal for a deliberative project, with the county being home to many individuals employed in technology fields and local political participation being relatively high, judging by election turnouts. The idea was to create an online forum meant to offer advice and house discussions on the topic of fostering and adoption provision, a topic where the likelihood of controversy was judged to be very low. An exchange of ideas and information was expected to lead to higher awareness of child welfare, improvements of the service and ultimately an increase of applications by individuals willing to foster or adopt. However, the project was a failure, running for not even a year before it was shut down. Very few people posted topics in the forum during this time, the number of discussions held were low, while maintenance by a private technology company was costly. Needless to say, the desired outcomes could not be achieved in the short run. Lessons can be drawn from the identified reasons for failure: "budget constraints and organizational instability; policy shifts inside the social service agency; political ambivalence among elected representatives; the perception of legal risks that led to a cautious depoliticized approach; and problems generated by the outsourcing of part of the initiative" (Chadwick 2011: 27).

4.3 Agenda Setting

4.3.1 E-campaigning

Campaigns are described by Baringhorst (2009: 10) as *"[...] a series of communicative activities undertaken to achieve predefined goals and objectives regarding a defined target audience in a set time period with a given amount of resources"*, whereby attention is called to the fact that the high variety of campaign types makes the term difficult to define. Consequently, our case studies in Part II of this book will only exemplify a small selection, especially bottom-up types of practices with potential for agenda setting. Campaigns can also be seen as strategically coordinated collective activities that seek the engagement and multiplication of followers, aiming to push specific topics (e.g. climate protection) and to put them on the political agenda. The main agents of campaigning activities are various civil society actors and political parties. Lindner et al. (2016) have shown how the first category profits from the advantages of digital networked environments and the wide variety of available tools (e.g. mailing lists, blogs, YouTube videos, discussion fora, wikis, social media) and how the Internet extends the repertoire of collective action, both regarding information and framing and as a tactical medium in political campaigning. Regarding the recent Gilet Jaune movement in France, social media have proven to be an essential tool. Another very recent example of extraordinary public attention raised is the case of the "youtuber"Rezo's activities in the run-up to the European elections 2019 in Germany.[1] His direct attacks, particularly against the conservative party CDU, may have substantially contributed to the high losses of votes especially amongst the younger voters, although the exact effect is difficult to determine.[2]

E-campaigning by political parties is expanding likewise, particularly including the role of social media. In recent years much literature has appeared on the use of digital tools for electoral campaigning, investigating the importance of social media during various national elections (see below). Regarding the use of digital tools with participatory objectives by politicians, Medaglia notes: *"The use of social network services, for instance, is paradoxically found to reflect the one-way communication structures of traditional political campaigning, and not to foster citizen involvement in decision-making (Andersen and Medaglia* 2009) *[...]"* (Medaglia 2012: 352). This is in line with Baringhorst's observation that government actors tend to use campaigns for informational and educational purposes, while civil society actors typically campaign in an attempt to influence ongoing political debates or current political decisions, mobilising for certain activities and building up public pressure (2009: 12). E-campaigns can also aim to bring controversial issues onto the political

---

[1]https://www.theguardian.com/world/2019/may/22/german-youtuber-rezo-video-attacking-merkel-party-cdu-goes-viral, accessed 02.06.2019

[2]https://www.faz.net/aktuell/politik/europawahl/rezo-und-die-eu-wahl-wie-spd-und-cdu-die-jungen-verloren-16210331.html, accessed 02.06.2019

agenda, which can then be formally introduced into the political system through the means of e-petitions (Lindner et al. 2016: 93).

Recent developments have underlined that narrowcasting and political marketing as specific types of campaign strategies can have a big impact on representative democracy (Edwards and De Kool 2016). A combination of social and traditional media can effectively be employed for political marketing in which political parties disseminate news and reports themselves. Narrowcasting describes the formulation of specific messages which are tailored to a particular target group. This is again an area social media can be very helpful in. Through the use of social networks and targeted email campaigns a very specific group of individuals can be reached with specific information. The 2008 Obama campaign was a huge success precisely because it combined narrowcasting with centralised coordination (Towner and Dulio 2012). Along with the 2016 US presidential election, however, digital campaigning methods reached an unprecedented level of "computational propaganda" (Woolley and Howard 2016, 2018). The combination of microtargeting and "political bots as automated scripts designed to manipulate public opinion" on social media spread all sorts of misinformation (Howard et al. 2018: 81). It is controversial whether this effectively swayed the election result in Donald Trump's favour (cf. Liberini et al. 2018; Woolley and Guilbeault 2017; Allcott and Gentzkow 2017), or to what extent automation and labour market issues shaped the outcome, as Frey et al. (2018) suggest. However, "the 2016 campaign highlighted the challenges that the Internet poses for American democracy, and perhaps democracy in general" and "that virality is now the coin of the campaign realm"(Persily 2017: 71–72). These challenges became salient once more as the Cambridge Analytica scandal broke in March of 2018, revolving around a data breach affecting the personal data of millions of Facebook users. This directed a spotlight on how strategic use can be made of data harvested on social media platforms to influence public opinion. Individual personality profiles were constructed and in combination with an ensemble of different machine learning approaches highly personalised advertising based on personality data was enabled (Hern 2018). The scandal encouraged public discussions not only about privacy and consumer protection but also surrounding misinformation and propaganda, with the CEO of Facebook Mark Zuckerberg being asked to testify in front of the US Congress.

Political marketing and narrowcasting touch on the work of parliaments, because they help define the context in which parliamentary democracy operates. They turn public opinion into a compass with which representatives align the exercise of their mandate. This means that the nature of political representation is changing from a contractual relationship between electorate and elected to a relationship in a permanent state of flux, with politicians constantly being challenged to determine their position vis-à-vis public opinion. The traditional and new media are reinforcing this tendency and facilitating the strategic behaviour amongst politicians to which it is giving rise (Coleman and Spiller 2003). As a consequence, the two methods do little to encourage citizens and politicians to interact and confront each other's opinions.

Circumstances in Europe appear to be less conducive to effective narrowcasting than in the USA. Party discipline is weaker there than in Europe, leaving more scope for differentiated messages. It is riskier to disseminate isolated electoral messages in Europe (Ward et al. 2003; Cardenal 2011). Studies carried out in Norway, Germany and Austria show that political parties still make little use of online opportunities to connect with specific groups. This is in part because party strategists are unsure about the effects of narrowcasting (Karlsen 2011; Russmann 2011). Koc-Michalska et al. (2014) examined the 2007 French presidential campaign, along with the 2012 campaign, on the basis of two surveys and a quantitative content analysis of candidate websites. They determined that in 2012 social networking platforms appeared as a new online public sphere in which younger and less politically involved individuals, who are unsatisfied with the democratic system, partake. However, it also could be shown that prior political attitudes such as interest and trust remain decisive factors. Another observation the authors could make was that the personal homepages of minor and fringe parties have started to even outperform those of major candidates, despite the difference in resources.

4.3.2 E-petitions

E-petitions represent a category of participation opportunities for citizens that is formally institutionalised and fully operational at many government levels, from local communities to the European Parliament (Lindner and Riehm 2011). An e-petition system allows citizens to submit to a government institution a formal request on a specific political issue following a set of formal procedural rules, whereby all steps can be carried out online. Petitions are a hybrid category of participatory practice, since formal procedures are organised top-down but petitions on specific subjects are initiated bottom-up by citizens. The instrument is mainly related to the phases of problem definition, articulation and agenda setting in policymaking. It should be noted that the label "citizens' initiative" is used for a participatory mechanism that can be more or less the same as, or at least very similar to, a petition. One of the most well-known examples is the European Citizens' Initiative which will be treated separately in Sects. 4.5.3. and 9.1.

E-petitions can be an efficient tool to empower citizens and address common issues, given the process possesses a certain amount of transparency (Alathur et al. 2012). E-petitions exist in various forms: petitions that are merely electronically processed internally at the institution addressed; petitions submitted electronically (via email or web-interface); petitions that are publicly accessible on the Internet and provide more or less additional information; and publicly accessible e-petitions that include extended communicative and participatory functionalities (Riehm et al. 2009, 40). E-petition tools, especially those implemented at national levels in Scotland and Germany, have been studied quite intensively. Most recent assessments (Bochel 2013; Riehm et al. 2014; Lindner and Riehm 2011) add to earlier evaluations, amongst others, by the Office of Technology Assessment at the German Bundestag, the German parliament (TAB), where "Public (electronic) Petitions" were introduced in 2005. This type of petition tool comprises the following components: submission via email attachment; examination by the petitions committee; publication on the Internet; possibilities for co-signing and discussing petitions online; processing, examination and replies to the petitioners; and publication of the decision on the Internet. Only those petitions that pass the examination by the petitions committee are published; during the pilot stage they amounted to only 2% (Riehm et al. 2009, 27).

The system of public electronic petitions at the German Bundestag enjoys much popularity and is deemed a success; the percentage of e-petitions amongst all petitions increased from 17% to 34%, and public petitions grew from 5% to 24% between 2006 and 2011 (Riehm et al. 2014: 9–18, 26–28). During this period more than 4 million people signed 2750 public electronic petitions and an accumulated total of more than 200,000 discussion contributions were recorded. The petitioners and the petitions committee are given the opportunity to discuss the issue jointly in a public committee meeting if over 50,000 people sign a petition. This innovation is seen positively by both petitioners and members of parliament. The vast majority also welcomes the implementation of discussion fora and finds them informative and objective. The petitions committee considers that between one third and a half of the petitions are positively concluded. Petitioners themselves are a little more critical: only one third were satisfied with the treatment of their petition.

A common observation reflected in this case study is that e-petitions do not typically mobilise new citizens to participate via petitions, but they tend to substitute conventional petitions, leading to no overall growth in petitioning activities. The average petitioner remains male and with a higher educational background than average citizens, with e-petitioners being younger than conventional petitioners. The move to the Internet alone does not lead to procedural transparency and increased participation opportunities. This is more likely in a combination of technological and politico-institutional reform, as was the case in Germany.

In England, Panagiotopoulos et al. (2011) examined the effectiveness of e-petitioning tools in English Local Government and came to a less optimistic conclusion, claiming the efforts of institutional compliance to be minimal and the actual use of e-petitions to be low. Often governments fail to provide official replies to petitions which hit their quota, or they take far too long to issue these replies until the matter at hand is of no more relevance (Wright 2012, 2016).

The case of the Downing Street e-petitions (UK) was widely lauded as a success and led to a wider adoption of e-petitioning processes (Wright 2012). However, it suffered from highly unequal participation. This was in part due to the high presence of so-called "super-posters", who either create more than ten accepted petitions or sign over 100 petitions. "The regular petition creators were particularly harmful because they posted on new topics quickly, and Downing Street would block subsequent petitions on similar topics. Many thousands of people attempted to become active citizens only to find their petition (and often several) rejected. However, the rule that blocked repeat petitions limited the chance for people to dominate the agenda [...] while still allowing people to set their own" (Wright 2012: 466). Wright further criticised the lack of a formal space to deliberate or counter-petition. El Noshokaty et al. (2016) examined what makes an e-petition successful and came to the conclusion that incorporating positive emotions into a petition will raise its chances of success. No changes in success rate could be observed in petitions with an emphasis on moral obligations. In fact, in petitions where moral and cognitive elements were very strong, El Noshokaty et al. (2016) even noted a decline in success rates. Petition quality also factors into success. In the case of a government-initiated programme in China, most attention and comments are granted to petitions with high salience and low complexity (Zhang et al. 2016). Despite its popularity amongst citizens, this case is criticised for the prevalence of so-called "participation chaos", stemming from low-quality proposals with little or no relevance and organisational issues such as misplacements of proposal types, whereas organised participation requires a certain level of civic knowledge or skills (Zhang et al. 2016). Analysing the growth of the Downing Street e-petitions with a big data approach (over 8000 petitions) over a time span of 2 years, Hale et al. (2013) discovered a few successful petitions with rapid growth, the number of signatures gathered on the first day being a good indicator for success.

But how do the petitioners themselves define the success of a petition? According to Wright (2016), citizens can perceive petition success in a number of additional ways to policy impact, such as the following: increased publicity/awareness, increased membership, increased credibility, galvanised/focussed support, sense of solidarity in local/national community, feeling of making a difference, show of acting, policy changes through government, government provided alternatives or partial changes, helped gain key support/links, helped gain access to ministers, got an official response, reached a set target of signatures, increased understanding in government and/or amongst general public, made a statement, were able to express concerns, fulfilled sense of civic duty, proved others also care about the issue (Wright 2016: 850).

Researchers in Sweden examined the relationship of e-petitions on trust in political institutions with survey data, seeing as e-petitions are considered one of the most commonly used variants of citizen participation and concluded: "In general, experiences with e-petitioning have not rendered any overall gain in trust; and for citizens more distant from the political mainstream, distrust is often reinforced. However, the results show that more citizens with a negative predisposition toward government have changed their perception in a positive direction than vice versa (positive predisposition-negative change). So even if negative reinforcement is more common than positive reinforcement, change is more positive than negative" (Åström et al. 2016: 3f.).

Largely positive experiences with another tool for e-petitions have also been reported in the context of the New Citizens' Initiative Act in Finland (see Lironi 2016, 18 ff.). Since its institutionalisation in 2012, nine successful initiatives reached the Parliament. Of these only one was translated into law so far. The main experiences were as follows: enhanced participation of citizens in policymaking, especially amongst the youth; mutual learning processes amongst citizens and decision-makers; policy-shaping new ideas brought in by citizens; and enhanced legitimacy of policymaking. However, this instrument rather mobilises already privileged groups than a more representative section of the society, and although it raised the level of trust in policymaking, there were also signs of political disenchantment, especially amongst the supporters of failed initiatives.

E-petitions systems can also lead to so-called "slacktivism". The idea is that individuals engage in "activist" actions with minimal effort and no strong real-world consequences, the act itself only serving to satisfy a sense of having accomplished something and decreasing the likelihood of engaging in further, perhaps more effective, political engagements. Schumann and Klein (2015) could show negative effects of slacktivism on willingness to participate in a demonstration or to partake in a panel discussion, for example. They note the importance of individuals to feel part of a group and be invested in the group's welfare and viability in order to mobilise for offline collective actions.

Parycek et al. (2014) evaluated OurSpace, an international project dedicated to improving the engagement of the youth of Europe with European decision-makers through the combination of ICT use, information and motivation to participate. It turned out to be very difficult to mobilise young citizens. Participants felt sceptical regarding the potential to improve trust in politics, but recognised the value of OurSpace as a tool to contact politicians and present their opinions to decision-makers. The research team also discovered Europe's youth to be "[...] very capable to engage in face-to-face and anti-hierarchal discussions with both politicians and other users, and to engage in respectful and inclusive deliberation online" (Parycek et al. 2014: 138). The engagement of decision-makers was an important factor in the success of the project, and the implementation of social features such as chat or profile options are advised. Identified barriers for discourse were language, navigational difficulties on the Internet platform and low interest in European-level matters.

4.4 Decision-Making

4.4.1 E-consultation

E-consultations belong to the group of top-down e-participation instruments most widely practised at all tiers of government—from the local to supra-national levels. In practice the function of this instrument may be confined to contribute to agenda setting but in principle it also carries potential to substantially shape decisions to be taken. Main objectives are to enhance the legitimacy of political decisions and to raise the quality of decisions by improving inputs as regards the social range and/or the knowledge base. The potential to rationalise political decision-making is typically activated in the phase of policy formulation (cf. Albrecht 2012: 13ff.). A variety of designs is being practised with e-consultations. In addition to open and closed consultations as basic categories the variants include simple question-and-answer discussion fora, e-polls or e-surveys, selected e-panels and so-called editorial consultations (e.g. participatory drafting of policy documents in the European Parliament's Citizens' Agora) (cf. Tomkova 2009).

Pammett and Goodman (2013) explored the consultation practices undertaken before the use of e-voting systems as well as the following evaluation practices in Canada and Europe. They deem consultations important for openness and transparency in the context of e-voting to foster trust in the electoral process. In their assessment consultations are limited in various respects. While in Europe they tend to involve parliamentary or government committees, political parties, expert committees and specific stakeholder groups, consultations in Canada appear to transpire between city councilors and government officials and often adopt the character of informing about decisions already made rather than consulting on a decision before the fact. Regarding the organisation of e-consultations, Loukis and Wimmer (2012) observed that one can achieve higher-quality focussed debates by structuring the consultations. They warn, however, that introducing structure can also lead to reduced participation as well as the exclusion of specific groups, resulting in a quality-for-quantity trade-off. They propose that structured e-consultations should be introduced complementary to unstructured consultations already taking place on many government agency sites. An evaluation of the first e-consultation ever held by the Irish House of Parliament showed successes regarding the Parliamentary reform and the mobilisation of citizens to participate in policymaking processes. However, it assessed e-consultations still as "appendages to existing, centralized decision-making power" (Murray 2013: 1), rather than constituting a development in the direction of e-democracy. Similar to Loukis and Wimmer (2012), Murray also warns of the quality of participation, with a reference to lack of Internet accessibility for many individuals.

4.4.2 E-participatory Budgeting

A new instrument termed "participatory budgeting" has practically been invented in Porto Alegre, Brazil, where citizens have been participating in processes to determine the distribution and investment of municipal budgets since 1989. This participatory arrangement, classified and much celebrated as a democratic innovation, has attracted special attention because of its special origin and participation in decision-making. E-participatory budgeting stands for the further development of this model using electronic communication tools. Over the past 25 years the practice of participatory budgeting first spread in Brazil and Latin America and subsequently all over Europe, with several hundred cities adopting the concept (Talpin 2012: 186). With the diffusion of the model, a differentiation process into a number of sub-types took place. Today traditional, online or hybrid communication channels are practised (cf. Mkude et al. 2014; Miori and Russo 2011), with varying degrees of success (Röcke 2014). In a study of projects in 20 European cities, Sintomer et al. (2008) identified six different models. Not all cases give citizens decision-making power; some are merely consultative or can have other impacts, for example, contributing to the modernisation of public administration or bridging the gap between politicians and citizens. Unlike the original model in Porto Alegre, the European cases only deal with 1%–20% of the municipal budget (Talpin 2012: 186). In Germany, participatory budgeting phases mostly comprise general information, discussion of ideas, specification of selected proposals and voting on selected suggestions. These are predominantly not final binding decisions. They are taken by city or community councils, mostly without a specific budget included (cf. Schneider 2018). A combination of online and offline channels to maximise inclusiveness is now state of the art. Discussions on how to distribute public funds are challenging for all stakeholders and consume much time and resources. Proper process design and ICT support to save time and resource demands are therefore essential elements (Heidelberger 2009).

In Europe, Sintomer et al. (2008, 2010) identified the following impacts: support for the demand for increased transparency, improved public services, accelerated administrative operations, better cooperation amongst public administration units and enhanced responsiveness. Positive contributions to the political culture and competences of participants can also be expected. This can include extended participation opportunities, enhanced transparency of public policy, better quality of decision-making, increased legitimacy and a stronger identification with the local community. Cost reduction and major structural reforms are less likely achieved.

Participatory budgeting has been carried out in over 1700 local governments from over 40 different countries, according to Cabannes (2015). Improvements can be achieved in the areas of basic service provision and management, due to the element of community oversight. Goncalves (2013) observes increased investments in sanitation and health services in Brazil as a result, leading to reduced infant mortality and showing that it can indeed impact public expenditures with noticeable consequences. Moreover, it "[...] is an effective mechanism of local authorities influence on territorial development" (Volodin 2014: 378), as with co-managed slum upgrading in Porto Alegre (Pimentel Walker 2016). However, as Gordon et al. (2017) point out, social media platforms remain underused in participatory budgeting processes because local community leaders in the USA perceive a lack of adequate infrastructure and hindrances caused by restrictive policies, as well as security concerns, which could be limiting success.

Lim and Oh (2016) compared offline and online participation channels of a participatory budgeting system in Korea, determining that citizen opinions were ultimately incorporated in the resulting budget or policy decision-making, with offline systems having been more successful due to higher deliberativeness and representativeness.

4.4.3 E-voting

E-voting is the form of e-participation with the most direct influence on a decision, i.e. the outcome of a choice between alternative options. However, since elections are a cornerstone of democratic institutions, not only the outcomes are important but also the whole process of voting needs special attention and must fulfil certain criteria. Therefore, our case studies in Chap. 12 will include a special focus on process aspects. The composition of topics discussed in Lindner et al. (2016) is still valid and reflected in the literature. An update of empirical case analyses offers the most valuable knowledge for the purpose of this section. For instance, as Estonia was the first country to introduce Internet voting for national and binding elections (in 2005 on a local level and since then for all kinds of elections—local, national, European), it is often analysed and rather dominant in the recent literature (e.g. Heiberg et al. 2012; Kitsing 2014; Sál 2015; Springall et al. 2014; Vassil and Weber 2011; Vinkel 2012, Hall 2012; Kersting and Baldersheim 2004). Interestingly, this does not imply success in e-democracy in a broader sense (Toots et al. 2011).

Another popular case, due to its long history and well-embedded and long-term political strategy, is Switzerland (e.g. Beroggi et al. 2011; Driza-Maurer et al. 2012; Germann and Serdült 2014; Hill 2015; Serdült et al. 2015). In the case of Norway, the very high level of public trust in the government and the high degree of caution and professionalism that accompanied the introduction of Internet voting in 2011 raised hopes that it could be established there. Nevertheless, controversies over the sufficiency of security mechanisms led to a discontinuation of the Internet voting project in 2014. In addition to these prominent European cases, interesting insights can also be gained from experiences made with Internet voting around the world, e.g. in Australia or the USA. Analyses of all of these empirical cases, focussing on a variety of topics, such as trust, security and transparency or impact on voter turnout, contribute to gain well-grounded knowledge about the current state of Internet voting.

4.4.3.1 Legal Theory and Computer Science

The introduction of Internet voting is confronted with a number of legal challenges. Elections, being a key element of democracy (Garrone 2005: 111), have to be protected carefully. While a legally binding constitution defines the procedural requirements for elections, computer science is in charge of developing the measures that ensure compliance with these requirements (Bräunlich et al. 2013). The main election principles, namely, universal, equal, secret, direct and free suffrage, find their manifestation in national legal frameworks, as well as in international election standards, for instance, the European Commission's Compendium of International Electoral Standards (EC 2016), the Venice Commission (2003) or the OSCE Election Observation Handbook (2010). In addition, the Council of Europe's (2005) recommendations on the legal, operational and technical standards for e-voting (Rec (2004)11) state that "e-voting shall respect all the principles of democratic elections and referendums" (Council of Europe 2005: 7) and refer to those five principles of voting. In fact, the Rec(2004)11 has been and still is a very influential international document (Stein and Wenda 2014). Aspirations to update and renew Rec(2004)11 are discussed on a regular basis in review meetings or expert meetings of the Council of Europe.

Compliance with these central legal principles poses great technical challenges for the implementation of Internet voting. Fundamental Internet security problems need to be taken seriously, and procedural issues such as guaranteeing both secrecy and transparency at the same time have to be considered. In addition, potential susceptibility to flaws accrues from the multiplicity of agents (computers, servers, networks) involved in the voting procedure, an aspect that can seriously influence the legitimacy of voting. Opponents claim that it is principally impossible to achieve this legitimacy with e-voting. McGaley and McCarthy (2004: 153) state, for example, that "the nature of computers is that their inner workings are secret. Since transactions and calculations happen at an electronic level, it is not physically possible for humans to observe exactly what a computer is doing". In 2015 Richard Hill reported his experience of an attempt to challenge the Geneva e-voting system in court. He filed court challenges against the use of Internet voting in 2011, when e-voting was offered to all voters in Geneva. He wanted the courts to examine if e-voting was consistent with the cantonal law and the Federal Constitution (Hill 2015). According to the Federal Tribunal it is not sufficient to merely claim a weakness of a system and that "an appeal can only be lodged if weaknesses have been actually exploited during a specific vote" (Hill 2015). Regarding vulnerability tests of voting systems, in a recent case in the USA, in Washington, DC, a unique approach was followed: a mock trial was held prior to an Internet election in order to offer everyone who is interested the chance to test the voting system in place (Wolchok et al. 2012). In fact, a research group from the University of Michigan, Ann Arbor, gained control of the election server, changed votes and revealed secret ballots. Their intrusion was not detected by the officials for nearly two business days. According to the "attackers", this case illustrates the practical challenges of securing online voting today (Wolchok et al. 2012). Another incident in connection with Internet voting in Australia was reported by Buell (2015), referring to a standard security flaw detected in a vendor software used for statewide elections. During elections in 2011 in Estonia, despite the fact that election fraud has never been detected, this possibility was much discussed after the parliamentary elections, when an Estonian student claimed that it would be easy to hack and manipulate the Estonian Internet voting system (Rikken 2011). His claim for nullification of the election results was rejected, with the argument that the sole possibility that a computer may have been affected without the voter's knowledge is not reason enough (Sivonen 2011). As a consequence, shortly before the European elections in 2014, a debate about security issues of the Estonian system came up again (Arthur 2014).

Regarding Estonia in particular, the OSCE that accompanied the elections in 2011 recommends some changes and sees room for further improvement of the Internet voting system (OSCE/ODIHR 2011). In 2007, a denial of service attack created problems for many Estonian websites (Jones and Simons 2012), exposing potential vulnerabilities. Evaluators of the security of the system in the 2013 Internet election in Estonia even recommend discontinuing Internet voting in Estonia, concluding "that a state-level attacker, sophisticated criminal, or dishonest insider could defeat both the technological and procedural controls in order to manipulate election outcomes" (Springall et al. 2014).

Similar challenges come up in various countries where Internet voting is in place on a regular basis: critics of Internet voting point to vulnerabilities of a system in place, sometimes even filing court challenges. However, their voices remain unheard, seeing as legally nothing can be done as long as a misuse cannot be proved. On the one hand, the sole possibility of fraud is not reason enough to take action; on the other hand, demonstrating flaws would mean committing a crime. Nevertheless, the possibility of indirect effects, such as revisions of e-voting systems due to court challenges or media and public attention, does exist (see also Hill 2015).

There are also several technical issues of practical implementation which remain to be resolved (Beroggi 2014; OSCE/ODIHR 2012, 2013) such as problems during the preparation, vote counting, login and connection as well as the vote casting phases during the test of the Internet voting system in the Canton of Zurich in 2004.

4.4.3.2 Socio-political Issues

Internet voting has the potential to increase voter turnout—this is one central argument brought forward by Internet voting proponents since the beginning of debates about Internet voting. Due to methodological issues, it is rather difficult to make profound claims about the relation between Internet voting and turnout. There is no inevitable causal relationship between the number of participating voters and online voting. Variables such as the immediacy of the issues, positions at stake or people to be elected must also be considered when looking at voter turnout. It is, however, possible to make some assumptions based on a variety of studies dealing with this relation. Reports of the impacts of e-voting initiatives on voter turnout are in fact rather sobering, with results indicating that the move from paper to Internet does not lead to the anticipated increase in total voter turnout. In Norway, for instance, an election evaluation revealed that the turnout levels in the trial municipalities slightly increased, but these are replicated in the whole country (MLGRD 2012). When examining survey data, individuals (primarily young, male, of higher income and education and engaging in frequent social media use) indicate that e-voting would mobilise them in situations where they would otherwise not participate (Spada et al. 2016) and that their interest in e-voting options is high (Carter and Campbell 2011). These survey results are, however, not reflected in data of actual e-voting experiments (Beroggi 2014; MLGRD 2012).

In 2004, a pilot programme for testing an Internet voting system was introduced in the Canton of Zurich, Switzerland, preceded by a survey on the expected benefits of e-voting, providing a very good example of how survey data and expectations on this issue can conflict strongly with findings (Beroggi 2014). Individuals indicated high interest in e-voting as opposed to traditional methods, while the findings showed predominant usage of postal voting. Overall, e-voting did not mobilise more young voters, as the overall age distribution stayed the same, but Beroggi (2014) notes that the average age of e-voters is lower than postal and ballot voters. In

Norway young voters were optimistic concerning online-voting, but emphasised the symbolic and ceremonial importance of walking to the polling station to submit their vote manually (MLGRD 2012). Based on an analysis of Estonia's Internet elections, Sál (2015) concludes that "the sought correlating relation between internet voting and the total voter turnout can't be convincingly proven".

Investigators of the 2011 election in Estonia explain the influence of e-voting on voter turnout as follows: they distinguish between usage and impact of e-voting and claim that "usage of e-voting is mostly restricted to the politically engaged, but the impact of the technology on the propensity to turn out is highest among 'peripheral' citizens" (Vassil and Weber 2011: 16). The term "peripheral citizens" describes rather disaffected and disengaged individuals, but those few who turn to the Internet option are fascinated by the e-voting application itself.

4.4.3.3 Socio-cultural Issues

Another dimension of e-voting that is discussed regularly deals with the issue of trust in technology and how it might influence election turnout and election outcomes. In order to engage in e-voting, one must have a reasonable amount of trust in the process, which appears to be present in Estonian and Swiss voters and Norwegian election stakeholders, according to the OSCE/ODIHR Election Assessment Mission Reports for the respective countries of 2011, 2012 and 2013. For Estonia, a steady increase of voters choosing to cast their ballot via the Internet from 2005 onwards can be noted (OSCE/ODIHR 2011). Looking at a comparatively high number of Internet elections, it seems that Estonians have gradually built up trust in the system. Concerning Internet voting in Estonia, Vinkel (2012) states that "[...] the factor of trust has been of the upmost importance. Without a doubt, trust will stay the most important factor of choosing internet voting also in the future and building and stabilising this trust is the most important but also one of the most difficult tasks of the election administration". In Norway in 2011 and 2013, the so-called Decryption and Counting Ceremony at election day had the aim to sustain trust in Internet voting by making the decryption and counting of electronic votes public (Markussen et al. 2014). To what extent the ceremony reached its aim remains open. Although the ceremony as such attests to the idea that IT is a socio-technical learning process, making specialised cryptographic elements of Internet voting comprehensible for anyone else than technical experts remains a challenge.

In sum, it is rather obvious that even after more than a decade of conducting and experimenting with Internet voting in various country-specific contexts, several challenges exist. In fact, their relevance is regularly emphasised when online elections in a variety of countries are accompanied by evaluations focussing, for instance, on turnout rates, security aspects, user friendliness or trust. Particularly striking is the large number of critics present in the literature. On a regular basis, system vulnerabilities are made public, sometimes even by filing a lawsuit. All in all, further developments are still needed with regards to technical aspects, legal frameworks, security, transparency and verifiability, as well as oversight and accountability. The Swiss trial is lauded by the OSCE/ODIHR (2012) for being good practice, the introduction being careful and limited, ensuring integrity of the systems and building public trust. At first sight, Internet voting might be perceived as an opportunity to alleviate the so-called democratic deficit of the EU. However, as shown empirically, such hopes have not been fulfilled. Essential for voting is not only the convenience aspect, but rather political reasons such as political interest or satisfaction with the political system. And regarding these challenges, Internet voting cannot be a technological quick fix.

4.5 Experiences with e-Participation at EU-Level

Over the past two decades, the EU has experienced a "participatory turn" (Saurugger 2010; see also Chap. 3) of its governance regime. Participatory democracy was implemented as a norm in the EU political system and a series of democratic innovations in practice were introduced to strengthen the connections with European citizens and civil society. Meanwhile, there are several contributions to an evaluation of the EU institutions' e-participation activities, such as the volume titled "Is Europe Listening to Us?" (Kies and Nanz 2013) or Lironi's (2016) study for the European Parliament. Based on these and a number of other sources, the following sections will review assessments of major e-participation instruments in use at EU level.

4.5.1 Deliberative Citizens' Involvement Projects (DCIPs)

Yang (2013) analysed a variety of 23 "transnational deliberative citizens' involvement projects" between 2001 and 2010 which were sponsored by EU programmes. They are described as a unique case of experimentation, but not as a paradigm shift in European communication policy, seeing as most projects were of a temporary and preliminary nature. Smith (2013) undertook a comparative analysis of design choices and democratic qualities on a subset of these cases, plus one additional case ("European Citizens Consultation—ECC09", "EuroPolis", "Agora", "Ideal-EU", "Your Voice in Europe—YViEu", plus "Futurum"), pointing out at least three novel challenges involved: large scale, language diversity and transnationality. Three different participation designs, including "deliberative polling" (randomly selected mini publics), "Twenty-first Century Town Meetings" (ICT-supported large-scale one-day events) and "online discussion forums", revealed the following results (Smith 2013: 202 ff.):

1. *Inclusiveness.* The two online examples "YViEu" and "Futurum" showed uneven participation, which damaged their legitimacy as perceived by policymakers. The solution to cope with large scales was open access to online participation and

randomised or targeted selection for face-to-face participation. An established pattern of EU-level participation is a focus on civil society organisations (CSOs). "YViEu" and "Agora" represent rare examples of institutionalised participation; however, both favour CSOs rather than individual citizens. People with English language skills had an advantage despite considerable efforts to allow for multi- or trans-lingual engagement.

2. *Considered judgement.* Opportunities for reasoned interactions and reflections on the judgements of fellow-participants were mixed. Interaction and deliberative quality of "YViEu" and "Agora" were seen as negligible, whereas "ECC09" and "Ideal-EU" allowed for some deliberation, mainly within national communities. "EuroPolis" and "Futurum" even achieved some trans-national exchange; however, none of these designs allowed for the trans-national development of recommendations.

3. *Publicity.* This aspect was assessed rather sceptically. The observed silence of the media is problematic, since publicity of democratic innovations is crucial for democratic legitimacy.

4. *Popular control.* Perhaps the most striking finding is the lack of any impact of these participation experiments on decision-making processes. Apart from empowering effects on the participants, there is practically no evidence that outputs were made use of in any form. This also holds for "YViEu", "the only consultation procedure that involves lay citizens to be institutionalised and to have a visible impact on decision-making" (Kies and Nanz 2013: 7). Possible reasons are the still experimental character of these democratic innovations, too broad topics, too general outputs and the failure to clarify how outputs should be integrated into the policy process.

Smith (2013: 212 ff.) points out that deliberative designs, particularly at European scale, bear high costs for organisers (and some also for participants), although the level of investments into these democratic experiments was rather small compared to traditional information campaigns on political issues. E-participation designs may allow saving costs and therefore tend to get priority. For example, implementing "YViEu" as an online platform also intended to save costs on an impact analysis. Inclusive and reasoned deliberation still requires substantial resources when carried out online.

Smith's comparative assessment underlines the feasibility of large-scale deliberative engagement at EU level and points out "Futurum" and "EuroPolis" as good practice examples. However, given the lack of commitment amongst decision-makers to formally tie the participation projects into the institutional policymaking process, he is rather pessimistic as regards a continuation of deliberative and consultative democratic innovations at EU level. In his opinion, a plebiscitary path as represented by the European Citizens' Initiative (ECI) will prevail as yet another tool benefitting organised interests rather than the citizens of Europe.

Kies and Nanz (2013: 9 ff.) largely share this view, and do not see the ECI specifically designed to further pan-European deliberation. Therefore, the two instruments should be seen as complementary as sufficient evidence has been accumulated of the deliberative instruments' positive democratic potential. To improve EU citizens' deliberation activities, they propose the following:

1. A combination of online and offline activities (an open online phase carefully connected with a phase of face-to-face consultations) and a topic of specific interest to promote citizens' inclusion.
2. National-level debates, discussions on propositions from other countries plus summarising national outcomes, followed by an optional pan-European debate, to achieve transnational debate.
3. Steps to increase impact on the political process: formal integration of new participatory instruments, input from citizens that is concrete and of real value for decision-makers and focussing on insights from deliberation processes on why certain decisions should be reached, rather than viewing outcomes as prescriptions for decision-makers.
4. Separate responsibilities for implementation and evaluation to increase the credibility and legitimacy of participatory processes.

Gastil (2013) offers a broader framework to assess the impacts of representative EU deliberation and consultation processes comparatively, distinguishing three types of influence: (1) shaping the views of the participants themselves, (2) informing the judgement of the wider public on an issue and (3) various forms of coupling deliberative events with formal decision-making. At the latter level, policy influence is understood to "improve the deliberation that occurs in these bodies" rather than to "direct government bodies to mindlessly affirm or abandon their previous policy judgements" (Gastil 2013: 221). The coupling between deliberation and decision-making can comprise influence on bringing an issue on the public agenda, on defining the problem(s) to be addressed, on naming the choices and alternatives, and finally, direct influence on the decisions taken. Comparing five major EU public participation exercises with the aim "to compare the principal intended paths of influence" (Gastil 2013: 222) leads to the following results: "ECC" and "EuroPolis" are mainly confined to an influence on the participants themselves and the wider public; the former was focussed on educative and civic effects in the agenda setting phase, whereas "EuroPolis" is attributed some potential for improving the understanding of decision-making issues. All three other cases are assessed as carrying potential for different degrees of influence on policymakers: The "Agora" 2008 event on climate change is seen as suitable for influencing policymakers in the form of yielding a broader understanding of the problems involved and of policy choices to be considered. Likewise, "Ideal-EU" had potential for advising public officials through framing available choices and could even reach into shaping the views of relevant alternatives. "YViEu" could have the most direct policy impact since the public is explicitly invited to deliberate on draft legislation and can substantially inform decision-making. Gastil also offers a review of participatory and deliberative arrangements practised around the world, suggesting their adaptation and incorporation into the EU governance system (Gastil 2013: 225 ff.).

4.5.2 E-consultation Instruments

Until recently, "Your Voice in Europe" and the European Citizens' Consultation were two key EU e-consultation instruments. In a comparative analysis focussing on institutional strategies in offering these tools, key actors mobilised and main effects, Badouard (2010) deplores the failure to develop a single and concerted strategy for EU-level e-participation offerings. The reasons are different political strategies and actors managing these mechanisms within the institutions, entailing a wide variety of projects.

The platform "YViEu" (today instead simply titled "Consultations") has been established in 2001 as the central site for all online consultations carried out by the various Directorates-General (DGs). These e-consultations aim to allow for the widest possible consultation of specific parts of the public on specific subjects and are regulated by general principles and standards (EC 2002). As stated by Badouard (2010: 101 ff.), the tool serves a three-part strategy: "Your Voice in Europe stages a democratization of the EU, regulates the relationship between the Commission and lobbies, and favours a more effective consultation process." Being regarded as both democratic and efficient, the instrument reconciles the often-assumed tension between openness and efficiency.

The European Citizens' Consultations (ECCs), held between 2007 and 2009, have quite a different mission as a communication tool (Badouard 2010: 102 ff.). Combining an online with an offline format, the aim was to initiate a pan-European debate leading to a European public opinion on the future of EU Europe. As such, the ECCs experimented with a new political mediation mechanism which allowed for a "transformative" type of participation by sensitising participants of EU policy issues and contributing to developing a European identity, citizenship and public sphere. In contrast, "YViEu" rather represents an "instrumental" form of participation, as it serves to contribute to specific public policies, institutional transparency and openness and is evaluated with regard to its results. While for "YViEu" the benefit for the Commission is in the foreground, the ECC focusses on the benefit for the citizens.

There are also clear differences concerning the actors involved in the two consultation mechanisms (Badouard 2010: 104 ff.). "YViEu" addresses the public using a variety of expressions including "public", "stakeholders", "European citizens" and "interested parties". However, there are some important barriers for "ordinary" citizens: many themes require a highly specialised technical expertise and relevant documents are often only available in a few languages, mostly in English. Consequently, civil society organisations represent the largest group amongst the participants, whereas lay citizens play a rather marginal role. An exceptional case was the European Commission's online consultation on European summertime arrangements held in summer 2018. It received the highest number of responses ever in any Commission public consultation (4.6 million responses from all 28 Member States), showing that this instrument can mobilise massive democratic participation. However, critics have called this form of mass procedures "unmanageable, unrepresentative and a source of confusion for the public" (Alemanno 2018: 7).

The ECC instrument contrasts with a special focus on 'ordinary' citizens and practising both a deliberative and an aggregative element. However, this has contributed to the highly complex setup of the process, complicated implementation and lowering the incentives for citizens to engage in deliberation (Karlsson 2010). Badouard's analysis finds that Europe-wide mobilisation of activist networks has been intensive and a further obstacle to the participation of individuals, so that "organised citizens' clearly outweighed "ordinary citizens", also in the ECC case. However, this does not preclude positive effects of successful online mobilisation of activist networks across national borders. This contributed to an important goal of the project, producing a European dynamic and transnational public.

As regards the impact on decision-making, the officially assigned role of consultations is to intervene upstream of the legislative process, so that participants rather contribute to preparing decisions than to directly taking part in decision processes. The conception of the "Your Voice in Europe" mechanism suggests a stronger link between consultation results and decisions, although the outcomes are not legally binding. Badouard argues that obligations to provide adequate feedback also create some pressure on the decisions to be taken and the recognition as a policy instrument, together with institutional accountability, brings the Commission to acknowledge the participants as legitimate political actors. Important conditions for the sustainability of these participatory instruments are their official status and a legal framework on their position in the decision-making process.

An analysis of the ECC by Karlsson (2011) shows that political representation has not been increased through the project as hoped. Members of the European parliament (MEPs) as well as participating citizens appeared to have been disappointed. Karlsson finds the design of the ECC project, at least in part, responsible for the failure. It had a lack of clarity over what inputs are desired by the MEPs and which inputs are expected from the citizens. The form of communication between MEPs and citizens, as well as its management must also be considered carefully. Kies et al. (2013) came to similar conclusions, finding there to be no impact of the deliberation results on decision-makers. They view the ECC as "a successful civic instrument but not a convincing policy instrument" (2013: 24), due to participants perceiving positive impacts such as higher confidence in the EU and informational gains, but politicians disregarding the propositions. A general problem with deliberative projects is the so-called "loss of plurality", in which ideas and inputs of citizens are lost during the phase of condensing all the information into a few limited recommendations. While this is inevitable, one must take care not to lose too much information, as was the case for the ECC (Kies et al. 2013).

Albrecht (2012) reviews the e-consultation practice at EU level with a focus on the "YViEu" platform, building on analyses of other scholars (cf. Quittkat and Finke 2008; Quittkat 2011; Tomkova 2009; Hüller 2008). His main points are: Online consultations have become a well-established instrument, regularly used by practically all DGs. This has certainly increased existing participation opportunities and brought more frequent public participation, especially of diverse interest groups, resulting in broadening the input into EU policymaking and extending its knowledge base. However, serious flaws include intransparent and sometimes inadequate processing of contributions; a shift of focus on closed question formats; little evidence of mutual learning and lack of impact on policy outputs; lack of feedback to participants on the use of contributions entailing frustration; one-way format of communication and no opportunities to debate contributions; only limited use of technologies (general purpose instead of specific e-participation and web 2.0 tools); and lacking integration of new arenas for debate, e.g. the political blogosphere (Albrecht 2012: 15 ff.).

He suggests three avenues of improvement: (1) deliberation to enhance input quality, (2) technological advancement and (3) moving towards popular spaces of online debate. Insisting on the double meaning of "deliberation"—an activity on an individual and a collective level—Albrecht advocates a model of deliberative e-consultations which not only consists of collecting comments on a policy proposal but also allows for discussions on these amongst the participants and with representatives of the EU institutions concerned. However, a number of unresolved problems hinder its implementation: to adapt small group and face-to-face formats to a large-scale setting, high costs, a minority of participants being willing to engage deeper, the need to facilitate the process and to inform and support the participants, and the reluctance of officials and policymakers to participate. As regards improving technological support, natural language processing and argument visualisation technologies are regarded as interesting candidates, although evaluation results to date are mixed. A third approach suggested is to integrate e-consultations in new ways with social media platforms such as the blogosphere and popular social networking sites, in order to counter the dominating top-down flavour of existing EU channels. The assumption is that a good deal of exchange on these sites includes political talk and that the separation between political content and living realities is being blurred more and more. Several EU projects have already experimented with linking e-consultations to social media (cf. Albrecht 2012: 19). Taken together the three strategies outlined show some promise to develop e-consultations further to a model which is more open and effective than the existing practice and which will also enhance the quality and legitimacy of policy decisions.

To exploit this potential, Albrecht suggests viewing e-consultations mainly as a knowledge management process and to focus on the views considered, rather than focussing on the participatory aspect and who participates. This would include attributing higher value to deliberated opinions than to opinions which are provided without interactive assessment and to integrate social media, not merely as an additional outlet or to inject political messages, but to analyse online discourse and controversies as part of the public opinion with the purpose to inform the formulation of policies. This would mean a turn from "passive listening" in the form of taking up contributions from citizens to "active listening" to civic discourse. Of course, this raises the issue of privacy protection, which has to be guaranteed in such practice. At the same time, in specific cases of e-consultation anonymity might lead to biased results, so that strategies must be developed to reconcile the need for identification and negative effects of a forced use of real names (cf. Ruesch and Märker 2012).

A summarised SWOT analysis of online EU public consultations is offered by Lironi (2016):

Specific *strengths* of EU e-consultations lie in reducing participation thresholds, encouraging participation and active citizenship, increasing democratic legitimacy of EU decision-making, enhancing the quality and transparency of EU rules and decisions, providing a cost-effective way of participation in decision-making, influencing the political process in addition to elections and political parties, reducing the democratic deficit, educating citizens about the EU decision-making and increasing its accountability.

The list of *weaknesses* is longer (Lironi 2016: 52 ff.): EU public e-consultations have low publicity, lack publication of clear feedback and results, are rarely representative for EU citizens and are not user-friendly; the platform "YViEu" is unattractive, intransparent, not user-friendly and ineffective; EU public e-consultations lack meaningful impact on decision-making, can lead to frustration of citizens and are rarely available in all 24 official EU languages; tool design lacks the specific expertise of consultation practitioners; assessments are difficult since evaluation criteria and key performance indicators are lacking; participants often lack the skills for effective participation; the instrument fails to empower individual citizens vis-à-vis organised interest groups; personal opinions rather than informed arguments predominate the contributions; and Commission DGs suffer from additional administrative burdens and diversion of resources.

Nonetheless, *opportunities* of EU e-consultation instruments include working on the perceived democratic deficit in the EU, the rise of alternative forms of engagement and (young) people's disengagement in "traditional" politics, progress towards more representative consultations with advances in representative statistical sampling methodology, lack of grassroots support for European policy, weak notions of "European Citizenship" and European demos, and technological advancements in ICTs.

Threats include the digital divide between countries (digital infrastructure and e-participation experience), lack of interest in EU politics, the perceived democratic deficit in the EU, and openness to e-participation offerings paired with resistance to fundamental change of decision-making structures.

Recommendations to improve online EU public consultations comprise:

- Upholding the use of this type of e-participation instrument and promoting it
- Making EU e-consultations better known, accessible to citizens and less technical, and always publishing the results with meaningful feedback, on time and with accurate analysis results
- Promoting EU e-consultations as an alternative engagement opportunity to attract those tired of "traditional" forms of politics and to stimulate grassroots discussions and engagement in EU affairs
- Considering a transformation from open consultations to a representative sample model

- Making sure that no citizen is excluded due to the digital divide and offering complementary offline options for citizens' participation in policymaking
- Efforts to enhance citizens' interest in EU politics and to facilitate their engagement

4.5.3 The European Citizens' Initiative (ECI)

The European Citizens' Initiative (ECI), which formally entered into effect on April 1st, 2012, is perhaps the first transnational instrument of participatory democracy worldwide. The ECI gives European citizens an opportunity to influence the legislative initiation process by submitting a proposal to the European Commission. It is now one of the main options amongst the formally institutionalised systems at EU level that provide for connecting bottom-up and top-down forms of participation with the support of digital tools. Principal requirements for the launch of an ECI are that the organisers constitute a citizens' committee with at least seven citizens from at least seven Member States, register the initiative on the ECI website, and collect at least one million support statements from citizens of at least seven of the Member States.

The ECI can be seen as an agenda-setting and policy-shaping instrument which produced great expectations but also scepticism amongst diverse observers, actors and stakeholders regarding the advancement of participatory democracy (cf. Pichler and Kaufmann 2012). Implemented to empower citizens, the ECI is now portrayed as a successful example of civil society mobilisation, seeing as civil society organisations (CSOs) have often been promoters of ECIs (Bouza García 2012: 338 ff.; see also Organ 2014). Bouza García identifies two important potentials: Firstly, the ECI may attract groups that are not highly institutionalised in Brussels, since CSOs that have been strongly active at the EU level may prefer a civil society dialogue. This could empower organisations that have been less able to attract the attention of EU institutions but are able to mobilise citizens, and thus more successful with ECIs. Secondly, with the emergence of new actors and issues, relations between EU institutions and civil society may change from "consensus-prone" to increased contention.

Empirical findings from an analysis of the first 16 initiatives suggest that the ECI has a special potential to enable citizens of small Member States to participate in the EU (Conrad 2013: 301), but the sample is yet too small to draw definitive conclusions. Hrbek (2012: 383) points to the fact, that despite political parties not yet having been organisers of an ECI, they may see potential in this instrument in the future and play a more active role. Whether the ECI will have the potential to realise a better integration of top-down and bottom-up approaches, given the existing social asymmetry amongst the promoters, remains yet uncertain.

4.5.3.1 Criticism

The procedural demands of the ECI require organisers to deploy extremely high levels of organisational capacities. Digital tools, in particular the Internet's advantage in mobilising support for an initiative, therefore play an important role. Duinkerken (2013: 30) even contends that collecting one million signatures without using modern ICTs would be almost impossible to achieve. However, the online collection software provided by the European Commission has in the past been subject of criticism, including shortcomings regarding its usability (Głogowski and Maurer 2013; Berg and Głogowski 2014; Starskaya and Çagdas 2012). Rustema (2014: 104) proposes that "a true open-source, community-developed" system would better meet the existing challenges. However, since its first release in December 2011, a number of updates have been made to improve the Online Collection Software provided by the European Commission.

4.5.3.2 Digital Support

In addition to reducing campaign costs organisers expect at least three advantages from using the Internet in an ECI process: spreading information about their campaign, disseminating arguments in support of it, and collecting sufficient signatures (Carrara 2012: 358). Sangsari (2013) also sees potential to facilitate the development of an ECI through prior deliberation in online forums as meeting places of organisers with like-minded people.

Typically, each ECI has a dedicated website serving to provide information on the initiative and facilitating online signature collection. Głogowski and Maurer (2013: 18) point out that ECIs "with transparent and user-friendly web pages translated into the majority of European languages have better chances to successfully collect signatures online" —a seemingly simple requirement, but not easy to implement. Carrara also points to the many facets of language barriers, e.g. due to cost reasons; most initiatives before 2012 refrained from opening multilingual online forums that could foster a debate. This poses another challenge to ECI organisers: in contrast to face-to-face collection, it is very resource-intensive to construct a deliberative space that allows for interaction, in many cases an insurmountable task. Therefore, the online presence needs to exhibit the campaign's central statement very clearly, and contain "*a strong, intelligible and universal argument register*" (Carrara 2012: 360). Meanwhile information on ECIs is distributed via social media which feeds into transnational discourse spaces, but particularly used by young (educated) elites (Knaut 2013; Greenwood 2012). While it is generally believed that the Internet allows for the inclusion of a variety of actors that would otherwise not be prone to public participation (Carrara 2012), Internet literacy is an indispensable prerequisite and Internet availability a decisive factor. Appropriate online channels are indispensable for an efficient transnational participation process; two thirds of the registered initiatives (up to March 2015) have collected statements of support online

(EC 2015: 9), in the case of the "Right2Water" initiative online collection even accounted for 80% (EC 2015: 7).

While the online collection of signatures can save time and resources, organisers cannot rely on digital support declarations alone for an initiative to be successful. In contrast to digital collection systems, face-to-face collection is more likely to strengthen citizens' identification with the initiative (Głogowski and Maurer 2013: 18). The role of online collection varies between the Member States, possibly due to differences in current e-participation cultures and levels of Internet access reasons (Carrara 2012: 366). Thomson (2014: 74) observes that campaigns are generally negatively affected by high data requirements, referring to the large amount of personal data, e.g. ID card numbers, signatories have to submit when stating their support for an initiative.

4.5.3.3 Points for Improvement

The current implementation of the concrete terms and rules of the ECI indeed demands significant improvements and modifications in design. Suggestions for major improvement of the online collection software and the entire process have been made (Kaufmann 2012: 240) and recognised to some extent. Additionally, calls were made to extend the period of signature collection to 18 months, to set up an independent helpdesk and to increase access to the signing of an ECI. There are also proposals on multilingual training tools, the clarification of EU data protection law and uniform requirements for signature collection in all Member States (Karatzia 2013). Berg and Thomson (2014: 122) advocate for the following 12 goals:

- "Reduce and harmonise personal data requirements across Member States;
- eliminate ID number requirements;
- ensure that all EU citizens can support an ECI—wherever they live;
- lower the age of ECI support to 16;
- redesign the online signature collection system;
- collect the e-mail address within the main ECI support form;
- lengthen the signature collection time to 18 months;
- give ECI campaigns time to prepare: let them choose their launch date;
- provide a support infrastructure for ECIs with legal advice, translation and funding;
- provide an EU legal status for ECI citizens' committees;
- remove or modify the first legal admissibility check;
- increase public and media awareness of the ECI."

Lironi (2016: 51) similarly argues for an intensified promotion of the ECI as a tool, increasing the user-friendliness of the ECI (e.g. through a reduction and harmonisation of identification and data requirements), and altering the signature collection timeframe.

A study commissioned by the European Parliament (Ballesteros et al. 2014) identified obstacles for the ECI in six areas covering the entire ECI process:

registration, certification of the online collection system, signature collection, verification and submission of statements and horizontal issues such as data protection or funding transparency. Here, measures to create a one-stop-shop for supporting ECI organisers as well as improving the signature collection software and support forms are seen as essential. The study concludes with recommendations to increase the ECI's effectivity, with concrete suggestions for revising both Regulation 211/2011 as well as EU primary law, the TEU (EP 2014). Key points include amending the TEU to either revising the ECI as an agenda-setting tool—in this case the Commission would not be obliged to follow a successful initiative with legislation—or revising the ECI as a tool for legislative initiative, meaning that citizens could have real legislative power within a certain framework. More specifically the study suggests a two-step system where, for instance, half a million signatures would request the EC to propose legislation, whereas one million signatures would oblige the EC to do so. The demand for introducing obligatory actions is strongly contested, as a million signatures cannot be considered representative for EU citizens.

The ECI as an institutional innovation for enhancing not only the citizens' influence on EU-level decision-making but also for contributing to the formation of a European public sphere has at best been of modest success to date. It would, however, be too pessimistic to conclude that the instrument has a predominantly symbolic function. It is to some extent still an experiment with many open questions and it was therefore wise to include a clause for a possible revision every 3 years after a period of gathering experience with the new instrument. For now, it seems that the ECI's relevance is far greater on the discursive level than in terms of the concrete policy-shaping impact.

The European Citizens' Initiative (ECI) was envisioned to increase direct participation in EU law-making, but seems to have failed in conveying its message to citizens as there appears to be no connection between knowing about the ECI and the image of the EU or being willing to use the tool (Gherghina and Groh 2016). Monaghan (2012) speculates that perhaps the output-based approach and the measurement of the ECI in Commission Green Papers or Proposals is not relevant to EU citizens, as they are more interested in changes in their political realities. The potentials of the ECI appear to remain untapped, which is unfortunate as Lironi (2016) refers to possible benefits such as strengthened participation of citizens in policymaking and consequently increased political legitimacy.

Most recent developments show some remarkable progress as regards the use and role of this instrument which underlines its democratic potential. After the conclusion of our study, the European Commission presented a legislative proposal to revise the European Citizen' Initiative, which entails several changes primarily addressing the liability of initiative organisers, the provision of information and advice, the registration phase of initiatives, the minimum age to support initiatives, the signature collection phase and the review provisions (EC 2017). Whether the interpretation of these developments as "impressive signs of previously unseen institutional matureness and political energy" (people2power 2017) of the ECI will be sustained remains to be seen.

4.5.4 E-Petitions of the European Parliament

The option to submit a petition to the European Parliament via the Internet is another form of using digital tools within a participatory instrument at EU level. The Committee on Petitions (PETI) is the body that is responsible for treating petitions and deciding on which kind of action to take.

According to a recent report (PETI 2015), citizens mainly petitioned about the environment, fundamental rights, justice, the internal market and European policy development and used the tool in order to contest or argue against decisions and rulings which were made. In 2014, 2714 petitions received marked a slight decrease from the previous year, the trend in the past few years having been rising. More than half (59.6%) of these petitions were closed at early stages due to three main reasons: the petition was deemed inadmissible, was closed after information on the relevant subject was communicated to the petitioner, or was closed due to being addressed to the wrong EP committee. A total of 1168 petitions were admissible, of which 1119 were passed on to the Commission for an opinion. English, German, Spanish and Italian are the languages most commonly used within the petitions (collectively accounting for 72%). While Germans, Spaniards and Italians were the most active petitioners, citizens from Estonia and Luxembourg were strongly underrepresented (PETI 2015).

Back in 2009, 63.2% of all petitions were sent via e-mail; this percentage has increased to 80% in 2014 (PETI 2015), the Internet being the preferred method for petitioning. In 2014, the PETI report documents 80% of the admitted petitions being closed within a year. An important observation made annually in these PETI reports is the fact that citizens "[...] confuse the EU institutions and those of the Council of Europe, in particular the European Court of Human Rights" (PETI 2015: 24). In November 2014 a new Petitions web portal was introduced, possessing more feedback features on the status of petitions and more information on the Parliament's areas of competence. The PETI report welcomes this development, though it points out that in order to reach the petitions page, a user must navigate through four pages from the Europarl homepage. Another criticism was the length of the whole petition process, particularly the long time needed by the PETI Committee to verify petitions (Lironi 2016: 37).

Tiburcio (2015) examined "The Right to Petition" to the European Parliament for the Committee on Petitions, noting that recent studies on petitions tend to neglect it, although it represented a "well-embedded process to deal with petitions" (Tiburcio 2015: 12). He comes to the following conclusion: "[...] the petition system of the European Parliament compares well overall with the petition systems of Parliaments of Member States. In terms of conventional features, it scores well in all dimensions: it ensures direct access (and not intermediate) by citizens; it is highly inclusive and open to both national citizens of Member States as nationals from third countries, if they reside within the EU territory; it offers possibilities for greater involvement of citizens, including through frequent holding of hearings, followed by public debate in committee" (Tiburcio 2015: 40).

He does, however, identify several weaknesses which have yet to be resolved, such as an information gap, and recommends working on the following points:

- Clearer information
- Publication of more detailed information related to the petition process
- Publication of all documents related to the petition
- A better and more focussed communication strategy
- Getting to know who the petitioners are (sex, age, education, occupation, etc.)
- Learning opinions and experiences of petitioners
- Conducting a public survey on citizen knowledge of the right to petition the European Parliament
- Investing in EU promotional material
- Collection of statistical data on the treatment of petitions on the PETI web portal.

4.5.5 Summary

The democratic innovations introduced in the course of the EU's "participatory turn" represent a variety of participatory instruments, practically all of which make use of digital tools in one form or another. They embody types of e-participation mainly contributing to political agenda setting or to be considered in decision-making (e-deliberative designs, e-consultations, e-initiatives or e-petitions). Similar instruments are also practised at national and sub-national levels; however, the supra-national nature of the EU poses three novel challenges: large scale, language diversity and trans-nationality.

As was shown, the experiences from over a decade of experimentation with various participatory designs, as well as in part regular use at EU level, have been mixed. The democratic potential of the existing participatory instruments, in particular the support of digital tools to enhance direct and participatory democracy, has been proved in many respects to different degrees. However, a number of serious challenges, unsolved problems and unfulfilled expectations have also been encountered.

Assessments of various types of deliberative participatory designs reveal many starting points to improve the democratic quality. The lack of any impact on decision-making is one of the most striking findings. The often experimental character is not the only reason; at times too broad topics, too general outputs and the lack of clear rules on how to integrate outputs into the policy process seem to be the biggest barriers. Opportunities for deliberation allowing for considered judgement are rare and usually limited to national communities. The "Europolis" and "Futurum" designs represented positive exceptions and demonstrated the possibility of trans-national exchange. The focus on civil society organisations rather than ordinary citizens, and the fact that this is a frequent pattern, challenges the ideal of inclusiveness. The lack of publicity of these democratic innovations, the silence of the media on them and the difficulties to mobilise citizens for participation are special points of grievance.

A more differentiated view of the issue of policy impact acknowledges several types of influence: on the participants themselves, the wider public and formal decision-making. Rather than being understood as a one to one translation of suggestions into policy decisions, the latter type of impact can mean improved deliberation in governmental bodies and more indirect impact by shaping the preparation of decisions along the various phases from agenda setting and problem analysis to framing choices and finally taking decisions. Likely impacts also depend on institutional strategies in offering particular participatory designs, for example, whether conceived as a policy instrument, such as e-consultations via the "Consultations" platform, or a communication instrument with a transformative mission aimed at sensitising participants of EU policy issues, such as the ECCs. Though e-consultations have become a well-established instrument in practically all DGs which has certainly broadened the input into EU policymaking and extended its knowledge base, serious flaws need to be worked on, such as intransparent processing, lack of feedback and lack of impact on policy outputs.

Finally, experiences with the ECI have shown that for the time being the potential to act as an effective bridge between bottom-up claims to participate in EU policymaking and formal institutions has not been realised as expected. Much acclaimed as the first formally institutionalised transnational instrument of participatory democracy, it has been more a tool for civil society mobilisation than citizen empowerment up to this point, since it requires enormous organisational capacities on the part of organisers of an ECI. However, most recently the signs of improved performance and increased use of this instrument look more promising. Digital support is indispensable and plays an even stronger role in most recent initiatives; still, it is all the more necessary to cure remaining deficits in support by the existing online collection system and other barriers identified. The European Parliament's e-petition system also requires some improvement by facilitating access and speeding up the whole petition procedure in order to raise its value as an instrument of participatory democracy.

4.6 Conclusions

4.6.1 Experience with Digital Tools in Different Types of e-Participation

The assessment of the European Citizen Consultations by Kies et al. (2013: 24) as "a successful civic instrument but not a convincing policy instrument" appears applicable for a great many e-participatory tools within various e-democracy sectors. It seems to be an ongoing theme that e-participatory projects provide added personal value for participants and community capacity, but suffer from a lack of direct, or even indirect, political impact. "There exist more opportunities than ever before for citizens wishing to have their say, via the media or directly to local and national governments, but there is a more pervasive sense of disappointment than ever before that citizens are outside the citadels of power, and that those within do not know how to listen to them" (Coleman and Moss 2012: 4).

A differentiated offer of *e-consultations* has been developing over the years at all government levels in a variety of formats (from simple questionnaires to open formats and crowdsourcing). However, it appears that at times a project which at first glance appears to be participatory will turn out to not have consultative or deliberative character, but have the objective to inform citizens about decisions already having been made. In the cases where citizen input is in fact the objective, there can be great uncertainty on what sorts of inputs are desired and how to produce them best. Designs of e-consultation processes need to cope with a tension between the goals of quality of inputs and inclusivity. Often the issues at stake require highly specialised expertise which average citizens do not possess but which are only available from civil society organisations. Well-designed e-consultation processes with transparent processing and appreciation of inputs contribute to heightened legitimacy of policy agendas. E-consultation processes are of low value when topics are too broad, the outputs too general and the rules or formal steps on how to integrate outputs into the policy process are lacking.

In the area of *e-petitions* successful examples of modernisation with the introduction of e-petition systems are observable. The increasing share of online petitions underlines high public acceptance but does not necessarily boost the overall amount of petition activity. Internet use does not automatically increase transparency and enhance opportunities for participation. There are indications that such effects require the cooperation of institutional and organisational reform and technological modernisation. A certain level of civic knowledge or skills on part of the petitioners was also stressed to be needed in order for petitions to be successful.

On concrete topics of life world relevance, *e-deliberation* systems enjoy high citizen interest and can be a cost-effective tool of engagement. A special advantage of e-deliberation can be that anonymity allows an exchange of ideas without regarding hierarchical factors such as social status. However, in order to cultivate successful deliberation and to ensure quality and a level of respect within the online discourse a moderation system and structure is important. A balance must be struck between structuring e-participatory events, such as adding moderators which can have positive effects on the quality and therefore the impact of the deliberation, and the aspect of inclusivity, which appears incompatible with high expertise levels and complexity. It is obvious that the success of deliberative e-participation events depends on the deliberative skills of the participants. These are not equally distributed in society and require training. New formats of large-scale citizen deliberation (combining offline and online formats) such as so-called citizen forums in Germany can have stimulating effects on a wider scale as regards civic discourse and awareness of public issues of relevance.

The area of *e-budgeting* may, at this point in time, have produced some of the strongest results when it comes to influencing decision-making, despite not necessarily leading to changed power relations between governments and citizens. Amongst the impacts identified are the following: support to demands for increased transparency, improved public services, accelerated administrative operations, better cooperation amongst public administration units and enhanced responsiveness. Positive contributions to the political culture and competences of participants can also be expected (e.g. extended participation opportunities, better quality of decision-making, increased legitimacy and a stronger identification with the local community). Cost reduction and major structural reforms are less likely.

As regards *e-voting*, even after more than a decade of experiences with trials and real use of Internet voting, several challenges exist and those elaborated in Lindner et al. (2016) have not lost any topicality, especially regarding the issues of turnout rates, security, user friendliness or trust. The literature contains a large number of critics addressing system vulnerabilities. They emphasise the need for further advances regarding technical design, legal regulation, security, transparency and verifiability as well as oversight and accountability. The reported Swiss trial can serve as a good practice example. However, hopes that Internet voting might cure the democratic deficit of the EU have not been met. Technology alone cannot address deeper causes for dissatisfaction and continuously falling voter turnout in EU elections.

An area to which much attention has been paid during the last years is *social media*. They have certainly become an important channel for political communication and targeted political propaganda. Opinions seem to differ greatly regarding the impact social media use (such as Facebook and Twitter) has on online and offline participation. Results range from Facebook use leading to decreased participation in all areas to online participation, and even offline protests, being promoted by the same site. In general, it does appear, however, that there is a tendency for mobilisation to be medium-specific. While political websites tend to still mainly serve an informative purpose, more and more politicians become accessible through the use of social media platforms such as Twitter, allowing for a dialogue between elected officials and citizens. An interesting phenomenon which adds to the difficulty of mobilisation is the fact, that being confronted with political opinions which differ from your own can lower political interest and engagement. Political deliberation and discussions on social media sites can therefore have negative effects on a person's willingness to engage in similar dialogues in the future. One must of course also not forget the various technical and privacy problems associated with e-democracy, as well as the fact that many countries still possess a significant digital divide.

A general problem that applies to all e-participatory procedures and tools is to strike a balance between quality or security enhancing design features and the aspect of inclusivity, which appears incompatible with high levels of complexity and expertise requirements. Currently amongst those making use of e-voting, e-deliberation and e-petitioning offers, there is an overrepresentation of young white males with a high educational background, whereby these individuals tend to migrate from offline voting, deliberation and petitioning to online versions without an increase of overall participation being achieved. "... [A] vast amount of research shows that the costs and benefits of participation are generally skewed in favor of those with higher socio-economic status (SES) and education levels. While other factors, such as membership in civic and political organisations and various social networks, can mitigate the impacts of SES and education, it is clear that unless practitioners take corrective measures, participation of all varieties will be skewed" (Ryfe and Stalsburg 2012: 1).

Naturally this problem has led to several mobilisation attempts, since a lack of diversity and representativeness of participatory projects inevitably results in decreasing interest from policy- and decision-makers and therefore in lower impact. Mobilisation has proven to be one of the great challenges of participatory projects in general, one of the explanations being that citizens have low confidence that their input in such projects will have any real weight in decision-making processes. This scepticism appears to be well-founded, judging by the low significance of e-petitions and e-deliberative events for legally binding outcomes, even if heightened legitimacy of policy agendas can be achieved. Deliberative civic engagements tend not to be embedded in political decision-making, often making them short-lived, temporary and focussed on single particular issues, characteristics which may contribute to the scepticism of citizens regarding their significance. Further barriers preventing mobilisation are language problems and low interest in European-level matters. Furthermore, promising projects such as the ECI are aimed at increasing participation on the side of civil society organisations rather than on the individual level. A factor for success which cannot be stressed enough for all of these civic engagement projects is the support and engagement of decision-makers.

4.6.2 Experiences with e-Participation at EU-Level

The democratic innovations introduced at supra-national level pose enormous novel challenges to cope with, in particular large scale, language diversity and transnationality. The experience from over a decade of usage and experimentation with innovative participatory designs at EU level has been mixed. The support of digital tools to enhance direct and participatory democracy has been proved in many respects, despite the fact that a number of problems have been encountered and exaggerated expectations of new democratic potentials have not been fulfilled.

A clear finding regarding deliberative participatory designs is their absolute lack of impact on decision-making. Reasons behind are inexistent formal rules for integration into the policy process, often too broad topics or unspecific outputs and sometimes still experimental status. As far as opportunities for deliberation leading to reasoned judgement exist at all, they are largely confined to communities at regional or national levels. "Europolis" and "Futurum" are positive exceptions, demonstrating that trans-national exchange is possible. The ideal of inclusiveness is seriously challenged by the dominance of civil society organisations as compared to giving ordinary citizens a say and the difficulties to mobilise these for participation. A special problem is also the disinterest of the media on these democratic innovations.

Taking a more differentiated view on the lack of policy impact of participatory designs reveals different modes and degrees of influence beyond the effects on the participants themselves or the wider public and beyond a one to one translation of input into formal decisions. This can mean improved deliberation in decision-making bodies, shaping the preparation of decisions in agenda setting, problem analysis and framing of choices up to the final taking of decisions. Institutional strategies in offering particular participatory designs also make a difference for their impact. The "Your Voice in Europe" platform was conceived as a policy instrument and the ECCs as a communication instrument. E-consultations are now a well-established practice across all DGs which certainly broadened the input into EU policymaking, however, serious flaws such as intransparent processing and lack of feedback need to be corrected.

Finally, expectations of the ECI as an effective bridge between bottom-up claims to participate in EU policymaking and formal institutions have not been fulfilled as hoped for. Up to now it is still rather an instrument for civil society mobilisation than citizen empowerment. The organisational capacities required by organisers are enormous. Digital support is indispensable, as are ongoing improvements of the online collection system and other barriers identified. On the side of the European Parliament the e-petition system also deserves higher visibility, efforts in facilitating access and speeding up the whole procedure to become a true instrument of participatory democracy.

What consequences to draw as regards the future of these democratic innovations is of course a political question. From the perspective of participatory democracy the definite recommendation to the EU institutions is to focus on improving the existing e-participation tools at EU level along the lines suggested by the assessments and the results of the SWOT analyses in the relevant literature presented. The institutional singularity of the EU as a supra-national entity prevents a simple transposition of experiences to the EU level. Instead careful selection and adaptation of positive models is required. This would suggest starting initiatives to promote new forms of e-participation and to gather experience through experimentation, for example, with crowdsourcing inspired by successful projects at national level. Another option worth thinking about could be how to strengthen the EU Parliament's representative character by building on MEPs as bridges to citizens with the support of digital platforms for facilitating citizens' participation in EU policymaking. Finally, further experimentation with appropriate new designs to foster deliberative engagements of citizens and, last not least, a further exploration of possibilities to integrate e-participatory designs with external "third places", i.e. social media platforms, seem worthy to be considered.

References

Aitamurto, T., & Landemore, H. (2016). Crowdsourced deliberation: The case of the law on off-road traffic in Finland. *Policy and Internet, 8*(2), 174–196.

Alathur, S., Ilavarasan, P. V., & Gupta, M. P. (2012). Citizen participation and effectiveness of e-petition: Sutharyakeralam – India. *Transforming Government: People, Process and Policy, 6* (4), 392–403.

Albrecht, S. (2012). E-Consultations: A review of current practice and a proposal for opening up the process. In E. Tambouris, A. Macintosh, & O. Saebo (Eds.), *Electronic participation* (pp. 13–24). Berlin: Springer.

Alemanno, A. (2018). *Beyond consultations: Reimagining European participatory democracy.* Carnegie Europe, reshaping European democracy. Accessed January 23, 2019, from https://ssrn.com/abstract=3304510

Allcott, H., & Gentzkow, M. (2017). Social media and fake news in the 2016 election. *Journal of Economic Perspectives, 31*(2), 211–236.

Andersen, K. N., & Medaglia, R. (2009). The use of Facebook in national election campaigns: Politics as usual? *Lecture Notes in Computer Science, 5694,* 101–111.

Arthur, C. (2014, May 12). *Estonian e-voting shouldn't be used in European elections, say security experts.* Accessed February 23, 2019, from https://www.theguardian.com/technology/2014/may/12/estonian-e-voting-security-warning-european-elections-research

Åström, J., Jonsson, M., & Karlsson, M. (2016). Democratic innovations: Reinforcing or changing perceptions of trust? *International Journal of Public Administration,* 1–13.

Badouard, R. (2010). Pathways and obstacles to eParticipation at the European level. A comparative analysis of the European Citizens' Consultation 2009 and the online consultations of the European Commission. *JeDEM, 2* (2), 99–110. Accessed January 23, 2019, from http://jedem.org/index.php/jedem/article/view/30

Baek, Y. M., Wojcieszak, M., & Carpini, M. X. D. (2012). Online versus face-to-face deliberation: Who? Why? What? With what effects? *New Media and Society, 14*(3), 363–383.

Ballesteros, M., Canetta, E., & Zaciu, A. (2014). *European citizens' initiative – First lessons of implementation.* Study. European Parliament, Directorate General for Internal Policies, Policy Department C: Citizens' Rights and Constitutional Affairs. Brussels: European Parliament. Accessed January 23, 2019, from www.europarl.europa.eu/RegData/etudes/STUD/2014/509982/IPOL_STU(2014)509982_EN.pdf

Barber, B. J. (1984). *Strong democracy: Participatory politics for a new age.* Berkeley, CA: University of California Press.

Baringhorst, S. (2009). Introduction. Political campaigning in changing media cultures – typological and historical approaches. In S. Baringhorst, V. Kneip, & J. Niesyto (Eds.), *Political campaigning on the web* (pp. 9–30). Bielefeld: Transcript.

Barrett, G., Wyman, M., & Schattan, P. C. V. (2012). Assessing the policy impacts of deliberative civic engagement. In T. Nabatchi, J. Gastil, M. Leighninger, & G. M. Weiksner (Eds.), *Democracy in motion: Evaluating the practice and impact of deliberative civic engagement* (pp. 181–204). Oxford/New York: Oxford University Press.

Berg, C., & Głogowski, P. (2014). An overview of the first two years of the European citizens' initiative. In C. Berg, & J. Thomson (Eds.), An ECI that works! Learning from the first two years of the European Citizens' Initiative. The ECI Campaign (pp. 11–18). Accessed January 22, 2019, from www.ecithatworks.org/wp-content/uploads/2014/04/An_ECI_That_Works.pdf

Berg, C., & Thomson, J. (2014). Lessons and recommendations for an ECI that works. In C. Berg, & J. Thomson (Eds.), An ECI that works! Learning from the first two years of the European Citizens' Initiative. The ECI Campaign (pp. 118–122). Accessed January 22, 2019, from http://www.ecithatworks.org/wpcontent/uploads/2014/04/An_ECI_That_Works.pdf

Beroggi, G. (2014). Internet voting: An empirical evaluation. *Computer, 47*(4), 44–50.

Beroggi, G., Moser, P., & Bierer, D. (2011). *Evaluation der E-Voting Testphase im Kanton Zürich 2008-2011: Testphase basierend auf RRB 1770/2007.*

Bochel, C. (2013). Petitions systems: Contributing to representative democracy? *Parliamentary Affairs, 66*(4), 798–815.
Boussaguet, L. (2016). Participatory mechanisms as symbolic policy instruments? *Comparative European Politics, 14*(1), 107–124.
Bouza García, L. (2012). New rules, new players? The ECI as a source of competition and contention in the European public sphere. *Perspectives on European Politics and Society, 13*(3), 337–351.
Bräunlich, K., Grimm, R., Richter, P., & Roßnagel, A. (2013). *Sichere Internetwahlen: Ein rechtswissenschaftlich-informatisches Modell*. Baden-Baden: Nomos.
Buell, D. A. (2015). Computer Security and the Risks of Online Voting. *Communications of the ACM, 58*(7), 13–14.
Cabannes, Y. (2015). The impact of participatory budgeting on basic services: Municipal practices and evidence from the field. *Environment and Urbanization, 27*(1), 257–284.
Cardenal, A. S. (2011). Why mobilize support online? The paradox of party behavior online. *Party Politics, 19*(1), 83–103.
Carrara, S. (2012). Towards e-ECIs? European participation by online pan-European mobilization. *Perspectives on European Politics and Society, 13*(3), 352–369.
Carter, L., & Campbell, R. (2011). The impact of trust and relative advantage on internet voting diffusion. *Journal of Theoretical and Applied Electronic Commerce Research, 6*(3), 28–42.
Chadwick, A. (2011). Explaining the failure of an online citizen engagement initiative: The role of internal institutional variables. *Journal of Information Technology and Politics, 8*(1), 21–40.
Cho, J., & Keum, H. (2016). Leveling or tilting the playing field: Social networking sites and offline political communication inequality. *Social Science Journal, 53*(2), 236–246.
Coleman, S., & Moss, G. (2012). Under construction: The field of online deliberation research. *Journal of Information Technology and Politics, 9*(1), 1–15.
Coleman, S., & Spiller, J. (2003). Exploring new media effects on representative democracy. *The Journal of Legislative Studies, 9*(3), 1–16.
Collingwood, L., & Reedy, J. (2012). Listening and responding to criticisms of deliberative civic engagement. In T. Nabatchi, J. Gastil, M. Leighninger, & G. M. Weiksner (Eds.), *Democracy in motion: Evaluating the practice and impact of deliberative civic engagement* (pp. 233–259). New York, NY: Oxford University Press.
Conrad, M. (2013). Small-states perspective on the European citizens' initiative. *Icelandic Review of Politics and Administration, 9*(2), 301–322.
Council of Europe. (2005). *Legal, operational and technical standards for e-voting: Recommendation Rec(2004)11 adopted by the Committee of Ministers of the Council of Europe on 30 September 2004 and explanatory memorandum*.
Davies, T., & Chandler, R. (2013). Online deliberation design: Choices, criteria, and evidence. In T. Nabatchi, J. Gastil, M. Leighninger, & G. M. Weiksner (Eds.), *Democracy in motion: Evaluating the practice and impact of deliberative civic engagement* (pp. 103–131). New York, NY: Oxford University Press.
Davis, R. (2005). *Politics online. Blogs, chatrooms and discussion groups in American democracy*. New York, NY: Routledge.
Driza-Maurer, A., Spycher, O., & Taglioni, G., Weber, A. (2012). E-voting for Swiss Abroad: A joint project between the confederation and the cantons. In M. Kripp, M. Volkamer, & R. Grimm (Eds.), *Electronic Voting 2012. Proceedings of the 5th Conference on Electronic Voting 2012 (EVOTE2012)* (pp. 173–187), Bonn.
Duinkerken, M. J. (2013). *Die Europäische Bürgerinitiative – Ein effektives Instrument direkter Partizipation?* Bachelor thesis. Accessed January 22, 2019, from www.epub.ub.uni-muenchen.de/15085/1/Duinkerken_Final_41.pdf
Dunne, K. (2015). ICTs: Convenient, yet subsidiary tools in changing democracy. *International Journal of E-Politics (IJEP), 6*(2), 1–13.

EC – European Commission. (2002). *Towards a reinforced culture of consultation and dialogue – General principles and minimum standards for consultation of interested parties by the Commission*. Communication from the Commission, COM(2002) 704 final Brussels, 11.12.2002.

EC – European Commission. (2015). *Report from the Commission to the European Parliament and the Council*. Report on the application of Regulation (EU) No 211/2011 on the citizens' initiative. Brussels, 31.3.2015, COM(2015) 145 final. Accessed January 23, 2019, from http://ec.europa.eu/transparency/regdoc/rep/1/2015/EN/1-2015-145-EN-F1-1.PDF

EC – European Commission. (2016). *Compendium of international standards for Elections*. Accessed January 23, 2019, from www.eeas.europa.eu/sites/eeas/files/compendium-en-n-pdf.pdf

EC – European Commission. (2017). *Proposal for a Regulation of the European Parliament and of the Council on the European Citizens' Initiative*. Brussels, 13.9.2017, COM(2017) 482 final. Accessed January 23, 2019, from http://www.europarl.europa.eu/RegData/docs_autres_institutions/commission_europeenne/com/2017/0482/COM_COM(2017)0482_EN.pdf

Edwards, A., & de Kool, D. (2016). *Digital democracy: Opportunities and dilemmas. The Dutch parliament in a networked society*. Den Haag: Rathenau Instituut.

El Noshokaty, A. S., Deng, S., & Kwak, D. H. (2016). *Success factors of online petitions: Evidence from change.org*. Paper presented at the Proceedings of the Annual Hawaii International Conference on System Sciences.

EP – European Parliament. (2014). *European Citizens' initiative – First lessons of implementation*. Directorate General for Internal Policies. Policy Department C: Citizens' Rights and Constitutional Affairs. Petitions and Constitutional Affairs.

Escher, T. (2011). *TheyWorkForYou.com. Analysis of users and usage for UK Citizens Online Democracy*. Retrieved from http://www.mysociety.org/files/2011/06/TheyWorkForYou_research_report-2011-Tobias-Escher1.pdf. Accessed January 23, 2019.

Fedotova, O., Teixeira, L., & Alvelos, H. (2012). E-participation in Portugal: Evaluation of government electronic platforms. In J. Varajao, M. Cunha, P. Yetton, & R. Rijo (Eds.), *4th Conference of enterprise information systems – Aligning technology, organizations and people* (Vol. 5, pp. 152–161).

Font, J., del Amo, S. P., & Smith, G. (2016). Tracing the impact of proposals from participatory processes: Methodological challenges and substantive lessons. *Journal of Public Deliberation, 12*(1), Article 3.

Frey, C. B., Berger, T., & Chen, C. (2018). Political machinery: Did robots swing the 2016 US presidential election? *Oxford Review of Economic Policy, 34*(3), 418–442.

Garrone, P. (2005). Fundamental and political rights in electronic elections. In A. H. Trechsel & F. Mendez (Eds.), *The European Union and E-voting – Addressing the European Parliament's internet voting challenge* (pp. 111–123). New York: Routledge.

Gastil, J. (2013). A comparison of deliberative designs and policy impact in the EU and across the globe, Chapter 9. In R. Kies & P. Nanz (Eds.), *Is Europe listening to us? Success and failure of EU citizen consultations* (pp. 217–237). Farnham: Ashgate.

Germann, M., & Serdült, U. (2014). Internet voting for expatriates: The Swiss case. *Journal of eDemocracy, 6*(2), 197–215.

Gherghina, S., & Groh, A. (2016). A poor sales pitch? The European citizens' initiative and attitudes toward the EU in Germany and the UK. *European Politics and Society, 17*(3), 373–387.

Głogowski, P., & Maurer, A. (2013). *The European citizens' initiative – Chances, constraints and limits, political science series*. Vienna, Austria: Institute for Advanced Studies.

Goncalves, S. (2013). The effects of participatory budgeting on municipal expenditures and infant mortality in Brazil. *World Development, 53*, 94–110.

Gordon, V., Osgood, J. L., & Boden, D. (2017). The role of citizen participation and the use of social media platforms in the participatory budgeting process. *International Journal of Public Administration, 40*(1), 65–76.

Graham, T., Jackson, D., & Wright, S. (2016). 'We need to get together and make ourselves heard': Everyday online spaces as incubators of political action. *Information Communication and Society, 19*(10), 1373–1389.

Greenwood, J. (2012). The European citizens' initiative and EU civil society organisations. *Perspectives on European Politics and Society, 13*(3), 325–336.

Grimmelikhuijsen, S. G., & Meijer, A. J. (2014). Effects of transparency on the perceived trustworthiness of a government organization: Evidence from an online experiment. *Journal of Public Administration Research and Theory, 24*(1), 137–157.

Guidetti, M., Cavazza, N., & Graziani, A. R. (2016). Perceived disagreement and heterogeneity in social networks: Distinct effects on political participation. *Journal of Social Psychology, 156*(2), 222–242.

Hale, S. A., Margetts, H., & Yasseri, T. (2013, May). Petition growth and success rates on the UK No. 10 Downing Street website. In *Proceedings of the 5th Annual ACM Web Science Conference* (pp. 132–138).

Hall, T. (2012). Electronic voting. In N. Kersting (Ed.), *Electronic democracy* (pp. 153–176). Opladen: Barbara Budrich Publishers.

Heiberg, S., Laud, P., & Willemson, J. (2012). The application of I-voting for Estonian parliamentary elections of 2011. In A. Kiayias & H. Lipmaa (Eds.), *E-Voting and Identity. Vote ID 2011*. Lecture Notes in Computer Science, 7187 (pp. 208–223). Berlin/Heidelberg: Springer.

Heidelberger, C. A. (2009). Electronic participatory budgeting: Supporting community deliberation and decision-making with online tools. *Conference Paper Midwest Decision Sciences Institute Conference*, Miami University, Oxford, OH, April 16–18.

Hern, A. (2018). *The Guardian. Cambridge Analytica: How did it turn clicks into votes?* (online). Published 6.05.2018. Accessed January 23, 2019, from https://www.theguardian.com/news/2018/may/06/cambridge-analytica-how-turn-clicks-into-votes-christopher-wylie

Hill, R. (2015). Challenging an E-voting system in court: An experience report. In R. Haenni et al. (Eds.), *VoteID 2015* (pp. 161–171).

Howard, P. N., Woolley, S., & Calo, R. (2018). Algorithms, bots, and political communication in the US 2016 election: The challenge of automated political communication for election law and administration. *Journal of Information Technology and Politics, 15*(2), 81–93.

Hrbek, R. (2012). National and European political parties and the European citizens' initiative. *Perspectives on European Politics and Society, 13*(3), 370–384.

Hüller, T. (2008). Gut beraten? Die Online-Konsultationen der EU Kommission. *Zeitschrift für Politikberatung, 1*(3), 359–382.

Im, T., Cho, W., Porumbescu, G., & Park, J. (2014). Internet, trust in government, and citizen compliance. *Journal of Public Administration Research and Theory, 24*(3), 741–763.

Jones, D., & Simons, B. (2012). *Broken ballots: Will your vote count? (CSLI lecture notes, Vol. 204)*. Stanford, CA: CSLI Publications.

Karatzia, A. (2013). The European citizens' initiative: Giving voice to EU citizens. King's student law review. London: King's College. Accessed January 23, 2019, from http://blogs.kcl.ac.uk/kslreuropeanlawblog/?p=452#.VIbxlsnm59M

Karlsen, R. (2011). Still broadcasting the campaign. On the Internet and the fragmentation of political communication with evidence from Norwegian electoral politics. *Journal of Information Technology and Politics, 8*(2), 146–162.

Karlsson, M. (2010). A panacea for Pan-European citizen participation? Analysis of the 2009 European citizen consultations. In E. Amna (Ed.), *New forms of citizen participation: Normative implications* (pp. 97–112). Baden-Baden: Nomos.

Karlsson, M. (2011). Connecting citizens to the European parliament: E-consultations as a tool for political representation. In Z. Sobaci (Ed.), *E-Parliament and ICT-based legislation: Concept, experiences and lessons* (pp. 80–102). Hershey, PA: IGI-Global.

Kaufmann, B. (2012). Transnational 'Babystep': The European citizens' initiative. In M. Setala & T. Schiller (Eds.), *Citizens' initiatives in Europe. Procedures and consequences of Agenda-setting by citizens* (pp. 101–116). Basingstoke: Palgrave Macmillan.

Kersting, N. (2005). *The quality of political discourse: Can e-discussion be deliberative?* Paper presented at the British Political Studies Association Annual Conference 5–7 April, Leeds.

Kersting, N. (2013). Online participation: from 'invited' to 'invented' spaces. *International Journal of Electronic Governance, 6*(4), 270–280.

Kersting, N., & Baldersheim, H. (Eds.). (2004). *Electronic voting and democracy. A comparative analysis.* London: Palgrave.

Kies, R., & Nanz, P. (2013). Introduction. In R. Kies & P. Nanz (Eds.), *Is Europe listening to us? Success and failure of EU citizen consultations* (pp. 1–16). Farnham: Ashgate.

Kies, R., Leyenaar, M., & Niemöller, K. (2013). European citizen's consultation: A large consultation on a vague topic. In R. Kies & P. Nanz (Eds.), *Is Europe listening to us? Success and failure of EU citizen consultations* (pp. 59–78). Farnham: Ashgate.

Kim, S., & Lee, J. (2012). E-participation, transparency, and trust in local government. *Public Administration Review, 72*(6), 819–828.

Kinney, B. (2012). Deliberation's contribution to community capacity building. In T. Nabatchi, J. Gastil, M. Leighninger, & G. M. Weiksner (Eds.), *Democracy in motion: Evaluating the practice and impact of deliberative civic engagement* (pp. 1–23). New York, NY: Oxford University Press.

Kitsing, M. (2014). Rationality of internet voting in Estonia. Electronic government and electronic participation. In M. F. W. H. A. Janssen, et al. (Eds.), *Electronic government and electronic participation joint proceedings of ongoing research, posters, workshop and projects of IFIP EGOV 2014 and ePart 2014* (pp. 55–64).

Knaut, A. (2013). Die Europäische Bürgerinitiative – innovativ, transnational und demokratisch? Paper zum Panel "Demokratische Innovationen im Kontext gesellschaftlicher Diversität", Politik der Vielfalt. Drei-Länder-Tagung der ÖGPW, DVPW und SVPW, 19.–21. September 2013, Universität Innsbruck.

Knobloch, K. R., & Gastil, J. (2015). Civic (Re)socialisation: The educative effects of deliberative participation. *Politics, 35*(2), 183–200.

Knobloch, K. R., Gastil, J., Reedy, J., & Walsh, K. C. (2013). Did they deliberate? Applying an evaluative model of democratic deliberation to the Oregon citizens' initiative review. *Journal of Applied Communication Research, 41*(2), 105–125.

Koc-Michalska, K., Gibson, R., & Vedel, T. (2014). Online campaigning in France, 2007-2012: Political actors and citizens in the aftermath of the Web.2.0 evolution. *Journal of Information Technology and Politics, 11*(2), 220–244.

Lampe, C., Zube, P., Lee, J., Park, C. H., & Johnston, E. (2014). Crowdsourcing civility: A natural experiment examining the effects of distributed moderation in online forums. *Government Information Quarterly, 31*(2), 317–326.

Leighninger, M. (2012). Mapping deliberative civic engagement. In T. Nabatchi, J. Gastil, M. Leighninger, & G. M. Weiksner (Eds.), *Democracy in motion: Evaluating the practice and impact of deliberative civic engagement* (pp. 1–23). New York, NY: Oxford University Press.

Liberini, F., Redoano, M., Russo, A., Cuevas, A., & Cuevas, R. (2018). *Politics in the Facebook Era. Evidence from the 2016 US Presidential Elections. Online Working Paper Series No. 389, Centre for Competitive Advantage in the Global Economy*, The University of Warwick. Accessed January 23, 2019, from https://warwick.ac.uk/fac/soc/economics/research/centres/cage/manage/publications/389-2018_redoano.pdf

Lim, S., & Oh, Y. (2016). Online versus offline participation: Has the democratic potential of the internet been realized? Analysis of a participatory budgeting system in Korea. *Public Performance and Management Review, 39*(3), 676–700.

Lindner, R. (2012). Wie verändert das Internet die Demokratie? *Gesellschaft, Wirtschaft, Politik (GWP), 61*(4), 517–525.

Lindner, R., & Riehm, U. (2011). Broadening participation through e-petitions? An empirical study of petitions to the German parliament. *Policy and Internet, 3*(1, Article 3), 1–23.

Lindner, R., Aichholzer, G., & Hennen, L. (Eds.). (2016). *Electronic democracy in Europe. Prospects and challenges of e-publics, e-participation and e-voting*. Cham: Springer International.

Lironi, E. (2016). *Potential and challenges of E-participation in the European Union. Study for the AFCO Committee, European Parliament, Policy Department for Citizens' rights and constitutional affairs*. Brussels: European Parliament.

Loukis, E., & Wimmer, M. (2012). A multi-method evaluation of different models of structured electronic consultation on government policies. *Information Systems Management, 29*(4), 284–294.

Loveland, M. T., & Popescu, D. (2011). Democracy on the web: Assessing the deliberative qualities of internet forums. *Information Communication and Society, 14*(5), 684–703.

Lu, Y., Heatherly, K. A., & Lee, J. K. (2016). Cross-cutting exposure on social networking sites: The effects of SNS discussion disagreement on political participation. *Computers in Human Behavior, 59*, 74–81.

Mahrer, H., & Krimmer, R. (2005). Towards the enhancement of e-democracy: Identifying the notion of the 'middleman paradox'. *Information Systems Journal, 15*(1), 27–42.

Markussen, R., Ronquillo, L., & Schürmann, C. (2014). Trust in internet election observing the Norwegian decryption and counting ceremony. *Conference Paper, Electronic Voting: Verifying the Vote (EVOTE), 2014 6th International Conference*.

McGaley, M., & McCarthy, J. (2004). Transparency and e-voting – Democratic vs. commercial interests. In A. Prosser, & R. Krimmer (Eds.), *Proceedings of the 1st International Workshop on Electronic Voting in Europe* (pp. 153–163). Lecture Notes in Informatics.

Mechant, P., Stevens, I., Evens, T., & Verdegem, P. (2012). E-deliberation 2.0 for smart cities: A critical assessment of two 'idea generation' cases. *International Journal of Electronic Governance, 5*(1), 82–98.

Medaglia, R. (2011). eParticipation research: A longitudinal overview. In E. Tambouris, A. Macintosh, & H. DeBruijn (Eds.), *Electronic Participation, Epart*, Vol. *6847* (pp. 99–108).

Medaglia, R. (2012). eParticipation research: Moving characterization forward (2006-2011). *Government Information Quarterly, 29*(3), 346–360.

Miori, V., & Russo, D. (2011). Integrating online and traditional involvement in participatory budgeting. *Electronic Journal of e-Government, 9*(1), 41–57.

Mkude, C. G., Perez-Espes, C., & Wimmer, M. A. (2014). Participatory budgeting: A framework to analyze the value-add of citizen participation. In *Proceedings of 47th International Conference on System Sciences (HICSS)*, 6–9 Jan 2014, Waikoloa, HI, pp. 2054–2062.

MLGRD, Ministry of Local Government and Regional Development. (2012). *Summary of the ISF report: Ministry of Local Government and Regional Development*.

Monaghan, E. (2012). Assessing participation and democracy in the EU: The case of the European citizens' initiative. *Perspectives on European Politics and Society, 13*(3), 285–298.

Murray, M. (2013). Politics at the touch of a button: An evaluation of the first ever Oireachtas (Irish Houses of Parliament) E-consultation. *Parliamentary Affairs, 66*(3), 597–616. https://doi.org/10.1093/pa/gsr072.

Organ, J. (2014). Decommissioning direct democracy? A critical analysis of commission decision-making on the legal admissibility of European citizens initiative proposals. *European Constitutional Law Review, 10*(3), 422–443.

OSCE. (2010). *Election observation handbook*, 6th edn.

OSCE/ODIHR. (2011). *Estonia Parliamentary Elections 6 March 2011: OSCE/ODIHR Election Assessment Mission Report*. Accessed January 23, 2019, from http://www.osce.org/odihr/77557?download=true

OSCE/ODIHR. (2012). *Swiss Confederation Federal Assembly Elections 23 October 2011: OSCE/ODIHR Election Assessment Mission Report*.

OSCE/ODIHR. (2013). *Norway Parliamentary Elections 9 September 2013: OSCE/ODIHR Election Assessment Mission Final Report*.

Pammett, J. H., & Goodman, N. (2013). *Consultation and evaluation practices in the implementation of Internet Voting in Canada and Europe*. Ottawa: Elections Canada. Accessed January 23, 2019, from www.elections.ca/res/rec/tech/consult/pdf/consult_e.pdf

Panagiotopoulos, P., Moody, C., & Elliman, T. (2011). An overview assessment of ePetitioning tools in the English local government. In E. Tambouris, A. Macintosh, DeBruijn, H. (Eds.), *Electronic participation, Epart,* Vol. 6847, pp. 204–215.

Panopoulou, E., Tambouris, E., & Tarabanis, K. (2014). Success factors in designing eParticipation initiatives. *Information and Organization, 24*(4), 195–213. https://doi.org/10.1016/j.infoandorg.2014.08.001.

Parycek, P., Sachs, M., Sedy, F., & Schossboeck, J. (2014). Evaluation of an E-participation Project: Lessons learned and success factors from a cross-cultural perspective. In E. Tambouris, A. Macintosh, F. Bannister (Eds.), *Electronic Participation, Epart.* Vol. 8654, pp. 128–140.

People2power. (2017). *Spring Comeback Kid: The European Citizens' Initiative*. Accessed January 23, 2019, from http://www.people2power.info/insight/spring-comeback-kid-the-european-citizens-initiative/

Persily, N. (2017). The 2016 U.S. election: Can democracy survive the internet? *Journal of Democracy, 28*(2), 63–76.

PETI – Committee on Petitions (2015). *Report on the activities of the Committee on Petitions 2014, 2014/2218(INI)*, European Parliament. Accessed January 23, 2019, from http://www.europarl.europa.eu/sides/getDoc.do?pubRef=-//EP//NONSGML+REPORT+A8-2015-0361+0+DOC+PDF+V0//EN

Pichler, J. W., & Kaufmann, B. (Eds.) (2012). *Modern transnational democracy. How the 2012 launch of the European Citizen's initiative can change the world*. Schriften zur Rechtspolitik, Bd. 33. Wien-Graz: Neuer Wissenschaftlicher Verlag.

Pimentel Walker, A. P. (2016). Self-help or public housing? Lessons from co-managed slum upgrading via participatory budget. *Habitat International, 55*, 58–66.

Quittkat, C. (2011). The European commission's online consultations: A success story? *Journal of Common Market Studies, 49*(3), 653–674.

Quittkat, C., & Finke, B. (2008). The EU commission consultation regime. In B. Kohler-Koch, D. De Bièvre, & W. Maloney (Eds.), *Opening EU-Governance to Civil Society. Gains and Challenges, CONNEX Report Series No 05*, University of Mannheim, Mannheim Centre for European Social Research (MZES), Mannheim, pp. 183–222. Accessed January 23, 2019, from http://www.mzes.uni-mannheim.de/projekte/typo3/site/fileadmin/BookSeries/Volume_Five/Chapter08_Quittkat_Finke.pdf

Riehm, U., Coenen, C., Lindner, R., & Blümel, C. (2009). *Bürgerbeteiligung durch E-Petitionen. Analysen von Kontinuität und Wandel im Petitionswesen*. Berlin: Edition Sigma.

Riehm, U., Böhle, K., & Lindner, R. (2014). *Electronic petitioning and modernization of petitioning systems in Europe*. Technology Assessment Studies Series – 6, TAB Office of Technology Assessment at the German Bundestag.

Rikken, K. (2011, February 10). *Student finds flaw in e-voting, seeks nullification of result*. Accessed January 23, 2019, from https://news.err.ee/99405/student-finds-flaw-in-e-voting-seeks-nullification-of-result

Röcke, A. (2014). *Framing citizen participation. Participatory budgeting in France, Germany and the United Kingdom*. London: Palgrave.

Ruesch, M., & Märker, O. (2012). *Real name policy in E-participation. The case of Gütersloh's second participatory budget*. Paper presented at CeDEM 2012, Krems, Austria, May 3–4.

Rumbul, R. (2014). *In the digital era, political activism can be individual as well as collective*. Retrieved September 2016, from Democratic Audit UK. Accessed on January 23, 2019, from http://www.democraticaudit.com/2014/12/16/in-the-digital-era-political-activism-can-be-individual-as-well-as-collective

Russmann, U. (2011). Targeting voters via the Web. A comparative structural analysis of Austrian and German party websites. *Policy and Internet, 3*(3), Article 3.

Rustema, R. (2014). Why the ECI needs a community-developed online collection system. In C. Berg, & J. Thomson (Eds.), *An ECI that works! Learning from the first two years of the European Citizens' Initiative. The ECI Campaign* (pp. 104–106). Accessed January 23, 2019, from www.ecithatworks.org/wp-content/uploads/2014/04/An_ECI_That_Works.pdf

Ryfe, D. M., & Stalsburg, B. (2012). *The participation and recruitment challenge. Democracy in motion: Evaluating the practice and impact of deliberative civic engagement.*

Sál, K. (2015). Remote Internet voting and increase of voter turnout: Happy coincidence or fact? The case of Estonia. Masaryk University. *Journal of Law and Technology, 9*(2), 15–32.

Sangsari, M. (2013). The European citizens' initiative: An early assessment of the European Union's new participatory democracy instrument, Policy Paper, Canada-Europe Transatlantic Dialogue: Saurugger, S. (2010): The social construction of the participatory turn: The emergence of a norm in the European Union. *European Journal of Political Research, 49*(4), 471–495.

Santos, H. R., & Tonelli, D. F. (2014). *Possibilities and limits of E-participation: A systematic review of E-democracy.* XXXVIII Encontro de ANPAD, Rio de Janeiro, 13–17 September.

Saurugger, S. (2010). The social construction of the participatory turn: The emergence of a norm in the European Union. *European Journal of Political Research, 49*(4), 471–495.

Scherer, S., & Wimmer, M. A. (2014). *Trust in e-participation: Literature review and emerging research needs.* Paper presented at the ACM International Conference Proceeding Series.

Schneider, S. (2018). *Bürgerhaushalte in Deutschland: Individuelle und kontextuelle Einflussfaktoren der Beteiligung.* Wiesbaden: Springer VS.

Schumann, S., & Klein, O. (2015). Substitute or stepping stone? Assessing the impact of low-threshold online collective actions on offline participation. *European Journal of Social Psychology, 45*(3), 308–322.

Serdült, U., Germann, M., Mendez, F., Portenier, A., & Wellig, C. (2015). Fifteen years of internet voting in Switzerland: History, governance and use. In Terán, L., & Meier, A. (Eds.), *ICEDEG 2015: Second International Conference on eDemocracy and eGovernment*, Quito, Ecuador, 8–10 April 2015, IEEE Xplore CFP1527Y-PRT, pp. 126–132. Accessed January 23, 2019, from https://doi.org/10.1109/ICEDEG.2015.7114482

Sintomer, Y., Carsten Herzberg, C., & Röcke, A. (2008). Participatory budgeting in Europe: Potentials and challenges. *International Journal of Urban and Regional Research, 32*(1), 164–178.

Sintomer, Y., Herzberg, C., & Röcke, A. (2010). *Der Bürgerhaushalt in Europa – eine realistische Utopie?* Wiesbaden: VS Verlag für Sozialwissenschaften.

Siu, A., & Stanisevski, D. (2012). Deliberation in multicultural societies. In T. Nabatchi, J. Gastil, M. Leighninger, & G. M. Weiksner (Eds.), *Democracy in motion: Evaluating the practice and impact of deliberative civic engagement.* New York, NY: Oxford University Press.

Sivonen, E. (2011). Supreme court rejects last voter complaint. News.err.ee, 21.3.2011. Accessed January 23, 2019, from http://news.err.ee/99529/supreme-court-rejects-last-voter-complaint

Smith, G. (2013). Designing democratic innovations at the European level: Lessons from the experiments. In R. Kies & P. Nanz (Eds.), *Is Europe listening to us? Success and failure of EU citizen consultations* (pp. 201–216). Farnham: Ashgate.

Spada, P., Mellon, J., Peixoto, T., & Sjoberg, F. M. (2016). Effects of the internet on participation: Study of a public policy referendum in Brazil. *Journal of Information Technology and Politics, 13*(3), 187–207.

Springall, D., Finkenauer, T., Durumeric, Z., Kitcat, J., Hursti, H., MacAlpine, M., & Halderman, J. A. (2014). Security analysis of the Estonian internet voting system. In *CCS'14: 21st ACM Conference on Computer and Communications Security* (pp. 703–715).

Starskaya, M., & Çagdas, Ö. (2012). *Analysis of the online collection software provided by the European Commission for the European Citizens' Initiative.* Working Papers on Information Systems, Information Business and Operations, 01/2012. Vienna University of Economics and Business, Vienna. Accessed January 23, 2019, from http://epub.wu.ac.at/3643/1/Binder1_(2).pdf

Stein, R., & Wenda, G. (2014). The Council of Europe and e-voting: History and impact of Rec (2004)11. *Conference Paper, International Conference on Electronic Voting EVOTE2014.*

Strandberg, K. (2015). Designing for democracy?: An experimental study comparing the outcomes of citizen discussions in online forums with those of online discussions in a forum designed according to deliberative principles. *European Political Science Review, 7*(3), 451–474.

Strandberg, K., & Grönlund, K. (2012). Online deliberation and its outcome-evidence from the virtual polity experiment. *Journal of Information Technology and Politics, 9*(2), 167–184.

Talpin, J. (2012). When democratic innovations let the people decide. An evaluation of co-governance experiments. In B. Geissel & K. Newton (Eds.), *Evaluating democratic innovations: Curing the democratic malaise?* (pp. 184–206). New York: Routledge.

Thomson, J. (2014). What didn't happen with the European citizens' initiative…and what did. In C. Berg, & J. Thomson (Eds.), *An ECI that works! Learning from the first two years of the European Citizens' Initiative.* The ECI Campaign (pp. 73–76). Accessed January 23, 2019, from www.ecithatworks.org/wp-content/uploads/2014/04/An_ECI_That_Works.pdf

Tiburcio, T. (2015). *The right to petition.* Study for the PETI Committee. Directorate General for Internal Policies, Policy Department C: Citizens' Rights and Constitutional Affairs, Brussels. Accessed January 23, 2019, from http://www.europarl.europa.eu/RegData/etudes/STUD/2015/519223/IPOL_STU(2015)519223_EN.pdf

Tomkova, J. (2009). E-consultations: New tools for civic engagement or facades for political correctness? *European Journal of ePractice, 7*, March.

Toots, M., Kalvet, T., & Krimmer, R. (2011). Success in eVoting – Success in eDemocracy? The Estonian Paradox. Accessed January 23, 2019, from http://ssrn.com/abstract=2757704

Torcal, M., & Maldonado, G. (2014). Revisiting the dark side of political deliberation the effects of media and political discussion on political interest. *Public Opinion Quarterly, 78*(3), 679–706.

Towner, T. L., & Dulio, D. A. (2012). New media and political marketing in the United States: 2012 and beyond. *Journal of Political Marketing, 11*(2), 95–119.

van Dijk, J. A. G. M. (2012). Digital democracy: Vision and reality. In I. Snellen, W. Thaens, & W. van de Donk (Eds.), *Public administration in the information age: Revisited* (pp. 49–61). Amsterdam: IOS-Press.

Vassil, K., & Weber, T. (2011). A bottleneck model of e-voting. *New Media and Society, 13*(8), 1336–1354.

Venice Commission. (2003). *Code of good practice in electoral matters: Guidelines and explanatory report: Adopted by the Venice Commission at its 51st and 52nd sessions* (Venice, 5–6 July and 18–19 October 2002). Opinion no. 190/2002. Strasbourg.

Vinkel, P. (2012). Internet voting in Estonia. In P. Laud (Ed.) *Information security technology for applications* (pp. 4–12). Springer.

Volodin, D. S. (2014). Participative budgeting as an effective approach for local budgets distribution improvement in Ukraine. *Actual Problems of Economics, 160*(1), 373–379.

Wang, X., & Wan Wart, M. (2007). When public participation in administration leads to trust: An empirical assessment of managers' perceptions. *Public Administration Review, 67*(2), 265–278.

Ward, S., Gibson, R., & Nixon, P. (2003). Parties and the Internet. In R. Gibson, P. Nixon, & S. Ward (Eds.), *Political parties and the internet. Net gain?* (pp. 11–38). London/New York: Routledge.

Weiksner, G. M., Gastil, J., Nabatchi, T., & Leighninger, M. (2012). Advancing the theory and practice of deliberative civic engagement. In T. Nabatchi, J. Gastil, M. Leighninger, & G. M. Weiksner (Eds.), *Democracy in motion: Evaluating the practice and impact of deliberative civic engagement* (pp. 1–16). Oxford/New York: Oxford University Press.

Wolchok, S., Wustrow, E., Isabel, D., & Halderman, J. A. (2012). Attacking the Washington, D.C. Internet Voting System. In A. D. Keromytis (Ed.), *Financial cryptography and data security* (pp. 114–128). Berlin: Springer.

Woolley, S. C., & Guilbeault, D. (2017). Computational propaganda in the United States of America: Manufacturing consensus online. In S. Woolley, & P. N. Howard (Eds.) Working Paper 2017.5. Oxford: Project on Computational Propaganda. Accessed January 23, 2019, from http://blogs.oii.ox.ac.uk/politicalbots/wp-content/uploads/sites/89/2017/06/Comprop-USA.pdf

Woolley, S. C., & Howard, P. N. (2016). Automation, algorithms, and politics. Political communication, computational propaganda, and autonomous agents – Introduction. *International Journal of Communication, 10*, 4882–4890.

Woolley, S. C., & Howard, P. N. (eds.) (2018). *Computational propaganda. Political parties, politicians, and political manipulation on social media*. Oxford Studies in Digital Politics, Oxford University Press.

Wright, S. (2012). Assessing (e-)democratic innovations: "Democratic goods" and downing street e-petitions. *Journal of Information Technology and Politics, 9*(4), 453–470.

Wright, S. (2016). 'Success' and online political participation: The case of Downing Street E-petitions. *Information Communication and Society, 19*(6), 843–857.

Yang, M. (2013). Europe's new communication policy and the introduction of transnational deliberative citizen's involvement projects. In R. Kies & P. Nanz (Eds.), *Is Europe listening to us? Success and failure of EU citizen consultations* (pp. 17–34). Farnham: Ashgate.

Zhang, W., Xu, X., Zhang, H., & Chen, Q. (2016). Online participation chaos: A case study of Chinese government-initiated e-polity square. *International Journal of Public Administration*, 1–8.

Open Access This chapter is licensed under the terms of the Creative Commons Attribution 4.0 International License (http://creativecommons.org/licenses/by/4.0/), which permits use, sharing, adaptation, distribution and reproduction in any medium or format, as long as you give appropriate credit to the original author(s) and the source, provide a link to the Creative Commons licence and indicate if changes were made.

The images or other third party material in this chapter are included in the chapter's Creative Commons licence, unless indicated otherwise in a credit line to the material. If material is not included in the chapter's Creative Commons licence and your intended use is not permitted by statutory regulation or exceeds the permitted use, you will need to obtain permission directly from the copyright holder.

Part II
Case Studies

Chapter 5
Introduction to the Case Study Research

Ira van Keulen and Iris Korthagen

Abstract Van Keulen and Korthagen introduce in this chapter the empirical study of 22 cases of digital tools which form a large and important part of this book. The authors indicate how the cases were selected based on different criteria such as diversity of institutional contexts and scales, geographical diversity and different types of citizen involvement. Each of the cases is described based on an evaluation framework for assessing the digital tools. The authors choose to put legitimacy and its key dimensions—input, throughput and output legitimacy—central in the framework. A logical choice since disengagement from the European democratic processes and distance of the European citizens from EU institutions remains a major problem. This short chapter explains furthermore how the data collection and analysis of the 22 cases have been done. Special attention is paid to explaining the method of Qualitative Comparative Analysis (QCA).

Next to the systematic literature review (see Part I), this research comprises the empirical study of 22 cases of digital tools, tools which have been used or are still used as instruments for citizen involvement in democratic processes. The cases were for a large part requested by the Panel for the Future of Science and Technology at the European Parliament, who commissioned this research. The other cases were selected based on the following criteria: (1) diversity of tools, (2) diversity of institutional contexts and scales (local, national, European and some international),[1] (3) geographical diversity and (4) different types of citizen involvement. The combination of these criteria provides a broad perspective on the kind of tools that

---

[1]We included two cases of application of digital participation tools from outside Europe (Belo Horizonte and Melbourne) because we hold that these can help to set up effective and efficient digital tools at the EU level (just like cases at the local and national level can).

I. van Keulen (✉)
Rathenau Instituut, The Hague, The Netherlands
e-mail: i.vankeulen@rathenau.nl

I. Korthagen
Netherlands Court of Audit, The Hague, The Netherlands

© The Authors(s) 2020
L. Hennen et al. (eds.), *European E-Democracy in Practice*, Studies in Digital Politics and Governance, https://doi.org/10.1007/978-3-030-27184-8_5

could be used to strengthen participatory democracy at the EU level. Of course, we do not claim that this set of case studies would be representative for all uses of digital tools as discussed on the basis of our literature review. It remains a selection which could be completed towards still greater correspondence with our conceptual framework and the arsenal of digital practices in political participation, if there were no space limitations.

5.1 Evaluation Framework

The description of the 22 cases is based on an evaluation framework for assessing the digital tools. The selection of the key elements of the framework has been made according to the project's central aim: To identify and analyse best practices with digital tools for participatory and direct democracy at different political and governmental levels (local, national, European) that in the future can be used at EU level to encourage citizen engagement and countervail the European democratic deficit.

In view of the current crisis of representative democracy, the disengagement from the democratic processes and the distance of citizens from EU institutions, restoration and enhancement of democratic legitimacy at the European level is needed. Therefore, we put legitimacy and its key dimensions (Schmidt 2013) centre stage in the evaluation framework and use it as the basis for differentiating further, more specific evaluation aspects. In this we follow the Council of Europe in its recommendation on e-democracy as referred to in the Introduction: "E-democracy, as the support and enhancement of democracy, democratic institutions and democratic processes by means of ICT, is above all about democracy. Its main objective is the electronic support of democracy" (Council of Europe 2009: 1).

In order to investigate how digital tools can contribute to stronger connections between EU citizens and EU politics, we distinguish between five types of citizen involvement: (1) monitoring, (2) formal agenda setting (invited space, i.e. initiated by government), (3) informal agenda setting (invented space, i.e. initiated by citizens), (4) non-binding decision-making and (5) binding decision-making (see Table 5.1) (Kersting 2014). In combination with the focus of the research on democratic legitimacy, this leads to an evaluation model along the lines of the input, throughput and output legitimacy of political decision-making processes (Schmidt 2013; Scharpf 1999).

Fritz W. Scharpf (1999) divided democratic legitimisation into input legitimacy, judged in terms of the EU's responsiveness to citizen concerns as a result of participation **by the people** and output legitimacy, judged in terms of the effectiveness of the EU's policy outcomes **for the people**. Vivien Schmidt (2013) has added to this theorisation of democratic legitimacy, a third criterion for evaluation of EU governance processes: throughput legitimacy, judging legitimacy in terms of their inclusiveness and openness to consultation **with the people**.

The distinction between the three criteria for democratic legitimacy helps to understand the particular relevance of the democratic deficit in times of the recent

Table 5.1 Overview of case studies

Monitoring		TheyWorkForYou	National	Great Britain
		Abgeordnetenwatch	National	Germany
Agenda setting	Informal	Petities.nl: Dutch e-petitions site	National	Netherlands
		Open Ministry Finland: crowdsourcing for law proposals	National	Finland
	Formal	Iceland: crowdsourcing for a new constitution	National	Iceland
		Future Melbourne Wiki: crowdsourcing for city planning vision	Local	Australia
		Predlagam.vladi.si: platform for e-proposals and e-petitions	National	Slovenia
		European Citizens' Initiative: citizens' proposals for new EU laws	European	EU
		Participatory budgeting Berlin	Local	Germany
		Internetconsultatie.nl: consultation on draft laws	National	Netherlands
		Futurium: consultation on EU (digital) policy making	European	EU
		Your Voice in Europe: (open) public consultation on EU policy	European	EU
		European Citizens' Consultation: pan-European consultation on the future of Europe	European	EU
Decision-making	Non-binding	Pirate Party Germany	National/district	Germany
		Five Star Movement	National	Italy
		Podemos	National	Spain
		Participatory budgeting Belo Horizonte	Local	Brazil
		Participatory budgeting Paris	Local	France
		Participatory budgeting Reykjavik	Local	Iceland
	Binding	Voting for Spitzenkandidaten in the 2014 EP elections within the Green Party	European	EU
		E-voting for elections	National	Estonia
		E-voting for elections/referenda	National	Switzerland

and current EU crisis. Due to the transnational character, EU institutions' legitimisation has difficulties to be rooted in strong channels of information by citizens (input legitimacy) and consultation with citizens (throughput legitimacy) and thus must rely on legitimising its policies by the quality of its output, that is its decisions and regulations being in the best interest of, and thus being supported by, the citizenry (output legitimacy). The fact that in the latter respect the means of the EU institutions are restricted as well has a special bearing in times of crisis. The missing input legitimacy becomes the more problematic, the weaker output legitimacy is getting, entailing apparent difficulties to establish consensus on a, for example, joint European policy to solve the refugee problem. In a situation where strong decisions have to be taken at the EU level (beyond national interests), input but also throughput legitimacy is urgently needed.

The three types of legitimacy pose different demands on digital tools for citizen involvement. In the following paragraphs we will address these different demands.

Regarding the **input legitimacy**, the use of digital tools will be assessed for how it enhances the voice of citizens in the political decision-making process. "Voice" concerns the way in which affected citizens are able to influence the political agenda (Manin 1987). To what extent are citizens enabled to express their wishes and interests in political decision-making? How can citizens get an issue on to the political agenda? Is there equal opportunity for citizens to voice their concerns? Are citizens supported enough in their efforts to voice themselves in the process (i.e. interaction support)? Is the tool user-friendly (i.e. tool usability)?

Regarding the **throughput legitimacy**, an evaluation will be made of how digital tools contribute to the quality of the deliberation process, in terms of an inclusive dialogue and a careful consideration of options (Cohen 1989). Relevant questions are: to what extent do the views of the citizens expressed by the digital tool represent the views of the general population (i.e. representation)? How is the diversity of views within the population (including minority views) reflected in the process? Are the different policy options carefully considered in the deliberation process? Do the citizens have access to all the relevant information about the decision-making process to which the results of the digital citizen involvement should contribute?

Concerning the **output legitimacy**, responsiveness to the arguments and proposals of citizens (Cohen 1989) and effectiveness (Scharpf 1999) will be evaluated, along with the accountability of decisions made. To what extent do the tools substantially contribute to the political decisions made (i.e. democratic impact)? How do the digital tools contribute to feedback? Is information provided about the decision-making process and its outcomes (i.e. accountability)?

The cases are described based on the questions mentioned in Table 5.2 on the evaluation framework. Each case description has at least four sections: an introductory section (i.e. short description of the digital tool), one on the participants, one on the participatory process and one on the results of the digital tool.

5.2 Data Collection

Each individual case is thoroughly studied. All aspects of the evaluation framework are covered in a structured template that forms the empirical checklist for the case studies. Empirical data on all these aspects come from different data sources and methods of data collection, namely:

- (grey) literature research
- standardised online questionnaire
- semi-structured interviews

Table 5.2 Evaluation framework for assessing digital tools

Key dimensions	Demands	Specific questions
Input legitimacy	• Information/equality of opportunity • Tool usability • Interaction support • Voice	• Has the possibility to participate been effectively communicated to the target group? • Is the tool accessible for every member of the target group to participate? • Are the participation tools considered usable, reliable and secure? • How and to what extent are participants enabled to express their wishes and interests? • How and to what extent are the participants able to set the (political) agenda? • Does the design help to involve citizens beyond the participation elite?
Throughput legitimacy	• Deliberation quality • Representation • Diversity/inclusion	• To what extent is information provided about the complete decision-making process and how is the citizen participation part of this (during the process)? • How is information provided to the participants about the issues at stake? • Does the tool encourage interactive exchange of arguments between participants? • Does the tool encourage interaction between the views of participants and views of the officials/politicians? • To what extent are the participants representative for the target group? • To what extent is the input of and/or conversation between participants moderated? • How is the diversity of views of the participants managed (aggregated?) in the process; are minority standpoints included?
Output legitimacy	• (Cost)-effectiveness • Democratic impact • Accountability • Responsiveness	• How does the instrument contribute to the decision-making process and its outcomes? • Does the tool increase the transparency of the issues at stake? • Does the tool help to enhance accountability: informing who is responsible for what action? • How are participants informed about the outcomes and about what has been done with their contributions (afterwards)? • Does the process provide space to the official/politician to make their own judgement, selection or assessment?

Key in our strategies for data collection is thus *methodological triangulation*. We used more than one method and source to gather data on the 22 cases. This was to cross-check our data and to obtain construct validity (an effective methodology and a valid operationalisation) (Fielding and Warnes 2009). The elementary data for the case studies came from the (grey) literature about the case. In addition, two respondents per case were interviewed. In our design the two respondents were (1) a professional that is involved in the case and (2) an expert who scientifically studied and/or contemplated the case. The data collection was finished in February 2017.

The interviews took place via two steps. First, the interviewees were asked to answer a standardised questionnaire online to evaluate the digital tool. For the e-voting experiences a separate questionnaire was created, because not all questions were applicable in these cases. The concept questionnaires were pre-tested in a pilot and feedback was received from two external experts. This led to several adjustments in the questionnaire.

Second, the respondents were interviewed face-to-face, by telephone or Skype, asking follow-up open questions which took no more than one hour. The individual responses of the professionals and experts guided these subsequent semi-structured interviews. The open questions addressed, in a more qualitative way, the motivations of respondents behind their evaluation scores. Moreover, the open questions focused on a better understanding of the success factors, risks, challenges and the EU suitability in relation to the specific digital tool. In addition, in the interviews unsolved issues within the case study—inconsistencies in the data or aspects on which no information can be found in the literature—were discussed with the respondents. The interviewees were able to comment on the transcript of the interview as well as on the draft case study.

The data collection was conducted in the year 2016 until February 2017. In a few of the cases the latest developments in the following months and year (2017–2018) are addressed in the case descriptions.

5.3 Qualitative Comparative Analysis (QCA)

To analyse case descriptions based on the findings of the desk research, the questionnaire and the interviews, the technique of Qualitative Comparative Analysis (QCA) was used.[2] QCA is a technique for making a systematic comparison of different case studies. The intention of the QCA is to integrate qualitative case-oriented and quantitative variable-oriented approaches (Ragin 1987). The QCA technique aims for "meeting the need to gather in-depth insight into different cases and to capture their complexity, while still attempting to produce some form of generalization" (Rihoux and Ragin 2009, xvii).

Our particular research has an intermediate-N research design, including 22 cases. This sample is too large to focus on in-depth analysis only and too small to allow for a conventional regression analysis, but QCA is an appropriate technique for analysis (cf. Gerrits and Verweij 2015). It is particularly in such intermediate-N research designs that QCA helps to acknowledge the internal case complexity on the one hand, while it enables cross-case comparison on the other hand (Rihoux and Ragin 2009, xvii).

---

[2]In Chap. 12 the QCA method is explained in more detail.

References

Cohen, J. (1989). *Deliberation and democratic legitimacy*. 1997, 67–92.
Council of Europe. (2009). *Recommendation CM/Rec(2009)1 of the Committee of Ministers to Member States on electronic democracy (e-democracy)*. http://www.coe.int/t/dgap/democracy/Activities/GGIS/CAHDE/2009/RecCM2009_1_and_Accomp_Docs/Recommendation%20CM_Rec_2009_1E_FINAL_PDF.pdf
Fielding, N., & Warnes, R. (2009). Computer-based qualitative methods in case study research. In D. Byrne & C. C. Ragin (Eds.), *The Sage handbook of case-based methods* (pp. 270–288). London: Sage.
Gerrits, L., & Verweij, S. (2015). Taking stock of complexity in evaluation: A discussion of three recent publications. *Evaluation, 21*(4), 481–491.
Kersting, N. (2014). Online participation: From "invited" to "invented" spaces. *International Journal for Electronic Government, 6*, 260–270.
Manin, B. (1987). On legitimacy and political deliberation. *Political Theory, 15*(3), 338–368.
Ragin, C. (1987). *The comparative method: Moving beyond qualitative and quantitative methods*. Berkeley: University of California.
Rihoux, B., & Ragin, C. C. (2009). Introduction. In B. Rihoux & C. C. Ragin (Eds.), *Configurational comparative methods. Qualitative comparative analysis (QCA) and related techniques* (pp. xvii–xxxv). Thousand Oaks, CA: Sage.
Scharpf, F. W. (1999). *Governing in Europe: Effective and democratic?* Oxford: Oxford University Press.
Schmidt, V. A. (2013). Legitimacy in the European Union revisited: Input, output and throughput. *Political Studies, 61*(1), 2–22.

Open Access This chapter is licensed under the terms of the Creative Commons Attribution 4.0 International License (http://creativecommons.org/licenses/by/4.0/), which permits use, sharing, adaptation, distribution and reproduction in any medium or format, as long as you give appropriate credit to the original author(s) and the source, provide a link to the Creative Commons licence and indicate if changes were made.

The images or other third party material in this chapter are included in the chapter's Creative Commons licence, unless indicated otherwise in a credit line to the material. If material is not included in the chapter's Creative Commons licence and your intended use is not permitted by statutory regulation or exceeds the permitted use, you will need to obtain permission directly from the copyright holder.

Chapter 6
Parliamentary Monitoring

Iris Korthagen and Hade Dorst

Abstract Korthagen and Dorst introduce two digital tools which enable voters to monitor the actions of their representatives: the British theyworkforyou.com and the German abgeordnetenwatch.de. Only the German tool is interactive; it also offers opportunities to ask questions to MPs, comment their voting behaviour and sign petitions. In their description and analysis of both cases, the authors put a strong focus on the participatory process and practical experiences of users. For a better understanding of these tools and how they are used in practice, interviews were conducted with the organisers and researchers familiar with both tools. Strengths and weaknesses are identified and possibilities for improvements explored. Although both tools are developed for the general public, they are mostly used by journalists and other professional users such as NGOs. The data of the websites therefore still reaches many people through mass media. The most important benefit of these tools is that they contribute to impartial information on political votes. However, unintended side effects are there as well, as several MPs in the UK increased the number of times they spoke just to increase their scores.

6.1 Parliamentary Monitoring in the UK: TheyWorkForYou

6.1.1 Introduction

TheyWorkForYou (theyworkforyou.com) enables voters to monitor the actions of their representatives in the Upper and Lower Houses of Parliament in the United Kingdom, the Scottish Parliament and the Northern Ireland Assembly. Visitors of the website can search information on any Member of Parliament (MP), debate or public bill committee or enter their postal code to find information on the MP

I. Korthagen (✉)
Netherlands Court of Audit, The Hague, The Netherlands

H. Dorst
Copernicus Institute of Sustainable Development, Utrecht University, Utrecht, The Netherlands

© The Author(s) 2020
L. Hennen et al. (eds.), *European E-Democracy in Practice*, Studies in Digital Politics and Governance, https://doi.org/10.1007/978-3-030-27184-8_6

relevant to them (Edwards et al. 2015). The available information on every MP includes facts and figures such as the number of written questions and speeches during debates, recent appearances, expenses and an extensive register of interests. For each figure, it is indicated whether this is above or below average (MySociety 2016c). The Policy Agreement Ratio is used to display MPs' voting records in gradations, such as *"consistently voted against"*, *"almost always voted against"*, or *"generally voted against"* regarding important policy issues (Edwards et al. 2015). Since the Brexit vote, information on how each MP campaigned concerning the European Union was added (MySociety 2016d).

The website was launched by volunteers in 2004 and became a project of MySociety in 2006. This organisation, a charity project of UK Citizens Online Democracy, aims to promote *"strong democratic accountability"* and a *"thriving civil society"* (Edwards et al. 2015: 261). It runs several other websites that aim to engage the public in politics, such as MyNextRepresentative, WhatDoTheyKnow and FixMyStreet. The organisation is not politically aligned and its projects and tools are for everyone to use to "make democracy a little more accessible" (MySociety 2016a). The main purpose is to provide neutral, non-partisan information about the actions, words and votes of MPs in a way that is understandable for everyone (Escher 2011). More specifically, the goals of the website are to create (1) value, (2) transparency and (3) engagement (Escher 2011). It aims to provide better information than official parliamentary sites do and to simplify access to this information for people who are interested. The official database of proceedings of parliamentary debates, Hansard, is *"notoriously difficult to navigate"*, according to the interviewed organiser. Another aim is to allow citizens to make a fair judgement of MPs on the basis of what they do and to make MPs feel accountable (i.e. citizens acting as watchdogs). A final aim is to make sure citizens are better informed and to engage citizens in politics.

The UK Parliament is characterised as a "strong debating parliament", but Edwards et al. (2015: 261) also note that its accountability seems to be eroding, due to several dents in the representativeness of MPs, for instance, because of their representation of special interests, party donations, non-parliamentary incomes from consultancies or other services to companies and expenses. An expense scandal in the media that erupted in 2009 was a blow to public confidence in Members of Parliament (Edwards et al. 2015). TheyWorkForYou provides insight into these factors, not only for citizens but also for journalists to see, and this period indeed saw an increased usage of the website (Escher 2011).

MySociety is a not-for-profit social enterprise. It receives funding and research grants from several organisations and donations from individuals (MySociety 2016b). There is not much funding for the tool, but to maintain it costs a lot of work (interview, head of research MySociety). Setting up the website costs a few thousand pounds, with Escher (2011) indicating that with annual maintenance costs of over £20,000 it is the most expensive MySociety project. There are no resources to pay a developer to expand the website or add new functions. The tool runs on software specifically designed for TheyWorkForYou. MySociety has expanded its mission by supporting parliamentary monitoring organisations abroad. The software code used to run TheyWorkForYou is open source and has been used to create similar websites in Ireland, New Zealand and Australia.

Relevant legal frameworks for the tool to function were, according to the interviewed organiser, the right to contact an MP and the right to access parliamentary and debate information. However, at the time TheyWorkForYou started, government information was protected under Crown copyright and therefore could, without permission, not be published elsewhere. The interviewed researcher notes that it is very likely that the release of the Open Government Licence in 2010, which works similar to the creative commons license, has been driven by TheyWorkForYou. It changed the legal landscape in the sense that government information is now more likely to be published under an open license instead of under Crown copyright.

6.1.2 Participants

The site has no specific target group; all British citizens over the age of 12 can use the tool (interview, head of research MySociety). Participation is based on self-selection, and registration is not required.

Since 2007 the website receives between 200,000 and 300,000 visits a month, with noticeable drops during summer recess and between Christmas and New Year (Escher 2011). The interviewed organiser states that the website is frequented more around election times and during political issues. In the run-up to the General Election in 2010, the website had over 230,000 visits in 1 week, making that week the busiest since its launch. In May and June 2009, a significant spike occurred as the media reported on extravagant expenses by MPs and people used the website to check on their MPs' expenditures (Escher 2011). The summer of 2016 saw another sudden increase in visitor numbers due to political upheavals such as the Brexit vote and the resignation of the Prime Minister (MySociety 2016d).

When it comes to the site's demographics there is a strong male bias, a strong participation of high-income groups and of people with a university degree (Escher 2011). TheyWorkForYou users with a high education make up the majority of the tool's users. This is a high proportion, higher even than that of FixMyStreet, another UK-based tool of MySociety (Rumbul 2015). People with full-time employment also make up the largest user group of the tool, with 41% (Rumbul 2015). When compared to the average Internet user, visitors over the age of 54 are overrepresented. The share of retired visitors of TheyWorkForYou is twice as high and sick or disabled people are also overrepresented in comparison to the online population (Escher 2011). There is insufficient data to say anything reliable about the inclusion of people with different ethnic backgrounds. However, as Escher (2011) shows, the available data suggests that white people are overrepresented compared to the average Internet user.

Making the parliamentary process more accessible for all layers of society is one of the main aims of MySociety (Escher 2011). However, respondents in Escher's survey are more politically engaged and more often participate in politics online than the average Internet user. Compared to the general knowledge of politicians and parliamentary proceedings—Escher states not even half the population can name their MP—the users of TheyWorkForYou are quite knowledgeable: four out of five users indicate they knew the name of their MP before they used TheyWorkForYou (Escher 2011). However, three out of five visitors had never looked for information on their representatives' actions before looking up their MP on TheyWorkForYou. A significant new group of users is also reached as two out of five users have not been engaged in politics before using the tool. The most recent data of MySociety shows that over 70% of TheyWorkForYou users read political news at least once a day. One-fifth of users had previously contacted a politician, government agency or public body (Rumbul 2015).

These numbers are an indication of a high proportion of the website's users being professionals. As Edwards et al. state (2015: 262): *"Although there is no concrete evidence of this, many NGOs, campaign groups and the like use the site to gather information, in particular on how MPs are voting (source: email communication, 30-07-2015)."* The interviewed researcher also states that many of the website's users are part of the "political class", using the website professionally: campaigners, journalists and civil servants. Each week some 1500 visits, 2% of all visits, are from members of the parliament (their IP address can be traced back to parliament.uk) (Escher 2011). Another 2.5% of visits can be traced back to governmental sources (.gov.uk and .mod.uk). In 2010 the Conservative Party Central Office accounted for 0.26% of site visits up until the General Election, after which the number of visits decreased again (Escher 2011). The interviewed organiser affirms that they observe a lot of traffic from inside the Houses of Parliaments. MPs and their aides use the website, for instance, when an election is coming up and they want to show constituents their actions so far. *"It is a bit like showing your CV when you're applying for a job"* (interview with head of research MySociety). The BBC accounts for almost 0.5% of all visits in 2010. As journalists use the tool as well and sometimes credit TheyWorkForYou for the information they retrieve, the media also function as an intermediary between the website and citizens (interview with organiser).

According to Escher (2011), MySociety does not promote its websites much because of financial constraints. There were a few promotional activities over the years. With the aid of a Google grant, Google Adwords were used to advertise the website so that when someone would search for terms such as "members of parliament" or names of MPs, a sponsored add for the website would appear. In 2010, a campaign was launched in the weeks running up to the General Election, consisting of a quiz that allowed voters to compare their views to those of candidates, which resulted in a temporary increase in visits to the website (Escher 2011).

MySociety has a blog and posts news on current political developments in relation to TheyWorkForYou or on updates of the tool. There are also Facebook and Twitter accounts for TheyWorkForYou which are regularly used. A communications and marketing manager promotes all MySociety's websites, but there is not a large budget to do so. At present, MySociety is organising focus groups for young people to find out how to engage them. The interviewed organisers state they would like to find ways in which to engage those people that are not already interested in politics, if budget permits. For this purpose, they do research on User Centred Design: What could the website do for its users if it was designed differently or had other features? A footnote here is placed by the interviewed researcher, remarking that *"ordinary people don't get their information about democracy from these sorts of tools. I think they get them from Facebook and the media"*. The interviewed organiser also states that the tool could be improved by increasing the repackaging of information for broader audiences via forums as Twitter, Facebook or Reddit.

6.1.3 Participatory Process

Users of the tool cannot give input through the website. It is not meant to be a platform for interaction, according to the interviewed organiser. TheyWorkForYou only displays information obtained from official public sources and tries to avoid creating a narrative out of information. *"We don't want to curate the information. We're not political and we don't want to appear like we're trying to craft any kind of story out of the information. What we do, is try to simplify the information for people so it can easily be compared"* (interview with head of research MySociety).

The interviewed organiser indicates that the tool's strong suit is that it enables citizens to participate in an informed manner. Also, they can hold their representatives accountable for the way they vote and challenge those who do not appear to represent their interests. Another MySociety tool, WriteToThem, is very closely connected with the TheyWorkForYou website. On every MP's profile page, a button can be clicked which links to WriteToThem, to directly contact the MP. Still, it is a somewhat passive tool, which does not give much opportunity for interaction, therewith possibly stifling debate. However, the interviewed organiser states that there are no resources to moderate full two-way participation.

6.1.4 Results

According to Edwards et al. (2015), the effects of this website on parliamentary work are difficult to assess.

In 2006, *The Times* suggested that the statistics displayed on the website contributed to an increase in non-necessary interventions by MPs (Edwards et al. 2015). Head of Research at MySociety (Rumbul 2014) states: *"When it came to the attention of some MPs that citizens were monitoring how often they spoke in the chamber, as reported by* The Times *in 2006, several MPs increased the number of times they spoke. In most cases however, they did not speak of anything of substance, and this therefore skewed the totals for individual MPs and compromised the integrity of the information being provided to citizens."* The tool may thus have led to *"symbolic accountability processes"* (Edwards et al. 2015). In order to convince users of the tool to look further than these figures and to counter the consequences of a too narrow interpretation of this data, MySociety has added some "silly" data as well, such as the number of times an MP uses an alliterative phrase (e.g. "she sells seashells"). On the website, MySociety (2016a) explains: *"Simply put, we realise that data such as the number of debates spoken in means little in terms of an MP's actual performance. MPs do lots of useful things which we don't count yet, and some which we never could. Even when we do, a count doesn't measure the quality of an MPs contribution."*

As Edwards et al. state (2015: 261): *"In the United Kingdom, the election system allows for a direct accountability relation between individual representatives and their voters, but the strict party discipline that is imposed on the representatives in the British House of Commons leaves little room for independent behaviour in parliamentary votes."* Members of parliament are expected—not obliged—to vote with their party. One impact of the website seems to be that parliamentarians vote less in line with their party and more for their constituents, according to an impact assessment by Becky Hogge (2016: 3): *"The greatest impact of TheyWorkForYou may be on Parliamentarians themselves. MySociety suspects, and some data also confirms, that Parliamentarians have changed the way they go about their work in response to TheyWorkForYou's vote monitoring and analysis tools, both by turning up for more votes and rebelling against their party more often."*

When evaluating the website's impact, Hogge (2016) points out that the possible monetised time savings for users, such as civil society groups and journalists, should be considered. If keeping up with parliamentary actions through the tool can free up time for smaller campaigning or lobby groups' time to use for other actions, more of a level playing field is created.

Almost all respondents in Escher's survey believe that it offers them neutral, non-partisan information (Escher 2011) and indicate they find the website well structured and easy to navigate. However, when a poll on the website asked visitors if they could find what they were looking for, 40% answered negative. Among survey respondents, this was 20%. Nine out of ten respondents indicated that the website improved their knowledge about their representatives. Rumbul (2015) found that a majority of the tool's users felt more confident in contacting their representatives directly as a result of these types of technological platforms.

However, Edwards et al. (2015) state that transparency on the parliamentary process does not automatically translate to its legitimacy. The fact that civilians are better able to see how these processes work does not imply they accept and acknowledge them, let alone trust the politicians and political institutions that form the foundation of these processes.

The interviewed researcher also remarks that although the tool works very well, it will not change the comprehensibility of the parliamentary system. The speech of parliamentarians is reported verbatim, and thus no translative action is provided.

6.2 Parliamentary Monitoring in Germany: abgeordnetenwatch.de

6.2.1 Introduction

The German parliamentary monitoring website abgeordnetenwatch.de was first developed for the state of Hamburg in 2004. Following its success there, it was extended to the federal level. It is an online platform that German citizens can use to monitor their representatives, ask them questions and sign petitions (but not start them). The website has a blog with posts on results of their investigative research on topics concerning parliamentary transparency, citizenship and participation in politics. Visitors of the blog can react to the posts. Parliamentary profile pages show public information such as voting behaviour, questions asked and answered and ancillary functions on representatives of the Federal Parliament (Bundestag), of German members of the European Parliament and of 11 state parliaments (Parliamentwatch 2015).

Abgeordnetenwatch.de is an independent, non-governmental and non-profit organisation. The website was launched by the campaigners of "Mehr Demokratie" (*More Democracy*) (Buzogány 2016), an organisation committed to promoting direct democracy. Political scientist Gregor Hackmack and computer scientist Boris Hekele are the main founders of the platform (Kleinsteuber and Voss 2012). Hackmack sees the website as a tool to "update" the democratic process, with the accountability of representatives and the transparency of the democratic process as important themes (Buzogány 2016: 74 and interview with researcher). In addition to performing a "watchdog" function, the platform has the goal of a more person-oriented democracy. Its main aims are to establish dialogue between voters and representatives, to make Parliament more accountable, transparent and less anonymous, and to provide a sort of archive or "memory" of what has been said and achieved by parliamentarians (Albrecht and Trénel 2010; Kleinsteuber and Voss 2012). In some instances—"*concerning our core topics*" (interview with fundraiser)—the organisation of abgeordnetenwatch.de will start a petition themselves, such as on transparency around lobby activities.

Users can search their representatives by entering their postal code and ask questions by clicking on the contact button at the personal pages of the Members of Parliament (MPs). Only when submitting a question are a name and email address required. A moderation protocol is in place to ensure a platform free of lobbying or offensive behaviour. All questions are moderated by a group of 20 volunteers. These questions and the answers of the MPs are published on the website (Albrecht and Trénel 2010). The moderators only post contributions that are identified as requests for statements on particular issues. A user is not allowed to post more than two questions on one issue to a politician, as monitors feel that it is unlikely a clear answer will be given after two attempts (Pautz 2010). Users can appeal to the abgeordnetenwatch.de board if their questions are rejected and politicians can even be sanctioned by losing their personal page if improper use or fraud is suspected.

Abgeordnetenwatch.de worked as a non-commercial social enterprise, depending on funds, donations and volunteers. In 2014 the platform was funded by recurring donors and individual donations (62%), donations from foundations (15%), companies (12%), premium profiles (3%) and other sources of income (8%) (Parliamentwatch 2015, 20). Transparency on funding—both where it comes from and where it goes—is important to the organisation in order to build users' and funders' trust (interview with fundraiser, abgeordnetenwatch.de). Later on, the organisation is professionalised with paid staff members and freelancers. In 2018 two managing directors, 15 staff members and about 20 freelancers work for abgeordnetenwatch.de. The Q&A platform takes up the most resources of all different functions of abgeordnetenwatch.de, due to intensive monitoring activities and technical development and maintenance (interview with fundraiser). Open source software is used as much as possible. It is difficult to say whether the platform is cost-effective, but the financially independent status of the organisation may be a marker for cost-effectiveness (interview with fundraiser).

6.2.2 Participants

Participation is based on self-selection. Any visitor can search for information on politicians and ask questions. Over 1.5 million visitors were recorded in 2016 that submitted over 193,000 questions, with a response rate of 80% (Parliamentwatch 2015). While the number of visitors per year has dropped, as there were 2.6 million visitors in 2012, the number of questions has increased in these 5 years (in 2012, 141,907 were recorded). The response rate holds consistently around 80% between 2012 and 2016 (Abgeordnetenwatch 2017, 12).

A survey into the background of its users shows that the platform attracts predominantly male visitors (81%), people with higher education (41.8%) and people with a higher than average political interest (Albrecht and Trénel 2010). The average age was 40 years. Over half of the respondents contacted their representative for the first time through this platform (Parliamentwatch 2015).

Reaching those who do not usually participate in the political process has not received specific attention of the organisation. The interviewed researcher states: *"The whole process is quite well explained on the website, but it's still a technical process. You have to know something about the role of parliamentarians and so on, and you have to be able to read longer texts [...]. That might exclude some people. [...] I'm not sure if they tried to specifically address people who are not comfortable with the way the site is presented at the moment. [...] You will have to sort of adapt yourself to the process you want to interact with. That is of course a bit problematic if there's a huge gap between the daily lives of people and the daily lives of politicians."* The interviewed organiser (interview with fundraiser) indicates that it may also be beneficial for users of the tool to delve into the political process before participating. *"Those people do take the time and make the effort. For them, it can be a good experience."* But he also states the platform could be made more straightforward and self-explanatory. *"If you're in your twenties and you're used to simple apps or Facebook or communication via those channels, then [abgeordnetenwatch. de, mainly the Q&A] is not that intuitive. It takes a bit of time. [...] You should usually have a look: what questions did that MP already answer?"* Simplifying the platform structure and experimenting with new ways to engage people might help to make the tool more inclusive (interview with fundraiser). An action undertaken before we interviewed the fundraiser in 2016, in the run-up to the Berlin state elections, was to enable people to ask their question through Facebook. This did not prove to be successful, however (interview with fundraiser).

Media partnerships are important for the success of abgeordnetenwatch.de. Over 50 news portals have a working relationship with abgeordnetenwatch.de and many journalists use the website to base their research on (Buzogány 2016: 75). "*In terms of data, it's a bit of a hidden treasure. We have so many voting records. We have so many answers given by MPs. It's all on the platform. That's the idea: it is on the platform and it remains on the platform. [...] There is a project about to start about the extra earnings of MPs, how that might relate to their voting behaviour. We provide the data [for this].*" Moreover, the 2014 annual report states that media partners "*serve as important crowd-pullers*", as one-third of the visitors found the platform through media (Parliamentwatch 2015). An additional attraction is the blog on which issues are researched and news is reported. There is also a weekly newsletter, featuring interesting questions and answers and recent successes. The number of newsletter subscribers is increased by campaigns that accompany petitions started or endorsed by the organisation (Parliamentwatch 2015).

6.2.3 Participatory Process

Users of the platform can (1) search information on their representatives' voting behaviour, ancillary functions and expenses; (2) query their representatives and receive an answer, both published on the website; and (3) sign petitions.

The main functionality of the platform is to accommodate interaction between citizens and parliamentarians, not the exchange of views between citizens. Users of the website can comment on the voting behaviour of individual parliamentarians, recommend answers by parliamentarians or share them on Facebook and Twitter. The site requires some personal data from people who want to interact with politicians: a name and an email address. Privacy and security are important to both citizens asking questions and parliamentarians answering them. Here, transparency and privacy may conflict. "*We try to be really careful with the data we get. If you fill in something, whether it's a donation or if you're signing a petition, your data is encrypted. That is really important. You can also call us and ask to have your data deleted*" (interview with fundraiser).

Politicians' data published on the website is publicly available via other channels as well, the interviewed researcher states, and risks of hacking are therefore minimal. "*At the moment, it has become accepted that people have the right to know more about parliamentarians than before. We [Germany] also have tougher regulations of what they can do beside their mandate, consulting or such matters. [...] I think Abgeordnetenwatch has become part of that process to make more data available. [Parliamentarians] are public persons, [and so] hacking would not make a difference, because today all the data on them is already publicly available*" (interview with researcher). Privacy of politicians is ensured through a code of conduct. "*We do not *allow questions concerning the private lives of politicians, for instance. We believe that does not foster an open dialogue. That is why moderation is really important*" (interview with fundraiser).

6.2.4 Results

The high percentage of questions asked and answered within a short time (in general a few weeks at most) show abgeordnetenwatch.de to be an effective platform with a strong reputation (Edwards et al. 2015). According to Albrecht and Trénel (2010), the quality of these questions and answers is also high. Pautz (2010) states that, although the possibilities of ICT have not substantially increased citizen involvement in politics, the fact that abgeordnetenwatch.de functions as a collective memory of the actions of representatives may at least increase politicians' accountability, at little cost to citizens.

A lack of direct impact of questions on decision-making may partly be caused by Germany's political system, where MPs often vote according to the party line, depending on the vote call. Because of this system, individual MPs can often not be held directly accountable for their voting behaviour. Abgeordnetenwatch.de fosters direct communication between citizens and their representatives and has impact "*on the way people care about transparency of the parliamentary process, on the personal integrity of members of parliament, and also on the debate on how much they have to be responsive to such platforms and to requests from individuals*" (interview with researcher). The interviewed organiser (interview with fundraiser) affirms that this attitudinal shift of politicians might possibly be abgeordnetenwatch. de's largest achievement. The platform actively supports the current development from contractual to permanent representativeness. The initiators of abgeordnetenwatch.de want to "*facilitate a shift 'from a democracy made up of spectators to a democracy of participants', thus effectively reshaping the functioning of the representative system*" (Pautz 2010). Politicians are, more than they used to be, under permanent evaluation by voters. "*What we did see was, in one or two cases, that MPs, when they were asked about their voting behaviour, they actually... First of all, they explained it. In one or two rare cases, they later on adapted their voting behaviour. But that is obviously not only due to a question asked. I think that is part of a bigger process, like the political situation changing.*" In the same interview it is stressed to value the impact of all the organisation's continuing efforts to make politicians accountable: "*I think our investigative research (the petitions, putting pressure on politicians) has a more direct impact on the political process than the dialogue platform has*" (interview with fundraiser). The success of abgeordnetenwatch.de contributes to the fragmentation of the parliament, as it affects the party structure by putting voters in direct contact with representatives, making the individual MPs stand out in relation to the parties (Pautz 2010).

Abgeordnetenwatch.de is a topic of discussion in the German parliament (Albrecht and Trénel 2010). On the one hand, there are those that perceive the questions asked on the website to be an extra load in an already overfull work schedule and see the website more as a pillory than a platform for citizen consultation. On the other hand, there are MPs who use the website as a place to promote themselves, or they put up links to the questions they have answered on their own websites. However, the opportunities to contact representatives directly may raise false expectations of the influence citizens have on the political process (interview with fundraiser, interview with researcher). In the case of Germany, this is because the role of parliamentarians is not necessarily to be responsive to their own constituency, but to consider the common good whenever they decide on an issue (interview with researcher). People monitoring and asking questions to "their" representative may therefore falsely expect that this MP is supposed to answer to them directly.

At the end of each year, abgeordnetenwatch.de publishes a ranking based on representatives' performance in answering questions. By using grades, the ranking shows which representative was most responsive. This ranking is reported in local and national media. Several years ago, the newspaper *Bild* found that some of the worst-scoring deputies did not only fail to answer the questions of voters but also neglected their other tasks in parliament, which has caused some representatives to resign. This increased awareness made it difficult for politicians to ignore the website (Buzogány 2016).

Another focus of abgeordnetenwatch.de is research into lobbies, ancillary positions and party expenses (Edwards et al. 2015; Abgeordnetenwatch.de 2016), which abgeordnetenwatch.de posts on its blog. In 2010, the speaking fees of former finance minister and member of parliament Peer Steinbrück were published on the blog, leading to the obligation of disclosing income from ancillary functions of representatives in 2013. With regard to lobbyists, abgeordnetenwatch.de took legal action against the Parliament, which refused to open up about their contacts. This was ruled as being unlawful. Since 2015, the Parliament has not only provided a list of all lobbyists (over 1100) but has also sharpened the rules of access to parliament members (Abgeordnetenwatch.de 2016). In general, the website does have impact on parliamentary processes, but it doesn't impact decision-making on specific policy issues.

References

Abgeordnetenwatch. (2017). *Jahres- und Wirkungsbericht 2016*. Accessed 13-12-2018, from https://www.abgeordnetenwatch.de/sites/abgeordnetenwatch.de/files/aw_jahresbericht_2016_web.pdf

Abgeordnetenwatch. Finanzierung. (2016). Accessed 13-12-2018, from https://www.abgeordnetenwatch.de/ueber-uns/mehr/finanzierung

Albrecht, S., & Trénel, M. (2010). *Neue Medien als Mittler zwischen Bürgern und Abgeordneten? Das Beispiel abgeordneten.de*. Berlin: TAB.

Buzogány, A. (2016). Wer hat Angst vor Abgeordnetenwatch? Repräsentation, Responsivität und Transparenzforderungen an Abgeordnete des Deutschen Bundestages. *Z Vgl Polit Wiss, 10*, 67.

Edwards, A., De Kool, D., & Van Ooijen, C. (2015). The information ecology of parliamentary monitoring websites: Pathways towards strengthening democracy. *Information Polity, 20*, 253–268.

Escher, T. (2011). *TheyWorkForYou.com. Analysis of users and usage for UK Citizens Online Democracy*. Accessed 10-10-2018. Retrieved from https://research.mysociety.org/publications/impact-of-uk-parliamentary-sites

Hogge, B. (2016, January). *Open data's impact, theyworkforyou, taking the long view*. Accessed 10-10-2018. Retrieved from Odimpact: http://odimpact.org/files/case-study-they-work-for-you.pdf

Kleinsteuber, H. J., & Voss, K. (2012). Abgeordneten.de – Bürger fragen, Politiker antworten. In S. Braun & A. Geisler (Eds.), *Die verstimmte Demokratie* (pp. 249–258). Springer.

MySociety. (2016a). *About*. Accessed 10-10-2018, from https://www.theyworkforyou.com

MySociety. (2016b). *Funding*. Accessed 10-10-2018, from https://www.mysociety.org/about/funding

MySociety. (2016c). *MPs*. Accessed 10-10-2018, from https://www.theyworkforyou.com/mps

MySociety. (2016d). *News – TheyWorkForYou*. Accessed 10-10-2018, from https://www.mysociety.org/category/projects/theyworkforyou

Parliamentwatch. (2015). *Annual report and activities overview 2014*. Accessed 10-10-2018, from https://www.abgeordnetenwatch.de/sites/abgeordnetenwatch.de/files/aw_annual_report2014_english_web.pdf

Pautz, H. (2010). The internet, political participation and election turnout. *German Politics and Society, 28*, 3.

Rumbul, R. (2014) *In the digital era, political activism can be individual as well as collective*. Accessed 10-10-2018, from http://eprints.lse.ac.uk/63244/1/democraticaudit.com-In%20the%20digital%20era%20political%20activism%20can%20be%20individual%20as%20well%20as%20collective.pdf

Rumbul, R. (2015) *Who benefits from civic technology? Demographic and public attitudes research into the users of civic technologies*. Accessed 10-10-2018, from https://www.mysociety.org/files/2015/10/demographics-report.pdf

Websites (All Accessed 10-10-2018)

https://www.abgeordnetenwatch.de
https://www.mehr-demokratie.de/ueber-uns/profil/
https://www.mysociety.org/category/projects/theyworkforyou/
www.theyworkforyou.com

Open Access This chapter is licensed under the terms of the Creative Commons Attribution 4.0 International License (http://creativecommons.org/licenses/by/4.0/), which permits use, sharing, adaptation, distribution and reproduction in any medium or format, as long as you give appropriate credit to the original author(s) and the source, provide a link to the Creative Commons licence and indicate if changes were made.

The images or other third party material in this chapter are included in the chapter's Creative Commons licence, unless indicated otherwise in a credit line to the material. If material is not included in the chapter's Creative Commons licence and your intended use is not permitted by statutory regulation or exceeds the permitted use, you will need to obtain permission directly from the copyright holder.

Chapter 7
Informal Agenda Setting

Ira van Keulen and Iris Korthagen

Abstract In this chapter, Van Keulen and Korthagen describe two tools which are used by citizens to put issues they think are important on the political agenda: the Dutch website petities.nl and the Finnish Avoin Ministeriö (Open Ministry) which ceased to exist but was aimed to help citizens' initiatives such as submitting a bill. Both are organised bottom-up. In their description and analysis of both cases, the authors put a strong focus on the participatory process and practical experiences of users. For a better understanding of these tools and how they are used in practice, interviews were conducted with the founders and researchers familiar with both tools. Strengths and weaknesses are identified and possibilities for improvements explored. While both tools show positive results in different ways, their impact in terms of policy tools leaves much to be desired. Interestingly, the low impact does not seem to create too much disillusionment among the participants. Quite the opposite, the amount of visitors of petities.nl have been steadily increasing. And participants of the Open Ministry are willing to accept not achieving the desired outcome, as long as they perceive the process to be fair. It turns out that e-participation tools are more often a successful civic instrument, but not a convincing policy instrument.

7.1 The Dutch e-Petition Case: Petities.nl

7.1.1 Introduction

The main goal of petities.nl is to facilitate citizens to sign or start a petition. The initiator of a petition is responsible for filing the petition and for gaining support, and petities.nl just offers the platform. Since the start of the website in May 2005, nearly

---

I. van Keulen (✉)
Rathenau Instituut, The Hague, The Netherlands
e-mail: i.vankeulen@rathenau.nl

I. Korthagen
Netherlands Court of Audit, The Hague, The Netherlands

9222 petitions were signed with one or more signatures (December 2018). The petitions cover a broad range of issues, from populist to technocratic ones. The petition which was signed the most so far—by nearly 400,000 citizens—was a proposal to advance the age of breast cancer screening. The amount of signatories in total is about 11 million. The website attracts about 2.5 million visits monthly.

Petitions can be defined as requests to a public authority, usually a governmental institution or parliament. In general, they have the purpose to change public policy, call for an official statement or evoke a certain act by a public institution (Lindner and Riehm 2011). Because of ITs such as the Internet and social media, it is now much easier to start a petition, gain support for a petition, monitor the petition and of course announce the results of the petition to the outside world. In all Member States of the European Union, citizens have the right to petition government, parliament or other public bodies which is mostly legally codified in the constitution and in addition often in specific laws and regulations too. In the Netherlands this right is codified in the constitution, that is article 5: *"Everyone shall have the right to submit petitions in writing to the competent authorities."* The legal provisions include the protection of the petitioner from adverse consequences of petitioning.

Petities.nl is a private initiative by Reinder Rustema, Arjan Widlak and Michiel Leenaars. Reinder Rustema is still the driving force behind petities.nl and edits new petitions lightly. He never removes a petition for content-related reasons. Only petitions on a company, an individual or a product are not allowed. The site runs on professional volunteers, private donations, support in kind (like hosting, office space) and irregular state subsidies, for instance, from the Ministry of Internal Affairs to build a new site (30,000 € in 2014).

The functionalities of petities.nl have increased over the years. Since 2016 the website can be used for crowdfunding among the signatories to pay for—for example—the help of a professional Public Affairs specialist for creating (political) impact with the e-petition. As a signatory you can also declare if and how you can or want to help to get the petition politically supported. Another interesting function of the petities.nl website is that petitioners can declare that they are available for their municipality to participate in citizen councils. One out of ten petitioners does so. The website also facilitates to send the e-petition directly to 22 local and regional governments. There is no such digital petition desk at petities.nl for the Dutch House of Representatives. The parliamentary administration assigns the petition to the most appropriate parliamentary committee. Citizens have to get in touch themselves with the House of Representatives to ask whether the concerned parliamentary committee is willing to accept the petition in public. There is no statutory obligation for parliamentary committees to hold a public meeting with the petitioners (like in Germany when 50,000 or more signatures are collected for one petition). If needed, petities.nl helps the petitioner to file the petition to the right public body. Since 2008 the recipients of petitions like local governments can open a virtual desk on the website to receive and answer petitions.

According to the interviewed initiator, agenda-setting is not the only goal of petities.nl. *"It is more about participating in a democratic process. To me, a petition is also a success when the answer of a recipient is: 'sorry, that is not going to happen, for this and this reason.' After which the signatories might even agree. [...] And sometimes the petitioners are plain wrong, because they know too little, they have heard something about it, but they do not know the rights of it. Well, that's fine. It happens, especially with today's overflow of information"* (our translation).

7.1.2 Participants

Petities.nl is a Dutch platform, with only the navigation translated in English. Any citizen can file or sign a petition: It is a question of self-selection. If someone wants to sign a petition, he or she has to fill in one's name, email address and place of residence. The signatory can choose whether he or she wants to reveal his/her identity below the petition or not.

On average a petition at petities.nl receives 1308 signatures (national level), 750 (state level) and 532 (local level); this is including the petitions which never started and/or received no signatures (courtesy of the initiator, assessed December 2018). The balance between local versus national issues is about fifty-fifty with slightly more locally oriented petitions. Millions of signatories are an indication of the low threshold of this form of political participation. Citizen involvement by way of an e-petition is of course much less time consuming than, for example, organizing a protest march. "Pyjama activism", "slacktivism" or "clicktivism" are terms for individual engagement in "activist" actions with minimal effort and no strong real-world consequences (Van Hulst et al. 2016). The act itself only serves to satisfy the individual's sense of having accomplished something and decreases the likelihood of engaging in further, perhaps more effective, political engagements.

7.1.2.1 Representativeness

A petition is not a representative opinion poll but only collects support statements. This raises the question of who is using petities.nl. The interviewed initiator believes that lower as well as higher educated Dutch citizens use the website to start a petition: *"How they describe and express themselves, the subject [of the petition], the e-mail address they are using. That gives me an impression of the kind of people I am working with"* (interview with initiator). In general petities.nl is used more than average by educated men above 50 years of age (Van Hulst et al. 2016).

The question whether the design of petities.nl attracts participants beyond the political participation elite is hard to answer. But when it comes to the diversity of the causes supported by the online petitions, it seems petities.nl is quite inclusive. The website is not dominated by one sort of (populist or technocratic) issue. The interviewed researcher notices: *"It [petities.nl] does not look like a regular American petition website where most of the visitors are serial signatories and where there is a lot of echo-chambering. Petities.nl is founded by someone who does not present himself in an ideological way and so the website has no specific political or ideological background*" (our translation). Petities.nl attracts mostly single signatories, because participants visit on average 1.3 webpage (interview with initiator). It does not seem to be an instrument for political organisations: *"Most of the professional organisations out there choose to register their own internet domain and install petition software on it. That way they themselves have access to the data.[...] But the problem they have then, is that the petition does not reach other groups than their own supporters or followers"* (interview with initiator).

7.1.2.2 Communication and Mobilisation Strategy

The low threshold implicates that a large-scale engagement strategy to give more name and fame to the platform was not needed. As the interviewed initiator says: *"We haven't spent one penny on advertisement."* The Ministry of Internal Affairs has helped petities.nl once to get in touch with some of the local governments, but mostly it works like a snowball via social media and e-mail. *"It's the signatories inviting others [to visit the website] through mail who create the most traffic"* (interview with initiator).

When it comes to a communication strategy on the e-petition itself, the website offers a handbook to help citizens to plug their petition. This handbook contains tricks and tips, for example on viral marketing and free publicity, based on the experiences the initiators had since 2005. The handbook addresses how to: increase traffic to the petition (e.g. by sending invitations to one's personal network, approaching journalists, placing messages on important sites, releasing the petition on a special day related to the cause of the petition), start a campaign website or blog with more information, write and spread a press release, how to get in touch with local or national TV or radio broadcasting centres and how to place a widget (so people can sign the petition from another social network or campaign site).

7.1.3 Participatory Process

The initiator of a petition captures the main message in a clear title of the petition and states in fixed text blocks: We..., Observe... and Request.... It depends on the petition how much information on the issue at stake is given but the design of the platform is such that there is not much space in order to keep the message as concise as possible. A link to a website can be added, like a Facebook page or an actual campaign website where more information can be found. Only language mistakes are edited before the petition is displayed.

The only input signatories can give is their name, email address, place of residence and their "signature" (pressing a blue button). Concerning privacy, the initiator mentions in the interview: *"Personal data is only shared in compliance with data protection laws"* (interview, initiator, our translation). The design of the site is such that participants cannot make any remark on the petition or discuss the petition among themselves: no views are exchanged. According to the interviewed initiator there is not much need for online deliberation in general: *"The moral of the internet is that you can endlessly 'fork' as we call it. If you know better, you move on to another website, another Whatsapp group, etc. There is no scarcity of space"* (interview with initiator). It is always possible to find like-minded people, somewhere else on the Internet.

The interviewed researcher concludes that the contribution of a participant is limited, but this is not always necessarily a bad thing. *"You can only sign or not sign. You cannot co-edit a text for example. At the same time, your voice is not lost as happens often in deliberative settings where a participant can take part in a discussion but where in the end it is difficult to ascertain where and how one's input has been used. With petitions, your voice just counts"* (interview with researcher).

7.1.4 Results

The collective result of a petition is never binding. It is a non-mandatory sign of discontent or a new idea which can be picked up or ignored by government or politics. A petition can in that sense be compared with an advisory, not binding referendum. Petitions can put an issue on the agenda of the recipients (i.e. agenda setting), but in the Dutch system they do not need to respond to a petition. The formal recipient of most of the petitions on petities.nl is a representative at the national, regional or local level. Although the right to petition compels the addressee to pay attention to a petition, it is very easy for the representatives to just accept a petition and tell the petitioners they will use it in their decision-making process (Edwards and De Kool 2016). They can decide for themselves how to proceed with the request. And if they decide to proceed, the petitioner is usually not involved in the ensuing debate and decision-making process anymore. Representatives provide virtually no feedback on how they have dealt with petitions. The initiator of petities.nl argues this is undesirable and may grow distrust: *"Petitions need to be answered. And that could be an honest 'no' as well."* But the "no" needs to be explained. The officials need to be transparent about their considerations.

"Pyjama activism" also characterises the initiators of the petitions, as most petitions are not presented in time for the relevant political debate when there is a "policy window". Actually, many individual petitioners do not see the use of presenting their petition to officials. *"It does not happen that often that ordinary citizens offer their petition to Members of Parliament. Citizens reason like this: 'Well, it's on the internet now. All of us are here with our names on a long list. 10,000s of us. Sometimes 100,000s of us. It should be clear enough now. We really do not need to come and hand over the petition as well'"* (interview with initiator). This differs radically from the perception of members of parliament: *"A petition does not exist when it is not handed over. Apparently, the issue has been solved or it is not so urgent anymore"* (interview with initiator).

The website is transparent in the sense that it gives an overview of all the petitions either open for signing, closed or filed. At the same time there is not much information on the political impact of the petitions on the site. The initiator wants to improve this. *"I have received funding of the Foundation for Democracy and Media to work on a structural solution for this. For a period of twelve weeks, I am going to give information on the impact of 25 e-petitions filed at the largest local governments. It is like investigative journalism. In the end, all the signatories get the information [linking to official sources] and it makes people very happy. [...] This is quite unique; nobody works like this at the moment. The Germans [openpetition.de] want it, but they don't get time"* (interview with initiator).

Regardless of the formal limitations, some petitions become politically influential because they collect many signatures and capture broad media attention. For example, in February 2016 an e-petition got signed 17,500 times in 3 days (and in the end it had nearly 30,000 signatures) against a new law on administrative requirements between freelancers and their clients. There was a lot of media upheaval about it and the state secretary did undertake action in the end by sending all Dutch freelancers a letter in which he explained the particulars about the new law. Petities.nl does generally get good press in the Netherlands. The press takes notice of the public signals from the website quite regularly. The interviewed initiator agrees: *"Not a week goes by without a petition from petities.nl mentioned in some local newspaper somewhere in the country. [...] Also the petitions on national issues are regularly in the news"* (interview with initiator).

The potential power of e-petitions is not so much to have an impact on decision-making but mostly as a form of "testimony politics" on moments of urgency. *"Petitioners are not really that much concerned with the impact, they just want to make a statement or leave a testimony"* (interview with researcher). The rise of e-petitions in that sense fits in the broader trend of what is called the "mood democracy" by Hendriks (2012). Citizens can make themselves heard at an international stage and mostly at their own terms (since petitions are initiated bottom-up and access barriers are comparatively low in terms of formal requirements). The conclusion that e-democracy tools are often successful as a civic instrument but not a convincing policy instrument (Kies and Nanz 2013: 24) seems to apply here as well.

7.2 The Finnish Citizens' Initiative and the Open Ministry

7.2.1 Introduction

Since 2012, Finnish legislation enables three types of citizens' initiatives: (1) initiatives asking the Eduskunta (the Finnish House of Representatives) to roll out new policy, (2) initiatives in which citizens themselves submit a bill to the Eduskunta and (3) initiatives for annulment of existing legislation. If such an initiative collects at least 50,000 signatures—less than 2% of the voting population—within 6 months, the Finnish Parliament is obliged to discuss the proposal and vote on it.

In October 2012 the online platform "Avoin Ministeriö" (Open Ministry) was founded by a citizen group to advocate well-functioning citizens' initiative processes and to support individual citizens' initiative campaigns. *"The Open Ministry (Avoin Ministeriö) is about crowdsourcing legislation, deliberative and participatory democracy and citizens' initiatives. It is a non-profit organisation based in Helsinki, Finland. We help citizens and NGOs with national citizens' initiatives, EU citizens' initiatives and develop the online services for collaborating, sharing and signing the initiatives."*

The online tool of Open Ministry was used to collect ideas for discussion and for co-creation purposes. In the first years legal experts tested and edited the initiatives pro bono at the online platform. Open Ministry also helped in getting publicity for particular initiatives, and volunteers of the platform sometimes acted as official representatives of an initiative, particularly to the government and the European Parliament. The digital process around the citizens' initiatives as organised by Open Ministry is often referred to as *crowdsourced lawmaking* (Edwards and De Kool 2016).

The procedure of Open Ministry consisted of five steps. First, registered users presented their own ideas online, inviting other users to comment, support or refuse the idea. Usually ideas needed further development: by clarifying the objectives, listing arguments for and against, an assessment of the possible consequences and so on. In the second phase, ideas were fine-tuned into an official legislative proposal that could be put at the official website for citizens' initiatives of the Ministry of Justice's website with—in the first years of Open Ministry—the help of legal experts and other experts on the topic. Next, the proposal would be uploaded at the official website. In a 6-month period, the initiative should collect at least 50,000 electronic and/or paper-based expressions of support. After the Population Register Centre had checked names and confirmed that at least 50,000 approved signatures had been collected, a spokesperson for the initiative could submit it to Parliament for consideration. Finally, the citizens' initiatives were debated in Parliament in the same way as other legislative proposals. The law obliged Parliament to deal with the initiative and to hear its initiator, but it is up to the Parliament to make the final judgement to accept or reject the proposal (Christensen et al. 2015). These legislative procedures were groundbreaking, as Heikka (2015: 288) argues: *"If one were to point to a key to the success of the CI-Act as a civic engagement experiment, I argue that the radical legislative framework itself—a result of a decade's work by three governments—was the defining element."*

Open Ministry received a financial contribution of 30,000 € from SITRA, a Finnish innovation fund for setting up the first version of the website and 15,000 € from the Ministry of Justice (interview with initiator). But due to a lack of further financial support, the Open Ministry was not able to continue its work: *"We were more active in the first two years of the citizens' initiative law. [...] We haven't been able to continue that and to develop it further. So now the operations are quite minimal. [...] In fact, this year, we switched to quite a simple, just a wordpress-based webpage basically"* (interview with initiator).

7.2.2 Participants

The purpose of the constitutional amendment that enables citizens' initiatives is *"to promote and support free civic activity and thus strengthen civil society, in which different parts of the population participate and have a say in developing society"*. This makes clear that the Finnish citizens' initiative is aimed at a broad range of people.

The target group of the online crowdsourcing at Open Ministry is in principle everyone with legislative ideas, comments or opinions. While the term crowdsourcing in theory includes anybody who has access to the Internet and is aware of the task, "the crowd" in practice refers to the individuals who self-select from that larger group of people (Aitamurto and Landemore 2016). The academics Nurminen et al. (2013) conducted a survey among users of the Open Ministry website at the end of 2012. Their respondents show an overrepresentation of the 21–40 age group, males, university graduates and urban residents in comparison to the general population. While these findings suggest the citizens' initiative mainly activates people who are well off, in later research on the citizens' initiative, Christensen et al. (2015) emphasise that also people who are unemployed or in bad health make regular use of the new possibilities. Moreover, *"actually the strongest finding that we have is that it appeals to young people. [...] So in that sense it's actually reaching a group that is often considered to be problematic from a democracy perspective, young people often don't want to participate"* (interview with researcher).

Co-founder of Open Ministry Joonas Pekkanen states in 2014 on YouTube in relation to the participants: *"Politicians and civil servants preparing the law need to understand that it is not a representative sample of the population obviously. Because people choose to participate and people with their own interests of course are vocal about their needs and requirements for the law. [...] The challenge is to get regular people who are not motivated by their personal interests to get involved. That's the big issue, that's the big question to answer in the future, I think."*

At the same time, as Edwards and De Kool (2016) are stating, the main aim of crowdsourced lawmaking is to encourage diversity, not representativeness per se. Aitamurto and Landemore (2016: 175) argue more or less the same in relation to crowdsourced lawmaking: *"lack of statistical representativeness [...] does not necessarily mean a poverty of views, information, and arguments and low quality deliberation"*. At the same time, the threshold of 50,000 signatures can be seen as a minimum check of the popular support for the proposal. And in the end, in the following parliamentary debate and parliamentary vote, political representativeness is ensured.

The communication strategy of Open Ministry included press releases and the Facebook page (interview with initiator). By being online 6 months earlier than the ministerial website for the citizens' initiatives, Open Ministry was able to focus media attention to their website and boost their user base (Heikka 2015). The people behind Open Ministry have therefore been *"important in the beginning in creating awareness of the possibilities the citizens' initiative gives. And they campaigned for many of the successful initiatives in the beginning. [...] But I think it was more about the people than the platform*" (interview with researcher). The academic researcher rates the effectivity of the communication strategy around the platform quite low, as he thinks Open Ministry is not well-known in general: "*It is a specific group of people that was reached. It's urban, well-educated men. And they're living in the Helsinki area.*"

Avoin Ministerio has helped several citizens' initiatives to collect the required number of signatures. But in practice campaigning appeared to be a very decentralised process, where different groups organised and mobilised themselves separately online and offline around the issues, especially when they had conflicting interests or views. In order to reach a new audience offline, participation was tested by distributing paper versions of the initiative. "*That we put into a few hundred libraries. And the idea was ... and pre-paid envelopes for the libraries to send those back to us. And easier to collect paper signatures also from those who can't take part in the digital platforms. [...] But that we also ended because nobody wanted to pay for the expenses for doing that.*" This option was used: "*Not a huge volume but it's more for the people who are in the kind of minority or in the fringes of society in a way*" (interview with initiator).

7.2.3 Participatory Process

In order to participate, citizens need to register via the APIs offered by banks, mobile operators or a chip ID. Initiators and representatives of specific legislative proposals also need to provide their contact details, which are published online. The process of crowdsourcing varied for different proposal trajectories. The (co-)founder stated in the interview that the ban on fur farming initiative, the same-sex marriage initiative and the copywriting initiative were "*the biggest ones. So those initiatives that brought people in and I think we had something like 6,000 registered users, people who opened an account on our site to be able to comment and write. [...] The most crowdsourced one was the copywriting initiative; there was more than a hundred people commenting on it. And more than a thousand people voting for the draft before it was finalised. [...] The same-sex marriages initiative was prepared a bit differently. We had a set of semi-open or set of semi-closed group of law students and professors helping them to write the proposal and then we just published drafts a few times. So, it wasn't kind of co-edited all the time. [...] We were testing out different processes and ways of working on different proposals*" (interview with initiator). In another trajectory about the donation legislation, they formed a proposal via a Wiki platform, but it was never launched on the websites to collect support from citizens, because it was put forward as an MP initiative in the end (a faster route to new legislation), as the co-founder further explained during the interview.

The 15 initiatives that have passed the threshold of 50,000 signatures within 6 months up till the end of 2016 concern the following issues:

2013(–2014)

- Fur farming (before governmental site was launched) (69,381)
- Copyright reform (51,801)
- Swedish language (61,306)
- Same-sex marriages (166,851 in 2013)
- Energy certificates (62,211)
- Drunk driving (62,835)

2014(–2015)

- Birthing hospitals (66,797)
- Child molestation (58,013)
- Right to refuse conscientious cessation of life (67,547)
- Expelling foreigners guilty of offense (54,324)

2015(–2016)

- Zero-hour contracts (62,516)
- Same-sex marriage and (adopted) children (106,195)
- Pension index (84,820)
- Referendum membership of the euro area (53,425)
- Maternity Act (55,707)

Many citizens' initiatives do not get enough support. Christensen et al. (2015) calculate that 44.9% did not even manage to collect more than 100 signatures. Another 48.1% stagnates before 10,000 signatures. Thus collecting 50,000 signatures is not an easy task and proves to be a threshold that prevents much extra workload for parliament (Heikka 2015).

7.2.4 Results

Until December 2016 only one of the citizens' initiatives has led to changes in the law: the gender-neutral marriage legislation. This win on the equal marriage law *"has big implications for the citizens' activism in Finland"*, because *"people have seen that their digital participation can make a difference"*, Bria et al. (2014) argue. Other initiatives have had indirect impact on legislation, increased the awareness of the issues and influenced opinions regarding the specific issues, like the one on energy certificates (Christensen et al. 2015). The successful law proposals that reached the 50,000 threshold are brought under closer public scrutiny, research concludes. The initiatives that collected the required number of signatures received so much media attention that Parliament felt the urge to proceed with them relatively swift and thoroughly (Christensen et al. 2015: 6).

Yet the quality of the legislative proposal was not always considered satisfactory. Even the initiative to legalise same-sex marriage was criticised by Eduskunta's Legal

Affairs Committee for having "technical deficiencies" (Edwards and de Kool 2016: 59). Nevertheless, the bill was passed by Parliament in November 2014 by a vote of 105 to 92, supported by Alexander Stubb, the liberal conservative Prime Minister, who had spoken out in favour of the proposal in an open letter before the parliamentary vote.

One of the interviewees mentioned positive changes instigated by the citizen initiative procedure, the debate around that and the contributions of Open Ministry: *"If we talk about the Citizens Initiatives, at least the process...those that made it through to parliament, the process has been relatively open. And also the meetings in the different committees have been fairly open and there's been a lot of media attention. So I think in that case, it has been an improvement to help how things are normally done in Finland"* (interview with researcher). The citizens' initiative can help increase throughput legitimacy by creating a more trustworthy decision-making process. *"The participants may well be willing to accept not achieving the desired outcome, as long as they perceive the process to be fair"* (Christensen et al. 2015). In general, the citizens' initiative is positively evaluated: 83% of citizens regard the contribution of the citizens' initiative to Finnish democracy as positive in the Finnish national election survey (Christensen et al. 2015).

Open Ministry promoted transparency and accountability by providing detailed information about parliamentarians' comments and voting records on its website (Edwards and De Kool 2016: 59). In addition to the support for citizens' initiatives, the people behind Open Ministry took part in various projects and discussions to improve citizen participation, transparency and accountability. Stefaan Verhulst, an academic in law and communications, wrote in a blog: *"Finland's program forces representatives to officially take a stand for or against proposals demonstrated to be important to a large portion of the population. As such, Open Ministry could lead to not only more immediate direct democracy, but greater accountability for government representatives."*

But in the end, the story of Open Ministry is less of a success. *"The failure of the Open Ministry to maintain its service after its initial success is a cause for concern, however, and resourcing of a civic technology ecosystem should be examined. The more radical experiments for crowdsourcing draft texts for legislation have suffered, since these technical features and practices were part of the work of the Open Ministry NGO. Lack of money was the likely cause of the downfall of the Open Ministry as a crowdsourcing service but allowing NGOs deeper integration with existing government technical resources could alleviate this problem"*, Heikka (2015: 288) argues. The online activities of Open Ministry around the legislative proposals were directed more at supporting initiatives with signatures and less at deliberating proposals. In the interview the researcher argued: *"There is a need for some sort of legal advice to ensure that the proposals actually achieve what they are supposed to. And that's a problem because of course most citizens don't have the knowledge that they would need to ensure this."* About the former legal support within the Open Ministry platform, he says: *"I don't think they succeeded in offering this legal advice. Not enough of it anyway"* (interview with researcher).

References

Aitamurto, T., & Landemore, H. (2016). Crowdsourced deliberation: The case of the law on off-road traffic in Finland. *Policy and Internet, 8*(2), 174–196.

Bria, F., Halpin, H., Pekkanen, J., Korhonen, J., Toret Medina, J., Arana Catania, M., & Mancini, P. (2014). *D 5.1 Pilot implementation of open social web for participatory democracy*. D-CENT Project no. 610349. Accessed 10-12-2018, from https://dcentproject.eu/wp-content/uploads/2014/12/D5.1-Pilot-Implementation-of-Open-Social-Web-for-Participatory-Democracy.pdf

Christensen, H. S., Karjalainen, M., & Nurminen, L. (2015). *Does crowdsourcing legislation increase political legitimacy? The case of Avoin Ministeriö in Finland*. Accessed 10-12-2018, from https://onlinelibrary.wiley.com/doi/full/10.1002/poi3.80

Edwards, A., & de Kool, D. (2016). *Digital democracy: Opportunities and dilemmas. The Dutch Parliament in a Networked Society*. Den Haag: Rathenau Instituut.

Heikka, T. (2015). The rise of the mediating citizen: Time, space, and citizenship in the crowdsourcing of Finnish Legislation. *Policy and Internet, 7*, 268–291. https://doi.org/10.1002/poi3.98.

Hendriks, F. (2012). *Democratie onder druk*. Amsterdam: Van Gennep.

Kies, R., & Nanz, P. (Eds.). (2013). *Is Europe listening to us? Success and failure of EU citizen consultations*. Farnham: Ashgate.

Lindner, R., & Riehm, U. (2011). Broadening participation through E-petitions? An empirical study of petitions to the German Parliament. *Policy and Internet, 3*(1), Article 3, 1–Article 3,23.

Nurminen, L., Karjalainen, M., & Serup Christensen, H. (2013). *Combining citizens' initiatives and deliberation – The case of Open Ministry*. Accessed 10-12-2018, from https://ecpr.eu/filestore/paperproposal/106c7149-616a-4782-a892-64b111ed3f3a.pdf

Van Hulst, M., Cuijpers, C., Hendriks, F., Metze, T., Leenes, R., & Hoekzema, D. (2016). *Digitale empowerment van de demos. Een onderzoek naar aansprekende e-democracy innovaties*. Ministerie van Binnenlandse Zaken en Koninkrijksrelatie.

Websites (All Accessed 10-12-2018)

http://openministry.info
https://www.kansalaisaloite.fi/
https://www.kansalaisaloite.fi/fi/ohjeet/briefly-in-english
https://www.kansalaisaloite.fi/fi/aloite/2212
https://www.kansalaisaloite.fi/fi/hae?searchView=pub&orderBy%20=createdNewest&show=ended&minSupportCount=50
https://www.eduskunta.fi/EN/lakiensaataminen/kansalaisaloite/Pages/default.aspx
http://thegovlab.org/finland-is-about-to-change-what-we-mean-by-law-making/
https://www.youtube.com/watch?v=sE-sUFGArdA
https://handboek.petities.nl/wiki/Hoofdpagina
https://www.petities.nl
https://jaarverslag.petities.nl/financieel2014/

Open Access This chapter is licensed under the terms of the Creative Commons Attribution 4.0 International License (http://creativecommons.org/licenses/by/4.0/), which permits use, sharing, adaptation, distribution and reproduction in any medium or format, as long as you give appropriate credit to the original author(s) and the source, provide a link to the Creative Commons licence and indicate if changes were made.

The images or other third party material in this chapter are included in the chapter's Creative Commons licence, unless indicated otherwise in a credit line to the material. If material is not included in the chapter's Creative Commons licence and your intended use is not permitted by statutory regulation or exceeds the permitted use, you will need to obtain permission directly from the copyright holder.

Chapter 8
Formal Agenda Setting (National and Local Level)

Iris Korthagen, Gloria Rose, Georg Aichholzer, and Ira van Keulen

Abstract Korthagen et al. describe and analyse five digital democratic tools which serve or had served to support formal agenda setting at the national and local level (crowdsourcing for a constitution in Iceland, Future Melbourne Wiki, the Slovenian Predlagam.vladi.si, participatory budgeting in Berlin Lichtenberg and the Dutch internetconsultation.nl). The authors place a strong focus on the participatory process and practical experiences. For a better understanding of these tools and how they are used in practice, interviews were conducted with administrators and researchers familiar with the respective tools. Strengths and weaknesses are identified and possibilities for improvements explored. Most of the tools have had their impact on a political or policy agenda, although the extent of the impact differs and cannot always be quantified. This success is partly due to the embeddedness of most of the tools in formal policy or political processes. An important finding of this chapter is that although e-participation can have an impact on the political agenda setting, it does not always imply that there is an impact on the final decision-making process.

8.1 Crowdsourcing for a New Constitution: Iceland

8.1.1 Introduction

This case is known internationally because it was the first time 'crowdsourcing' was used to draft a new constitution. It is considered a classic example of how digital tools—next to offline participatory events—can contribute to democratic processes.

I. Korthagen (✉)
Netherlands Court of Audit, The Hague, The Netherlands

G. Rose · G. Aichholzer
Institute of Technology Assessment, Austrian Academy of Sciences, Vienna, Austria
e-mail: gloria.rose@oeaw.ac.at; aich@oeaw.ac.at

I. van Keulen
Rathenau Instituut, The Hague, The Netherlands
e-mail: i.vankeulen@rathenau.nl

© The Author(s) 2020
L. Hennen et al. (eds.), *European E-Democracy in Practice*, Studies in Digital Politics and Governance, https://doi.org/10.1007/978-3-030-27184-8_8

Internet and social media were used to involve citizens and experts from Iceland but also from abroad in the process of writing the actual text of the constitution. The idea behind crowdsourcing is that when ordinary citizens and experts combine their judgements, the results are qualitatively better than when based on the experts' judgement alone (Surowiecki 2004).

In November 2009, Prime Minister Johanna Sigurdardottir of Iceland sent a bill to the parliament to start a constitutional revision process. There was a clear motive. Since 2008 the country suffered from a national economic meltdown which caused the country's stock exchange, currency and banks to crash. The public asked for fundamental reforms, like the separation of legislative and executive powers, more direct public participation, electoral reforms supervision of the financial sector, public ownership of natural resources (Kok 2011) and less influence for the president, who was severely criticised because of his close connections with the banking world (Meuwese 2012). In that same month, different grass-roots organisations calling themselves 'The Anthill' organised a national forum to discuss the future of Iceland. With 1500 Icelanders (0.5% of the population) joining the organisers, they hoped to obtain some sort of mandate representative enough to make the Althingi (the Iceland Parliament) listen (Landemore 2015). The Althingi decided that citizens should be involved in drafting a new constitution replacing the first one, dating 1944 after independence from Denmark. During the four phases of the constitutional revision process, citizens have had quite some influence on the decision-making process in different ways (Meuwese 2012):

1. The initiative to revise the constitution (2009)

    (a) Public protest resulted in a bill to start the revision of the constitution (agenda setting).
    (b) The first National Assembly was organised bottom up and lead to a decision by parliament that citizens should be involved in the drafting process (agenda setting).

2. The choice for a constitutional assembly and working method (2010).

    (a) The Constitutional Assembly of 25 people were elected by popular vote (decide).
    (b) The assembly organised a second National Forum with 950 randomly selected citizens who laid down key notions to be included in the new constitution (co-decide).

3. The actual drafting of the constitution (2011).

    (a) Citizens were invited to make suggestions and give comments (co-decide).
    (b) The assembly discussed the last amendments and voted on the final draft (decide).

4. The approval (2012).

   (a) In a non-binding referendum, the draft constitution was approved by a majority of the Iceland population (co-decide).
   (b) The new government, however, did not adopt the crowdsourced constitution (contest).

In the end, the parliament never took up the proposed constitution. It was never brought to vote, so it never went into effect. The new government that took office following the 2013 elections has established a committee to prepare further decision-making about the new constitution. The committee published a provisional report in the spring of 2014 identifying the Constitutional Council's draft as one of several possible alternatives for a new constitution (Edwards and De Kool 2016). Since then the constitution remained on ice. Bjarni Benediktsson became Prime Minister on 11 January 2017, but he has never been a great supporter of the whole crowdsourcing process. Since the end of November, however, Katrín Jakobsdóttir became president of Iceland. Under her guidance, the current government has been preparing a new constitutional process aiming for a revision of the constitution in a period over 7 years. The draft constitution of the Constitutional Council will be taken into account, but will not be the foundational text in this new process. Most important is that extensive public consultation will be again part of the process.

The costs of the first constitutional reform process from 2009 to 2011 were paid by the Icelandic Parliament. The total budget is, however, unknown (Kok 2011).

8.1.2 Participants

Participants were involved in different ways and at different stages of the constitutional reform process. In general, the target group of the whole process were not only citizens and experts from Iceland but also from abroad.

At the start, the 25 members of the Constitutional Council were selected from a group of 522 citizens who nominated themselves. They had to gather signatures to place themselves on the ballot. Of the 25 members, 15 got less than a thousand votes, which has been considered as a lack of authority and legitimacy on behalf of the assembly (Kok 2011). Besides this, the members were not representative for the Iceland population and turned out to be highly educated. A disproportional amount of them were professors and students of political studies. The 950 people who participated in the National Forum were randomly selected from the national population register. Quota sampling was used to ensure representativeness in terms of age, gender and geographical distribution, which was only successful for gender (Landemore 2015).

The phase of writing the constitution was open to everybody, as mentioned, even to non-nationals. Translating techniques were used and Council members communicated often in English on their Facebook or Twitter accounts, making the process very accessible for foreigners. The only thing required on the website of the Council was an email address (Kok 2011). The 5% Icelandic citizens without Internet access could participate through letters ("*hundreds of letters*", interview with Council member) and telephone calls to the Council members. There were also public deliberations with the Council that all people could attend but it was not possible to participate in the discussions.

No reliable data has been published to indicate the level of online engagement. However, the fact that just over 4000 people have "liked" the Council's Facebook page during the constitutional drafting seems to indicate that it was not very intensely used. It is therefore unclear whether the revision process has succeeded in truly engaging the Icelandic population (Kok 2011). On the other hand, when it comes to the contributions of the participants, Meuwese (2012) reports that the Council received about 3600 comments, as well as 370 "*formal suggestions*" on the official website. Tushnet (2015: 9) thinks the amount of contributions was quite substantive: "*Not a trivial number in a nation with a population of under 400,000.*"

The majority of the participants of the online crowdsourcing process seem to have been mostly ordinary Iceland citizens. Many professionals disregarded the whole process or gave their comments only after the draft constitution was finished, according to the interviewed Council member. The interviewed researcher says: "*Maybe boycotting is not the right word, but I have the impression that the viewpoint at the Faculty of Law of Reykjavik was that: 'Writing a constitution is for experts.' To some extent there been done some preparatory work done by experts and in the end the draft version of the constitution was also edited by experts. So my impression is that professionals were not involved in the digital participation process but did intervene in everything around it*"(interview with researcher).

Although there was a clear urgency that helped to mobilise the population, a communication strategy was needed. The Ministry of Justice and Human Rights introduced the candidates for the Constitutional Assembly on a special website and published a brochure with information about the candidates and the elections which was distributed to all homes in the country. The national Icelandic broadcasting service broadcasted over 50 radio shows. In the end, 36% of the total population voted, which is a low turnout for Iceland's standards (Kok 2011). Reasons mentioned were amongst others: low media coverage, lack of debate between the candidates about basic issues, disagreement about the importance of a Constitutional Assembly and most probably also a general election fatigue. Looking at the first two reasons mentioned, it seems that the communication strategy failed in that respect.

It is difficult to discover how the crowdsourcing process worked and how different groups of citizens were actively approached to get involved. One interviewee (researcher) confirms that she did not hear of any communication strategy: "*It wouldn't fit with the overall ad hoc character of the process.*" Tushnet (2015: 9) adds: "*It is also not clear whether specific attempts were made to include different groups of citizens—beyond the so-called participation elite—like minorities in the crowdsourcing process.*" Also, not much can be found in the literature on what Althingi did to get as high a turnout as possible for the non-binding referendum on the final draft of the constitution. The turnout was 47%, which is comparable with the turnout at similar referenda in other countries (Edwards and De Kool 2016).

8.1.3 Participatory Process

During the 4 months the drafting process lasted, the Council published preliminary drafts online for public review in 12 rounds and in three different working groups consisting of the Council members. Participants could comment on these drafts. Some of these suggestions which were approved for consideration by the Council were posted on the website. The suggestions could be debated online by participants. The Council would then consider the arguments for and against the suggestions and decide whether to include them in the next draft. During the last round the Council discussed the draft per article which was followed by voting by the participants (Kok 2011).

Participants could follow the activities of the Council closely. During the drafting process short interviews with delegates were uploaded on Youtube and Facebook daily. On Thursdays at 13:00 there was live broadcast from the Constitutional Council meetings on the webpage and on Facebook. There were schedules for all meetings, all minutes from meetings of groups, the Board and the Council as well as the Council's work procedures. News from the Council's work was posted on the webpage as well as a weekly newsletter. This made the process very transparent and reflected a high degree of accountability towards the public. It was quite innovative for the Council to use digital means—especially social media to actively solicit input from citizens (Gylfason and Meuwese 2016). According to the interviewed Council member, privacy or safety issues were a *"complete non-issue"* because *"there was no confidential information at stake or anything"*.

However, the drafting process seems to have been organised ad hoc with little time available and under a lot of pressure, without a method to structure all the input from the participants (interview with researcher). The interviewee saw this confirmed at a conference in Iceland on the whole constitutional process. As an example of the unstructured process she mentions: *"If some comment came in on Facebook, then I believe that an intern or someone else working at the Council and started working on it. [...] There was not a protocol or something, like: how do we deal with the comment coming in and how do we send this information to the meetings of the Council?"* (interview with researcher).

Meuwese (2012) mentions that most of the posts of participants on social media were generic and a fair number of suggested substantive provisions for inclusion in the draft constitution. Kok (2011) argues that many of the suggestions were more policy recommendations—for example, the prohibition of livestock maltreatment—rather than constitutional rights. On the other hand, the contributions to the official Council website were, according to the interviewed Council member, quite substantive. The concern about the crowdsourcing method that Council members had at the start turned out to be unfounded. *"We were concerned that maybe this would be abused by too many people; that our website might sort of be filled by people writing rubbish as you see on many newspaper websites. But that did not happen"* (interview with Council member).

During the drafting process there were forms of deliberative democracy—amongst participants and between the Council members and the participants (mostly through Facebook and the website)—as well as aggregated forms of democracy (presenting preliminary texts and voting). The process of writing by the Council members and then presenting to the public and receiving comments made it a predictable process (Van Hulst et al. 2016). In other phases of the process there was a similar kind of balance between deliberation and aggregation.

However, the comments themselves were not aggregated. According to the interviewed Council member, neither aggregation nor a systematic approach was needed. The reason was that it was possible for the Council to take a look at every contribution and comment, because of the small size of the population of Iceland. *"But if this was the US for example, you had to multiply everything by a thousand and then it would be impossible for them to read everything, so they would simply make a random selection"* (interview with Council member).

In the end, the offline process might have been more important than the online process, according to the interviewed researcher: *"I think the deliberation within that group of 25 people [the Council] was more important than the processing of all the input from participants. The Council members were elected for a certain reason, for their ideas, so they were mandated. And there was of course the pre-work of the National Forum [in which 1,000 citizens participated] which they were using. So, the input from citizens did not only come from the digital participation process but also through the Forum. Cause 1,000 citizens, in Iceland that is 0.3% of the population"*.

The transparency of the process seems to have created a lot of public appreciation and a sense of co-ownership with the participants (Van Hulst et al. 2016). The fact that people could monitor the writing of the constitution, that they were regularly informed, that they got personal emails from the members of the Council in response to their suggestions and comments, could have contributed to the perceived legitimacy of the design. It created a sense of responsibility for the document in the entire population, including those who have not even tried actively to take part in the experiment, but, crucially, they knew that they could participate if they would have liked. The public appreciation is partly reflected in the result of the referendum where the yes camp won 67% of the vote and on every issue.

Tushnet (2015) has some doubts in relation to the co-ownership. He thinks that constitutions drafted by laypersons, who have no continuing interest in actually implementing it, may be defective because in the end they have no responsibility for the operation of the government or society they have been creating.

8.1.4 Results

During the first three phases, the people of Iceland have had quite some influence on the process, but in the last decision-making phase, citizen involvement was strongly reduced. The strategy of writing a draft constitution through crowdsourcing could lay claim to legitimacy. Still, it is not possible to track back the input of participants to the final draft. *"We can only find out because members of the Council tell us so, but there is no archive of any sort. It is all anecdotal. The only thing we know for sure is that there has been a deliberative process in the Council itself"* (interview with researcher).

The Constitutional Council's strategy was to let the parliament vote on the proposal before they had to resign in March 2013. This was important because the Iceland constitution can only be changed by a majority of two successive parliaments. After the election, another second vote by the new parliament could take place. However, contrary to the parliamentary procedures, the draft constitution was never put to a vote, so it never went into effect. The final outcome ran up against considerable resistance from institutionalised political circles, for example, on the provision on public control of the natural resources.

Gylfason (2014: 29), member of the Constitutional Council, notes in his article: *"Even so, in a direct affront against democracy, Parliament hijacked the bill as if no referendum had taken place. It is one thing not to hold a promised referendum on a parliamentary bill [...]. It is quite another thing to disrespect the overwhelming result of a constitutional referendum by putting democracy on ice as is now being attempted in Iceland by putting a new constitution already accepted by the voters into the hands of a parliamentary committee chaired by a sworn enemy of constitutional reform as if no referendum had taken place. Parliament is playing with fire."*

It is only until recently that a new constitutional reform is announced by the new government. Possibly, elements of the earlier crowdfunded draft constitution will be used in this new process. However, since the link with the formal political process has never been made in the process from 2009 till 2012, Edwards and De Kool (2016: 52) are still right, when they conclude: *"This makes the Iceland case study a significant example of the tension that can arise between representative democracy and participative democracy."*

8.2 Future Melbourne Wiki: A Strategic City Vision by the Community

8.2.1 Introduction

In 2007, the City Council of Melbourne, Australia, decided to replace its strategic vision for the city with a plan drawn up by the community: The Future Melbourne project. Starting March 2007, six visions for Melbourne—a city for people, a creative city, a prosperous city, a knowledge city, an eco-city and a connected city—were drafted in cooperation with several stakeholders such as community groups, academics and civil society organisations. This draft was then published as a wiki webpage. Consultations were organised: First, 2 weeks in which changes in the document were made by specific stakeholders, followed by a month of public consultation in which the wiki was open for anyone to edit. Various meetings and events were organised to gather input for the document, making the project a combination of on- and offline community activity, taking place over the course of 18 months.

The City Council, consisting of nine members supported by an urban planning management team, initiated the plan (Kang 2012). The aim was to enhance community collaboration on the future of Melbourne, to create a plan that had "*a political buy-in, not only from an electoral point of view but also from an institutional point of view*" (interview with initiator), by engaging the whole community: citizens, institutions, businesses and organisations. The Council was the first in Australia to incorporate e-democracy practices in policymaking. All activities, both on- and offline, were funded from the Council's budget (Melbourne Planning Committee 2008).

The Future Melbourne Reference Group was established to manage and critically monitor the process, consisting of prominent ambassadors from Melbourne. The city's urban planning team's role was to service this leading group (interview with initiator). Various groups of people were actively invited to provide input via a range of events, such as public meetings, roundtables, Internet forums and exhibitions sponsored or organised by the Melbourne City Council. The final method of participation, to publish and edit the outlines of the plan on a wiki, can be seen as a form of crowdsourcing for policymaking (Van Hulst et al. 2016).

The wiki was made using the open source application TWiki. It consisted of two components: pages on each vision of the draft plan and a chat page for each wiki page. This made it possible to edit the content and to discuss the content and the edits made. For editing the document, registration with an email address was necessary. All contributions throughout the process and outcomes of offline activities were fed back into this wiki by City of Melbourne officers (Kang 2012; van Hulst et al. 2016). "*The wiki played a very particular role at the end of the project as a vehicle to transparently do a final edit and publish the plan in a way that it was accessible*" (interview with initiator). A dedicated Future Melbourne Wiki team answered questions by participants, corrected errors of facts made in edits, linked citizens to relevant documents and updated participants on events and developments concerning the project. An evidence library was added so that contributors could reference their edits and a "*Do-it-yourself community meeting kit*" (interview with organiser) could be downloaded from the library. It explained the process of organising a community meeting, and it included forms for collecting and filing input into the library. These options helped to integrate on- and offline processes and bridged larger geographic distances in collaborative processes.

The use of a wiki sparked some controversy within the City of Melbourne administration, as it was perceived as a threat to some employees within the administration and a risky mode of communication for the city. The initiators' response was to suggest it would be just another layer to the process, not a substitute to any part of the normal urban planning process (interview, organiser). "*What we said to council was, 'you don't have to agree to this plan. [...] All you have to do is acknowledge that this is a plan by the community. And in future when the council starts to take actions that have a strategic component, it will use this as a resource.' So, we split those processes*" (interview with initiator).

8.2.2 Participants

The City Council sought contributions of the citizens of Melbourne, but also welcomed input by a broader community (Kang 2012). During public consultation, the website received around 30,000 page views. The draft was visited by over 7000 unique visitors in 1 month. And 131 members of the public registered to edit the contents of the plan and collectively made several hundred contributions to the draft (Collabforge 2009). The Post Implementation Review of the project reveals that of the 129 registrants of whom demographic data was recorded, 59% were men (Collabforge 2009). Of participants that made changes to the document, an even larger share was male: 88% (Van Hulst et al. 2016). Over one-third of the users were aged between 27 and 35, but most changes to the wiki were made by participants between 36 and 45 years old. There is no data on the socio-economic status of participants.

Most edits were not made by the public though, but by City of Melbourne officers. They were responsible for around 60,000 views and made 11,500 edits (Collabforge 2009, van Hulst et al. 2016). This is a substantially larger share than the several hundred edits made by citizens during 1 month of public consultation. For the officers, the wiki was open for editing for a longer period of time. On the other hand, the officers acted as messengers, transferring input from meetings and events with stakeholders and citizens into the wiki (Van Hulst et al. 2016). Using a direct-editing tool such as a wiki works as a filter, the interviewed organiser notes: *"If you have an idea and you have enough energy and interest and understanding to demonstrate your idea in context by going in and editing a strategy document or a policy document, that's pretty high on the ladder of engagement. And so, out of your total base of engagement, there is only a small subset who's going to ultimately take up that opportunity. [. . .] It acts as a filter and it filters out a lot of the noise in many respects."*

The Future Melbourne project approached issues of access and engagement using several strategies. Local library staff was trained to offer support and the wiki was enhanced with translation options. Content could immediately be translated into seven out of ten most spoken languages in the Melbourne area (Collabforge 2009). There was also an online help function or personal assistance by City of Melbourne employees during business hours. Community engagement sessions were organised for community representatives and leaders, helping them to engage in the plan and to edit it.

The project was advertised through the city's regular communication channels, such as the website and newsletters. The main newspaper ran a series for 6 weeks, monitoring the process (interview with initiator). Officers of different departments were also asked to engage "their" stakeholders in the city, to ensure all the various sectors of the community would get to know the process and the opportunities it offered. Mark Elliott, owner of Collabforge, the organisation involved in designing the wiki, indicates that perhaps the process was not promoted enough: *"A key problem was coordination between internal units at the City of Melbourne; key* units whose role it was to promote the opportunities to participate weren't fully supporting or understanding of the online wiki component" (Van Hulst et al. 2016).

An analysis of the wiki views shows spikes of activity towards the end of both the public consultation and the stakeholder engagement periods (Collabforge 2009). As the interviewed initiator states, *"What we didn't want – and we did end up getting some of this unfortunately—is officers [...] writing down what they thought should happen. And so it was a mixture. It wasn't a pure result in the end."* Better targeting and inclusion of "normal citizens" would have strengthened the process, according to the interviewed researcher, as would better training in how to use the tool.

8.2.3 Participatory Process

The wiki was the principal means of online participation. Here, the draft plan based on (offline) stakeholder engagement was published. Citizens had several ways of participating: reading and monitoring the document online, making changes to the text in the wiki, discussing the draft through the wiki's discussion pages and face-to-face at the various events, and co-writing on envisioned scenario's for Melbourne's future, a process assisted by author Steve Bright. The only condition to participate online was a working email address (Van Hulst et al. 2016). The interviewed organiser states that the main strength of the tool is the shift it creates in participants' mindsets, *"from a critical outlook—do I agree with this?—to a constructive frame of mind—how can I improve this?"*.

The wiki was one part of a larger participatory process. The strategy of the process was to build the collaborative community organically, incrementally increasing the number of participants and opening the tool to larger groups. But initially only a few stakeholders took the chance to participate in the consultations. *"I think that was because, at that time, people did not understand what the opportunity was. [...] Most of them just used the traditional channels"* (interview with organiser). This was partially solved by taking a proactive approach. *"They [City officers] would take a laptop around. And they might go to one of the major universities and speak with the vice chancellors and talk through where the plan was at, at that point. And as they were getting feedback they would just start writing and either feed that directly into the wiki, or as a comment in the wiki to come back to. And then they were able to just tell them: 'This is how we're writing it. Everybody has access to it. You can have access to this later if you want to go and correct what I'm saying, but I'm just putting it in on your behalf right now.' And just right there, that was a big breakthrough... It's almost like the community sentiment started to shift right there with that. [...] And just that opportunity changed the way people thought about the organization that was running the consultation"* (interview with organiser). Van Hulst et al. (2016) also indicate that a strength of this project is the possibility of directly contributing to texts.

The subsequent phase was the public consultation of 4 weeks in which the wiki was opened up to the public for editing. This was supported with offline meetings and events. This combination between on- and offline participation made this project most successful (interview with researcher). The wiki provided the means for large-scale offline consultation to work. *"Face-to-face engagement is [...] much richer. But it is just not scalable, and that is the key issue"* (interview with organiser).

During the public consultation period there was no clear ownership of the document and no clear assessment of the proposals put forward (Collabforge 2009). *"Last one in gets final say [...] isn't a very constructive collaborative process"*, stated one respondent (Collabforge 2009: 7). One city department *"literally waited until ten minutes before midnight on the deadline to go in and make their contributions that they'd already planned, so that nobody could change what they'd put in there, basically"* (interview with organiser). No rule was established on deleting input either. One respondent stated: "It was hard to put so much time and work into contributions, just to see them deleted without knowing why" (Collabforge 2009: 9). This also impeded negotiation on contributions. Another issue was the lack of transparency on who was editing. It was unclear whether individuals were editing on behalf of a larger organisation or not. And as only an email address was needed for verification *"in theory, all changes could have been made by the same person"* (van Hulst et al. 2016: 31). A "neutral" point of view or a jury would have been helpful to mediate the different vested interests (Collabforge 2009). However, *"the role of the moderator then becomes quite powerful. Who moderates the moderator?"* (interview with researcher).

After the public consultation, the draft was shaped into a presentable form by city officers. Many of these edits were about making sure the final document read as if it had been written by a single author. Issues of privacy and security were hardly addressed, perhaps because around the time of the process (2007–2008), online safety and privacy was not as big an issue as it is these days (interview with researcher). No abuse was reported (interview with organiser).

8.2.4 Results

Including a wiki in the development of a new strategic city plan was innovative. The Future Melbourne project won the 2008 Victorian Planning Award and the 2009 President's Award, bestowed by the Planning Institute of Australia (Kang 2012).

The draft plan was published in the run up to the council elections, and a number of candidates and the new mayor then adopted several of the plan's principles for their electoral programme. When the new council was selected, it was already partially in favour of the Future Melbourne project, and it reformed their committee structure to echo the plan. All committees now fell under the header of "Future Melbourne committee". Councillor portfolios were to represent the different parts of the plan (such as "eco-city", "connected city" and "knowledge city"). This way, a large part of the plan was incorporated in the Council's strategic plan. When the council was re-elected after 4 years, they again incorporated many of the plan's ideas into their 4-year strategy. This meant the implementation of the plan effectively ran 8 years (interview with initiator).

In fact, the wiki component was essential to the political uptake of the plan, states the interviewed initiator: *"I think the wiki ended up being a very key component of the buy-in as much as anything because of the symbolic value that it brought to the process. The, if you like, slightly outrageous and outlandish transparency and empowerment that we were offering through that."* Respondents in the analysis by Collabforge (2009) state that as a collaborative tool the wiki was helpful in bridging organisational silos, to let the city's officers connect and communicate ideas.

Van Hulst et al. (2016) point out that the final plan was only assessed and accorded by the Council, but not by the citizens. There was no opportunity for them to indicate whether they still agreed with the final outcome of the plan. One respondent in the analysis by Collabforge (2009: 11) states: *"My big questions were, the work that I did, where is it going, how will it be considered and used?"* The City Council received many ideas for the development of the city through the public consultation process, but after reporting on some of these ideas in a news article on its website, it states in between brackets: *"Please note: There is no guarantee that all suggestions can be incorporated into the Future Melbourne draft plan. A number of the recommendations fall outside the City of Melbourne's areas of responsibility"* (Melbourne Planning Committee 2008). Expectations were also managed during the various offline meetings with the public, by being clear about the parameters of the process, for what the wiki was used and that the ultimate decisions on political issues was the responsibility of the Council (interview with initiator).

In many cases of online participatory processes, trust in government tends to actually decrease as a result of the lack of embedding the participation process and results in the decision-making process, according to the interviewed researcher. In other words, participants have their say, but don't see their opinions considered in the further process. Consequently, their trust in these processes diminishes. This wiki case seems to be an exception to the rule, as the online participation was well anchored in the rest of the decision-making, including monitoring and accounting for actions taken (interviews with organiser and researcher).

What helps, states the interviewed organiser, is if the document is "digital by default": The content created and edited must be the final work product. Which does not mean that the organisers do not have final say over the content, but that this must happen transparently and by way of dialogue. The wiki tool manages revisions, showing participants what has happened with their contributions. *"Participants readily accept the role that government must play when it is done openly and responsively"*, according to the interviewed organiser. Guidelines for participation ensure clarity on where responsibilities lie. *"So before somebody even is allowed to start, they need to tick a box which says: I understand the terms here"* (interview with organiser).

Despite its success, the wiki was not made a standard component in the urban planning process of the city. Drafting a new plan for the city in 2014 included public consultation, but this time without the use of a wiki (State of Victoria 2014; Van Hulst et al. 2016). The interviewed initiator states that the council did not want to start from scratch but only needed to refresh the plan. They wanted to do this in a much shorter timeframe. Instead of a wiki, a citizen's jury was formed to revise the plan into *Future Melbourne 2026*.

8.3 Predlagam.vladi.si in Slovenia

8.3.1 Introduction

Predlagam vladi is a Slovenian government-initiated e-participation platform which was launched on 11 November 2009. It is an Internet-based interface for petition-type proposals by citizens which seek to amend the current regulation in certain areas or matters. It is described as *"[...] the first practical attempts to institutionally democratise the link between the citizens and the Slovenian government through use of the Internet's emancipatory potential"* (Oblak- Črnič and Prodnik 2015: 100–101). The greatest potential of the tool is perceived to lie not in the area of political decision-making, but in the possibility of introducing socially relevant issues to the public sphere and contributing to rational opinion-formation. Seeing as the platform allows an exchange of opinions between Slovenia's citizens and policymakers at the state government level, it can be described as falling into the agenda-setting phase of the policy cycle (Predlagam vladi 2016a). During one of the interviews conducted within our study, an administrator of Predlagam vladi stated: *"[...] it is kind of a notification system on what issues are out there and what things do people think that we should change or what are the problems, so that bureaucrats and politicians are informed on even those smaller issues that don't get media attention [...]."*

While there is no option to submit suggestions offline within the Predlagam vladi structure, Slovenian citizens have the fundamental right to petition and are given the option to address their suggestions to the competent ministries or Prime Minister offline. The website is currently being managed by the Office for Communication (UKOM), with various ministries formulating responses to proposals. Governmental departments and agencies are obliged to respond to proposals submitted to them within 20 days by the order of the Government 38200-11/2009/9 dated 23.7.2009 (Predlagam vladi 2016b). It is currently entirely within the judgement of the government officials in which way input is incorporated, or whether it is taken into consideration at all (interview with researcher).

8.3.2 Participants

Within the first year of the website launch, a total of 2897 users registered. For the following 5 years the Government Communication Office reported 12,891 registered users (Offerman 2014). According to the interviewed administrator, the number of registered users is steadily increasing over the years: *"I would say that we see an increase in citizen participation when we have a change of government. I believe because the people are more hopeful that now maybe the new government will be more susceptive to their ideas [...]."*

In their analysis, Oblak- Črnič and Prodnik (2015) deem Predlagam vladi to have a demographically open and inclusive architecture, not technically limiting the participation of individuals based on age, gender or ethnicity. There is, however, a language bias, since the platform operates in Slovenian. During an analysis of Oblak- Črnič et al. in 2011, a sample of 218 users showed that almost a quarter were between 35 and 44 years of age, with 34% having a high degree of education, 30% a secondary school education and 10% a higher education (Oblak- Črnič et al. 2011). Data on representativeness concerning minority groups or the share of professionals participating is not available, seeing as personal data from the users is not collected.

Proposals are published primarily by individual actors. Only registered users can submit their own proposals, participate in discussions and vote on proposals. The data requirements for registration are quite low, with the system merely requiring a name, surname and email address. Seeing as the validity of names is not verified, there is no obligation to use real names. *"The only thing that we require is that they use a valid email [...]. At the beginning [we] were going with the idea that everybody should use their own name. [But then] how would we ensure that? Well, then they would have to use a government certificate that is issued by the government [...], but we didn't want to [introduce] any obstacles that would hinder participation [...]"* (interview with administrator). According to Oblak- Črnič, the portal could also be accessed through OpenID or Facebook accounts, describing the usage as "plain and simple" and *"suitable even for people with low computer literacy"* (Oblak- Črnič 2013: 416). Nicknames are used to identify users within the comment section and the vote casting, which contributes to a sense of anonymity (Oblak- Črnič 2013).

During the launch of the website, there were numerous press releases, press conferences and media reports made on the possibilities of participation. Currently no communication campaign exists specifically for the promotion of the tool. At one point there was a weekly 10-minute segment on national television in Slovenia, where a particular issue brought up on the website was discussed by a representative of the government or a citizen who drove the proposal. During the interview, the administrator explained: *"We felt that the media coverage that we got at the beginning was quite big and we were under the impression, that even if we spent ten thousand or twenty thousand euro for advertising, we wouldn't get the numbers that one media report gets in the evening news."* In the past, a banner and advertisement for the tool could also be found on the government website. It was reported that on average journalists will inquire about the statistics of the site about two to three times a year, in order to formulate a media report. According to an interviewed researcher, however, the general public is not sufficiently aware of the existence of this tool: *"I don't think the general public knows about the [tool]. I don't think it has been systematically promoted [...].*" They speculate this lack of systematic promotion may be tied to there not being enough staff to tackle an increase in workload.

8.3.3 Participatory Process

All registered users can post proposals for new government policies. The proposal can then be voted on during the course of 14 days, with other Predlagam vladi users being able to cast their vote in favour of or against the proposal. During this phase public deliberation takes place within the comments section and it is possible for the author to modify their original proposal based on this deliberation process. Governmental agencies can theoretically also enter this deliberative process (Oblak- Črnič 2013).

The ability to amend the initial proposal based on the forum deliberation was not initially provided, but is based on user feedback, as explained to us by an administrator: "*At the beginning we had two stages. One was the deliberation, or the discussion stage and the other was the voting stage. The difference was that once the deliberation stage was over, the user who proposed the suggestion could not change it anymore and so the editing of the proposal was then locked, and it was put to the vote. But we got the suggestion from the users that the voting could be started immediately, so now when the proposal is published by the moderator the users can comment on it and also vote on it immediately. The user who proposed the suggestion can still edit it, but if he or she does, then all the votes are deleted and all the users who voted on the proposal are informed by email that the proposal has changed, and they should vote again. The change, that was implemented on user request has simplified the voting procedure and resulted in a higher number of proposals being voted through*" (interview with administrator).

Moderators help initiators improve their proposals, for example, by applying keywords. They are in close contact with the relevant authorities for each proposal and get in touch with them when the proposal is launched with a request for active involvement. The moderators also judge the adequacy of the response of the competent authority (Oblak- Črnič 2013). The process of submitting proposals is described by the interviewed administrator as follows: "*When users send forward a suggestion it is not published immediately. We read it, and what we check is if we had a similar suggestion in the past. [...] There are two options then. If a similar suggestion is still under consideration and it is in debate by the users, we reject the second suggestion and reply that they should participate in the debate on this issue which is already going on, and we send them the link where they can participate. In the other case, if the suggestion was already answered by the Ministry under the current government, we [...] reject their suggestion and send the link to the [response] and invite them to read the [response]. If they still think their suggestion is different or if they still think that their suggestion should be put forward, [...] they should take into account the [response] and maybe amend their suggestion a little and we [will] publish it.*" The comments are also moderated. Seeing as they are posted in real time, moderation consists of checking whether the comments comply with the terms of use.

The proposal is submitted to the competent authority of the government of the Republic of Slovenia for an official response if at least 3% of users active in the last 30 days vote in favour of the proposal and if there are more votes in favour of than opposed. In the case of a positive response, follow-ups are posted annually or every 6 months on the implementation status of the proposal. In the case of a negative response, the users are informed that the procedure is finished, with an explanation as to why there will be no action on the suggestion made within the proposal (interview with administrator).

8.3.4 Results

Regarding transparency, the website itself provides data on the number of open topics and responses from the first year after launch, dating from 2009 to 2010. During our interview with a researcher familiar with the tool, we were informed that there are statistics on the number of open topics, which are sent to everyone recorded on an email list. Information on how many proposals ended up being effective, however, is harder to come by. The responses of the governmental bodies are all published online. When inappropriate comments are hidden, they are replaced by a message from the moderators explaining the reason for its removal.

Predlagam vladi offers fairly detailed statistics on the first year of proposals handled on the website, giving us the following insights: In less than 24 hours of the website going online, more than 80 proposals and draft proposals had been created. Between November 2009 and November 2010, a total of 1.201 proposals had been generated, 7.021 comments published and a total of 11.521 votes cast. Of these 1.201 proposals, 251 went on to be submitted for consideration to the competent government authorities, with 458 being rejected for not receiving sufficient votes. Other reasons for exclusion were, for example lacking concrete solutions to the matter at hand or being too similar to a proposal which already existed (Predlagam vladi 2016b). Within the first year there were 235 responses issued by the competent governmental authorities. On average these responses were sent within 23.9 days. A total of 11 proposals of the first year were ultimately successful in subsequent measures being taken.

One such successful example is the proposal for a reduction in the rate of value-added tax for baby diapers: On 9 March 2010, the Ministry of Finance supported the proposal and stated that it would be included in the following amendment of the Law on Value Added Tax. On 2 April 2010 this was implemented. Further examples of proposals which have been successfully implemented in some way are the proposal to upgrade the software of state administration computers to allow the viewing of . odf formats, a motion for a clear position on the pandemic flu vaccination, a proposal to increase the number of parking spaces for motorcyclists, a motion to be allowed anonymous votes on the Predlagam vladi website and a proposal to extend the voting time of Predlagam vladi from 7 to 14 days (Predlagam vladi 2016b). When looking at the successful cases from 2010, one can observe that many of these issues didn't have to do with policy changes but were related to software and the Predlagam vladi tool itself. It would be of interest whether the more recent successful proposals are of a similar nature. Additionally, some issues tackled in successful proposals were already present in the public sphere and part of discussions prior to being submitted to Predlagam vladi. It is therefore unclear whether it was the e-tool which led to a successful implementation or if the issues would have been implemented regardless (interview with researcher).

According to the website of Radiotelevizija Slovenija (www.rtvslo.si), Slovenia's national public broadcasting organisation, only 1.5% of 1505 responses from government authorities were positive by 2015. By the end of January 2015, a total of 13,088 users were registered with 5185 proposals having been submitted, 1748 of which garnered enough votes to be submitted to the competent authorities. Of these 1748 proposals, 1505 received a response. According to the report, half of the proposals were rejected on the basis of the proposed solution already being (or having been) in the process of implementation. Of the 1.5% positive responses, many were related to the accessibility of e-services (Cerar 2015). Many of the proposals are difficult to address, such as defining nuisance dog barking, the prohibition of church bells, the castration of rapists, a decrease of television commercials and the reimbursement of schooling costs by physicians who go abroad. This can help explain the low number of proposals receiving positive feedback from government authorities.

The interviewed administrator reported a total of around 35% of proposals being submitted to competent authorities, while the number of consequent actions taken by the government is very low, an estimated 40 out of 2000. Even if the response is positive, there are still further obstacles to overcome regarding implementation. An example of this was a case in 2009 where the decision was taken that the suggestion should be implemented, but due to the amendment being relatively small, it was decided to wait for a different matter to initiate the process of the law being opened and revised. In March of 2016, 7 years later, this finally happened and the suggestion from 2009 could be implemented. Bureaucratic procedures often hinder the realisation of positive responses in this way.

Something which managed to successfully increase positive responses from government authorities was the decision to endorse five or six proposals on a monthly basis: "*We at one point wanted to give these suggestions, before we send them to the competent ministries, a bit more weight. [...] What we did was, we, with the cooperation from the General Secretary of the government and the chairman of the Committee for State Order and Public Affairs, pick 5 or 6 suggestions monthly that we think are really good and that should be implemented, and then we put them forward to the committee and they discuss the suggestions. The committee consists of representatives of all the ministries*" (interview with administrator). These proposals are then submitted to the competent authorities, the idea being that they now carry more weight and are more likely to succeed. Interestingly, not only the success rate of endorsed proposals was raised through this method, but that of all proposals in general, indicating that the importance of the entire tool was raised in the eyes of the ministry representatives. Within a year the amount of positive responses received from government tripled compared to the six previous years (interview with administrator).

When there is a change in government, some users attempt to pass proposals which were previously rejected, a strategy which has proven successful in the past with a new government positively responding to a suggestion which had received a negative response before (interview with administrator). The same interviewee speculated that despite the high amount of negative responses, users appreciate the feedback the ministry provides, as it shows the ministry is giving adequate consideration to their suggestions. They point out that there is, however, no data available as hard evidence. The whole system is currently being upgraded, with the idea of presenting positive examples of successful proposals on the front page. This way it can be communicated that good suggestions can lead to implementation. The interviewed researcher was less optimistic concerning the government feedback: rather than letting the participants feel heard, they claim the responses are often perceived as standardised.

This interviewee also raised interesting criticism with the observation that the format of the tool was too open and the recommendation that it should be more structured with more information given on what kind of input the government wants from citizens. This of course goes hand in hand with limiting the scope of participation and bureaucratising the manner in which a proposal must be made. The interviewed researcher added that the open structure of the Predlagam vladi tool would not be an issue if there was enough staff which could process the ideas.

8.4 Participatory Budgeting in Berlin Lichtenberg

8.4.1 Introduction

After a large corruption scandal in 2005, the plea of civil society activists for participatory budgeting in Berlin was granted by the borough council that structurally implemented a participatory budget (PB) process in Berlin Lichtenberg. The instrument became part of a citywide administrative reform project to increase the effectiveness and efficiency of public spending (Röcke 2014: 133). The council formulated the following purposes for the PB: *"mutual agreement in policy decisions; effective and fair budgeting; transparency; and educating citizens about financial matters"* (Shkabatur and Fletcher 2016).

Increasingly PBs are employed in Germany, starting from 1 in 1999 to 14 in 2007 and on to 96 in 2013 (Ruesch and Wagner 2014). Most of them have the objectives to modernise local governments by participation and to become more responsive to the needs and wants of citizens. But they are no instruments for direct democracy. *"Citizens do not have the right to make a final decision, this is a consultative procedure"* (interview with administrator). The PB process in Berlin Lichtenberg thus concerns citizen involvement in agenda setting and providing concrete input for policy options.

The PB model was created in a workshop with policymakers, party foundations, civil society members and experts and was organised by the Federal Agency for Political Education. The basic structure of German Participatory Budgets has three phases (Ruesch and Wagner 2014):

1. Information provision about the budget and the participatory budget procedure
2. Consultation and participation of citizens, who contribute by making proposals, providing feedback on proposals and/or by making a planning of the budget
3. Decision-makers and civil servants explaining the outcomes of the process and justifying their decisions

The rules of the process in Berlin Lichtenberg are decided upon by the administration and the district executive. Some public meetings were organised to discuss the process and a group of organised citizens can put forward suggestions for changes in the process (Röcke 2014: 148–149). As in all German PB processes, the outcomes of the participatory process do not have a binding status and largely depend on the willingness of the borough council or citizen jury to adopt them (Van Hulst et al. 2016, interview with researcher). In annual reports effects of the PB and choices for or against citizens' proposals are justified (Van Hulst et al. 2016). Since 2012, the software applied by Berlin Lichtenberg is based on an open source software and adapted to the needs of the tool (interview with administrator).

The maintenance costs of the participatory budgeting are estimated by the former mayor: "*Each year Berlin's borough of Lichtenberg spends 60,000 euro on participatory budgeting. This is used for the Internet presentation, brochures and rentals of event space*" (Emmrich 2010: 69). The municipal budget that is opened up for citizen participation and consultation in an annual cycle is about 10% of the total borough budget. "*The budget in Berlin-Lichtenberg comprises 576 million euro, of which almost 90% are obligatory payments. This leaves 32 million euro as the subject of participatory budgeting*" (Emmrich 2010: 69). These discretionary expenses comprise: support of public health, business counselling, planning parks and free space, public libraries, general support for children and adolescents, cultural services of municipal institutions, the music school, voluntary services for elderly people, sports, maintenance of green spaces and playgrounds, planning of green spaces, support of the local economy and an adult education centre (Van Hulst et al. 2016; Röcke 2014: 198). Within this budget personnel costs are included, which makes the actual budget for PB much less.

8.4.2 Participants

The target group of the participatory budgeting in Berlin Lichtenberg which is described on the website is "everyone who lives or works in Berlin Lichtenberg". However, it doesn't seem to be verified if participants really live or work in

Lichtenberg unless they want to cast a vote (Van Hulst et al. 2016). The requirements to participate can be found on the website as the "Rules of the game". In the online discussions participants are encouraged to use their own name and surname, but it is not obliged. When participants propose a plan, they are obliged to give their contact details (interview with administrator).

From 2008 onwards a randomly selected group of citizens (10% of the population) receives a personal invitation letter for the public neighbourhood meeting signed by the mayor. In 2013, flyers with information about the PB in German, Russian and Vietnamese language are offered to inhabitants, which also included an invitation to make a proposal. Other flyers are designed especially for youngsters (interview with administrator). The researcher we interviewed states that next to these flyers, decentralised meetings in particular were an important way for community workers to reach people with a wide range of interests, backgrounds and experiences.

Different channels for communication and interaction were used for the whole participatory budget process, which enlarges the possibilities for different groups of inhabitants and employees in the area:

- The website (in German), including a blog, a section for praises and criticism, an agenda with events, an online voting tool (and its results) and a link to the total budget overview in xls.
- Offline information by a newspaper and possibility to write letters and proposals.
- Community centres that organise public meetings and can be reached by phone. In addition, childcare is provided during every public meeting and a sign language interpreter is present.
- Local borough coordinators spread information on participatory budgeting proposals.

This multichannel approach and the timeline with short information about the decision-making process around the proposal are used to increase the user-friendliness and accessibility of the PB process.

Despite these measures and the positive reviews, there is still room for improvement: "*I think here the problem is that it's a bit too formal, too technically sophisticated, but not really anchored in a sort of political activism or community activism of really going out, getting to the people, getting them involved. [...] I think this kind of political communication and inclination of why this is important [and] what change it makes [...] is probably missing a bit*" (interview with researcher).

Röcke (2014) reports not a very large mobilisation of citizens participating in the whole process (online and offline), but the "digital turn" increased the number of participants every year. In addition, Lichtenberg profits from a growing participatory culture: "*We have the luck and the good conditions in Lichtenberg of a high willingness of citizens to participate. Participatory budgeting is just one component of citizens' participation*" (interview with administrator). However, participation always depends on time restraints and personal interests (interview with administrator). Although the participation process only attracts a small part of the population, the main goal is to collect good proposals for the neighbourhood. Assessing preferences among a high number of participants is therefore not the most important requirement for a successful process.

Not much research has been done about characteristics of participants and whether PB in Berlin Lichtenberg is inclusive. *"The fact that participation is based on self-selection often excludes the less well-off residents of Lichtenberg. The under-represented groups include immigrants, elderly residents, uneducated residents, and young families,"* suggests Van Hulst et al. (2016: 42). Shkabatur and Fletcher (2016) report on Participedia.net that *"Participants were mostly young and middle-aged citizens of up to 50 years old, with a level of education higher than in the general population."*

8.4.3 Participatory Process

Participants can make proposals to spend money, to save money or to make proposals that do not entail costs for the discretionary budget. Participants can formulate proposals worth a maximum of 1000 € for activities or facilities in the neighbourhood. Since 2008 participants can also make proposals regarding construction investments in the district (of around four million euros) and neighbourhood projects that are provided by voluntary associations but financed by the district (Röcke 2014). The proposals can be put forward in written form, via the Internet and at neighbourhood assemblies (Röcke 2014: 145, interview with administrator). The process runs both on- and offline. *"There should always be parallel means. Because not everyone is comfortable with just one way [of participating"* (interview with administrator). Most proposals on the Internet are formulated in only one to three lines, without links, further justification or elaboration (Röcke 2014). Participants can also make comments on proposals of other participants, vote on a proposal and write blog posts.

To aggregate and weigh the proposals several strategies are combined. Participants make a list of the project proposals in an order of priority within public meetings organised in the 13 neighbourhoods. The next step is that the lists with the five priorities of the 13 neighbourhood meetings and the top ten from the Internet "vote" is sent as a survey to a representative sample of the population (50.000 randomly selected households) (Röcke 2014: 145–146). The respondents are asked to make their own list of five projects that they perceive to have most priority. Successively, the district council and the Parliamentary Committees make the final decisions on the allocation of the budget, which they explain in a public meeting (Röcke 2014). The citizen jury decides upon the allocation of the neighbourhood budget proposals (Van Hulst et al. 2016). Proposals that do not fit the established budget can be rejected by the district council or it can be decided that people may vote on it (online or offline). If there are sufficient votes in favour of the proposal, the district council considers whether the proposal is financially feasible, and it will be implemented (Van Hulst et al., 2016). Feedback on the implementation of the proposal or an explanation of the rejection is provided per proposal.

Participants can monitor the decision-making process online. The proposals are shown on the website and their status is indicated with the help of a three-colour system. Green indicates that a proposal has been carried out, red for a proposal that has been rejected, and yellow for a proposal that is still under discussion. This contributes to the user-friendliness, but sometimes proposals have the status of "under discussion" for quite a long time: in that case it's not clear for participants what will happen to these proposals (Van Hulst et al. 2016). In addition, *"the whole process is monitored by a committee (Begleitgremium) composed of around 15 people (civil society representatives, civil servants and politicians)"* (Röcke 2014: 145). The understanding of the participatory and political processes by Lichtenberg citizens has matured over time.

The tool gives the possibility of interaction and exchange of views. Van Hulst et al. (2016) only found a maximum of 15 comments on a proposal, which limits the diversity of views exchanged. Also, in the public meetings participants mainly focus on their individual wishes and an overarching perspective and assessment of the budgets is not attained (Röcke 2014). *"A rather weak point is this facilitative discussion aspect—to really have an informed discussion about why do we take this decision and not another one"* (interview with researcher). The interviewed administrator also affirms that participants not often use the possibility to interact or discuss proposals, and the organisation wished that would happen more often. This functionality will receive more emphasis in the near future (interview with administrator).

The website displays information on data protection: What data is saved, what it is used for and how it can be protected. It is an issue with the organisation, but no abuse has been reported so far (interview with administrator). Sometimes they check whether proposals are put forward by "real" people. But no hacks or influencing of voting outcomes have occurred (interview with administrator).

8.4.4 Results

In June 2016, the website counted 821 proposals since 2005, from which 426 proposals have been implemented. Although the participatory budgeting is consultative, it is quite influential on the decisions made (Ruesch and Wagner 2014: 12). For each proposal a brief account of the government is available online that explains why a project is or is not yet achieved or pending, which becomes visible by just clicking on the title of a proposal. Decisions are explained and evaluated in public meetings as well (Röcke 2014, interview with administrator). The participatory budgeting committee also has the task to discuss the evaluation of proposals with the participants (interview with administrator).

In addition, an annual accountability document is published on the website. However, Röcke (2014: 148) is quite critical on this form of accountability, because she saw many examples of only very short, simple rejections. This is an important concern, as most procedures in Germany are consultative and citizens do not make decisions concerning implementation; accountability is crucial for German PB. Without sufficient feedback on the final use of their input in budget planning, citizens are not motivated to invest their time (once again) in participating. This process of accountability can be further developed in the design of the online tool for participatory budgeting. Ruesch and Wagner (2014: 10) point to another example of PB in the city of Bonn, whereby means of visualisation of the overall structure of the municipal budget is presented in an understandable way for the public.

Röcke (2014: 134) concludes that the selected approach is "*technically sophisticated, but citizens have hardly any procedural and political powers in the process; in addition, the process of accountability is not very well developed*". On the other hand, she concludes that the procedure has led to a greater dialogue between citizens, officers and politicians, although the deliberative quality of the procedure could be better (Röcke 2014: 149f.). At least this process works in a way that it increases politicians' trust in citizens: "*[The administration] now also sees that citizens have expert knowledge, and that decision-making is not just based on files produced behind a desk. And that the triangle of politics, administration and citizens has already worked in other contexts*" (interview with administrator). The tool did receive the European Public Sector Award and the Theodor Heuss Medal (Ruesch and Wagner 2014: 12).

The costs of the maintenance of the participatory budgeting are 60.000 euros; however, high costs for personnel are not included here. We cannot make a harsh judgement on the cost-effectiveness. The (former) Mayor Christina Emmrich argued PB leads to a win–win situation: "*The citizens gain more transparency, a say on the budget and requirement-suited priorities and they see they are taken seriously. Political bodies gain objectivity and higher quality of budget-political discussions, more legitimacy and more identification of citizens with the community. The administration gains more information and proximity to the people, as well as more transparency in the setting of priorities*" (Emmrich 2010: 69).

As stated earlier, Lichtenberg seem to have a participation culture. Throughout the years, it has been shown to citizens that they can participate in various decision-making processes. "*This has a positive effect: it motivates [to participate]*" (interview with administrator). Increasing trust in government by obtaining legitimacy for decisions and making the decision-making process more transparent was the motivation from the start, she further elaborates. But whether PB has in fact had this effect on local citizens is hard to tell (interview with administrator). The interviewed researcher sees the potential as well, but agrees it is difficult to assess: "*I think it [is] a really well-organised, transparent process, which clearly states the different roles and duties and rights of the different stakeholders in the process. And which also gives information on where the money comes from, where [it goes], what we do with it and why. So I think that maybe it's more in the potential way. It has the potential to increase trust. [. . .] But if this actually is the case is another question*" (interview with researcher). Those who participate in these types of processes often already have a certain level of interest in politics, "*So it is very difficult to reach those who have lost any contact with the political atmosphere*" (interview with administrator).

8.5 Internetconsultatie.nl

8.5.1 Introduction

In the Netherlands, the official governmental website www.internetconsultatie.nl has been built as a platform to organise online consultation in the national legislative process. The public is consulted about draft bills, general orders in council, ministerial decrees and policy notes. E-consultation is part of the preparatory stage, the stage before the Council of State assesses the legislative proposal and the parliamentary debate about it.

The first e-consultations took place in 2009. After 2 years, the experimental e-consultation procedure was evaluated. The positive evaluation led to a structural implementation of e-consultation within the legislative process. The aims of the official website for online consultation are to increase the transparency of the lawmaking process, to offer new opportunities for participation and to improve the quality and practical feasibility of laws and regulations (website). The site has a function for "monitoring citizens" (van den Hoven 2005) (and monitoring organisations) as well. There are a lot of people that visit the site without contributing to the online consultation but only look for information about legislative proposals. Before, the lawmaking process was a black box and the consultation often included only a limited group of organisations they always consulted (interview with two administrators). An official procedure to consult individuals and organisations did not exist.

Two administrators of the Ministry of Security and Justice have been the main initiators and organisers in the past. Later on, most of the ministries were involved in the development and use of the tools (interview with administrators). One of the two originators is still responsible for the management of the website. For the specific consultations administrators involved with the specific legislative proposal are in charge. The website to consult the public is used by different ministries. As of our reference date (October 2018), 1036 online consultations have been completed (Internetconsultatie.nl). The House of Representatives has used the site only ten times to consult the public.

The website shows all online consultations that are running in chronological order. The user can look for specific topics via the search function, which results in a list of running and closed consultations. Clicking on a specific consultation leads to information about: the aims of the legislative proposal, the target group(s), the expected effects, the aims of the consultation, the procedure of the online consultation, a link to the proposal and sometimes links to additional information on the subject (as policy documents, parliamentary documents or even media articles).

In another click one can participate in the online consultation. Sometimes specific questions are formulated around the legislative proposal; in other cases the general question "what do you think about this proposal" is posed. One can participate by providing a response to the question(s). In the next screen, participants are invited to upload their own document with their reaction on the legislative proposal. One can skip one of these two. In the third step, participants are asked for their name and email address and if they want their reaction to be published.

8.5.2 Participants

In principle, the target group is as broad as the Dutch population, private individuals as well as staff of businesses and civil society organisations. More specifically, the target groups of actors that are affected by the particular legislative proposal naturally vary amongst proposals. The e-consultation is especially directed at groups of individuals and organisations beyond the "*usual suspects*" that would normally be included in consultation processes of ministries (interview with two administrators).

Broek et al. (2016) record more than 17.000 public contributions of participants in e-consultations from 2009. The actual number of contributions is, however, much higher, because visitors can decide whether they want their response to be published or not (Ministerie van Veiligheid en Justitie 2011). The number of responses per bill differs considerably and depends in part on the subject, the anticipated effects of the bill and the stakeholder groups that are affected by the legislative proposal. On average around 20—public—reactions per consultation are measured by Broek et al. (2016). Most—public—reactions seem to be placed in relation to legislative proposals around education (Broek et al. 2016: 41–42). A survey among users of the site ($N = 171$) showed that the group of participants consists mainly of highly educated individuals and that white males dominated the group of participants (Broek et al. 2016).

It is not allowed to respond completely anonymously in the e-consultation. Participants are obliged to enter their name and email address (which can only be used once). The official Digital Identity system of the government is not used. The administrator explains that they (the organisers) sometimes wonder: "*Shouldn't we do more to check a person's identity, with regard to security? That is, I think one of the issues that do ... At the same time, our main goal in an internet consultation is collecting ideas and it does not really matter if the ideas are offered by let's say Shelwin or the grocer at the corner.*"

The name of the organisation or initials of the individuals, their last name and place of residence are published on the website unless participants object against the publication of their input (website internetconsultatie.nl). Publication could be an obstacle for people or organisations with relevant specialist knowledge to participate if they don't want to share the information publicly with their competition. For instance, "*tax issues are always sensitive issues*" where confidentiality is often appreciated. And, "*in economic affairs, the know-how is often located outside the ministry. So, if you want to come up with legislation to bring to an end certain trends or developments in the industry people within that industry know more about that than people at the ministry*" (interview with researcher). With regard to this input confidentiality is clearly appreciated, but the public and parliament do want to know what information has been included from whom in the formulation of the legislative proposals and request publication. The confidentiality has thus become controversial.

Communication strategies show enormous variation in the different trajectories of legislative proposals (Broek et al. 2016). In some cases, there was no publicity at all; in other cases specific organisations that are contacted via letters, emails, phone or social media as LinkedIn are used. Social media are not only used to gain attention, but also to organise and stimulate an interactive discussion with citizens and professionals around the policy issue. For example, social media have been employed to engage individuals and organisations to discuss proposed regulation around drones or proposed regulation about energy (Broek et al. 2016). However, these interactive strategies are only used once in a while. The website internetconsultatie.nl itself is not interactive at all.

In general, the communication and engagement strategies to involve particular target groups can be strengthened, conclude Broek et al. (2016: 74). The administrator argues this is largely a task that must be tailored for every specific proposal (interview with administrator). She also stated that they work on a connection of the e-consultation site to the website that provides more information on legislative processes, which is "*a system of a legislation calendar where you cannot only see 'this is a bill and it's in this phase of the procedure' [but] that you can also see when an e-consultation is organised, and which consultation responses are entered to that proposal. That would enable people to follow the different phases of the legislative process*" (interview with administrator). This has not been realised yet.

8.5.3 Participatory Process

Participants can respond to proposed bills, general orders in council, ministerial decrees and policy notes by answering questions posed by the administrators involved or by raising questions or concerns themselves (with the possibility to upload their own document). Subsequently, participants can subscribe to receive information on the further process: "*Then you'll get a notification when a report is placed on the website or when the proposal is submitted to parliament or when it proceeds from the Lower House to the Senate*" (interview with administrator). It is unknown how many participants make use of this service.

8.5.3.1 Lack of Interaction

As discussed before, the website for the e-consultation doesn't entail possibilities to interact with stakeholders. Some administrators that apply Internet consultation feel a need for more interaction between participants and between participants and administrators, and participants feel this need even more (Broek et al. 2016). In contrast, most administrators involved would rather see interaction in earlier stages of the legislative process than in the phase of the online consultation. Broek et al.

(2016: 75) note that a general strategy with regard to interactivity would probably be undesirable; this needs to be deliberately decided upon per consultation.

The researcher in the interview suggests that a categorisation of reactions can stimulate interaction and the quality of the contributions. *"I actually think that the dialogue that would arise if people see their reaction to the site, that others see the reactions and some kind of interaction could occur, then I think that would lead to a much richer result"* (interview with researcher). Earlier reactions may inspire other participants, the researcher argues, and this could lead to a kind of co-creation. However, the administrator has her doubts in relation to such moderation. She questions whether such moderation could be done neutrally—without steering the discussion in a certain direction—and whether capacity within the ministries can be reserved to moderate such interactions (interview with administrator).

8.5.3.2 Interpretation of the Input

Procedural conditions are formulated about the Internet consultation process. These procedural requirements range from securing privacy to communication targets: that actors who might be affected by new regulation should receive information about the consultation and participants should receive feedback about the results. The requirements could be further improved and complemented, Broek et al. (2016) argue, on how to process the input. Some civil servants feel the need for a clearer assessment framework for taking the decision to deploy Internet consultation or not.

The input is interpreted by the administrators involved with the particular legislative proposal. How the input of participants is handled depends on contextual factors like the number of reactions, the quality of the input, the administrators involved and the time available to process the input (Broek et al. 2016). Sometimes an organisation is invited to the ministry on the basis of its input to further discuss the issue (interview with administrator). Further procedures could make the processing of input more solid.

The process of interpreting the input is not always publicly clarified by the administration. And although the goals of different consultations vary, the researchers question whether this interpretation process is as professional, systematic and methodically sound as it can be. *"I spoke with someone who said 'I got 1100 responses, I went to my boss and asked 1100 comments, how many do you think I can process per day?'. I think that's an example of a totally non-systematic approach. But others say, no you just get 1100 or some number of responses and you are going to read these one by one but you will first cluster these reactions, are these from organisations and individuals; in supporting and not supporting reactions; new arguments or existing arguments. Others said we put everything in an Excel file and then we deal with them systematically before we read them in detail. I think it's important that other ministries would do that as well"* (interview with researcher). Hence, one of the recommendations in the evaluation of Broek et al. (2016: 74) is a professionalisation of the interpretation method with which the input of all participants is handled. More attention is needed for a systematic procedure to process the input, for the analysis and the interpretation. Civil servants at the ministry need to have these research skills.

8.5.4 Results

The results of the participatory process are somewhat ambiguous. On a positive note, participants, as well as administrators, do indicate that Internet consultation contributes to the transparency of and participation within the legislative process. The transparency of the legislative process has increased, as argue 87% of the administrators and 65% of the participants surveyed by Broek et al. (2016). Moreover, in the studies of 2011 and 2016 two-thirds of the administrators evaluated the contribution to the quality improvement of legislation positively; they received useful input via the e-consultation. At the same time, the administrators indicate that often little room exists to manoeuvre: not much can be done with the input of participants, since the proposals are already seen as almost finalised.

Although the policy is to structurally e-consult legislative proposals, the researcher and the administrator question this default. *"That leads to several ministries thinking 'well okay then, but then it shouldn't be too complicated [for us]. We just throw it on the site with a general question and then we'll see"* (interview with researcher). The administrator of internetconultatie.nl confirms that civil servants within different ministries want to "tick the box" within the legislative process, without seeing the utility. Moreover, public consultation is not always that appropriate, as for technically complicated juridical law proposals or the implementation of laws, as the researcher suggest: *"That can sometimes be really hard ... Firstly, to consult about it because there is not always a lot of room to manoeuvre."* And secondly, with regard to the time schedule: *"The European Commission has of course penalties for non-timely implementation which are considerably high, so the government has made special arrangements to deal with implementation proposals more quickly"* (interview with administrator). Internet consultation could frustrate this tight schedule.

On the side of the participants, they feel that they do not have that much insight into what has been done with their input. Often a report about how the input of the e-consultation has been used in the legislative process is missing (Broek et al. 2016: 76). However, the output of the e-consultation process is often described in the explanatory memorandum alongside the legislative proposal for parliamentary debate, though the reflections in the memorandum are not always as elaborate and transparent as they could be. The extent to which it is explained how the participatory input is exactly used varies considerably. And participants are not always able to find this information themselves. It is thus understandable that participants have great doubts about the impact of their contribution on the quality of laws and regulations (Broek et al. 2016: 64). In an earlier evaluation this was also a point of concern. Often quite some time elapses before the website report on the most important results and the changes made to bills as a result. *"Participants indicate that participation should be rewarded, for example by ensuring that responses are published on the site without delay" (Edwards and De Kool* 2016: 42). *"From the perspective of learning processes, the system can be considered as too slow. People respond, but [information about] what's been done with that reaction reaches them way too late. [. . .] I think you can learn so much from the dynamics of that process, around which a dialogue should be organized*" (interview with researcher).

References

Broek, S. D., Kats, E., Van Lakerveld, J. A., Stoutjesdijk, F. D., & Tönis, I. C. M. (2016). *Doelrealisatie internetconsultatie*. Den Haag: Wetenschappelijk Onderzoek- en Documentatie Centrum.

Cerar, G. (2015). *Ali bodo predlogi državljanov vladi (še) bolj uslišani? Radiotelevizija Slovenija*. Accessed 18-01-2019, from https://www.rtvslo.si/slovenija/ali-bodo-predlogi-drzavljanov-vladi-se-bolj-uslisani/358413

Collabforge. (2009). *Future Melbourne Wiki post implementation review*. Accessed 12-10-2018, from http://www.futuremelbourne.com.au/wiki/pub/FMPlan/WebHome/Future_Melbourne_Wiki_Post_Implementation_.pdf

Edwards, A., & de Kool, D. (2016). *Digital democracy: Opportunities and dilemmas. The Dutch Parliament in a Networked Society*. Den Haag: Rathenau Instituut.

Emmrich, C. (2010). Mayor of Berlin-Lichtenberg (Germany): Participatory budgeting in large cities: Berlin-Lichtenberg. In: InWEnt gGmbH. *Dialog global 24. International Congress on Models of Participatory Budgeting. Documentation*, pp. 67–69.

Gylfason, T. (2014). *Iceland: How could this happen?* CESIFO Working Paper No. 4605. Accessed 12-10-2018, from https://notendur.hi.is/gylfason/cesifo1_wp4605.pdf

Gylfason, T., & Meuwese, A. (2016). *Crowd-sourcing vs. vested interests: The derailment of Iceland's new constitution*. Edward Elgar Publishing.

Kang, H. (2012) *A comparative study of e-democracy practices in Australia and in South-Korea*. PhD thesis. University of Canberra.

Kok, A. (2011). Icelandic national forum 2010. *Participedia*. Accessed 12-10-2018, from https://participedia.net/en/cases/icelandic-national-forum-2010

Landemore, H. (2015). Inclusive constitution-making: The Icelandic experiment. *The Journal of Political Philosophy, 23*(2), 166–191.

Melbourne Planning Committee. (2008). *Future Melbourne 2020 Draft Plan – Planning committee report*, 6 May 2008. Accessed 12-10-2018, from https://www.melbourne.vic.gov.au/about-council/committees-meetings/meeting-archive/meetingagendaitemattachments/40/740/pc_56_20080506.pdf

Meuwese, A. C. M. (2012). *Grondwetsinnovatie in IJsland: Het vervolg*. TvCR, pp 440–449.

Ministerie van Veiligheid en Justitie. (2011). *Kabinetsstandpunt internetconsultatie wetgeving: Resultaten van het rijksbrede experiment internetconsultatie wetgeving*. 5698502/11/6.

Oblak- Črnič, T. (2013). *Idea(l)s on e-democracy and direct online citizenship*. Southeastern Europe. L'Europe du Sud-Est.

Oblak- Črnič, T., & Prodnik, J. A. (2015). Online deliberation between the weak and strong public sphere. *JeDEM, 7*(1), 99–116.

Oblak- Črnič, T., Prodnik, J. A., & Trbizan, N. (2011). Deliberation and online participation: The case of the Slovenian portal "I propose to the government". *Journal of Comparative Politics, 4*(2), 90.

Offerman, A. (2014). *Slovenian portal allows citizens to participate in government decision making.* Accessed 18-01-2019, from https://joinup.ec.europa.eu/community/epractice/case/slovenian-portal-allows-citizens-participate-government-decision-making

Predlagam vladi. (2016a). *About the Project. (Google Translate)* Accessed 18-01-2019, from https://translate.googleusercontent.com/translate_c?depth=1&hl=en&ie=UTF8&prev=_t&rurl=translate.google.at&sl=auto&tl=en&u=http://www.vlada.si/teme_in_projekti/predlagamvladisi/o_projektu/&usg=ALkJrhiB6bJcaDuHvKOs4Y9nDhAzazF5dg

Predlagam vladi. (2016b). *Statistics Project. (Google Translate)* Accessed 22-10-2017, from https://translate.google.at/translate?hl=en&sl=sl&tl=en&u=http%3A%2F%2Fwww.vlada.si%2Fteme_in_projekti%2Fpredlagamvladisi%2Fstatistika_projekta%2F&sandbox=1

Röcke, A. (2014). *Framing citizen participation. Participatory budgeting in France, Germany and the United Kingdom.* London, New York: Palgrave.

Ruesch, M. A., & Wagner, M. (2014). Participatory budgeting in Germany: Citizens as consultants. In: Dias, N. (ed). *Hope for democracy: 25 years of participatory budgeting worldwide* (pp. 287–300). A more extensive version of this paper retrieved from: https://www.internationalbudget.org/wp-content/uploads/Ruesch-Wagner-PB-in-Germany.pdf. Accessed 12-10-2018.

Shkabatur, J., & Fletcher, S. (2016). *Participatory budgeting in Berlin-Lichtenberg.* Participedia.net http://participedia.net/en/cases/participatory-budgeting-berlin-lichtenberg. Accessed 12-10-2018.

State of Victoria. (2014). *Plan Melbourne.* Accessed 12-10-2018, from https://www.planning.vic.gov.au/policy-and-strategy/planning-for-melbourne/plan-melbourne-2014

Surowiecki, J. (2004). *The wisdom of crowds: Why the many are smarter than the few and how collective wisdom shapes business, economies, societies and nations.* London: Little Brown.

Tushnet, M. (2015). *New institutional mechanisms for making constitutional law.* Harvard Public Law Working Paper. No. 15-08. Consulted via SSRN: http://ssrn.com/abstract=2589178 of https://doi.org/10.2139/ssrn.2589178. Accessed 12-10-2018.

van den Hoven, J. (2005). E-democracy, E-contestation and the monitorial citizen. *Ethics and Information Technology, 7*(2), 51–59.

Van Hulst, M., Cuijpers, C., Hendriks, F., Metze, T., Leenes, R., & Hoekzema, D. (2016). *Digitale empowerment van de demos. Een onderzoek naar aansprekende e-democracy innovaties.* Ministerie van Binnenlandse Zaken en Koninkrijksrelatie.

Websites *(Accessed 12-10-2018)*

http://stjornlagarad.is/english/
http://www.futuremelbourne.com.au/wiki/view/FMPlan
https://www.buergerhaushalt-lichtenberg.de/datenschutz
https://www.buergerhaushalt-lichtenberg.de/info-material
https://www.buergerhaushalt-lichtenberg.de/spielregeln
https://www.facebook.com/Stjornlagathing/
https://www.internetconsultatie.nl
https://www.internetconsultatie.nl/veelgesteldevragen

Open Access This chapter is licensed under the terms of the Creative Commons Attribution 4.0 International License (http://creativecommons.org/licenses/by/4.0/), which permits use, sharing, adaptation, distribution and reproduction in any medium or format, as long as you give appropriate credit to the original author(s) and the source, provide a link to the Creative Commons licence and indicate if changes were made.

The images or other third party material in this chapter are included in the chapter's Creative Commons licence, unless indicated otherwise in a credit line to the material. If material is not included in the chapter's Creative Commons licence and your intended use is not permitted by statutory regulation or exceeds the permitted use, you will need to obtain permission directly from the copyright holder.

Chapter 9
Formal Agenda-Setting (European Level)

Gloria Rose, Ira van Keulen, and Georg Aichholzer

Abstract Rose et al. introduce four digital democratic tools which serve or have served to support formal agenda-setting on the European level (European Citizens' Initiative, Futurium, Your Voice in Europe, and European Citizens' Consultations). The authors place a strong focus on the participatory process and practical experiences. For a better understanding of these tools and how they are used in practice, interviews were conducted with administrators and researchers familiar with the respective tools. Strengths and weaknesses are identified and possibilities for improvements explored. While each tool shows positive results in different ways, their impact in terms of policy tools leaves much to be desired. Lessons learnt include the need to communicate clearly what input is desired from the participants and transparency about what outcomes can be expected and how the collected input is utilized. The tools must also be flexible enough to adapt to user feedback in order to provide for a learning process to take place.

9.1 European Citizens' Initiative

9.1.1 Introduction

The European Citizens' Initiative (ECI) is the first supranational instrument of participatory democracy in the European Union. The purpose of the ECI is to allow citizens to participate directly in the law-making process of the EU, giving citizens—under certain conditions—the opportunity of inviting the European Commission to legislate on a matter through the submission of a proposal. Currently this is the only tool granting EU citizens such a right (Lironi 2016: 34).

G. Rose (✉) · G. Aichholzer
Institute of Technology Assessment, Austrian Academy of Sciences, Vienna, Austria
e-mail: gloria.rose@oeaw.ac.at; aich@oeaw.ac.at

I. van Keulen
Rathenau Instituut, The Hague, The Netherlands
e-mail: i.vankeulen@rathenau.nl

© The Author(s) 2020
L. Hennen et al. (eds.), *European E-Democracy in Practice*, Studies in Digital Politics and Governance, https://doi.org/10.1007/978-3-030-27184-8_9

The key condition is that a million participants of at least seven Member States support an initiative by means of their signature within 12 months after its registration. Signatures can be collected offline as well as online through digital collection systems certified by national authorities in Member States. In order to sign a citizens' initiative, one must be an EU citizen and of voting age concerning European Parliament elections. Support forms are verified by the respective competent national authorities (EC 2016b). Initiatives which have reached the signature goal are then examined by the European Commission within a timespan of 3 months and a decision is made on whether or not the initiative warrants legislative steps to be taken. During the examination phase organizers are granted the opportunity to appear at a public hearing in the European Parliament to present their initiative. While there is no legal obligation for the EC to propose legislation, they must justify their decisions within a communication. This communication must detail how the Commission will proceed and what actions will be proposed (if any), and explanations for the decisions are given. It is made available in all official EU languages and adopted by the College of Commissioners (EC 2016c). The Europe Direct Contact Centre offers information and assistance concerning ECI rules and procedures in all EU languages, with over 1080 questions having been processed according to the 2015 Report from the Commission (EC 2015a).

Between the launch of the ECI and our analysis conducted in January of 2017, there have been 59 submissions to the EC. Only three of these were successful in terms of reaching the signature goals and proceeding to the next phase of the process, namely: "Right2Water", "One of us" and "Stop vivisection". Concerning the use of online channels, the "Right2Water" initiative collected up to 80% of its statements of support online, the "One of us" initiative merely around 30%, and "Stop vivisection" around 60% (EC 2015a: 7). At the time of analysis, four of the initiatives were still open. A total of 20 initiatives were refused for registration, of which 18 gathered insufficient support, and 14 initiatives were withdrawn by the organizers. Since the conclusion of our study, a fourth initiative, "Ban glyphosate", has successfully reached the required number of statements of support.

9.1.2 Participants

In general, the structure of the ECI appears to favour existing civil society organizations above individual citizens (Organ 2014), despite the fact that organizations cannot run a citizens' initiative. Civil society organizations are, however, permitted to promote or offer support for initiatives if this is done in a transparent manner (EC 2016c). The most common promoters of initiatives are well-established organizations with the aim of promoting a very specific policy and European organizations promoting public participation in EU policymaking in general (such as the King Baudouin Foundation or environmental groups such as Greenpeace). The third most prominent type consists of companies and organizations representing business interests with a specific focus on the health sector (see also Greenwood 2012: 333).

A fourth group consists of EU officials and representatives that use the ECI in order to raise attention to issues already being discussed in the EU.

Concerning the signatories of initiatives, no data are collected by the Commission concerning demographic information such as level of education regarding specific ECIs. The collection of statements of support is carried out by organizers of initiatives. The ECI Regulation provides inter alia for the specific rules on the procedures and conditions for the collection of statements of support, including the information to be provided by signatories for the different Member States, and the protection of personal data (ECI Regulation 2011, Articles 5 and 12). While consequently no specific observations can be made by the Commission regarding the representativeness or share of professionals supporting specific initiatives, it is commonly believed that ECI participants tend to be well educated with a high interest in EU matters. General information on the ECI instrument, also regarding awareness, participation and socio-demographic data, has been collected for the ECI as a whole via Eurobarometer Surveys (c.f. Flash Eurobarometer 430). Overall over 6 million people have participated in the ECI to date (interview with Commission official; see also EC 2015b). Despite there being no data on representativeness, the fact that the ECI is an offline and online tool makes it reasonable to assume it is more widespread and can reach out to certain groups which would not be reached exclusively through online means. *"The offline campaign for the ECI is very strong, especially on the national level. I know of organizers who were really going to different events, trying to reach out to different groups physically and not only virtually. [...] If the organizers want to reach out to minority groups, there is a possibility to do so with a tool like the ECI"* (interview with researcher).

Responsibility for raising awareness, collection of statements of support and mobilization of support for specific initiatives primarily lies with the initiator of an ECI. The Commission carries out information and awareness-raising actions on the ECI instrument. Information on the specific initiatives is provided via the ECI official website. State of play on ongoing initiatives is also provided as part of the Commission awareness-raising and communication actions. When asked about current efforts to improve this situation and raise awareness of the ECI, the Commission mentioned inter alia the ECI official register and website dedicated to this purpose which provides comprehensive and updated information on the ECI available in all EU languages (website accessed 18.01.2019). The Commission also provides the Guide on the ECI available in all EU languages and provided free of charge by the Commission both online and in paper version (website accessed 18.01.2019). The Commission is also working on several actions for awareness-raising on the ECI instrument, and also cooperates for instance with the European Economic and Social Committee (EESC), the Member States authorities in the ECI Expert Group and the EC Representations in the Member States in communication actions. In order to increase representativeness civil society events such as the ECI Day are being organized by the EESC. The Commission participates in this event and cooperates with the EESC in several ECI-related actions. There are also increased cooperation and synergies with the "Europe for Citizens" Programme (interview with Commission official).

According to the Report of the Commission from 2015, the ECI register has offered over 300 translations in total, with the average initiative being available in 11 languages and four initiatives offering translations in all official EU languages at the point of the Report being written (EC 2015a). Since April 2015, the EESC provides direct assistance to ECI organizers via translation services, which include the translation of the 800-character ECI submission text in all EU languages for all registered ECIs. Organizers can submit the request to the EESC to translate the main elements of their ECI (i.e., title; subject matter; main objectives; and relevant EU Treaties provisions) and then can submit these translations to the Commission for its validation and publication in the ECI official register. These translation services are therefore available to all organizers of ECIs since April 2015 (interview with Commission official).

9.1.3 Participatory Process

In order to submit an initiative, EU citizens must form a "citizens' committee" which can then launch an initiative by registering on the ECI website. A citizens' committee must be made up of at least seven EU citizens of seven different Member States and the members must be of voting age in European Parliament elections according to their respective national law. The conditions for registering are as follows: the initiative must fall within a field of EU competence (e.g. environment, agriculture, transport, public health) and there must be a Treaty provision to serve as a legal basis. Once an initiative has been registered it requires a total of 1 million supporting signatures; additionally, a minimum number of signatures is required for each Member State, which must be reached for at least seven Member States (EC 2015a; Lironi 2016: 34).

An important possible restriction for participants is the fact that there is no available EU funding for citizens willing to start an ECI. In addition, ECI initiators often have to engage with legally qualified personnel, data protection specialists, fundraisers and marketing specialists (Greenwood 2012: 332). For transparency reasons organizers have to provide information on all financial sources exceeding 500 € per year and per sponsor (EC 2015a).

9.1.4 Results

An estimated 6 million people have participated in the ECI according to the Commission report on the application of the ECI Regulation of March 2015. The start of citizens' initiatives has contributed to participation at the EU level and the launch of pan-European debates. There is, however, clear room for improvement regarding the amount of initiatives which are successful in terms of reaching the one million signature goal (interview with Commission official). One of the main challenges of the ECI therefore lies in supporting ECI initiators in collecting signatures within the given timeframe. While the success rate of the ECI is not very high when measured in these terms, it can be argued that initiatives which fall short with regard to signatures can still have an impact, seeing as they can stimulate a debate on their respective subject matter (interview with Commission official). This sentiment was also shared by the interviewed researcher: "*I do think that it is not true that the ECIs, even the ones that did not reach a million signatures, did not have impact. [...] I know, for example, the [initiative] on water, even though the Commission didn't start any sort of logistical proposal on it, in some national countries such as Italy, the fact that the ECI existed and the fact that there was a debate going around it and the fact that people were campaigning for the ECI also made national politicians realize there was a problem. And they actually debated it in national government.*"

It could be observed that ECIs are expensive on part of the organizers, which consequently means that "ordinary citizens" are at a disadvantage. Over 100,000 € have been spent on initiatives passing the million signature mark (Malosse 2015) with the initiative "Water is a human right" having raised 140,000 € in support and funding, "Stop vivisection" having raised 23,651 € and "One of us" having raised 159,219 €. Sangsari (2013) points out the need for organizers to possess human and financial resources, networks, alliances, coalitions with civil society, media and NGOs in order to gather the promotion and awareness needed for success.

One of the most fundamental shortcomings of the tool, as perceived by interviewee 17 (researcher), is that the ECI is not cost-effective. Large investments are required, also in terms of organization, for relatively low rewards in terms of certainty of impact. "*It just requires too much effort to implement, design and everything, and it just gives the people very little impact [...] and a lot of frustration because they don't see where the results are going.*" While the information supplied by the ECI website itself is generally very good, the feedback of results to the participants is lacking, which can in turn contribute to a lack of visibility of impact and contribute to the frustrations of citizens. Currently the results of the ECI are not legally binding, "*[h]owever, most respondents clarified that 'binding results' do not necessarily mean a direct change in EU legislation because of a successful ECI, as it would both be undemocratic and lead to 'dangerous waters'. What they mean is that there should be more efforts by the European Commission to reach a binding follow-up, for example an inter-institutional debate on the ECI results*" (Lironi 2016: 47–48). As could be witnessed with the first three ECIs to reach the required support, the Commission has committed to a set of follow-up actions in response to two of these successful initiatives (these can be found on the ECI website, accessed 18.01.2019). Even if no legal outcomes are achieved, it can be argued that the legitimacy of the policy agenda can be increased through deliberation (see also Organ 2014).

It can be observed that the ECI suffers from a lack of presence. Many citizens have never heard of the tool, due to there not being much media coverage, with the level of awareness likely differing between Member States. Single initiatives and campaigns can become well known, while the underlying tool of the ECI remains unfamiliar to most citizens. The EESC carries out awareness-raising events such as the "ECI Day". Already in 2012, the Commission established a point of contact providing information and assistance, based in the Europe Direct Contact Centre. Through this point of contact it answers any questions from citizens on the ECI rules and procedures, in all official EU languages. As referred to in the report on the application of the ECI Regulation (March 2015), during the first 3 years of the ECI operation, the point of contact has answered over 1080 questions. The ECI Support Centre (a not-for-profit service and initiative of the European Citizen Action Service, Democracy International and the Initiative and Referendum Institute Europe) has also worked on the development of an Android smartphone ECI-App meant to keep people updated and raise awareness. The App allows users to sign initiatives via their mobile phones (ECI Support Centre 2016). These efforts also address another point of common criticism pertaining to a lack of user-friendliness. In order to sign an ECI, a number of personal data is required from citizens. This entails a strong discouraging effect, particularly in connection with the low expectations with regard to impact and security concerns. Thomson (2014: 74) states that every single campaign "*has suffered, often gravely, from a myriad of problems stemming from these data requirements*", referring to the large amount of personal data, for example ID card numbers, signatories have to submit when stating their support for an initiative. While the amount of information gathered from citizens is deemed "*excessive*", email addresses are not collected, making it difficult to provide feedback about the initiative. The issue of user-friendliness remains problematic, as the issue needs to be balanced with questions of privacy and security. New updates of the OCS are released regularly, with an adapted version for mobile devices and improved functionalities being expected already in 2017. In addition, the collection of data, which is considered to be a big stumbling block for would-be signatories, is decided by each individual Member State (interview with Commission official). Due to a lack of harmonization between different countries regarding identification requirements and signature collections, expatriates are often excluded from the online signature collection process. The Commission is working with the Member States on this issue and has launched a study in 2016 to assess the options for the simplifications of data requirements in the ECI context (interview with Commission official).

Another difficulty lies in the online collection system for signatures. The various technical and security requirements make this a challenge, though the Commission provides and updates an open source Online Collection Software (OCS) which organizers can use. The ECI Campaign offers an alternative software named OpenECI for signature collection (The ECI Campaign 2016).

After the conclusion of our study, the European Commission presented a legislative proposal to revise the European Citizens' Initiative on 13 September 2017 (EC 2017). A draft report of this proposal was published by the Parliament's Committee on Constitutional Affairs (EFCO) on 9 March 2018 (EP 2018). These proposed changes are not considered in our analysis of the ECI case study. If adopted, however, the proposed ECI revisions could entail several changes which could potentially impact the case assessment. A select number of proposed changes are as follows:

- The minimum age to support an initiative is to be lowered to 16 (art 2).
- The Commission shall establish an online collaborative platform with a dedicated discussion forum (art 4).
- The Commission shall provide the translation of content into all official languages of the Union for its publication in the register and its use for the collection of statements of support (art 4).
- Organizers can form a legal entity in accordance with national law (art 5).
- Clarification of the conditions of liability of the group of organizers (art 5).
- Partial registration of an initiative in cases where only part or parts of the initiative meet the requirements for registration (art 6).
- Organizers shall have the possibility to resubmit a revised initiative (art 6).
- The 12 months for collection of statements of support shall start with the beginning of the collection period determined by the group of organizers (art 8).
- Statements of support shall be simplified by providing only personal data set out in one of the Annexes (art 9).
- There shall be a central online collection system operated by the Commission for the collection of statements of support (art 10).
- Institutions and advisory bodies of the Union and interested stakeholders should have the opportunity to participate in the hearings of successful initiatives (art 14).
- Groups of organizers or the Commission should have the ability to collect email addresses for communication purposes (art 17).
- There shall be a periodical review of the functioning of the ECI at least every 5 years (art 24).

The changes are to apply from 1 January 2020. These changes would primarily impact the liability of initiative organizers, the provision of information and advice, the registration phase of initiatives, the minimum age to support initiatives, the signature collection phase and the review provisions. The Council of the European Union announced that it is ready to enter into interinstitutional negotiations on the legislative revision of the ECI on 26 June 2018. The Council supports the Commission's proposal in large parts but rejects the suggestion of lowering of the minimum age to 16 and suggests banning the use of individual online collection systems (Council of the European Union 2018).

Overall, after 5 years of existence, the ECI as an institutional innovation has certainly achieved some success in mobilizing citizens across Europe and thus in contributing to the formation of a European public sphere to some extent; however, it has achieved modest success at best as regards enhancing the citizens' influence on EU level decision-making to date. It would definitely be too pessimistic to conclude that the instrument has a predominantly symbolic function. The fact that the ECI offers citizens an opportunity to set the agenda at the EU level must be recognized as an important benefit. The EU institutions can profit from this citizen input, by gaining more insight into public opinion (Lironi 2016: 47). The promising signs of progress the instrument has shown within the most recent developments underline the democratic potential which it can further unfold in future. It is to some extent still an experiment with many open questions and it was therefore wise to include a clause for a possible revision every 3 years after a period of gathering experience with the new instrument. For now, it seems that the ECI's relevance is far greater in contributing to issue-specific discourse and citizen mobilization at the EU level than in terms of concrete policy-shaping impact.

9.2 Futurium

9.2.1 Introduction

Futurium is an e-participation tool developed by Directorate General for Communications Networks, Content and Technology (DG CONNECT) of the European Commission. They created it as part of "Digital Futures", a project that ran from autumn 2011 until December 2013. The first version of this participatory foresight tool stimulated citizens, businesses, public administrations, NGOs and professionals to reflect on possible futures together (not on existing policies) and aimed to generate ICT policy visions that could inspire strategic choices at the European level. At the same time, it was an attempt to respond to the growing demand for citizen participation in policymaking by implementing a so-called "Policy Making 3.0" model (EC 2016a) based on the metaphor of emerging collective intelligence. *"In opening Futurium to broad public participation, Digital Futures created an experiment in crowdsourcing policy foresight"* (EC 2016a: 20). Futurium is meant to substantiate the legal obligation for the European Union to consult society in general as mentioned in article 11 of the Lisbon Treaty.

In the first experimental phase Futurium used social networks, participatory engagement and an online foresight toolkit to facilitate policy co-creation. The model was based on four main ingredients:

- Futures: Visions of what the world might look like, and the associated challenges and opportunities.
- Policy ideas: Ideas for possible future policies co-created to realize a chosen future or vision.
- Evidence: Data used to provide scientific ground to visions and policy ideas (links, data, etc.).
- Events: Bringing people offline together to discuss particular futures or policy ideas.

The tool was supposed to combine *"the informal character of social networks, the simplicity of wikis and the methodological approach of foresights"* (EC 2016a: 5). At the moment, Futurium is serving a number of units at the Commission as a platform where new policymaking experiences can be conducted through both scientific evidence and stakeholders' participation (Lironi 2016: 39–40). The tool can be used to discuss ongoing trends or to simply gather input on possible future policies. In its transition to a regular EU participation tool, Futurium became less sophisticated as an interviewee (developer) notes: *"The new platforms are based on a much simpler engagement model than the very structured foresight approach of Digital Futures."* Other features of Futurium as mentioned in the final report of Digital Futures, such as *"knowledge harvesting tools for policy-makers and stakeholders, data-crawling tools to extract knowledge from social networks and data-gathering tools to fetch real world data"* (EC 2016a: 39) are not incorporated in the platform at the moment. Latter tools have been made available for the different DGs of the EC as a separate data analytics module called Doris (interview with developer). But as the interviewed developer states: *"Realising the Policy Making 3.0 vision of combining the opinions of the crowd with evidence coming from big data may require long term investments, which goes beyond the scope of Futurium."*

On the Futurium platform there are currently 15 areas ("engagement activities") where participants can share their ideas, ranging from contributions to the Urban Agenda or how to improve eGovernment services in the EU, sign a petition or cast a vote for the Innovation Radar Prize (November 12th 2018). Every engagement activity has its own topic, landing page, platform and selected tools. Many of these engagement activities also include offline meetings, feeding into the online discussions and vice versa. In this case description we will focus on two specific projects that used (Digital Futures) or are using (eGovernment4EU) Futurium as a tool in their stakeholder engagement activities.

Futurium is an open source project based on Open Source Drupal developed specifically for the European Commission. The tool is secured and there are corporate EC measures taken to protect the tool from misuse of data and hacking. The different platforms are only mildly moderated. The development of the initial tool itself costed around 100,000 € (interview with developer). The budget for maintenance, hosting and curation is not included in this amount.

9.2.2 Participants

Futurium has been host and still is host to (currently 15) different projects. At the moment more than 6000 people have registered at Futurium, which means they have been or are contributing to one or more of the projects currently running. The current projects—contrary to Digital Futures according to the interviewed developer—attract more than the usual stakeholders, for example, the experts on the subject who are otherwise also consulted by the European Commission.

Digital Futures was one of the first experiments by the European Commission in adopting a bottom-up, participatory process in a foresight project. From the final report (EC 2016a: 116), it seems the participants included mostly scientists, innovators, students and policymakers. The interviewed developer was quite content with the diversity of the participants: *"Digital Futures was able to capture everyone, students, the people in schools, teachers, also thanks to the accompanying in-person events. We were able to get on board people who had never heard of DG Connect."*

Following the initial experience with Digital Futures, other policy areas have also been using Futurium as a tool for crowdsourcing ideas for future policies. One of them is eGovernment4EU which aims to accelerate the digital transformation of government. The platform enables stakeholders to publicly exchange their views in an open, transparent way by proposing concrete actions for implementation. The target group includes citizens, stakeholder organizations and associations, IT companies working with and/or for public administrations. In 2016 about 230 people have subscribed to the platform and about 50 people have contributed (interview with Community manager; it is not clear from the website if these numbers have increased recently). One-third of them are professionals from public administrations; another third from associations, businesses or organizations working in the field. The other third are citizens (interview with community manager). The online activities are being complemented by in-person meetings. The participants of the current platforms like eGovernment4EU are self-selected and invited to participate.

The engagement strategy of Digital Futures was one of the success factors according to the final report. Every participant could invite friends and colleagues to be engaged in Digital Futures and every participant could host a Digital Future conversation on the platform. That way the initiators wanted to create a viral process. All the online and offline meetings of Digital Futures together involved over 3500 participants in more than 100 participatory brainstorming events (on invitation) throughout the project, including more than 30 webinars. The community built around the project consisted of more than 2000 members who actually subscribed to the tool. Online participants could sign up themselves for the webinars or give their input on the website (self-selection). The interviewed developer was less enthusiastic about the communication strategy: *"We were not experts in engagement. That was linked to the exploratory nature of the foresight project. It was via social media and in-person meetings and events that people came to know about it [...] I need to say that getting viral is a very hard goal, especially on policy topics and foresight. We learnt all of this with Digital Futures."*

The possibilities to participate on eGovernment4EU have been communicated through on-site workshops about the eGovernment Action Plan, news items at websites, different newsletters, social media (mainly Twitter), presentations and distribution of flyers and post cards at different events on e-government. They also tried to get certain NGOs interested and to have other institutions link to the platform. One of the challenges the community manager is taking up is trying to have national administrations, or even regional administrators, link from their website to the platform of eGovernment4EU (interview with community manager). However, the engagement has not been very high. One explanation might be that all the information on the platform is in English. The interviewed community manager also mentions that a lot of eGovernment initiatives take place at national, regional and/or local levels, so participants wonder why to put their ideas or best practices forward at the European level.

9.2.3 Participatory Process

Digital Futures had and eGovernment4EU still has both online and offline activities organized that enrich the consultation process. The community manager sums up the relevancy of the online part of the consultation: *"I think that one of the things an online platform offers is first of all the transparency of the process. That when you do it offline, people don't know exactly what has been done, they don't know who has participated and worked on the proposals."* The online participatory processes of Digital Futures and eGovernment4EU are explained below.

9.2.3.1 Digital Futures

There are five different ways in which participants could contribute to Digital Futures: co-creating visions and policy ideas, organizing events, attaching evidence and linking it to visions and policies, grouping people and content into communities and commenting on content posted by others (interview with developer). The input of participants was aggregated in different ways, for example by voting or according to keywords. In the exchange of arguments between participants the deliberative performance of the platform was optimal, but less between participants and decision-makers (interview with developer). The content on the website was more aimed at experts and moderately comprehensible.

After the consultation Digital Futures was finished, DG CONNECT organized three public workshops in 2015–2016 to collect best practices, ideas and feedback on how to engage with stakeholders online and how to shape the eGovernment Action Plan 2016–2020, especially through Futurium. In the report of this workshop (EC 2015c) some improvements are mentioned: add a status overview of the process and account for the follow-up of proposals, more social media options, better structured discussions, more feedback, identification of most active users, more gamification and differentiated voting. Some of the comments lead to changes in the design of the tool.

According to the interviewed developer the information on the decision-making process on Digital Futures was very clear: *"Because we said to the participants, you give us your vision, then you give us the policy ideas and any evidence, and then we will summarise and offer it as an input it in the context of the renewal of the commission."* Also *"every participant got an email with the final report"*. In the end, however, Digital Futures focused on the visions and less on the policy ideas because DG CONNECT wanted to retain their independent role and not anticipate on the ideas and plans of the new Commission.

9.2.3.2 eGovernment4EU

Participants can contribute to the eGovernment4EU platform in six different ways: express their needs regarding eGovernment services or propose a solution, start discussions about these needs or solutions which could help modernize public administrations using ICT, add documents to the library, start a poll, list an event or write a blog. Once an idea has been submitted other participants can also contribute to its definition or justification with their own input. The features "needs" and "library" are used the most, but participants are hesitant to list an event or write a blog (interview with community manager). The last entry in "needs/ideas" is from end of July 2018. There is not much activity going on. Discussion between participants is facilitated, but this functionality also has not been used for a long time. The last entry is from September 2017. In order to stimulate an evidence-based discussion Futurium allows participants to upload documents, statistics or data from any source to substantiate their proposal, solution or the discussion. Here the last entry is of January 2018, also quite a while ago. The platform also provides a number of datasets and tools for visualization. However, according to the community manager it might not be clear to all users why this option is there and how it works: *"The bigger purpose and functions are not very well explained, I think."*

The entire decision-making process of eGovernment4EU is presented in a flowchart and help in the preparation and assessment of a proposal is offered by putting up selection criteria. Every 6 months the steering board, consisting of representatives of the Commission and the Member States, should evaluate the proposed actions and decide which ones they will commit to in the Action Plan. Therefore, the core of the eGovernment4EU platform consists of an actions dashboard that lists the status of current actions. *"We [...] inform about the owners, their status of implementation, the due date, etc. It creates transparency on the state of play of each of the actions"* (interview with community manager). The latest update is however from May 2017. It seems that—although on the website it is stated that feedback on the proposals and what has been done with them is communicated through the platform—not much feedback is given lately. It is only in two blogposts (see Results) that some reference is made to "themes" based on ideas expressed on the platform that are taken up by the Steering Board.

9.2.4 Results

The Digital Futures campaign "A journey into the 2050s visions and policy challenges" lasted about 1 year, and produced within Futurium produced over 200 "futures", 35 interviews with high-standing experts and futurologists, and more than 1800 evidence library entries. The stakeholder engagement strategy also included social media presence on the major networks (Facebook, Twitter and LinkedIn).

The interviewed developer was very enthusiastic about the impact of Digital Futures: "*Many people were inspired by the participatory approach to open up foresight to potentially everyone. [...] Also, some of the challenges or opportunities identified by Digital Futures are nowadays becoming hot topics. For instance the prospect of a super centenarian society or that robots will take over jobs from humans.*" The evaluation report mentions valuable impacts (EC 2016a: 10–11). The 11 final themes provided interesting futures to inspire policy exploration and design. DG CONNECT services used these for example as input to prepare briefs for the 2015–2019 EU College of Commissioners. Digital Futures also contributed to major foresight exercises carried out at the EU level, such as the interinstitutional project European Strategy and Policy Analysis System (ESPAS) and the Horizon 2020s strategic programming exercise 2016–2018. In the third place, the project has "*helped building skills and capacities which has been re-used to support other initiatives within DG CONNECT and the Commission*". And in the last place: "*The Futurium platform has been adopted as a corporate platform as part of the EC-wide offering as well as by other institutions such as the Economic and Social Committee. Furthermore, the platform has generated the interest of several academic and industrial actors working on foresight and stakeholder engagement methodology*" (EC 2016a: 10).

According to the developer, one of the strengths of the tool is the possibility to structure conversation without making it complicated or tied to rigid structures and rules like in surveys. The tool has a possibility to summarize content using the most advanced data-related algorithm, the earlier mentioned Doris system. Other strengths, according to the interviewed developer, are (1) the possibility to download for free and use the tool by any public administration in Europe via the ISA JoinUp repository, (2) the possibility to integrate evidence stemming from real world (big) data into the policymaking process, and (3) the customizable participatory process that can be used to engage everyone in the policymaking process at any level.

However, the interviewed community manager thinks Futurium can be improved: "*I think it is not very attractive and also not very user-friendly in the sense that, some things are available, but they're not explained very well. [...] And I think that this is an issue not only for the Futurium platform but more at the general level for the European Commission website. And anyway, it's based on the European Commission look and feel. We cannot escape from that completely.*" The interviewed developer thinks the usability and functionality tool can be "*dramatically improved, but this may require governance decisions and time. Currently the tool implements only about 40% of the policy making 3.0 model*". But he also admits that the original idea behind the tool—a policymaking model combining evidence and participation—might be too ambitious and future-oriented.

In February 2017 the first ideas from the platform eGovernment4EU were presented at a meeting of the Steering Board. The board consisting of representatives of the EU Member States and EFTA countries is responsible for assessing—and ultimately select—the proposals for newly identified actions in the eGovernment

Action Plan (and coordinating the effective implementation and monitoring of it). In May 2017 new actions were added to the Action Plan but it is not clear from the website whether these new actions are originally ideas from the eGovernment4EU platform. In a blog post it is only mentioned that *"During its first cycle [of the eGOV4EU platform], more than 30 ideas were expressed, and four themes were picked up for further developments."* Again in February 2018 another set of ideas were presented to the Steering Board. In a blog post—including a PowerPoint presentation of the ideas—it was mentioned that *"Although many of the ideas need to be developed further to reach their full potential, the Steering Board agreed that they would like to look further into the following themes: implementation of the Once Only Principle, digital skills for civil servants, personal data management, public procurement for start-ups."* It seems though that no new actions have been added to the Action Plan since then.

9.3 Your Voice in Europe

9.3.1 Introduction

Your Voice in Europe (YViE) is the European Commission's "single access point" to a variety of consultations and feedback opportunities for citizens and various stakeholders which is now being integrated into the Better Regulation Portal "Contribute to law-making". The Commission aims to take into account views of citizens and stakeholders throughout the policy cycle, ranging from the conception of a new idea to the adoption and evaluation of a proposal. The YViE portal is also part of the Commission's minimum standards for consultation, meant to introduce better regulation and improve European governance (EC 2016d). Next to the open public consultations on Your Voice in Europe, the Better Regulation Agenda also provides citizens with the following opportunities to be part of the EU law-making process: they may provide feedback on roadmaps, inception impact assessments, legislative proposals and related impact assessments, express their views on how to make EU laws and initiatives more effective and efficient and share views on draft acts (EC 2016d, e).

Your Voice in Europe is a web portal initiated by the European Commission's Directorate General for Informatics (DIGIT) and was launched in 2001. As of January 2017, there have been over 880 consultations. Participants are invited to share suggestions within a questionnaire or to formulate their contributions in an open format. Depending on the context, the questionnaire is typically designed with a mix of closed and open questions. Exchanges via email are not standard and are limited to rare cases with high technical difficulty and a low expected number of expert replies (interview with Commission official).

The consultations are initiated by the Directorates-Generals (DGs), who determine the topic and the desired publics. The "Better Regulation" guidelines outline which topics require an open public consultation. It is the responsibility of the DGs to communicate the duration of the consultations, the minimum period being 12 weeks, and to provide feedback to the participants who were consulted (Badouard 2010: 104). In the past, the internal "unit culture" greatly affected how consultation inputs were assessed and the extent to which the consultations results were considered in a particular EU policy (Winkler 2007: 176). Since the adoption of the Better Regulation Agenda there is now clear guidance on how stakeholder input is to be processed. There is no censorship based on current policy lines; however, responses which go against the general values of the European Union will not be published. Responses which do not uphold EU values are rare, possibly due to the fact that opinions are not given anonymously (interview with Commission official).

The Your Voice in Europe tool is currently undergoing new developments with the aim of unifying the separate consultation pages. These are currently prepared and managed by the different Directorates using different templates (interview with Commission official). Furthermore, there are also plans to inform users about which targeted consultations are taking place. The interviewed Commission official described the new developments as "[...] a complete revamp of the way we interact with stakeholders. There will be and partly already is a complete new web-design and communication on consultations". Next to the consultations there have been feedback opportunities on roadmaps and Commission adopted proposals since last year. "These different feedback mechanisms and the consultations as we know them from Your Voice in Europe, they will all be integrated to one big portal that gives access to all the different types of consulting" (interview with Commission official). The first phase has been launched in June of 2016, with the integration of Your Voice in Europe being planned for 2017. After the conclusion of our study, the described integration of "Your Voice in Europe" into the Better Regulation Portal has progressed and the webpage is no longer actively using the name "Your Voice in Europe". It is instead titled "Consultations". In addition to these changes, a new data analysis tool named "Doris", developed by DG CONNECT, EC, is meant to assist in processing the textual input arriving in different languages. Doris has the ability to cluster words which are frequently used and group responses. While the program is not flawless, it assists the interpretation and analysis of the large amounts of incoming data (interview with Commission official).

While the guidelines of the general principles and minimum standards for stakeholder consultation of the European Commission state that input gathered through consultations should be analysed and contribute to policy preparation, "neither the general principles nor the minimum standards are legally binding" (Commission of the European Communities 2002: 9) and "the DG at the origin of the consultation reserves itself the right to consider whether a contribution is relevant or not" (Badouard 2010: 104, see also Badouard 2013: 156). Badouard concludes that the impact of Your Voice in Europe on the decision-making process is based on its institutionalization and the recognition as an e-government tool by the Commission. The guidelines also provide information on how to establish a consultation strategy, conduct the consultation work, inform policymaking and provide feedback among other things.

9.3.2 Participants

By definition the Your Voice in Europe tool only hosts open public consultations, with targeted consultations not being published on the page. Targeted consultations, workshops and conferences for very specific groups are being communicated outside of Your Voice in Europe. Despite only being for public consultations in principle, in practice hybrid questionnaires incorporating both elements can be employed: *"Sometimes it makes sense to separate the questionnaire into two parts. One part for the general public and then the second part being more technical, more detailed, usually only for expert stakeholders. So, there is a mix between a public consultation and a targeted consultation"* (interview with Commission official). Anyone is entitled to join public consultations as a respondent and may represent organizations and businesses.

A study dating back to 2009, undertaken by the French Economic Social and Environmental Council (ESEC), examined a total of 31 consultations which were held between September 2008 and March 2009. During these consultations 5553 replies were made, of which 18.5% were from public authorities, 46.5% from civil society organizations, 7.3% from research centres, universities and think tanks, 14.2% from individual citizens and 13.5% from businesses (Badouard 2010: 104, 2013: 159–160).

The home page of the website is available in all 24 official languages of the European Union, with around 25% of the consultation pages being available in all EU languages (interviewee, Commission official). Participants are therefore often required to possess English skills. In addition, many consultations are highly specialized, requiring the participants to have much knowledge and expertise on the subject (Badouard 2010: 104). One can observe that the more documents are translated into other languages, the more Eastern European participants will contribute and make use of the tool (interview with researcher). The amount of civil participation is expected to vary depending on the subject matter, with broad subjects or subjects relating to social issues inviting more civil participation than subjects of a technical nature (interview with researcher).

The consultations are not used as a tool to assess representative European views, as there is no way to ensure equal representation. Separate tools, such as the Eurobarometer by Eurostat, are used to fulfil this purpose (interview with Commission official). During our interview, the Commission official also mentioned that most big organizations can devote more resources to participating in a consultation, but it is much more difficult to gather individual responses from SMEs when dealing with policies which may affect small companies.

Typically, the possibilities to participate are communicated through interest representatives or civil society organizations, as well as on the Your Voice in Europe website (interview with researcher), and a notification system alerting subscribers of published consultations in the area of their interest (interview with Commission official). According to the interviewed researcher, particularly consultations on broad issues would benefit from media attention. For example, an association in

France placed an advertisement in a local journal asking for opinions for the "Public consultation on the European Citizens' Initiative" held from 2009 to 2010. This association then collected the responses and passed them on to the Commission. *"I think this kind of procedure is quite interesting because I don't think that the Commission has the power to target individual citizens that are far from the institution. [...] They can target some organization or association that [...] could be a relay to talk to people and to make them participate"* (interview with researcher).

Each Directorate is responsible for the communication strategy of their public consultation. *"Whenever the DG has to consult stakeholders, the DG is obliged to produce a consultation strategy, which so far didn't focus too much on outreach and communication [...] but it will do so more in the future"* (interview with Commission official). In order to reach out to minority groups or people living in remote areas in Member States there is a need for targeted action. When attempting to invite groups such as local farmers to a consultation, one can use methods such as making an announcement in the local press. The consultation itself will still be Internet-bound, seeing as it is not logistically feasible to print out the questionnaires.

9.3.3 Participatory Process

The highly specialized consultations clearly favour expert responses (Badouard 2010), but attempts are being made to design the questionnaires in a manner which allows participants to first answer more basic questions before getting to more technical questions (interview with Commission official). The process of introducing more user-friendly ways of designing consultations is difficult, requiring a change in mindsets (interview with Commission official). Training sessions to this end are conducted on a voluntary basis. Questionnaires are scrutinized by a team of 10–12 people before being published on the consultation platform, with the aim of increasing the quality of the questionnaires. Following complaints of visually impaired people the issue of accessibility is also being looked into.

The tool does not provide a forum for deliberation, with there being no space for interaction among a larger number of participants. When asked whether a more deliberative function would be desirable, the interviewed Commission official responded: *"I believe that the intention is to have replies being published instantly, which would basically allow the second person to have a look at the first person's replies and then make his or her comments accordingly or react to that. [...] There will be more of that, even though it is still very far from a discussion. But I'm not entirely sure whether the main aim of that tool should actually be about discussion. For that we have other ways of reaching out to stakeholders [...]."* In this context, feedback mechanisms, which allow stakeholders to instantly comment on roadmaps, inception impact assessments, delegated/implementing acts and legislative proposals early in the development, were mentioned.

9.3.4 Results

Your Voice in Europe is a participatory mechanism linked to the decision-making process; the goal is to gather views and evidence from stakeholders, including European citizens. It has the advantage of being institutionalized, meaning it is recognized by the Commission as an e-government tool for public policy (Badouard 2013). There is a duty to consult, but there is no legal obligation to use consultation contributions in any way. Although the general principles and minimum standards for stakeholder consultation do request consultations be analysed and contribute to policy preparation, they are not legally binding, resulting in the policy impact differing with political cultures within EU units as well as with policy intentions (Winkler 2007). A case study could, however, show considerable impact on a draft which was then sent to the Parliament and Council: *"Not only did the Commission consider propositions that did not support its views, it also changed its mind according to contributions, or developed half-way responses in order to take into account the advice expressed during the consultation"* (Badouard 2013: 158). Weaknesses of the previous propositions were exposed and relevant solutions proposed through the consultation. Seeing as the consultations mostly take place during the impact assessment phase before the final proposal is shaped, it is difficult to determine in retrospect how the final proposal would look like had the consultation not taken place (interview 24, Commission official).

Your Voice in Europe can boast several successes, such as the fact that various interest groups are represented in the online consultations. Access to EU-level consultation processes has also been increased for individual actors. All in all, participation through the web portal can be considered high and diverse with many different interests being represented (Quittkat and Finke 2008). According to Winkler (2007), EC experts reported a high quality of consultation contributions. *"[…] our analysis showed that most online consultations seem to be more than simple opinion polls. Yet, their quality as instruments of participatory policymaking varies with their format: especially consultations with open, albeit structured, questions offer real possibilities of participation, but participation rates are much higher when online consultations are based on (multiple-choice) questionnaires"* (Quittkat and Finke 2008: 218). A benefit of online consultation tools is also to be found within statistical evaluation opportunities at relatively low cost (Badouard 2010: 101; Winkler 2007).

Transparency, however, remains a big issue concerning the methodology chosen for consultation evaluation and a lack of feedback to the participants concerning their inputs (Researcher 26, see also Chalmers 2014, Quittkat 2011, Winkler 2007). All responses of the Commission are published on the website. Currently it is obligatory that each initiative has a consultation synopsis report summarizing the consultation outcome and including how different views were considered. Many of these reports are not yet available and are going to start gradually appearing on the website (interview with Commission official). Participants have in the past reported being disappointed and feeling "fooled" about the impact of their contributions (Winkler

2007), which may in part have been due to a lack of communication about what happened with their inputs, underlining the importance of transparency order to foster interest and trust in EU politics.

The amount of public input achieved is also not always as high as would be desired, this being related to how successful the choice and execution of a communication strategy is. "*[...] we would like to increase the number of replies and feedback we get. So what we are going to do is to work with our communication experts in the house to have a few case studies working on a few different types of public consultations and see how we can best promote them and which impact we have*" (interview with Commission official). The Commission official also emphasized the need to increase the response rate, noting that consultations which are promoted via social media or press releases show notably higher response rates: "*In general we need to improve or increase the response rate. On average we have about 400–450 responses for each consultation [...].*" There is also a connection between the participation of different sectors and their satisfaction with the process. "*For instance [...] if we do a consultation in the field of the finance sector, all main stakeholders, they know [the tool], they can easily participate, they know it exists, [...] so they may have a higher satisfaction rate than for instance when we do a consultation in the field of agriculture. A lot of farmers are a lot less used to internet or difficult to reach, and they may then rather complain 'we were not consulted' or 'we didn't know'*" (interview with Commission official). Also, the satisfaction rate of stakeholders who are present in Brussels is expected to be higher in terms of being able to participate.

A study by Kies (2016) identified four main issues with Your Voice in Europe, some of which have already been discussed above: lack of broad participation, lack of a forum for discussion with no space to "*foster the emergence of European public*" or "*promote a transnational political identity*", no education programs addressing knowledge gaps concerning EU decision-making programs and lack of information as well as incentives for citizens to participate.

All in all the Your Voice in Europe platform as the European Commission's "single access point" to a variety of consultations and feedback opportunities shows certain achievements as well as flaws and needs for improvement. It is recognized by the Commission as a tool for public policy which reaches out to a large number of potentially interested stakeholders and citizens, whose contributions are to varying degrees considered as one among various information sources in decision-making processes. It contributes to a level of accountability of the institution and there is some evidence of good quality in many consultation contributions as well as some impact on EU policies, favouring mainly the participation of civil society organizations rather than citizens. Main points for improvement are deficits in wider communication of this participation opportunity and involving the general public, more user-friendly and accessible web interface and consultation formats, more transparency of the use of contributions made and opportunities for exchange and deliberation among consultation participants.

9.4 European Citizens' Consultation

9.4.1 Introduction

The European Citizens' Consultations (ECC) were part of a "Plan D" (Democracy, Dialogue and Debate) launched by the European Commission in 2005. This plan was a direct reaction to the voters' rejection of the European Constitution. Plan D sought *"to foster communication and debate on the activities of the EU by addressing the need to listen to citizens' expectations"* on the future of the European Union. The plan contained six initiatives that had an online deliberative component. One of them was the European Citizens' Consultations in 2006–2007. This consultation process brought together more than 1800 citizens from 25 member countries on three topics chosen by participating citizens themselves: family and social welfare, environment and energy, and immigration and Europe's global role. The ECC was relaunched in 2009 under the Debate in Europe Program (2008) of the European Commission. In this case description we will focus on the 2009 initiative (ECC09).

The ECC 2009 aimed to be the first pan-European deliberative consultation involving the 27 Member States of the Union around the main question: *"What can the EU do to shape our economic and social future in a globalised world?"* The instrumental objectives—as mentioned in the evaluation report—were to promote interaction between citizens and policymakers, establish citizens as policy advisors and develop citizen participation as a policy tool for the future. The transformative aims were to close the gap between the EU and its citizens, to increase the general public's interest in the EU and to expand civil society networks across the EU, resulting in a more developed culture of active citizenship. The entire consultation was divided into five major phases which resulted in 15 shared propositions for EU economic and social policy in a globalized world:

1. In the first phase, that lasted from December 2008 until March 2009, all European citizens were invited online to discuss and elaborate proposals on what role the EU can play in shaping our economic and social future in a globalized world. The web portal consisted of one general European website with basic information and access to national websites.
2. In the second phase (March 2009) two days of group deliberation, meetings with experts, debates with (candidate) Members of European Parliament (MEPs) and voting were organized in each of the 27 Member States. The aim of this consultation round was to choose and elaborate on the 10 best propositions for action at the EU level at each national event.
3. In the third phase (April and May 2009) the generated 280 propositions were rephrased into 88 recommendations and divided into different domains (economy, employment, social policy, health, etc.). These recommendations were presented at each national website and all 1635 participants were asked to vote online or by mail for the 15 most interesting recommendations.

4. The fourth phase was a European Citizens' Summit held on May 10-11 in Brussels. About 150 citizens who took part in the national events were invited, reviewing their own 15 recommendations once more before handing them over and discussing them with top EU policymakers.
5. The final phase consisted of four thematic conferences (climate change, health, education and poverty) which took place in France, Ireland, Denmark and Slovakia. Citizens—also from neighbouring countries—were invited to discuss the final recommendations with newly elected MEPs.

In almost all phases of the consultation online and offline actions were combined. Each national website had the same structure: one information section (with texts written by a professional journalist), one debate section and one proposal and voting section. A web-based deliberation tool called VoDoO (Voting and Documentation Online) was used during the national consultations. The online discussion was moderated, allowing the moderator to delete messages without leaving any traces visible for the participants. Next to the moderator, somebody was responsible for outreach activities, encouraging stakeholders like political parties, NGOs and political bloggers. to participate in the online discussion or advertise the ECC project with banners on their own websites. The entire process was managed by the Belgian King Baudouin Foundation and a consortium of 40 European civil society organizations, foundations, universities and think tanks. The budget of 3.8 million euros was financed by 40 European charitable trust organizations and co-funded by the EC.

9.4.2 Participants

The target group of the ECC09 were the European citizens in general. In order to make an active contribution they were required to register at their national ECC09 website with a valid email address. They could still participate anonymously (interview with organizer and researcher). At the same time, people could easily register multiple times and no special attention was paid to security or privacy issues. A second interviewee (organizer and researcher) does not object to that: "*It is not like an important vote. It is just to give your opinion.*"

In the first online phase, this system of open and self-selective recruitment "*created strong opportunities for interest groups and networks organized online to affect the outcome of the online consultations*" (Karlsson 2012a: 14). At the same time Badouard argues that the successful online mobilization of activist networks across national borders contributed to an important goal of the project: producing a European dynamic and transnational public in "spaces of creative action" (Badouard 2010: 107).

In order to obtain a demographically diverse group the second phase of national consultation started with a randomized selection process on general quotas for age, gender, professional status and region. Fifteen percent of the total budget of the

ECC09 was spent on the recruitment of 1600 participants by professional recruitment agencies. There was no specific method to include minorities like disabled people. Kies et al. (2013: 132) mention that there was a lot to be desired when it came to the representativeness of the national consultations, since there was over-representation of people who were "*highly educated, politically interested, and pro-EU*". Only 3.8% of all participants were EU-sceptical, which "*produced an outcome that reflected what a predominantly and, in close to half of the cases, exclusively EU-positive body of participants recommended*" (Karlsson 2012a: 12).

Especially in the first phase an engagement strategy was important to get the target group of the ECC09—the European lay citizens—mobilized. An interviewee (organizer) reckons that "*it is always a system of auto-selection and it is difficult to captivate the interest of people for things they would not naturally [do]*". The online communication campaign was especially successful in mobilizing EU-friendly networks and institutional websites that are visited by a well-educated public already familiar with European matters. In order to attract its target public, the lay citizens, "*the online phase could be improved by reinforcing the advertisement of the project among categories of the citizens who are generally not interested in (EU) politics*" (Kies and Wojcik 2010). Kies and Wojcik also argue that a collaboration between the mass media (in particular TV) and the Internet proves to be most effective to involve new citizens in the political process.

During the online consultation the web portal and national websites had almost 150,000 unique visitors, 29,536 registered users from January until May 2009, resulting in 5640 postings and 1142 proposals. Each national site received an average of just over 30 different visitors per day. In the second phase each national consultation had between 30 and 130 participants, involving a total of 1635 European citizens. In the third phase the broader European public was originally intended to be allowed to vote. Out of fear for organized groups being able to sway the voting, the organizers decided to only give a vote to the participants from the national consultations. In the end only less than 60% voted, caused by the absence of Internet for some users as well as a decreased interest after the consultation process. Kies et al. (2013: 62) also add: "*It could also be that the organizers underestimated the knowledge and capacities required for expressing preferences on such a large number of specialized proposals.*" The citizen summit in Brussels was attended by a selection of 150 representatives, selected on the basis of age, gender and nationality and also on the basis of proficiency in English.

Members of European Parliament and candidate MEPs were also participants in the consultation process of ECC09. Interestingly, according to Karlsson (2012b: 95) the online engagement between politicians and participants showed much more signs of cooperation than in the national offline deliberation, where they were polarized into the roles of producers and receivers of recommendations by the design of the project.

9.4.3 Participatory Process

In the first phase, participants could (1) post ideas or suggestions for a proposal for others to vote on, (2) take part in a debate about a proposal and (3) vote for (but not against) a proposal on their national websites. At this stage no transnational exchanges were possible (Badouard 2010). An important incentive for people to participate online was that the 10 most voted propositions were going to be discussed during the national face-to-face consultations. In total 1142 proposals were produced, which were distributed unevenly among the countries. Many proposals did not relate either to the topic of the consultation or to the EU. Among the most popular proposals we find environmental issues, drug legalization and the introduction of Esperanto as a work language in the EU (Kies and Wojcik 2010: 10).

Reviewing this online phase, Kies et al. (2013) conclude that some participants were very active, but over 80% were so-called lurkers who only read and voted on the proposals but did not get involved in the online debates. According to a survey these debates were in general reflexive and respectful with insightful and intelligent contributions.

In advance to the second phase, factsheets on the goals and intentions of the EU with regard to several social and economic issues were sent to the participants (Leyenaar and Niemoller 2010: 17). The 2-day national deliberation started with a shared decision that 10 ideas should be focused on. According to one interviewee (organizer) the online collected propositions did not play a big part: "*It could serve as an inspiration. But the participants of the face-to-face consultation, which was really the heart of the process, were not obliged to follow.*" On the second day, the participants co-drafted and voted on their recommendations. In each country experts were present to facilitate the participants' discussion, share their views with participants and provide them with information about certain topics. A survey among the participants shows that they deliberated in an open, well thought-out and converging process and received good guidance and instructions whenever necessary (Leyenaar and Niemoller 2010: 5).

In the third phase, the resulting 280 proposals were downsized in 88 recommendations and made available on the national websites. All national participants were allowed to place one vote on each proposal, except for the proposals they had posted themselves. Registered participants of the first phase could also make comments on the recommendations. Each country determined, after debate and voting, 15 recommendations that would be presented during the Citizens' Summit in Brussels. During this fourth phase 150 participants reviewed the final recommendations that had been selected on the first day. On the second day, the participants met with several top EU policymakers including the President of the European Parliament, the President of the European Commission and the President of the Committee of Regions. The recommendations were briefly presented to the policymakers by two participants and there was a discussion between them and the participants. One of the interviewed organizers refers to it as a "show": "*Then the politicians started doing a sort of political propaganda. Not really taking the propositions seriously, which were so vague anyway that you couldn't do anything about them."*

Kies et al. (2013: 64) mention one particular downside of a pan-European consultation process of the scale of the ECC09: loss of plurality. *"This danger results from the tension between, at one end of the spectrum, the plurality of opinions and proposals generated by hundreds of participants on- and offline and, at the other end of spectrum, the requirements for obtaining a limited number of clear recommendations supposedly shared by all the participants."* During all the phases the amount of proposals are downsized by either voting or editing. Although the loss of plurality is inevitable in consultation processes, in comparison to other more current citizens' consultations, with the ECC09 there is comparatively a large loss of plurality.

9.4.4 Results

ECC09 was *"a successful civic instrument but not a convincing policy instrument"* (Kies et al. 2013: 24). The interviewed organizer and researcher reflects: *"It was an effective way of gathering ideas and priorities bottom-up, from citizens all over Europe, but it lacked some important elements: a connection to the policy process, interest from politicians and political parties, transnational deliberation and sufficient marketing."* The second interviewee (organizer and researcher) adds: *"The main strength was civic power. [...] They even felt more European afterwards. They were feeling this sensation of European publics. [...] A second strength is probably the procedure itself. [...] It should have been integrated into the decision-making process, but in itself it's a very innovative procedure trying to consult people from twenty-eight countries."*

There are different reasons for the ECC not having had any policy impact. The most important one is probably that there was no official link between the consultation and the decision-making process. The European institutions were not obliged to provide feedback on the recommendations to the participants or give an official response for example. The ECC recommendations did not have any political mandate (Karlsson 2012b). In the interviews there were complaints that the ECC09 was not working towards a structural solution: *"They [European Union] are aware that we need to try to find new ways of involving citizens. So that's why they have been spending all this money. But then they are doing a one-shot experiment and they don't include it into the decision-making process. That is a problem. They don't think of a long-term solution for implementing citizen participation at the EU level. So, it cannot work. Then it's better to do nothing"* (interview, organizer).

Another reason for a lack of policy impact is a design problem: The scope of the subject of the consultation was too broad and vague. Kies et al. (2013: 64): *"The question of the social and economic future of Europe in a globalized world is indeed likely to attract almost infinite number opinions and critics on what should be done and how it should be implemented."* Karlsson adds that the wide scope of the issues under debate also demanded a broad area of expertise of the participants. At the same time there was not enough information for the participants on what current policies there were in the areas under discussion. This resulted in recommendations of a very general character, too broad *"to give sufficient indication of citizen preferences, and in turn too broad to be useful as guiding recommendations in policymaking"* (Karlsson 2012b: 92–93).

Karlsson evaluated the ECC09 amongst MEPs. They expressed dissatisfaction with the content of the recommendations and the issues they highlighted. Karlsson recommends that there should have been a meet and greet between the MEPs and the participants at an earlier stage. That way they could have exchanged perspectives and knowledge before the content of the proposals was decided upon. Another reason why the consultation process was dissatisfying for the MEPs was that there were no specific groups of citizens involved. This makes the process less interesting for MEPs because it did not offer them *"new ways to communicate with their own constituents, or with a specific group of citizens sharing knowledge or experience that was needed within the realm of a specific policy debate"* (Karlsson 2012b).

With regard to the transformative objectives for developing a European identity, *"the survey results suggest a very high level of efficiency: with the exception of the time available, positive judgments of 85% or higher were recorded"* (Leyenaar and Niemoller 2010: 6). When the instrumental objectives are considered (i.e. whether the process had any policy impact), the consultation can neither be considered efficient nor cost effective. *"It had absolutely no impact. For me, it's a scandal. It's a lot of money. A lot of experiments that have been done. A lot of people that have been involved. A lot of energy with no outcome and no concrete proposal to say what are we doing now with all this experience that we've been gathering"* (interview, organizer).

References

Badouard, R. (2010). Pathways and obstacles to eParticipation at the European level. A comparative analysis of the European Citizens' Consultation 2009 and the online consultations of the European Commission. *JeDEM, 2* (2), 99–110. Accessed January 18, 2019, from http://jedem.org/index.php/jedem/article/view/30

Badouard, R. (2013). Combining inclusion with impact on the decision? The Commission's online consultation on the European Citizens' Initiative. In R. Kies & P. Nanz (Eds.), *Is Europe listening to us? Success and failure of EU citizen consultations* (pp. 153–172). Farnham: Ashgate.

Chalmers, A. W. (2014). In over their heads: Public consultation, administrative capacity and legislative duration in the European Union. *European Union Politics*, 1465116514529849.

Council of the European Union. (2018). *Item note on proposal for a regulation of the European Parliament and of the Council on the European Citizens' Initiative – General approach.* Brussels, 19 June 2018. 9783/18. Accessed January 18, 2019, from http://data.consilium.europa.eu/doc/document/ST-9783-2018-INIT/en/pdf

EC – European Commission (2002). *Consultation document: Towards a reinforced culture of consultation and dialogue – Proposal for general principles and minimum standards for consultation of interested parties by the Commission.* COM/2002/0277 final. Accessed January 18, 2019, from http://eur-lex.europa.eu/legal-content/EN/TXT/PDF/?uri=CELEX:52002DC0277&from=EN

EC – European Commission. (2015a). *Report from the Commission to the European Parliament and the Council. Report on the application of Regulation (EU) No 211/2011 on the citizens' initiative.* Brussels, 31.3.2015, COM(2015) 145 final. Accessed January 18, 2019, from http://ec.europa.eu/transparency/regdoc/rep/1/2015/EN/1-2015-145-EN-F1-1.PDF

EC – European Commission. (2015b). *Guide to the European Citizens' Initiative. A new right For EU citizens – You can set The Agenda!* Accessed January 18, 2019, from https://publications.europa.eu/en/publication-detail/-/publication/d5c945cb-06ba-11e6-b713-01aa75ed71a1

EC – European Commission. (2015c). *Workshop report: Third workshop on new EU eGovernment Action Plan 2016–2020.* https://joinup.ec.europa.eu/sites/default/files/isa_field_path/workshop_report_3.pdf

EC – European Commission. (2016a). *Digital futures: Final report. A journey into 2050 visions and policy challenges.* https://ec.europa.eu/futurium/en/system/files/ged/futurium_scientific_report_v10revcl_v2_0.pdf

EC – European Commission. (2016b). *The European Citizens' Initiative: FAQ.* Accessed on January 18, 2019, from http://ec.europa.eu/citizens-initiative/public/faq#q1

EC – European Commission. (2016c). *The European Citizens' Initiative: Basic facts.* Accessed on January 18, 2019, from http://ec.europa.eu/citizens-initiative/public/basic-facts?lg=en

EC – European Commission. (2016d). *Contribute to law-making.* Accessed November 7, 2016, from http://ec.europa.eu/yourvoice/about/index_en.htm

EC – European Commission. (2016e). *Better regulation. Lighten the load – Have your say!* Accessed November 7, 2016, from http://ec.europa.eu/smart-regulation/refit/simplification/consultation/consultation_en.htm#up

EC – European Commission. (2017). *Proposal for a Regulation of the European Parliament and of the Council on the European Citizens' Initiative.* Brussels, 13.9.2017, COM(2017) 482 final. Accessed January 18, 2019, from http://www.europarl.europa.eu/RegData/docs_autres_institutions/commission_europeenne/com/2017/0482/COM_COM(2017)0482_EN.pdf

EP – European Parliament. (2018). *Briefing. EU legislation in progress. Revising the European Citizens' Initiative.* Accessed January 18, 2019, from http://www.europarl.europa.eu/RegData/etudes/BRIE/2017/614627/EPRS_BRI(2017)614627_EN.pdf

Greenwood, J. (2012). The European Citizens' Initiative and EU civil society organisations. *Perspectives on European Politics and Society, 13*(3), 325–336.

Karlsson, M. (2012a). Democratic legitimacy and recruitment strategies in eParticipation projects. In *Empowering open and collaborative governance* (pp. 3–20). Berlin: Springer.

Karlsson, M. (2012b). Connecting citizens to the European parliament: E-consultations as a tool for political representation. In *E-parliament and ICT-based legislation: Concept, experiences and lessons* (pp. 80–102). IGI Global.

Kies, R. (2016). *The 7 golden rules to introduce citizens' consultations at the EU level: Reforming "Your voice in Europe".* Paper presented at the Fourth International Conference on Legislation and Law Reform, World Bank, Washington, 17–18 November 2016.

Kies, R., & Wojcik, S. (2010). European web-deliberation: Lessons from the European citizens consultation. In *Online Deliberation: Proceedings of the Fourth International Conference-OD2010* (pp. 198–211).

Kies, R., Leyenaar, M., & Niemöller, K. (2013). European citizen's consultation: A large consultation on a vague topic. In R. Kies & P. Nanz (Eds.), *Is Europe listening to us? Success and failure of EU citizen consultations* (pp. 59–78). Farnham: Ashgate.

Leyenaar, M., & Niemoller, K. (2010). *Evaluation report. European Citizens' Consultations 2009.* http://www.aueb.gr/statistical-institute/european-citizens-II/ECC09-Evaluation-Report.pdf

Lironi, E. (2016). *Potential and challenges of E-participation in the European Union. Study for the AFCO Committee, European Parliament, Policy Department for Citizens' Rights and Constitutional Affairs.* European Parliament, Brussels

Malosse, H. (2015). *Opening speech by the EESC President at European Citizens' Initiative Day*. Accessed January 18, 2019, from http://www.eesc.europa.eu/?i=portal.en.members-former-eesc-presidents-henri-malosse-speeches-statements.38201

Organ, J. (2014). Decommissioning direct democracy? A critical analysis of commission decision-making on the legal admissibility of European citizens initiative proposals. *European Constitutional Law Review, 10*(3), 422–443.

Quittkat, C. (2011). The European commission's online consultations: A success story? *Journal of Common Market Studies, 49*(3), 653–674.

Quittkat, C., & Finke, B. (2008). The EU Commission consultation regime. In B. Kohler-Koch, D. De Bièvre, & W. Maloney (Eds.), *Opening EU-Governance to Civil Society*. Gains and Challenges, CONNEX Report Series No 05, University of Mannheim, Mannheim Centre for European Social Research (MZES), Mannheim, pp. 183–222. Accessed on January 18, 2019, from http://www.mzes.uni-mannheim.de/projekte/typo3/site/fileadmin/BookSeries/Volume_Five/Chapter08_Quittkat_Finke.pdf

Sangsari, M. (2013). *The European Citizens' Initiative: An early assessment of the European Union's new participatory democracy instrument, Policy Paper, Canada-Europe Transatlantic Dialogue*.

The ECI Campaign. (2016). *ECI Software that works! OpenECI is designed by and for ECI Campaigners*. Accessed 18 January, 2019, from http://www.citizens-initiative.eu/open-eci

Thomson, J. (2014). What didn't happen with the European Citizens' Initiative...and what did. In C. Berg, & J. Thomson (Eds.), *An ECI that works! Learning from the first two years of the European Citizens' Initiative* (pp. 73–76). The ECI Campaign. Accessed January 18, 2019, from www.ecithatworks.org/wp-content/uploads/2014/04/An_ECI_That_Works.pdf

Winkler, R. (2007). *Electronic participation. Theoretical reflections and empirical assessment: The EU's online platform Your Voice in Europe*. Dissertation at the University of Vienna.

Websites

Accessed January 18, 2019

http://ec.europa.eu/citizens-initiative/public/initiatives/successful
http://ec.europa.eu/citizens-initiative/public/legislative-framework
http://ec.europa.eu/citizens-initiative/public/welcome
https://bookshop.europa.eu/en/guide-to-the-european-citizens-initiative-pbNA0415686/
https://ec.europa.eu/info/consultations_en
https://ec.europa.eu/info/law/contribute-law-making_en
https://www.eesc.europa.eu/en/agenda/our-events/events/eci-day-2018-working-together

Accessed November 10, 2018

http://ec.europa.eu/dorie/fileDownload.do;jsessionid=xh8KNzbZWdKNPe9Y5IJOuQYSu%20CtWIZXrytbUD2yo-7LREdYe14qC!-898031139?docId=155076&cardId=155076
https://en.wikipedia.org/wiki/European_citizens'_consultations
https://eur-lex.europa.eu/legal-content/EN/ALL/?uri=uriserv:a30000
https://participedia.net/en/cases/european-citizens-consultation-2009

Accessed November 11, 2018

https://ec.europa.eu/futurium/en
https://ec.europa.eu/futurium/en/blog/update-ideas-submitted-egovernment4eu-platform
https://ec.europa.eu/futurium/en/content/process-egovernement-action-plan-2016-2020
https://ec.europa.eu/futurium/en/content/selection-criteria
https://ec.europa.eu/futurium/en/egovernment4eu
https://eur-lex.europa.eu/legal-content/EN/TXT/PDF/?uri=CELEX:52016DC0179&from=EN
https://joinup.ec.europa.eu/sites/default/files/event/attachment/workshop_report_3.pdf

Open Access This chapter is licensed under the terms of the Creative Commons Attribution 4.0 International License (http://creativecommons.org/licenses/by/4.0/), which permits use, sharing, adaptation, distribution and reproduction in any medium or format, as long as you give appropriate credit to the original author(s) and the source, provide a link to the Creative Commons licence and indicate if changes were made.

The images or other third party material in this chapter are included in the chapter's Creative Commons licence, unless indicated otherwise in a credit line to the material. If material is not included in the chapter's Creative Commons licence and your intended use is not permitted by statutory regulation or exceeds the permitted use, you will need to obtain permission directly from the copyright holder.

Chapter 10
Non-binding Decision-Making

Iris Korthagen, Casper Freundlich Larsen, and Rasmus Ø. Nielsen

Abstract Korthagen et al. introduce six quite successful digital tools used in decision-making processes. Three tools are used by political parties (Spanish Podemos, the Italian Five Star Movement and the German Pirate Party) aiming for direct democracy and more transparency. The other three tools are online participatory budgeting (PB) tools initiated by municipalities (the Brazilian city Belo Horizonte, the French capital Paris and the Icelandic capital Reykjavik). The authors place a strong focus on the participatory process and practical experiences. For a better understanding of these tools and how they are used in practice, interviews were conducted with administrators and researchers familiar with the respective tools. All tools except one, the Podemos tool, prove to have an impact on decision-making processes with the party or municipality. The authors explain this success rate by the fact that the tools are embedded in actual formal decision-making processes: the internal party decision-making process and the budgeting process of local democracies.

10.1 The German Pirate Party

10.1.1 Introduction

The Pirate Party Germany was founded in 2006 by 53 inhabitants of Berlin. In 2009, the German Pirate Party got officially represented in politics, with one seat in the European Parliament and seats in four state parliaments. Because of scandals and internal disputes, the Pirate Party lost the trust of the voters and is no longer represented in any state parliament. Key party issues of the German Pirate Party are direct democracy, copyright, digital communication, privacy and transparency

---

I. Korthagen (✉)
Netherlands Court of Audit, The Hague, The Netherlands

C. F. Larsen · R. Ø. Nielsen
The Danish Board of Technology Foundation, Hvidovre, Denmark
e-mail: rn@tekno.dk

© The Authors(s) 2020
L. Hennen et al. (eds.), *European E-Democracy in Practice*, Studies in Digital Politics and Governance, https://doi.org/10.1007/978-3-030-27184-8_10

(www.piratenpartei.de). Their internal approach is characterized by many possibilities to participate (online) in the decision-making process. The Pirate Party makes extensive use of new technology to communicate and collaborate on policymaking. The technology facilitates the intension of the Pirate Party to—in terms of Bolleyer et al. (2015: 159)—maximize the democratic equality both between followers and members and between members and elites.

The use of technologies as Liquid Feedback was introduced to cater to the aims of this new party: democracy and transparency. Because of these values, anyone could come to the party conventions and have a say: *"This rendered the convention to a point where you weren't able to make a decision, because people were always discussing formalities. It wasn't really effective. At that point liquid feedback came in. If we want to be different from the other parties and if we take seriously that people want to participate via the Internet, then they have to be able to do that and join the decision making of the party. If we want to propagate this as the big difference of the Pirate Party, we need usable software, which is able to do this. So, they started creating the software, because we exploded so fast in members"* (interview with a politician).

The Liquid Feedback software has been the backbone for the inter-party decision-making process and incorporates four steps (Paulin 2014: 221–223, see also Klimowicz 2016). It all starts with an initiative that can be proposed by any registered member. This proposal must receive support of at least 10% of the registered users within a predefined period of time. If the proposal has received enough support, time for discussion and eventual modifications of the initiative is allocated, again within a defined time frame. Eventually, members can cast their vote on the final proposal directly or (temporarily) delegate their votes to a confidential whom they trust. Liquid Feedback has been used from May 2010 till May 2015, although use of the tool had been gradually declining since then (interview with a researcher).

German law prescribes that all important decisions have to be democratically decided on at party conventions—so not online. These regulations mean that input from participants through the Pirate Party's Liquid Feedback tool is not necessarily of influence on decisions of the Party's members of parliament. *"If you decide something in Liquid Feedback, it can never be binding"* (interview with a researcher). This had its impact on the effectivity of the tool for party members. The real decision-making process was taking place outside Liquid Feedback (interview with a researcher).

Internal procedures are written down in the Statute of the Pirate Party, which can be found on their website. About internal party policies and candidates, the Statute postulates: *"In the German Pirates, candidates are elected by members on the regional or local level (Section 1, §10.2). The national executive is elected individually on an annual basis during the national membership meeting (Section 1, §9a.3). Changes to party policy and statutes can be initiated by all members and require a two-thirds majority during the annual membership meeting (Section A, §§12.1 and 12.3). Further, all members, if they have sufficient support, can initiate a membership referendum, the outcome of which is binding and equal to a membership meeting vote (Section A, §§16.1–16.6)*" (Bolleyer et al. 2015: 165). The finances of the party can be found on a website; the main financial sources are the contributions of the State and membership fees.

10.1.2 Participants

The target group of participants are people who share the main values of the German Pirate Party. The voter profile for the Pirate Party is young, male, Internet-savvy and well educated. The German pirates attracted many protest votes and only 14% of the voters for the Pirate Party made this choice because of concrete programmatic or content-based issues (Greenstein 2013). Membership of the German Pirate Party is inclusive; it is not a problem if you are already a member of another political party. Decisions about membership are made at the lowest organizational level. The regional branch is allowed to reject membership applications. "*The concept of 'membership' in their national constitution explicitly refers to the obligation to work for the party as well as to the rights linked to membership. [...] members must be Germans who live in Germany, and must be aged over 16 (Section A, §2.1)*" (Bolleyer et al. 2015, 164–165).

At first, the Pirate Party in Germany mainly attracted a community of people interested in the Internet itself, in issues around the Internet (such as copyright), and in digital instruments to realize horizontal decision-making. In 2009, the party gained more attention and popular support due to a few events: an Internet censorship law proposed by minister Van der Leyen (CDU) that would ban German Internet users from accessing child pornography (and the fear that the government would ban other Internet sites in the future), the SPD parliamentarian Tauss who switched over to the Pirate Party and the success for the Pirate Party in Sweden. In addition, the Pirate Party principles of openness helped to gain public support as well as the wider attractiveness of the digital instruments (Hensel 2014: 248). The number of members increased more than tenfold in 2009. After the party won seats in Berlin's state parliament in 2011, they also won seats in Saarland, Schleswig-Holstein and North Rhine-Westphalia in 2012.

The online design of the tool has always been intended to open sharing of all information and towards horizontal decision-making procedures, striving to include participants beyond the participation elite. But when the party managed to attract a broader and more diverse member base, the result was not that inclusive after all. In practice, it appeared that making meaningful interventions within online conversations presumed some digital competences, knowledge on the subject and strong connections within the Pirate Party. Not only did the new group lack abilities or knowledge to contribute to the internal discussion, their contributions in the debates were also seen as light-spirited and unprofessional (Hensel 2014: 249). What actually happened was that informal structures between a small group of members overruled the digital horizontal structures in the party decision-making processes, although this practice is in contradiction with all principles of the Pirate Party.

Despite the aims of the party of participatory decision-making, the German Pirate Party [as well as the Swedish (Bolleyer et al. 2015) and the Dutch Pirate Party (interview with two members of the Dutch national Pirate Party)] shows relatively low member commitment in participation. *"In the German Pirate Party, recent figures indicate that only 28 percent of members on the national level pay their fees and have full voting rights"* (Bolleyer et al. 2015: 170). Another problem is that the German Pirate Party is a very male-dominated party; only few women are represented (Kulick 2013). Also, questions are raised with regard to the representativeness of participants in relation to the "super voters": *"In a discussion on the effect on super-voters—i.e. users with a large share of incoming delegations—the democratic nature of the system was questioned, and many users became inactive"* (Kling et al. 2015: 3).

10.1.3 Participatory Process

Members of the German Pirate Party can give many different sorts of input online. They can discuss issues, formulate proposals, provide feedback on proposals and they can vote on a proposal or delegate their vote to another party member they trust. For a long time, Liquid Feedback was the most important tool for internal decision-making processes. Kling et al. (2015: 3) described the Liquid Feedback process clearly: *"In Liquid Feedback as used in the German Pirate Party, members can create initiatives which are to be voted on to obtain the current opinion of the party members, e.g. for collaboratively developing the party program. Initiatives are grouped into issues which group competing initiatives for the same issue. [...] Furthermore, issues belong to areas which represent main topics such as environmental policies. Each user can create new initiatives, which need a minimum first quorum of supporters for being voted upon. In Liquid Feedback, votes can be delegated to other voters on three levels: On the global level, meaning that all initiatives can be voted for by the delegate on behalf of the delegating user; on the area level, so that delegations are restricted on an area; or on the issue level. The actions of every voter are recorded and public, allowing the control of delegates at the expense of non-secret votes."* The threshold of a minimum support by 10% of party members also effectively obstructs counterproductive contributions, because this threshold makes sure that unsupported views can be ignored without further discussion. *"The only possibility to give feedback in Liquid Feedback is to do it in a positive and constructive way. [...] If you want to change something, then you have to suggest what has to be changed"* (interview with a politician). Voting on proposals in Liquid Feedback works through a preference system, in which multiple, prioritized votes can be cast. Participants can thus choose and prioritize several policy options at the same time (interview with a politician).

The use of the Liquid Feedback tool had been contested within the party since the beginning (interview with a researcher; interview with a politician). Many Pirates did not perceive the security to be well organized. Also, practical failures and fundamental democratic issues within the systems were noticed (Hensel 2014: 248). On complex matters, the tool does not provide enough information to enable sufficient participation, according to the interviewed researcher. This has had the effect that too few people actually participated for decisions to be legitimate. The system itself was quite complicated as well, which made contributing difficult for some people: *"I'm one of these supposed digital natives because [...] I grew up with computers and internet more or less. [But] I find it very hard to find my way around this Liquid Feedback and to find what's discussed at the moment and who is voting for what and why. And, for example, if you delegate your votes, you will never see where your votes land in the end. [...] It looked like it was programmed by nerds, for nerds, and not for the general public"* (interview with a researcher). Eventually many of the supporters of the Liquid Feedback tool left the party and it fell out of use (interview with a researcher).

Hensel (2014) argued that the most important tools for the communication within the Pirate Party are the Wiki, mailing lists, a party-related blogosphere, digital party magazines, video and streaming services and the video conferencing software Mumble.

- Mumble *"is an open and free voice conferencing software. Mumble allows us to carry out decentralized meetings and short action planning, without having to travel across the country."*
- PiratenPad *"is a widely used virtual notepad in which several people can leave messages synchronously. This makes it possible to construct complete texts, action plans or protocols for meetings. The Piratenpad server can be reached at www.piratenpad.de and is available to everyone. This way, this Pirate Party software has become a popular tool for companies, NGOs and even other political parties."*
- Piratenwiki functions as *"the information and coordination platform of the Pirate Party Germany. Here, content that has been previously constructed through other means (for example, in Piratenpad) is collated and archived—it is, so to speak, a kind of Wikipedia for the Pirate Party. On the Wiki you can find our principle programs, minutes of meetings of all subdivisions, plans for events, application links to party conferences, lists of roundtables and working groups, and much more"* (www.piratenpartei.de).

As noted earlier, the Liquid Feedback software did not leave much room for discussion, only for alternative proposals (Paulin 2014). Discussions were deliberately excluded from the system of Liquid Feedback and needed to find their way to the PiratenPad online platform, which provides chatrooms, wikis, mailing lists or other forums that are not related to the party. This software ensures constructive discussion and decision-making: *"You have quite a dynamic discussion process. You have to propose something, you can't say 'Everything is bad' [...]. You have to say: 'I want it this way'"* (interview with politician).

10.1.4 Results

Liquid Feedback makes it possible for political parties to improve the accessibility and transparency of decision-making and the quality of members' participation (Edwards and de Kool 2016). But although direct democracy is an important aim of the German Pirate Party, the results of the Liquid Feedback system are not binding for the party leadership (Paulin 2014). Sometimes the party leaders do make a different consideration than the members. This is an unresolved normative conflict in the party. "*Should a parliamentarian act as a trustee, accountable only to his own conscience (a norm constitutionally enshrined in Germany)? Or should the parliamentarian act as a delegate of party members, who can indicate their policy preferences through Internet devices such as Liquid Feedback, thereby implementing the equality between office holder and 'ordinary' members? The representatives in Berlin were most open towards the 'delegate model' and committed themselves to considering the membership position via Liquid Feedback in parliamentary decisions. However, member feedback is considered to be non-binding advice even in this case*" (Bolleyer et al. 2015: 173).

Because transparency within the decision-making processes is highly valued, in principle members discuss their own standpoints out in the open. That was also the idea of the developers of the software. Edwards and de Kool (2016) saw this, however, as an important dilemma, and a very sensitive issue within the Pirate Party. Being transparent about party members' opinions and decision-making behaviour may generate information that those concerned regard as a violation of privacy. The Pirate Party therefore offered an opportunity to participate anonymously. The developers of the software (Jan Behrens, Björn and Andreas Nitsche) subsequently distanced themselves from the application of the software by the German Pirate Party in an open letter. They argue that the federal board has not installed the system properly. Anonymous participation complicates the process overall. The developers do not think that anonymous votes (with a pseudonym) and an accountable, transparent decision-making process can go together.

Liquid democracy has inspired other actors to use parts or variation as a system of collective, online decision-making. But the interviewee related to the German Pirate Party warned: Do not use the Liquid Feedback software for show. Nothing is more frustrating than participating in a process in which ultimately nothing happens with the result—this makes it very hard to motivate people to participate again, he emphasizes. In reaction to the Pirate Party and its use of digital technologies, Chancellor Merkel set up the 'Kanzler Dialog'. "*They set up an Internet website which was thoroughly programmed and which had a voting system. It was just clicks. You opened a new window in your browser and you could vote again. It was with cookies. One topic on this website was legalizing marihuana. What happens? Nothing*" (interview with politician). This can damage the trust people have in politics.

10.2 The Five Star Movement in Italy

10.2.1 Introduction

Officially founded in 2009, the 5 Star Movement (Movimento Cinque Stelle, hereafter 5SM) is currently Italy's largest political party with 14 European Parliament representatives. The meteoric rise of the 5SM in Italian and European politics has been closely connected to the movement's ability to organize and mobilize using web-based communication platforms. In this case study, we attempt to identify the strategies and tools used by the movement to connect online community-building with real-life mobilization in a successful bid for political power. Our focus in this study is especially on the phase before the movement's electoral successes, in which an online "fad" around the movement's charismatic founder was harnessed and structured into an effective political organization.

Online communication was central to 5SM from the beginning. The movement was co-founded by Italian comedian Beppe Grillo and Gianroberto Casaleggio, an entrepreneur acquainted with web strategies. Grillo has been the face of the movement, leveraging his existing public profile in a turn to political critic. At the same time, Casaleggio's communications company (Casaleggio Associati Ltd) has been the practical initiator and coordinator of the movement's digital infrastructure. Today the company also maintains the web platform used by 5SM on the national level. The movement's online presence is essential to its structure. Sæbø et al. (2014: 244) cited movement members who describe the movement as a "non-association" with a "non-statute" and with *"its headquarters on the web"*. The 5SM is a self-declared 'populist' movement (IlFattoQuotidiano.ti 2013) with a *"post-ideological"* approach (Kirchgaessner 2016). The aspirations of the movement to give voice and influence to "people" come together in the movement's championing of "direct democracy", which for the movement is embodied in its use of a number of different online tools for communication and mobilization.

The web platform of 5SM combines different tools, which are used for a variety of purposes such as debate, knowledge sharing, voting, e-learning and more. At the time of our study (2016–2017), all online tools rested on a common platform named Rosseau. This platform provides the resources for different services. One such resource, LEX, provides a space to share documents. Over the years, practices have emerged for how to use this space. These practices are key to how the movement works. One example is that elected officials representing the movement will share all reports that they must respond to with movement's members well in advance. This enables the possibility of an open dialogue process about how the movement should react to that report (interview with platform developer). This is one way that the movement seeks to operationalize the central populist tenet of exerting a more direct form of control over representatives than is traditional in representative democracy.

Another, perhaps even more central service is the voting function. Here, all registered and eligible members of the movement can announce their candidacies for upcoming elections, and the group of voting members decides who becomes listed as official candidates (interview with platform developer). Other services include e-learning modules designed to prepare newly elected candidates for their official duties and to introduce the tools at their disposal (interview with platform developer), as well as facilities for online streaming of official meetings. New services are added on a regular basis (interview with platform developer).

The use of online tools has been central to the movement from the beginning, but this has developed gradually. Only in recent years have the different tools become integrated in a common platform. The movement emerged around Grillo's blog, which he started in 2005. Here, Grillo continued a history of publicly sharing anti-establishment views and criticisms as part of his comedy. Once followers of the blog began to identify themselves as a political movement, they adopted Meetup[1] as a means of coordinating small meetings among movement supporters. From around 2007, Grillo's blog supplied space for contact and debate within and between these groups (Sæbø et al. 2014: 245).

The centrality of the blog, which until 2015 was still formally Grillo's, as well as the allegedly opaque internal processes of the movement, led to criticism of centralism and even autocratic tendencies in the movement (De Rosa 2013a). Conceding the point, in 2015, the movement changed the URL of the blog (to www.movimento5stelle.it). While the movement may thus have its "headquarters" online, it has combined this virtual structure from early on with "real-world" mobilization of supporters. In this way, according to De Rosa (2013b: 20), *"the web [is] the connective tissue, the megaphone and the organizing principle behind a campaign that offers seamless movement between different reality spaces (online/offline)"*. Meetings and rallies have been central to the movement since its inaugural "V-day" in 2007, where Grillo began the process of gathering signatures for a proposed change to the Italian electoral law (Beppegrillo.it: 2007). At around the same time, some of the Meetup groups began to organize to run for local elections on civic lists162. This turn to local politics culminated in 2016 with the election of 5SM mayors in Rome and Turin. This turn also started the process by which the movement began to turn into a party (Kirchgaessner 2016). The "non-association" was formally founded as an association in 2009 to provide an organizational platform for the coordination of civic lists and to make it legally possible for movement members to run for the Italian Parliament and, from 2014, for the European Parliamentary elections.

Regarding the political context of 5SM and its online participatory tools, the choice to seek representation in political institutions has been a crucial milestone for the movement. *"The 5SM has started to come to terms with representative democracy, choosing to act from within political institutions"* (Bordignon and Ceccarini 2015: 456). As already noted, this choice has been highly successful with 5SM now being represented in the European and Italian parliaments as well as many Italian municipalities (ibid.). Sæbø et al. (2014) noted that while the movement has thus had

---

[1] See https://www.meetup.com/

to make concessions to the "offline" world of institutions, the statute of 5SM reiterates that *"the Internet plays a crucial role for 5SM"*, that *"the headquarters of the 5SM is the blog itself"*, and that the movement uses the Internet to *"let citizens enter into the movement for consulting, deliberating, decision-making and electing purposes"* as well as *"governance"* of the association (246). Italian regulations for party associations give extensive leeway for the design of internal processes and, thus, provide a legal space that the movement has sought to utilize to give as much direct influence to movement members as is possible and feasible (interview with platform designer).

The online platform of 5SM claims to be funded largely by crowdfunding (IlFattoQuotidiano.ti 2013). The funds received by parliamentarians for support staff are directed back to the organization to support these and other communication efforts (ibid.).

10.2.2 Participants

As of January 2017, close to 1500 Meetup groups with more than 145,000 members in more than 20 countries had been established. In principle, anyone registering on the 5SM website can participate in the preparation and discussion of the movement's decisions, although they must stick to the debate guidelines. To be able to participate in the different voting activities of the movement (see below), voters must be 18 years of age and eligible to vote in Italy (interview with platform designer). To document their eligibility, subscribers must submit a scanned ID (Federici et al. 2015: 288). Despite this openness, however, Grillo has been criticized for eliminating online users unilaterally and for using his administrative position to "blackmail" movement voters into voting according to his own preferences (Sæbø et al. 2014: 247). These criticisms aside, the participatory functions of the platform are extensive, and with the electoral results achieved by the movement in recent years to the European Parliament, the Italian Parliament, and local and regional Italian governments, the movement claims to have *"one of the most effective platforms in the world"* (interview with platform designer).

10.2.2.1 Engagement and Communication Strategies

5SM is in a sense synonymous with its engagement and communication strategy. From the perspective of the movement itself, members do not participate in activities of the movement; they are the movement, and the central administration and elected officials merely serve the movement. This high-minded philosophy of radical engagement is implemented in a number of ways, as outlined under 'Participatory process' below.

A central claim of 5SM is to be more open and therefore more representative than traditional parties (Federici et al. 2015: 288). There is no data gathered on the statistical representativeness of the movement's members in relation to the Italian and/or European elections (interview with platform designer). However, the movement website as of 2015 had 800,000 unregistered "followers" and around 100,000 certified "subscribers"—numbers which compare favourably with traditional party membership in Italy, where the most-voted-for party (PD) boasted a membership in 2015 of around 240,000 (down from 800,000 in 2009) (Federici et al. 2015: 288). Up to 30,000–40,000 subscribers to the website usually participate actively in important online discussions (ibid.: 294).

While statistical representativeness is neither a goal, nor a point of observation for the movement, the movement's claim to represent "people"—as long as this is understood in terms of representing a partisan, self-selected part of the population—could on the face of it be on par with traditional parties. De Rosa (2013a) documents that for the 2012 Italian Parliamentary election, the group of 5SM candidates—of which only 13% were female and only 10% were below 29—was in no way sociologically representative of the Italian population. Again, this is noted here with the caveat that the movement does not aim or claim to achieve statistical representativeness among its candidates.

10.2.3 Participatory Process

Participation and deliberation are central to the 5SM platform design. All content in the LEX and on the blog is thus open to debate among registered subscribers. Debate activity levels among subscribers are "good" in comparison with similar platforms (interview with platform designer). Movement members, however, have options for participation and co-creation that go beyond debate. These options are outlined here.

A first option is agenda setting. From the outset, the digital platform of 5SM focused on agenda setting. Participants can post about ideas and views and debate posts by other participants and party/movement officials. There is also an element of providing input for policy options in that posts can be in the form of policy proposals, and participants can co-create law proposals in wiki-style processes. Results are listed on the main web platforms of 5SM. Subscribers who have participated in debates and/or votes are notified by email about outputs and outcomes. A second option is voting. A central function of the blog has been as a platform for what the movement calls "digital primaries" (interview with platform designer). Sæbø et al. (2014) noted that this use of the blog has taken various forms, flexibly adapted to each purpose. In one example, digital primaries conforming to direct democracy principles of "one user, one vote" were held to select candidates for 5SM national Parliamentary election lists, whereas, in another example, the digital primary took on a more deliberative democratic form when movement members had to decide on which presidential candidate to support (246). A third option, which as far as we have been able to determine is not yet implemented, is assuming direct control of elected officials (proxy voting). Registered blog users may propose legislation and—on the condition of 20% of the online vote—compel the elected officials to put forward the proposal in Parliament (interview with platform designer). This has been a projected goal since the founding of the movement, but had by mid-2016 not been implemented, causing some internal criticism (interview with researcher). Such criticism would be natural, since the possibility to assume direct control over representatives is at the core of the republican populist tradition, which seems to be the movement's ideological ancestor (see above). A fourth option is the monitoring of elected officials. Adopting what De Rosa (2013b) calls a "no-confidence stance" on the relationship between the movement's members and its representatives, extensive direct monitoring of the actions of elected officials is possible. The blog thus acts as a hub for transparency with video streaming ensuring the transparency of meetings, also meetings with political allies and opponents (De Rosa 2013a; Sæbø et al. 2014: 247). The funds received by parliamentarians for support staff are directed back to the organization to support these and other communication efforts (op. cit.), while simultaneously 5SM parliamentarians actively use social media to disseminate information about their activities.

The fact that subscribers have to submit ID to be confirmed creates a potential privacy threat to subscribers. However, in terms of privacy protection, the statute of the association contains provisions for privacy that prevent the association from sharing personal information with third parties (Federici et al. 2015: 292). Extensive security measures have been put in place to ensure the integrity of the movement's voting results (interview with platform designer).

10.2.4 Results

The impact of the largely online mobilization and organization efforts of the movement has been substantial in terms of providing voter support for elected officials. The electoral successes of the movement seem to prove the hypothesis that by providing an online infrastructure that gives voice to citizens, political initiators can in fact organize and mobilize voters.

In terms of policy impacts, we have no hard data on the relationship between, on the one hand, the online deliberations among citizens, the proposals produced by citizens and the proposal votes among registered subscribers, and, on the other hand, the voting and negotiation behaviour of the elected officials of the movement. We thus cannot conclude either for or against the assumption that the elected officials of 5SM represent more directly the political will of their constituents. This will likely be a theme for evaluation of the movement's government record. As described above, extensive information is made available to movement members to allow them to judge for themselves the correspondence between debate outcomes within the movement and positions taken by elected officials.

10.3 Podemos in Spain

10.3.1 Introduction

Podemos was founded as a political party in 2014, following the anti-austerity Indignados protests. Podemos is represented in both chambers of the Spanish Parliament, Cortes Generales, and has five seats in the European Parliament. By all accounts, the influence of the party remains on the rise. In this case study, we look at the different digital participation tools the party has adopted as part of developing its organizational structure. Some of these tools provide a day-to-day online infrastructure for organization and participation in the Party, while others are used ad hoc to support specific political processes.

Podemos has made inclusive and transparent decision-making as the main asset and indicator of its politics. The basic claim is that direct participation of citizens is indispensable for a system to be democratic and legitimate. One of the main channels for public participation is the Podemos website,[2] which enables online voting and decision-making. Since its foundation in 2014, Podemos has launched several online platforms based on open source software, such as Reddit (adapted by Podemos under the name Plaza Podemos[3]), Agora Voting (now nVotes),[4] Loomio,[5] Titanpad (now abandoned[6]) and, more recently, the UN-backed citizen participation platform Consul.[7] The latter is the software behind the new platform to which Plaza Podemos has been moved. Generally, the use of different digital tools is initiated and managed by the political party Podemos. Plaza Podemos specifically was initially created as a "subreddit" (a dedicated forum on Reddit) by a supporter of the Party in 2014. The Party later contacted the creator of Plaza Podemos in its search for new digital tools to connect with people. As a result, the page became the official subreddit of the Party and the creator joined the managing team of the Party (Borge and Santamarina 2015). The aim of the digital tools is to organize direct democratic involvement, transparency and accountability through the application of direct democracy ideals in practice. This is done inside the institutional framework of the political party of Podemos.

Podemos seeks bottom-up support for Party activities through crowdfunding and fundraising. Podemos is mainly financed through donations and crowdfunding for specific projects by individual citizens. To achieve financial transparency and *"corruption-free politics"*, it is possible to scrutinize the accounts and balances of the party online (Klimowicz 2016: 67). The main website of Podemos contains an

---

[2] See https://podemos.info/
[3] See https://plaza.podemos.info/
[4] See https://nvotes.com/agoravoting-com-redirect/
[5] See https://www.loomio.org/
[6] See https://blog.titanpad.com/2016/11/shutting-down-titanpad_12.html
[7] See https://consulproject.org/en/

opportunity to financially support the Party's activities directly by donating to the Party or its specific activities.

The combined toolbox used by Podemos lets participants engage in different phases of Party decision-making; from agenda-setting to policy deliberation and prioritization among policy proposals. In setting the agenda, Podemos uses the debate blog platform Osoigo, and Plaza Podemos, for open as well as focused debates, providing platforms to influence and deliberate on the political agenda. In providing input for policy options, proposals can be submitted on these same platforms or follow from debates held there. Whenever a proposal reaches a certain number of positive votes, the proposal is moved to the Podemos participation portal (participa.podemos.info), where it is processed among registered users as an introductory policy proposal. The user proposals that gain sufficient support are turned over in their final phases to a work group, which drafts a proposal document to be put to a vote. A work group consists of officials as well as the initiator(s) of the proposal, giving a very tangible element of co-deciding along with the binding vote that follows.

10.3.2 Participants

The target group of Plaza Podemos users is quite broadly defined. At 14 years of age, citizens can register in Podemos and gain access to the digital tools. However, some of the different platforms also contain opportunities to participate without registering, as well as a great deal of information on ongoing debates and topics of possible relevance to visiting non-members. Although certain citizen profiles may be more specifically targeted that others, Podemos and the digital participatory tools of the party address Spanish citizens on a broad scale: *"That was the aim of this Party—you know—to reach to la gente, the people... So, in that sense, the target group was not, you know, a specific minority group or a specific section of the population, it was the whole society"* (interview with a researcher).

Initially, this broad outreach strategy may have contributed to the popularity of and public interest in Plaza Podemos. Following the launch of the party and Plaza Podemos on Reddit, the novelty of a broadly inclusive and participatory forum for political debate gained media attention: *"Plaza Podemos was very famous in the beginning. When they started in 2014, some traditional mass media (...) were following the debates in Plaza Podemos. It was very extraordinary in the sense that an online platform within a Party was given a lot of voice and a lot of echo in mass media"* (interview with a researcher). However, as Podemos has become more established as a party, the Plaza Podemos platform seems to have become less influential. Although Podemos has gained great numbers of members and participants—estimated at around 400,000 users (interview with researcher)—media attention as well as participant activity on Plaza Podemos has decreased. It could be simply that the platform has lost its novelty. However, both our interviewees expressed considerations that something else might be at play: *"It's not very lively* now... *I suppose because [there] was a lot of enthusiasm before, and now people are a little bit fed up because no proposal (...) has achieved to be voted on by the whole of the party... It was not accepted by the executives of the party. People, I think, are maybe disappointed in that sense*" (interview with a researcher).

Podemos has also raised barriers to participation as an effect of increasing safety and Party control of the census of participants: "*[...] they are becoming more restrictive, and so now this year you have to register as a member of Podemos and then you can participate in Plaza Podemos. But at the beginning, they were so open that it was possible to participate in Plaza Podemos and to have their say, even to vote... With only a nickname and without any restriction*" (interview with a researcher). Until recently, Plaza Podemos users have all been handled as one census, including passive and active members alike. This has caused some internal discussion (Borge and Santamarina 2015), resulting in a distinction between the census in its entirety and a census of active participants. The point of this distinction was to qualify the group of people contributing to binding decisions inside the Party: "*One of the main questions when you take into consideration decision-making mechanism is the census. If you don't have an accurate census, then it is difficult to give to this tool... binding decisions. And that was one of the main problems with Reddit: We didn't control the census*" (interview with politician). This restriction, adopted in the period from 2014 to 2015, limits the right to participate in internal votes to only the active census. Problems of primaries being compromised by organized groups of right-wing voters also made higher-level security necessary (Borge and Santamarina 2015). In practice, the requirement for gaining voting privileges is connected to one's additional participation: "*So, if in the last year you have done anything related to Party processes(...), you enter into the active census. (...) I think the requirement is to at least have participated electronically or physically once in the last year*" (interview with a researcher). Being fully dependent on self-selection among participants, there is no mechanism of representative selection, and both our interviewees believe that it is skewed towards highly educated men: "*In Plaza Podemos, the participants [...] I think they are not very representative of the whole Spanish population because I think that most of them are men for example, and I think that most of them are high-educated (...) But it is only an illustrative impression that I have*" (interview with a researcher).

There is also a matter of digital and social divide: "*I must say the majority is men and not all age groups are equally savvy with technology. There is also something about the economic status [...] The facility to have access to Internet and use it regularly, still nowadays—not only in Spain —depends on your cultural background and economic possibilities.*" (interview with a politician). In turn, the mechanism of self-selection and the generally flat structure of discussion can provide opportunities for minority groups to make themselves heard: "*I think we are a in a way a party full of minority groups with a vocation of being a majority party. If you see data from polls and demographics and so on, we may have the most diverse base of supporters... Including maybe the strongest base of for instance disabled people*" (interview with a politician).

10.3.3 Participatory Process

Participants provide input in several ways on the platform. First and foremost, participants can submit proposals to the deliberative platforms. Such proposals are subject to comments and being voted up or down by participants. In later phases of the decision-making process, participants can support a given proposal to get it accepted for proposal development by the organization and initiator. Anyone can post a proposal and the phases of making a successful proposal on Plaza Podemos are as follows: When a proposal has gained a certain number of positive votes (equivalent to 0.2% of registered users), it is moved to another section of the Participa platform. A proposal must then gain support from 2% of members before a notification is sent by email to all registered Podemos members. If the proposal then reaches 10% support within a set deadline (typically around 3 months), the proposal reaches the final draft phase. Here, the initiator(s) enter into a work group with party officials to co-draft a final proposal document, which is then voted upon by registered members. If agreement cannot be reached in this phase, two competing draft proposals are put to a binding vote on the Agora Voting platform.

"*Agora is the software for online voting. (...) This is the tool that we use for primaries and this will be the tool that we use also for consultations. For instance, it is mandatory to ask our members about any pact or any agreement for instance to get or not into our government. Agora Voting is basically the interface that gathers the data from our census (...) to have online voting anonymously and all these guarantees*" (interview with a researcher). Recently, the number of channels for participation has been reduced and simplified: "*Apart from Plaza Podemos, they have Appgree [...]. They have ListenToYou (Osoigo), which is a direct channel of citizens [to connect] with parliamentarians. They have these three channels now [...] One year ago, they had like, I don't know, ten different channels [...] Maybe it is smarter to simplify*" (ibid).

In these ways, proposals are aggregated in several phases. First, proposals are voted up or down on the Agora Voting platform in order to gather initial support. Proposals that prove popular can then progress to a second platform, Participa, where only registered members can contribute. This accumulation of support continues as participants discuss, challenge, counter and qualify proposals. Successful proposals are ultimately aggregated—voted upon—in a binding vote. Between participating citizens, the "*two most important proposals discussed* [on Plaza Podemos] shows a high level of discourse equality, reciprocity, justification and civility" (Borge and Santamarina 2015: 33). Generally, proposals experience substantial discussion, suggesting an active group of participants.

When a proposal is sent for development in a work group, the author(s) of the proposal is included, and participants and Party decision-makers can exchange views in the process of developing the proposal. In this way, successful proposals from the online platform must see some interaction and deliberation between officials and initiators. The final vote is binding towards the political representatives, by which the aggregated view of participants is communicated to decision-makers. No initial information is given on the issues at stake, other than what the initiator submits to his/her proposal. However, information relevant to an issue can often be found because of the structure of the platform. Podemos itself merely provides information on the tools and processes, although our interviewee representing the Party expresses some concern about leaving documentation entirely to users: "*I think we provide basic information about how to use the tool. I think when it comes [to] raising issues for discussion or for decision, maybe we should be more methodic... Explaining the context, the process, the pros, the cons and so on*" (interview with politician).

10.3.4 Results

Results of the online participation of members contribute to the decision-making process in two main ways. First, the deliberation on proposals contributes to political agenda-setting in the Party. Second, the results of binding votes on proposals contribute to the policy output of decision-making processes. This output, however, is to be understood as policy aims of the Party. To be implemented as a policy, Podemos is still dependent on reaching majorities in relevant parliaments. Whenever a proposal from Plaza Podemos enters a representative democracy institution, obvious limits are posed to the political output efficiency of participation. Similar considerations are relevant when designing an online platform like that of Podemos. In the words of our interviewee: "*If you don't give the possibility to have an actual impact on the outcome, then they are not interested in the mid-term... They lose interest, and we need to find ways to make it more binding and meaningful*" (interview with a politician).

The interviewed researcher was more critical towards the political efficiency of participation on Plaza Podemos, and the feedback on the influence on policy: "*In an indirect way, [Podemos] are paying attention to the discussion on Plaza Podemos, but it's in a very indirect way. [...] They take decisions without explaining themselves and without entering in Plaza Podemos and saying 'Well, you see, we are listening to you'. So, the listening is very indirect. It's not that those participatory tools have a direct impact. They have a kind of indirect impact that you can see between the lines in some decisions*" (interview with a researcher). Regarding the different thresholds of support and the process of participant proposals, the interviewee continues: "*The only way you can monitor [the process], is if the organizers tell you about it*" (interview with a researcher). The researcher of Podemos finds that this seeming lack of political efficacy could be influencing the engagement of members: "*I think that in the case of Podemos, people are very disappointed with these instruments. They were very fond of them at the beginning and now I think that the registered members are kind of... Well, they are abandoning. (...) If you enter in Plaza Podemos you will see that participation is very low. And if you compare this to Plaza Podemos in 2015[...] That was incredible*" (interview with a researcher).

10.4 Participatory Budgeting in Belo Horizonte

10.4.1 Introduction

In 2006, the Brazilian city of Belo Horizonte took a decisive step forward in moving the Porto Alegre model of participatory budgeting (PB) online. The Belo Horizonte digital participatory budget (DPB) is a process for discussing and voting on preselected projects proposed by City Hall. During the DPB period, participants can post comments in five discussion forums on the DPB website as well as vote on the proposed projects. Each citizen can vote for one project in each of the municipality's administrative regions (Coleman and Sampaio 2016). Through a platform accessible not only via the Internet, but also via voting kiosks and voting by phone, the city managed to engage 10% of the voting population in decisions on budget allocation. The participatory platform, however, was exclusively digital, meaning that voting would only take place online. Voting kiosks were set up to make ICT hardware available to all, as well as to provide guidance: *"To minimize problems related to digital divide in the project, the City Hall established several voting kiosks throughout the city. Associations' headquarters, cooperatives and schools were also listed as official voting locations"* (Sampaio et al. 2011).

The city has applied participatory budget processes since 1993, following the Porto Alegre PB model, which is based on physical deliberation meetings and neighbourhood representatives collaborating with city officials. In this model of annually recurring PB, online tools play a secondary, supplementary role. But for 2006, the Belo Horizonte municipality decided to add to the Porto Alegre model by having a parallel PB process that would run entirely online, that is, a Digital Participatory Budgeting (DPB) process. In this parallel process that ran on a dedicated website *"any citizen with his or her voter's registration number from Belo Horizonte could choose 9 out of 36 projects (being one project per region), pre-selected by the City Hall, and by the associations linked to the PB"* (Sampaio et al. 2011). The funds for the DPB were additional to that already dedicated to the ongoing Porto Alegre-style annual PB process. In 2006, *"City Hall would invest US$ 11.25 million in its nine regions [while the] US$ 44.2 million budget for offline PB were maintained"* (ibid.) The first application and creation of the tool was initiated by then Mayor Fernando Pimentel of the Workers' Party (Partido dos Trabalhadores) and the Belo Horizonte municipality were involved in all phases of the (DPB) process. City officials were not, however, involved in development or management of the website, which was performed by the communications agency Nitrato (ibid.).

After the initial DPB in 2006, further changes have distinguished it from the original Porto Alegre model. From 2008 onward, the process no longer focused on issues pertaining to specific neighbourhood but focused instead on a single issue on a city level. Here, *"voters from Belo Horizonte should choose one among five pre-selected projects. All the options referred to road projects, with the goal to improve Belo Horizonte's traffic"* (ibid.). Again, all project proposals were preselected without citizen involvement. Later applications of the DPB in Belo Horizonte were undertaken in 2011 and 2013 (Coleman and Sampaio 2016). The Municipality of Belo Horizonte finances both use of the DPB web tool and the implementation of policies following the process. The distribution of funds via the DPB is based on an index created by the municipality in partnership with a local university "*high priority areas receive more funding, in order to stimulate economic growth and social prosperity*" (Sampaio et al. 2011).

As a local government initiative, there are some legal constraints as to what sort of decisions are delegated to the citizens. However, this is no different from the legal limitations that the ordinary participatory budget of the city functions under: "*the legal framework is kind of important in this sense that [...] there are some limits as to what City Hall can actually do. [...] So, people could not vote for, let's say, laws or bills or something like that. [...] As we had the face-to-face PB for several years, I guess it was not a big concern for anyone*" (interview with a researcher).

10.4.2 Participants

In the design of the DPB process, openness to all citizens of the city was prioritized over sociological representativeness. Thus, in contrast to the Porto Alegre model, no selection mechanisms were applied to engage participants in a representative way. Nor were voting results weighted to reflect the demographics of the population. Instead, efforts were made to ensure that voters were actual citizens.

The general target group of the Belo Horizonte DPB includes all adult citizens with a voter registration ID. This automatically means that participants must be a minimum of 18 years of age. In comparison with the original Porto Alegre model for PB, in Belo Horizonte, it has been an aim to broaden participation beyond those already affiliated to the PB, and make participation more inviting, specifically for young people and the middle class—both groups that were underrepresented in the face-to-face PB processes (Coleman and Sampaio 2016): "*We wished both to promote the expansion of popular participation and extend the participatory budget process to segments of the population that usually don't get involved, such as the middle class and youth*" (Veronica Campos Sales, PB coordinator, personal interview in Coleman and Sampaio 2016: 5). This is supported by our interviewed city official who was affiliated with the 2006 and 2008 DPB's: "*We were interested in increasing involvement by the population. We had already the presential participatory budget (...). The main target groups [of the DPB] were youth and middle class, who did not take part in the presential process.*"

Thus, citizens of Belo Horizonte with a voter ID could already register to participate in 2006 (using their voter ID). In 2008, participants were also required to type in a random series of numbers (CAPTCHAs) as a security measure against computer bots. Although thorough registration processes were in place in 2006, security requirements were introduced by legal officers of the state in response to allegations of corrupt voting practices in the 2006 and 2008 DPBs (Coleman and Sampaio 2016). In 2011 and 2013, requirements for registration were supplemented by the download of a security app, dual voter ID (electoral and personal), email confirmation and questions on age and gender (Coleman and Sampaio 2016).

The number of participants has varied over the applications of the DPB tools between 2006 and 2013. The population of Belo Horizonte is just under 1.5 million. In the first DPB in 2006, well over 10% of the city's population, precisely 172,938 people, participated online. This resulted in 192,229 website visits and over 500,000 votes. In later applications, participation has fallen significantly from 124,320 citizens in 2008 to 25,378 in 2011, and 8900 in 2013 (Coleman and Sampaio 2016: 6). *"It was a huge success in this first edition. I mean, the whole city was commenting about these topics and ideas. And you could see in the streets, people engaging and mobilizing for this case. (...) You have a tipping point after 2008. Because it was considered by everyone as a very good success and now today you see the same program with 100,000 less participants. There was a huge failure between 2008 and 2011"* (interview a with researcher).

What happened between 2008 and 2011 to explain such a steep decline? The scientific researcher interviewed points to one particularly damaging error: the failure to implement the 2008 project chosen by the voters: *"In 2008, the framework was just about choosing one single work in the whole city. And in the end, this work was not carried out"* (interview with a researcher). In the researcher's view, this meant that citizens in general and participants in particular, lost trust in the process: *"When the 2011 process started, people felt very frustrated about the DPB... Because they had mobilized, they had, you know, made everything to gain this work, to win this election. And then the work was not carried out. So, most people did not want to participate any more. Even though City Hall tried to explain that it was not its fault that the work was still to be done, but in the end, people did not trust the process anymore"* (interview with a researcher).

The application of the online platform was first and foremost an attempt to involve younger citizens and the middle class, who were disaffiliated with PB. The main reason given for this was the assertion that these groups simply found participation in the face-to-face process too extensive and time-consuming, and that minimizing this would increase engagement: *"The digital participation, we thought, was already the instrument to bring in the target group"* (interview with a city official). On this basis, the process was simplified to allow quick and easy voting, although maintaining channels for more extensive participation as well: *"If somebody wanted only to vote, he could vote in 30 seconds, but if he wanted also to participate, to discuss, to give his opinion, to lobby for what he thought was the best option, he had many instruments [online] to discuss with City Hall and also to promote discussion in-between citizens"* (interview with a city official). However, no data was collected in these years to support conclusions that the DPB succeeded in engaging citizens in the target groups.

10.4.3 Participatory Processes

In 2008, two online features for further participation in the DPB were implemented. One was a chat feature, where citizens could contact city officials responsible for the PB. The other was a comment section on each project, where anyone (registered user or not) could submit comments (ibid.).

The five discussion forums make up the foremost platform for exchange of views. In 2006, 1209 messages were posted. A study of two of these forums (including two issues from each forum) indicated that only around 30% of messages were dialogical, while around 70% were monological (Sampaio et al. 2011). This suggests a somewhat low degree of "deliberativeness" in the forums. City officials and incumbents did not participate in these forums to encourage deliberation nor to answer citizens' questions: *"People would address the City Hall in the questions, 'Why don't you do this work instead of that?', 'Why don't you select works in my region?', and the City Hall would just leave these messages unanswered. This was very frustrating for people"* (interview with a researcher).

The 2006 DPB website provided basic information about each of the projects available. This included information on location and costs, as well as pictures. In the 2008 process, which dealt exclusively with city infrastructure projects, background information included visualizations of the roads "before" and "after" reconstruction, as well as informational videos. Virtual maps were also employed to visualize project locations, as well as where to find voting spots around the city (Sampaio et al. 2011).

10.4.3.1 User-Friendliness

Generally, our interviewees expressed satisfaction with the user-friendliness and efficacy of this tool for online participatory budgeting, and dissatisfaction with the scope and ambition of its application. The technological simplicity of the tool is considered to motivate more participants to take part and make participation more efficient: *"The main strength is that it was easy. Digital democracy platforms can be kind of hard to understand, or even demand too much, especially if it's based on comments—that you have to comment, to read, and to respond—it is not everyone that has the time or the energy to participate. So, it was kind of a platform for, let's say, ordinary people who wanted to say what they prefer"* (interview with a researcher).

This consideration runs parallel to the initial idea that minimizing the inconvenience of participation would increase participation among the specific target groups. One could also view this in the context of citizen empowerment versus simplicity of use: *"The technology was very, very simple (...), but the empowerment of people, on the other hand, was very high"* (interview with a researcher). This seems to mostly be the case concerning the voting process and less so regarding the deliberative processes: *"I think we had a weak participation of citizens in terms of discussing which public works should be voted. This is the weak part of the process*" (interview with a city official).

10.4.3.2 Trust-Building (or Not)

DPB voting results are intended to become policy. This occurs in most instances, but "*The [only project] voted in 2008 has not yet been finished because there is a problem in terms of land use and land property - it's a legal problem that involves federal government and local government and this has not been [finalized]*" (interview with a city official). Although the outcome of the process is in this way a disappointment, participants did influence the output of decision-making. The failure to deliver their choice lies in the configuration of the successful project: "*It was not that [the DPB participation] did not influence the decision making... Yes, it did influence, but later on, City Hall had administrative and legal problems [in the implementation]*" (interview with a city official). This may explain a measurable decline in feelings of political efficacy among participants. Expressions of external efficacy in posted messages fell from 40% in 2008 to 20% in 2011 (Coleman and Sampaio 2016). In total, 6.7% of messages in 2011 specifically mentioned the 2008 project: "*I encouraged many people to vote for this Project of São Vicente Square and where is the work? It's only deception [...] Why should I vote again?*" (Participant in a discussion forum on 28 November 2011, DPB 2011 as quoted in Coleman and Sampaio 2016: 11; Sampaio et al. 2011).

In evaluating the methodology of the tool, one interviewee emphasizes the limitations in political scope of participation in the DPB: "*I think the participatory budget process in Belo Horizonte should change (...) into a process that discusses which city we want. (...) The methodology should discuss largely with citizens what are the public works because actually it is not 'what are the public works' but 'which is the city that we want?'*" (interview with a city official). This in turn leads to the conclusion, that although the DPB in Belo Horizonte has had some positive effects, it has done little to establish new trust in political actors and institutions: "*I think the tool has not contributed in terms of changing trust of the target group in local politics. I think what they thought before is the same they think after the process*" (interview with a city official). Factors that are emphasized as inhibitory in this regard are the focus on city planning projects (rather than policy) and especially the breach of trust that occurred when not implementing the 2008 project. To our other interviewee, the latter indeed makes the Belo Horizonte DPB most illustrative as "*an example of what not to do*" (interview with a researcher).

10.5 Participatory Budgeting in Paris

10.5.1 Introduction

In 2014, Paris began a multi-annual process in which Parisians are invited to participate in the distribution of an annually increasing share of the city's budget. The general purpose of *Budget Participatif* (BP) is to promote democratic innovation in the city, giving citizens the opportunity to participate in decisions that affect their daily lives. BP should be *"an inclusive device, (...) a tool against social inequalities"* (translated from Mairie de Paris 2016). Citizens can be involved in the phases of agenda setting, giving input for (and co-selecting) spending options and in deciding by public vote which ideas are to be implemented. The participation process runs at four levels: the City, the 20 arrondissements (district level), some low-income neighbourhoods and all public schools at primary, college and lycées levels (Cabannes 2017).

In the first year, 17.7 million euros were spent on the BP. Parisians were able to vote on 15 projects designed by the City of Paris (Budget Participatif 2016). One year later, in 2015, Parisian residents were able to submit proposals themselves. They initially submitted more than 5000 proposals. A process of preselection reduced the number to approximately 600 projects, out of which 8 were selected at the level of the city for a total budget of about 35 million euros. In addition, 181 less expensive projects were selected at the level of Paris' 20 arrondissements for a total budget of about 59 million euros (Holston et al. 2016: 6). In 2016, the total budget reached a 100 million euros (compared to Paris' overall budget of close to 10 billion euros). An innovative aspect of the Paris participatory budgeting project is that an overall value of 500 million euros for the whole 2014–2020 period was announced; that way trying to help to build confidence between the city and the citizens of Paris.

Participants can propose their ideas on the BP website. When submitted, proposals are available for comment and support by participants. A permanent team of nine people conducts day-to-day activities of the participation process. This team also connects with many other employees of the city of Paris administration, which help out in different ways. There are different commissions at the district and city levels that are responsible for the preselection of the proposals; they evaluate all the proposals on cost, feasibility and eligibility. Both commissions are composed of an elected body and a citizen body. There are four criteria for selection (decided by the City, not by citizens): the project needs to (1) be proposed by a Parisian, meaning a resident, (2) satisfy general interest, (3) be part of the city's responsibility and (4) the running costs of the investments related to projects need to be limited and primarily should not imply generating a public job (Cabannes 2017). After the selected projects are published online, candidates can run promotional campaigns for their ideas. The city provides an online toolkit to make flyers, posters, social media posts and organizes in-person workshops to help the candidates. Each project is presented during city sponsored events. In the end, the proposals are put to a public vote on the BP website as well as on paper ballots. Participants have 10 votes, from which they can assign five to city-level proposals and five to district level (interview with an organizer). Following the final selection, citizens can monitor the implementation of winning projects on the website.

The participatory process is closely tied to the political and administrative institutions of Paris. First, online participation takes place on the city's web platform. The city is obliged to process citizen proposals and to follow the results of the voting processes. Following the first PB—presented by Mayor Anne Hidalgo in 2014—the application of participatory budgeting was approved by the Paris Assembly as a rule of law. This means that the next mayor of Paris cannot reverse the process of participatory budgeting unless the Paris Assembly does so (Napolitano 2015). In this way, Paris is legally committed to budget participative *"every year until 2020. And if we get a new mayor, the new mayor [must] still ask the council to vote on the cancellation of the participatory budget"* (interview with an organizer). This legal framework is especially relevant as it depoliticizes the use of Budget Participatif and commits the city to its outcome. As the interviewed journalist points out: *"So now that it's a rule of law, the next mayor cannot just decide to scrap the participatory budgeting. It has to go through the assembly of the city again. (...) Now, it's a thing of the city and not just of the mayor. (...) I think it contributed very positively in this sense."*

Procedures and responsibilities are formalized and communicated by the City, often on the website. As Paris is divided in 20 local districts (arrondissements), a lot of the groundwork to engage the public is delegated to districts. The district mayors are not all a member of the Socialist Party of Paris Mayor Anne Hidalgo and could thus be thought to be less enthusiastic about the participatory budget. The Hidalgo administration solved this by financial motivation: *"We actually made a very interesting deal with them, at the very beginning, which was that any district that would get into the game will have their local budget doubled... So they're all playing the game, and are actually very involved"* (interview with an organizer).

10.5.2 Participants

Budget Participatif as a participatory tool targets all residents of Paris. Anyone can participate by way of self-selection—regardless of age and nationality. There seems to be an acceptance that not all citizens have access to the Internet or are comfortable using the platform for one reason or another. Some district city halls and public buildings have offered personal help and/or workshops (Napolitano 2015).

And Parisians do participate. Around 40,000 citizens participated by voting in 2014 and around 67,000 voted in 2015 (Joignot 2016) and 92,809 in 2016, which represent 5% of the total urban population of Paris (Cabannes 2017). This *"is a lot compared to other cities but not that much compared to the entire Parisian population"* (interview with an organizer). To put it in perspective, 1,018,280 Parisians registered to vote for the local elections in 2014, of which close to 600,000 voted.

10.5.2.1 Communication and Mobilization Strategies

The tool is marketed broadly and has seen a lot of media attention, especially in its first year. *"We do have a lot of press, but it's a concept that seems to be hard to explain. So, it's not that easy"* (interview with an organizer). The advertisement from the city's hand has focused on visibility on city streets and online, as the interviewed organizer points out: *"[We use] big advertisements and posters in the streets, because the city controls that. So, we use it a lot, and it's a big, big budget. [...] We started to buy some online advertisement which is quite new for the city"* (interview with an organizer).

In 2014 and 2015, around 60% of the voters choose to use the online tool (Napolitano 2015 and interview with a journalist). *"For me, that's still a lot of people voting offline"* (interview with an organizer). The backup of an offline voting method, our expert interviewee believes, prevented critique on the web solution: *"Probably, if it had been only an online vote, there could have been some kind of [public] discussion, but the fact there was also a paper ballot meant also that the people that didn't feel safe, instead of complaining, they said 'okay I'm just going to vote on paper'"* (interview with a journalist).

It is an explicit goal of the tool to involve participants beyond the political or participatory elite. It seems to succeed in doing so. Whether this is caused by advertising the process and tool, by design characteristics or other factors is arguable. Some design characteristics that lead to more inclusion can be pointed out. First of all, the parallel process of physical voting and project submission is implemented to prevent a digital divide. The initiative to offer advice and support could qualify layman participation in comparison to that of elite actors. The same applies to the organization of project workshops. Finally, registration is kept very easy: *"We don't want any obstacle on the participation and we know that the more detailed the form is... Like to register to vote... The less votes we're getting"* (interview with an organizer). In fact, identification is so limited that *"you just have to declare on your personal honour, when you say that you live in Paris. And you give an address, but it's fully possible to fake it"* (interview with an organizer). Combined, these and potentially other characteristics seem to lower the barrier of participation, promoting broader involvement—as well as empowerment—of ordinary citizens.

No specific mechanisms have been implemented to ensure representativeness, and it does not seem a primary focus. *"In my perspective, the participants are representative in the view that, like, all those people were allowed to vote and all those people were involved. Of course, I don't know the people who voted... Nobody knows"* (interview with a journalist). Little data is collected to pursue or assess the representativeness of participants, due to legal constraints and considerations towards participation barriers: *"Because the French law is very strict, we cannot ask questions about for instance race. (...) it would be interesting to target minorities, but we cannot do that"* (interview with an organizer). Officials do have some general ideas of socio-economic and demographic characteristics, although the basis of this is limited: *"You can tell from the part of Paris where they live, what kind of social [level] it is. (...) Where there is more poverty or young people, [people] participate a lot. But surprisingly, the conservative areas and very family working areas are also very involved... Like in the 15th district"* (interview with an organizer).

10.5.3 Participatory Process

On budgetparticipatif.paris.fr, participants can submit proposals on city level as well as on arrondissement level. These proposals are featured on the website, where participants can then offer their comment and/or support. At a fixed deadline, the City collects the proposals and assesses them with regard to technical and legal feasibility. Participants can vote on all the accepted projects either online or on paper ballots. Ten votes can be cast, divided in city level and arrondissement level: *"You can choose five projects in the whole Paris area and five projects in one particular district that you get to choose, like wherever, where you live or you can choose the district where you work..."* (interview with an organizer).

The participatory process has changed already in its first years. In 2014, all proposed projects were designed by the City. A year later, in 2015, the proposals came from the citizens and 10 million euros was earmarked for projects concerning schools. This, however, did not stop participants from focusing on another topic: *"one thing we were not happy about last year was that a lot of projects were addressing the same topic. (...) Anything green, which is good, but we have a lot of money already dedicated on green in the regular budget, so it was actually too much"* (interview with an organizer).

In 2015, when citizens were encouraged to submit their own ideas, 5.115 proposals came in. Around half of these were rejected by the administration due to technical, legal and social criteria. A total of 71% of these proposals were sent in by individuals and 29% by associations, companies, etc. (Budget Participatif 2016). A lot of effort has been put into teaching participants the formalities of proposing projects, and the 2016 process has seen a greater success rate in meeting the criteria (interview with an organizer). Lessons from the 2015 process may have been illustrative in this regard. *"One of the main difficulties in (...) involving citizens in the process is that people usually—because it's not their job—don't know about feasibility of projects, they don't know what the city can do, what the local council can do, and also what the city cannot do, because sometimes it's a competence of the county or the region"* (interview with a journalist).

10.5.3.1 Aggregation

The input of participants is aggregated in at least two ways. First and foremost, the process of voting is one of aggregating support for citizen projects to decide which to implement. In the phase of project assessment, there is also room for the City to combine, pair and interpret proposals, being another form of weighing and aggregating citizen input. In 2016, this phase was opened up for citizen involvement. *"We made a big effort to involve citizens into the merging phase and really encourage them to come and defend the project together. First of all, that way we have less projects to deal with, but also, we will have more comprehensive projects. And finally, because we need people to get more involved in the campaigning phase"* (interview with an organizer).

10.5.3.2 Deliberation

Interaction and exchange of views between participants is encouraged by the design (e.g. comment and support options). Between participants and political decision-makers, the exchange of views is arranged indirectly. The participants' proposals (including qualifying comments, etc.) are not given to the decision-makers, but to the broader population of Parisians to vote upon (albeit after being processed by the City Administration). The results (representing the aggregated views of the citizens) are given to the political decision-makers after the vote, who are obliged to adopt the results as policy measures under the constraints of the budget (Plesse 2014).

10.5.3.3 Information on the Process

Information is provided by the City of Paris in several phases of the BP process. First, the website provides a fair share of infographics, FAQs and information, which explain the process of BP and how to participate. In the proposal submission phase, information regarding the legal framework and support for financial approximations is provided by the administration to the submitting participant(s). After the submission of proposals, the reasons of rejection are explicitly explained to the owner of the project by the administration.

Furthermore, distribution of decision-making responsibilities is clarified in the thorough information material on the website and the different phases of the decision process are documented on the website. Participants and other interested readers can also monitor winning projects on a devoted section of the BP website, where progress is reported. Throughout the process, participants can give feedback on the result and impact of their contributions. Participants who have submitted proposals are informed by email about acceptance, changes, regrouping, rejections and the reasoning or regulation behind it that may be relevant to the proposal (Budget Participatif 2016). *"We've done a lot of data visualization, videos, there is this chart where the rules are written... There is a big part of the website doing pédagogie. (...) We do a lot of meetings, explanations, drawings and everything"* (interview with an organizer).

10.5.4 Results

In the first phase of public participation, citizens contribute to the proposals, from which the acceptable ones (with regards to technical and legal feasibilities) are selected and put to a public vote. In the second phase of participation, the participating citizens fully decide by way of voting what is to be the political output of the process. Voting results on city level and for the arrondissements are communicated publicly shortly after the vote.

Most of the proposals concern quality of life (like renovating micro public spaces like a street corner, a garden or a wall), transportation and mobility (like safety of pedestrians and alternative forms of transportation to cars) and the environment (like green energy, educational programmes on recycling, etc.). In 2017, the city started to encourage development of projects around less popular topics like sport, cleanliness, security, housing, solidarity, cleanliness, new technology, economy and citizen participation.

Citizens are not generally involved in the implementation and thus can merely monitor outcomes: *"It's the city that's going to do the projects"* (interview with a journalist). This is also reflected in the distribution of funds to winner projects. The city has pre-set a budget for each project and pre-distributed funds to the different arrondissements dependent on the number of inhabitants (interview with organizer) and on social development: *"They didn't give the same amount of money to every local council, to every arrondissement. They gave more money to the underdeveloped areas, so the richest part, the central part, they get very little money comparatively"* (interview with journalist). This priority is surely an expression of a social political position but can also be seen as a means to gain higher effect on development—or incremental value—of public investments.

The BP is not only thought of as a tool of ideation and voting—another level of abstraction is apparent: *"For us, participatory budgeting is just a tool of trust, and a symbol and a demonstration of a new way to do politics. So that's something we don't measure. I mean, we measure the trust people have in [Paris Mayor] Anne Hidalgo and it's working well, but we don't know if it's related to the participatory budget"* (interview with an organizer). Thus, institutional and incumbent trust is a key consideration. But the attraction of the process as well as the (digital) tool towards younger citizens is highlighted: *"The main strength for me is transparency and also reaching a new audience for democracy and renew the population, that is a success for sure. If you go to a traditional local meeting with only retired old people, and you compare it now to the number of children who participated at public schools, it's striking, so that's an amazing success"* (interview with an organizer).

10.6 Participatory Budgeting in Reykjavik (Betri Reykjavik)

10.6.1 Introduction

Betri Reykjavik (Better Reykjavik) is an open source website platform for participatory budgeting (PB) under the Reykjavik municipality's budget. It combines deliberative and participatory democracy and gives citizens the opportunity to suggest, debate and vote for budgetary decisions and other communal projects (Participedia.net 2018). Betri Reykjavik is an ongoing process, which commits City Hall of the capital of Iceland to collect proposed ideas and projects every month. This way, the website is used as a participatory tool throughout the ongoing decision-making processes of the local government.

Betri Reykjavik is based on two processes. One is a monthly agenda-setting process, which translates to Your Voice at the City Council, where participants submit ideas and vote on them. The top ideas are discussed at City Council meetings and either approved or rejected. More than half of the presented ideas are accepted by the City Council as policy. Your Voice at the City Council provides thus specific input for policy.

The second process allows citizens to submit ideas for new construction projects in My Neighborhood. Here, the city assesses the ideas and assigns costs to the projects. People then vote in an online process, providing a binding vote for ideas, which will be included in the budget by the City Council (Bjarnason and Grimsson 2016). The participation process can therefore be characterized as co-decision-making. Formally, however, the final decision on the process and handling of individual ideas presented on Betri Reykjavik remains in the hands of the city government (Participedia.net 2018).

The overall aim and purpose of Betri Reykjavik is to involve citizens in decision-making and to engage them in politics. Specific purposes are (Lackaff et al. 2014):

- To build trust in political institutions and increase legitimacy political decisions
- To increase political participation and inclusivity in-between elections
- To educate citizens about city governance

Betri Reykjavik is initiated and maintained by the local not-for-profit organization Citizens Foundation, which devotes its work to improving relations between citizens and administration. The foundation receives financial support from the Reykjavik municipality to maintain and develop the platform (Participedia.net 2018). The financing of the final projects is through the municipality's public budget.

The municipality did not design the tool itself for a reason: They wanted to avoid possible constraints of legal restrictions. In spite of the political commitment to Betri Reykjavik, the design and maintenance is done by Citizens Foundation. The interviewed scientific researcher explains the process as such: *"One of the things that I think is really interesting about the original Better Reykjavik project, is that the city didn't have to change any policies. So, they wanted to do this project, but they would have had to change a lot of policies to run it themselves. [...] They just let this non-profit, the developers, run it and manage it. And they sent someone from the city to gather the top ideas that came out of that every month. And then that person physically put them on the agenda of the individual city boards that would address those ideas. So it was kind of a run-around of the regulatory environment of the city to take advantage of this new type of engagement."*

10.6.2 Participants

Since its establishment, Betri Reykjavik has had over 22,800 unique visitors and now—October 2018—has over 23,000 active users. The tool is designed to be broadly applicable and relevant to all citizens of the municipality—be it stakeholders, experts, officials or laymen. *"One of the interesting things about the Better Reykjavik project, especially in its early days, is that they were targeting anyone who was literate and had access to a computer"* (interview with a researcher). Participants register using their electronic citizen's ID. They do not go through any sort of selection. Apart from a minimum voting age of 16 years, no characteristic (dis) qualifies ideas or participants. In other words, the selection of participants is strictly self-selective.

10.6.2.1 Communication and Mobilization Strategies

The website was initially advertised broadly around the city and online. There was also a specific appeal to political parties to use the tool. *"This was a fairly high-profile project in the city. There was a lot of discussion in the mass media, so it was in the newspapers, on the radio... Of course, there was a social media campaign. They also did outdoor advertising, I think, so there were posters up. (...) It was a legitimate, serious effort to pull people in, I think"* (interview with a researcher).

10.6.2.2 Representativeness

The tool does not weigh votes for representativeness. In fact, there has been little consideration regarding representativeness—the focus in this regard has been on mobilizing participants with applicable interest, knowledge and opinions (interview with an organizer). Some thought has gone into assessing representativeness in retrospect: *"In our participatory budgeting system, where people have to vote with an electoral ID-card, we get anonymized, demographic-style data. Gender, age groups and things like that"* (interview with an organizer). The expectation from the developers that an online tool would automatically attract young citizens was shot down: *"Most problems are with young people. And we thought that after the first year, when we did the participatory budgeting, being an online tool and everything, that we would see a lot of action of 20–30 year olds*" (interview with an organizer). The interviewed organizer finds this difficulty of engaging the youngest age groups almost a law of nature, as they often are not very interested in their neighbourhood: "*When people start to have children, then it seems to be that the near neighborhood (...) becomes certainly a lot more important in people's lives... It's just one of those things, right? (...) You're never going to be able to have someone who's 20 years old, single (...) as interested as a 35-year old who has two children, you know?*" (interview with an organizer).

There has been some attention paid to minority protection and participation on the Betri Reykjavik platform. This is done through the sorting of arguments—thus paying attention to the minority *view*—rather than the efforts of selection or mobilizing of participants from minority groups (see next paragraph). This is contrasted by the fact that the vast majority of the website is only available in the Icelandic language, making it difficult for some minorities to participate: "*In Icelandic context, I think the biggest issue, the biggest barrier in a lot of cases, is the Icelandic language. So, the immigrant community uses mostly English but not everything was necessarily available in a language they could understand*" (interview with a researcher).

It is an explicit focus of Betri Reykjavik to make participation in decision-making more egalitarian and inclusive to layman citizens. Design-wise, this is evident in "*a direct connection with social media networks like Facebook and Twitter [which] reduces barriers to participation while situating policy discussions within the users' real social networks*" (Lackaff et al. 2014). Participation is designed to be simple, quick and easy, adopting "like"-style mechanisms and limiting text contributions to 500 characters (Bjarnason and Grimsson 2016).

10.6.3 Participatory Process

Betri Reykjavik combines two main tools or platforms, tied to the two forms of processes. *Your Voice at the City Council* starts with a brainstorm phase, in which participants deliberate on the political agenda by proposing and debating policy ideas. The technology behind this is *Your Priorities*, an open-source idea generation platform. Here, participants can submit ideas in text and graphics, informally vote ideas up and down and debate ideas by placing arguments for and against. The arguments are sorted into columns to keep the debate on track and relevant to the proposal. Finally, after the most popular projects are determined (10–15 every month), citizens can have a final vote on the projects on the website using Open Active Voting software, which is also open source (interview with an organizer). New versions of both platforms are released on a somewhat regular basis in order to enhance user-friendliness and lower participation barriers: "*We are always working on simplifying the process, in terms of how to participate. And that, I think, is in general a weakness of participatory processes, that they can be too complicated*" (interview with an organizer).

During the online citizen deliberation on project proposals, the diversity of views is managed by allowing equal visual impact to both sides of the debate. The most popular arguments against any proposal are presented at the same level as the most popular arguments in favour of the proposal, regardless the distribution between the two sides (Lackaff et al. 2014): "*What we tried to do was to split the screen in two so people who support the idea can write points for it on the left side of the screen (...), and on the right side of the screen, people who are against the idea can put their points... And almost overnight (...) the quality level of the debate increased a lot*" (interview with an organizer). Thus, views are exchanged between participants strictly by arguing for or against proposals. This minimizes the extent to which a comment can refer to another comment rather than the proposal itself: "*If you see a point, you don't agree with, there's no way to comment on it. You have to write a counterpoint*" (interview with an organizer). Both our interviewees emphasize several advantages to this design:

- Firstly, securing that minority views can gain attention, and "*make sure that the minority view is heard. When you go to the website you can see the idea, then the best points for the idea are at the same level as the best points against it. Even if there's a thousand people who support the idea and only 10 that don't support it*" (interview with an organizer).
- Secondly, user-friendliness in the sense of debate overview for newcomers: "*The thing that I like about it is that after a while, when a new participant comes to this particular issue, they can very quickly get a sense of the thinking on it, that's gone on previously*" (interview with a researcher).
- Thirdly, user-friendliness in the sense of minimizing the time necessary to participate: "*Participants can participate very little or they can participate very much, depending on how interested they are, which I see as a strength*" (interview with a researcher).
- Finally, this way of designing the debate module works to improve ideas. "*This has been very helpful to help the city make the ideas better*" (interview with an organizer).

It is clear from the dual process participation model which decisions are up to the City Council and which processes are subject to binding online votes. Reports of City Council meetings are publicly available. The public participation processes are public to everyone while ongoing and remain available in the website's archive until they are finished.

Participation results contribute (in some cases directly) to policy output. Citizens are informed about this output via the website platform of Betri Reykjavik and on the municipality's main website. The participants of a specific process are notified by email when there are developments in the decision-making process, as well as on implementation and later developments (Bjarnason and Grimsson 2016). "*If there's an idea that is going into processing, people can track it on the website (...) and each time there's a status update, you know, when it goes into a committee and is discussed and there are meeting notes, they are sent to all the participants*" (interview with an organizer). The interviewed organizer is quite insistent on the importance of proper feedback: "(...) *And obviously at the end, when the idea is agreed on or rejected, then everybody gets an email as well. It's super important (...). Otherwise, you're really not respecting people's time.*"

10.6.4 Results

In the first 3 years of Better Reykjavik, over 150 citizen ideas were approved by City Council. *Better Neighbourhoods* has seen over 200 different project ideas being implemented, following an investment totalling 5.7 million euros from the city (Participedia.net 2018). With Betri Reykjavik, results of the participatory process contribute directly to the formal decision-making process. This happens either by presenting and discussing the top proposals directly in the City Council's meetings or by providing construction projects, which are more or less co-created by citizens and civil servants, which are then voted on by the public and accepted by the municipality as binding. Of course, the results of binding votes are more directly influential on policy and/or planning output, but the participatory process in all cases is nevertheless directly tied to the decision-making process in City Hall or the municipal administration.

Some reservations can be made regarding the genuine political influence of Betri Reykjavik: "*The Reykjavik PB project is expertly focused on kind of small things. So, it's focused on, you know, park benches, parks, and repairs and things... So yes, within this kind of small domain, participants have a very direct impact. But it could also be argued that we're not talking about zoning or infrastructure development or what kind of... Bigger issues, that citizens might also be interested in*" (interview with a researcher). In other words, the possibility of affecting city policy on a higher level—for example, an overall strategy of "what kind of city do we want"—is rather limited.

It is also important to note that even binding votes do leave some room for interpretation of decisions in the implementation phase: "*The city does have some leeway to interpret the results*" (interview with a researcher). Surely, this is even more so the case when it comes to the proposals and ideas from the ideation process *Your Voice at the City Council* being presented to City Hall.

Whatever political, strategic or planning level is in question, this tool does—as agreed by both our interviewees—seem to improve City Hall and administration decisions. Being the co-founder of the Citizen's Foundation, the organizer puts it like this: "*That's really the biggest strength of using this tool: better decisions*" (interview with an organizer).

References

Beppegrillo.it. (2007). *'Vaffanculo-Day'*. http://www.beppegrillo.it/2007/06/vaffanculoday.html. Cited and translated on Wikipedia.org: 5 Star Movement. Accessed January 15, 2017.

Bjarnason, R., & Grimsson, G. (2016). *Better neighborhoods 2011 to 2016 – Participatory budgeting in Reykjavik. Presentation material*. Accessed October 15, 2018, from https://www.slideshare.net/NordicInnovation/citizenled-urban-planning-better-neighbourhoods

Bolleyer, N., Little, C., & von Nostitz, F. C. (2015). Implementing democratic equality in political parties. Organisational consequences in the Swedish and the German Pirate Parties. *Scandinavian Political Studies, 38*(2), 158–178.

Bordignon, F., & Ceccarini, L. (2015). The Five-Star Movement: A hybrid actor in the net of state institutions. *Journal of Modern Italian Studies, 20*(4), 454–473.

Borge, R., & Santamarina, E. (2015). *From protest to political parties: Online deliberation in the new parties arising in Spain*. Paper presented at the IPSA Conference Communication, Democracy and Digital Technology. Rovinj, Croatia, 2–3 October.

Budget Participatif. (2016). *Tout savoir sur de budget participative*. Accessed October 15, 2018, from https://budgetparticipatif.paris.fr/bp/la-demarche-sommaire.html

Cabannes, Y. (2017). Participatory budgeting in Paris: Act, reflect, grow. In Y. Cabannes (Ed.), *Another city is possible with participatory budgeting* (pp. 179–203). Montréal/New York/London: Black Rose Books.

Coleman, S., & Sampaio, R. C. (2016). Sustaining a democratic innovation: A study of three e-participatory budgets in Belo Horizonte. *Information, Communication and Society*, 1–16.

De Rosa, R. (2013a). Voice of the people or cybercratic centralism? In: *Conference for E-Democracy and Open Governement*, 89.

De Rosa, R. (2013b): *Voice of the people or cybercratic centralism?* Slideshare presentation of De Rosa. Accessed January 18, 2017, from http://www.slideshare.net/dgpazegovzpi/rosanna-de-rosa-voice-of-the-people-orcybercratic-centralism-the-italian-case-of-beppe-grillo-and-movimento-cinque-stelle-five-starsmovement?from_action=save

Edwards, A., & de Kool, D. (2016). *Digital democracy: Opportunities and dilemmas. The Dutch parliament in a networked society*. Den Haag: Rathenau Instituut.

Federici, T., Sæbø, Ø., & Braccini, A. M. (2015). 'Gentlemen, all aboard!' ICT and party politics: Reflections from a mass-eParticipation experience. *Government Information Quarterly, 32*(3), 287–298. https://doi.org/10.1016/j.giq.2015.04.009.

Greenstein, C. (2013). *Position, salience, and ownership theory and the Pirates: The rise and fall of an atypical party*. Master thesis, University of North Carolina at Chapel Hill.

Hensel, A. (2014). Erfolgreich gescheitert? Die Entwicklung der Piraten als Partei der Internetkultur. Der Bürger im Staat. *Politik und Internet, 64*(4), 246–251.

Holston, J., Issarny V., & Parra C. (2016). Engineering software assemblies for participatory democracy: The participatory budgeting case. In: *Software Engineering in Society at ICSE*.

IlFattoQuotidiano.ti. (2013). *Grillo, confessione a eletti 5SM: Finzione politica l'impeachment di Napolitano*. Cited on Wikipedia.org: 5 Star Movement.

Joignot, F. (2016). *La démocratie autrement. 1/6: Le budget participatif*. Loaded September 28, 2016. Accessed October 15, 2018, from http://www.lemonde.fr/festival/article/2016/07/14/la-democratie-autrement-1-6-le-budget-participatif_4969435_4415198.html

Kirchgaessner, S. (2016). We are for what is logical: How Italy's 5SM became a real contender. In: *The Guardian*. Accessed on January 20, 2017.

Klimowicz, K. A. (2016). The role of digital tools in the development of citizen-centered politics. In L. Jonak, N. Juchniewicz, & R. Włoch (Eds.), *Digital ecosystems. Society in digital age* (pp. 59–72). Warsaw: DELabUW.

Kling, C. C., Kunegis, J., Hartmann, H., Strohmaier, M., & Staab, S. (2015). Voting behaviour and power in online democracy: A study of LiquidFeedback in Germany's Pirate Party. *Proceedings of the International Conference on Weblogs and Social Media*. Accessed October 12, 2018, from https://arxiv.org/pdf/1503.07723.pdf

Kulick, M. S. (2013). Die Piratenpartei und die Genderproblematik. In O. Niedermayer (Ed.), *Die Piratenpartei* (pp. 149–174). Wiesbaden: Springer.

Lackaff, D., Bjarnason R., & Grimsson, G. (2014). *Better Reykjavik: Municipal policy crafting from the autonomous grassroots.* Accessed October 15, 2018, from https://rafhladan.is/bitstream/handle/10802/8000/IPP2014_better_reykjavik.pdf?

Mairie de Paris. (2016). *Vous avez voté Paris l'a fait. Budget participatif. Bilan des éditions 2014/2015.* Accessed October 15, 2018, from https://budgetparticipatif.paris.fr/bp/document?id=2278&id_attribute=102&working_content=true

Napolitano, A. (2015). *Lessons from Paris. Home to Europe's largest participatory budget.* Accessed October 15, 2018, from http://techpresident.com/news/25441/paris-experiments-participatory-budget-codesign

Participedia.net. (2018). *Electronic participatory budgeting in Iceland.* Accessed October 15, 2018, from http://participedia.net/en/cases/electronic-participatory-budgeting-iceland

Paulin, A. (2014). Through liquid democracy to sustainable non-bureaucratic government. Harnessing the power of ICTs for a novel form of digital government. *JeDEM, 6*(2), 216–230.

Plesse, R. H. (2014). *Parisians have their say on city's first €20m 'participatory budget'*. Loaded September 17. Accessed October 15, 2018, from https://www.theguardian.com/cities/2014/oct/08/parisians-have-say-city-first-20m-participatory-budget

Sæbø, Ø., Braccini, A. M., & Federici, T. (2014). From the blogosphere into real politics: The use of ICT by the five star movement. In L. Mola, F. Pennarola, & S. Za (Eds.), *From information to smart society. Environment, politics and economics.* Springer.

Sampaio, R. C., Maia, R. C. M., & Marques, F. P. J. A. (2011). Participation and deliberation on the Internet: A case study of digital participatory budgeting in Belo Horizonte. *The Journal of Community Informatics, 7*(1–2), 1–22.

Webpages

Accessed October 12, 2018

http://finanzen.piratenpartei.de/guv.php
http://wiki.piratenpartei.de/Hauptseite
http://wiki.piratenpartei.de/Mumble
http://www.spiegel.de/netzwelt/netzpolitik/piratenpartei-veraergert-entwickler-von-liquid-feedback-a-856698.html
https://darkbln.wordpress.com/2011/01/03/offener-brief-liquid-democracy/
https://en.wikipedia.org/wiki/Pirate_Party_Germany#cite_note-6
https://www.n-tv.de/politik/Wie-demokratisch-sind-die-Piraten-article10233026.html
https://www.piratenpartei.de/mission/politikmuede/
https://www.piratenpartei.de/partei/satzung/

Accessed October 15, 2018

http://municipales2014.paris.fr
https://betrireykjavik.is/community/777
https://betrireykjavik.is/domain/1
https://betrireykjavik.is/group/47
https://budgetparticipatif.paris.fr/bp/
https://budgetparticipatif.paris.fr/bp/jsp/site/Portal.jsp?page=search-solr&conf=list_projects&sort_name=5560755979855408750_random&sort_order=asc

Accessed January 2, 2019

https://blog.titanpad.com/2016/11/shutting-down-titanpad_12.html
https://consulproject.org/en/
https://nvotes.com/agoravoting-com-redirect/
https://plaza.podemos.info/
https://podemos.info/
https://www.loomio.org/
https://www.meetup.com/

Open Access This chapter is licensed under the terms of the Creative Commons Attribution 4.0 International License (http://creativecommons.org/licenses/by/4.0/), which permits use, sharing, adaptation, distribution and reproduction in any medium or format, as long as you give appropriate credit to the original author(s) and the source, provide a link to the Creative Commons licence and indicate if changes were made.

The images or other third party material in this chapter are included in the chapter's Creative Commons licence, unless indicated otherwise in a credit line to the material. If material is not included in the chapter's Creative Commons licence and your intended use is not permitted by statutory regulation or exceeds the permitted use, you will need to obtain permission directly from the copyright holder.

Chapter 11
Binding Decision-Making

Kerstin Goos and Iris Korthagen

Abstract Goos and Korthagen present a detailed analysis of the three case studies "Green Primary", "Voting in Estonia" and "Voting in Switzerland", which all describe different practices of online ballots. Relevant contextual factors of the digital tools with regard to the key dimensions input legitimacy, throughput legitimacy and output legitimacy are assessed in order to better understand the role these digital tools can play in the political decision-making process. The case studies are based on desk research and interviews with organizers and researchers of the e-participation processes and analyse the digital tool, the participants, participatory process and the results of the digital tool. The analysis shows that online voting tends to be more inclusive and that the process as such requires different steps to strengthen security and privacy of the online ballot. Furthermore, no clear indicators for an often-claimed increase of turnout exist, and, in general, scaling up online elections to a larger framework than the rather restricted ones analysed in this chapter requires major efforts with regard to legal, technical and social aspects.

11.1 Green Primary

11.1.1 Introduction

In 2014, the online Green Primary was organized: An online election to choose the two lead candidates (*Spitzenkandidaten*) for the European Green Party (EGP). During the elections for the European Parliament in 2014, the aim was to reinforce the link between the European Parliament and the European Commission via the election of leaders of political parties who could become the President of the Commission (see Hobolt 2014). Before the Lisbon Treaty, the President of the Commission was appointed on the basis of a consensus decision of European leaders

---

K. Goos (✉)
CyberForum e.V., Karlsruhe, Germany

I. Korthagen
Netherlands Court of Audit, The Hague, The Netherlands

© The Author(s) 2020
L. Hennen et al. (eds.), *European E-Democracy in Practice*, Studies in Digital Politics and Governance, https://doi.org/10.1007/978-3-030-27184-8_11

in the European Council. In the Lisbon Treaty, this procedure for choosing the President was modified. Five European political parties nominated their lead candidate for the position of the Commission President. For the internal election of the *Spitzenkandidaten*, the political parties followed different procedures. The European Green Party chose to organize an online election.

More specifically, the selection procedure determined that "*any European Green politician with the ambition to run as the leading EGP candidate needs to be nominated by his/her national party and receive the support from at least four to a maximum of eight of the 33 EGP member parties. Moreover, all EU member parties have the right to exclusively support one candidate*" (Put et al. 2016: 16). In the process of determining the lead candidates for the EGP, two other procedures are of importance:

- In the voting process, every vote counts as one: No weights for member parties or countries were applied in assessing the total amount of votes for a candidate.
- Two winning candidates are to be elected, who cannot be of same sex or Member State (Put et al. 2016: 17).

Four nominees had been endorsed by the EGP member parties to be the contenders in the open online election: José Bové, Ska Keller, Rebecca Harms and Monica Frassoni. The organization of this online election by the EGP was called the online "Green Primary". Green Party leader Natalie Bennett argued: "*This primary is an experiment in extending European democracy well beyond its former limits. [...] It will be the first-ever pan-European primary election, a chance for 16 and 17-year-olds to influence a vote from which they are otherwise excluded, and we hope will provoke a wide debate not just about the contenders but about the possibility of giving citizens a much broader say in European decision-making.*"[1] The purpose of this online procedure was to make a visual appeal for European Union (EU) decision-making that actively involves European citizens. Moreover, the Committee of the European Green Party (2014: 3) also mentioned boosting the—future—campaigns of member parties by creating publicity and increasing capacities through the collection of email addresses of Green-minded voters as a goal. The interviewed academic researcher also described an increase of "*the commitment of the electors to the actual voting as they have their say about the candidates*" as a possible effect of the e-voting procedure (interview with a researcher).

The EGP has spent about 200,000 € on the Green Primary (including online voting implementation costs, security and legal advice) and about 250,000 € for the campaign (for staff, meetings, design of campaign material, publicity and translation; Committee of the European Green Party 2014: 6).

The online voting took place at the website www.greenprimary.eu between 10 November 2013 and 28 January 2014. This procedure was more inclusive than the selection procedure of other European parties. As the scholars Put et al. (2016:

---

[1] https://www.greenparty.org.uk/news/2013/11/10/bringing-democracy-to-europe---the-european-green-primary-kicks-off-todayhas-begun, accessed 15 October 2018.

17) conclude: *"Self-evidently, this primary election is located at the extreme inclusive end of the inclusiveness–exclusiveness continuum. The other four Europarties each organized party conferences to select the final candidate for EC presidency. These party agencies were composed of party delegates in the cases of PES, ALDE and EL, and additionally high-level intra-party officeholders in the case of EPP. In other words, selectorates of these four parties are situated towards the more exclusive end of the continuum when compared to the EGP procedure."*

11.1.2 Participants

The voting was not only accessible for Green Party members, but to every EU resident of 16 years or older. Participants thus did not have to be a member of the Green Party, but only had to tick a box that they shared green values. A total of 22,676 persons voted and they originated from all EU Member States (Put et al. 2016: 16). The Committee of the European Green Party (2014) reports that after an initial peek at launch, participation decreased until the last 14 days. The Committee of the EGP also concluded that the accessibility could be improved. The necessity of certain digital skills and usage of a mobile phone appeared to be causing problems for some people, especially for older generations (Committee of the European Green Party 2014: 5).

This final number of voters is evaluated as disappointing by different media: *"With a total of 375 million voters across the EU, the paltry participation numbers were a flop. The Greens had originally set to mobilize 100,000 participants—a far cry from actual turnout."*[2] But even within the Green Party the goal of 100,000 participants might have been utopian, the National Democratic Institute (2015: 73) argues: *"With EU-wide party membership totalling around 150,000 voters, the EGP's goal for participation was ambitious."*

Because only name, country, postal code, phone number, email address and a confirmation of the voter that he or she is above 16 were requested in the online voting, the representativeness of voters cannot be determined on the basis of those data (interview with a campaign manager). The only criteria the party had for representation was national participation. *"So the only assessment we did, was if we had a good representation of countries and yes, we had participants from all over Europe, so this gave us the confidence that this was a pan-European vote"*, the campaign manager argued in the interview, but *"there are differences of course between the number of participants between countries and [...] the number of participants were not proportional to the number of citizens from the country and the European Union. And so it was not a perfect representation of course and also*

---

[2]https://www.dw.com/en/online-voting-flops-for-european-green-party/a-17395839, accessed 15 October 2018.

the number of participants was not very high in total" (interview with a campaign manager).

To engage people for the open online primary, offline debates were held around Europe to give voters the chance to see the candidates in action. These meetings were open to anyone and not just aimed at members of the Green Party. Moreover, the meetings were also broadcasted online. The engagement strategy also informed voters with press releases, news reports on the website and an online blog on the different steps before and during the online election process and other information on the online voting process on the primary website as well as on the website of the European Greens. Interaction was promoted and channelled on social media (interview with a campaign manager). Through Twitter and the EGP Facebook page, people were also invited to ask questions to the contenders. A video about the primary was made and viewed 2746 times on YouTube.

The Committee of the EGP reported a high amount of mostly positive media coverage for the Green Primary. In contrast, political scientist Arzheimer strikes a more negative tone claiming that those who were not frequent visitors to the Green Party websites, probably did not know about the e-voting opportunity. *"The Greens need to market it more aggressively, and the media need to report on it more. That would increase participation." [...] "The purpose of this measure was to generate attention. That just didn't work."*[3] Both interviewees—the academic researcher and the campaign manager—assessed the effectiveness negatively. The online campaign manager argued: *"the most important factor that led to low participation was that we didn't make enough promotional mobilisation in the national countries on the ground. [...] It's very hard to run a campaign on a European level only from Brussels"*.

Insiders of the European Parliament Beck et al. (2014: 93–94) evaluated the engagement strategy in Germany, France and Spain in the Green Primary. For Germany, they concluded: *"There was a lack of communication following the Council of the European Green Party of April 2013, when the idea of a Green Primary was first decided, between the delegates who attended and the general party membership. Although this was a useful first experience, it is clear that the procedures for campaigning and voting will have to be started earlier and made technically easier to persuade more people to participate next time."* For France, they evaluated: *"The media coverage was modest but rather positive in France, probably due to the popularity of candidate and green MEP José Bové. The main difficulty for the Green European Primary was that it took place during the campaigns for local elections which ultimately drew away attention leading to a disappointing turnout."* In Spain, primaries are popular in the political debate. The relatively high number of Spanish voters in the Green Primary is quite a low number in comparison to the total number of votes Podemos had reached in his primary. The overall judgement about the engagement in Spain is therefore also quite negative.

---

[3]https://www.dw.com/en/online-voting-flops-for-european-green-party/a-17395839, accessed 15 October 2018.

Also, a broader public debate about the European elections or Spitzenkandidaten failed to materialize (Committee of the European Green Party 2014: 5).

11.1.3 Participatory Process

Out of the four contenders, two final figureheads needed to be selected to lead the EGP campaign. To vote in the online Green Primary, people had to register on the Green Primary website and provide an email address and a mobile number. After registration, the participant received an email with an activation link and was able to vote by selecting the two Green leading candidates of their choice.

The campaign manager we interviewed rated the voting system as quite user-friendly, but he admitted: *"sometimes we had to prioritise security over user friendliness or, let's say, easiness. So, sending an email and an SMS and basically sending people two passwords, or two ways of identification, or logged in data, let's call it like this, is already...you can say not as user friendly as possible. But we had to compromise with security and anonymity"*. The system counted more registrations than votes, but the number of people they "lost" on the way is not that high according to the campaign manager: *"It's not that high. [...] you could say we lost twenty percent on the way."* As the campaign manager rightly argues, casting a regular vote via a paper ballot also involves several barriers for voters along the way. The loss of voters might be partly explained by one minor technological issue regarding SMS across the different countries in the EU, the campaign manager stated: *"We were sending out SMS and that means that there was an interaction between our platform and the national phone provider. And with some very small number of national phone providers, this interaction didn't work properly. Because we don't have a European phone provider and it was not that much the fault of our platform or technology, but more of the other end. But this was a minor problem that we observed."*

Although the main participation consisted of voting for the two Spitzenkandidaten, the process around the Green Primary also included other forms of participation, such as via the debates in nine countries or Facebook chats with the contenders. On the website of the Green Party, updates with the highlights in this campaigning process are provided that give a glance of the public interest in these events. The Facebook chat with one of the contenders, Ska Keller, was summarized as follows: *"The chat, which took place on the EGP Facebook page, was a truly European affair. Questions came from Belgium, Bulgaria, Finland, France, Ireland, Spain and the UK. Ska faced difficult questions about not only her qualifications, but also her views on crucial issues facing Europe today—massive youth unemployment, access to affordable third-level education, migration and refugee rights, the transatlantic trade agreement (TTIP) that's currently being discussed by the EU and US, and the transition to sustainable energy."*

Also the chat with another contender, José Bové, was framed as a European one, with questions from Belgium, Croatia, Hungary, Ireland, the Netherlands, Portugal and Spain. The blog sketched a conversation about issues on which Bové has been active before—GMO food, agriculture, shale gas—as well as other areas like EU foreign policy and immigration. The Committee of the EGP reported that the chats reached an audience of between 4000 and 10,000 per chat. Daily messages with the hashtag #GreenPrimary were reported on the EGP website during the process. The hashtag has been used almost 15,000 times (Committee of the European Green Party 2014). The EGP's Facebook page was liked 30,000 times during the online campaign (from 10,000 to 40,000).

11.1.4 Results

The 22,676 participants voted as follows: 11,791 votes for Ska Keller; 11,726 for José Bové; 8170 for Rebecca Harms and 5851 for Monica Frassoni (Committee of the European Green Party 2014). This made Keller and Bové the winning duo, who became the leaders of the Green Party in the European Parliament election and the Green candidates for the President of the European Commission.

The turnout in the online elections was disappointing. In relation to the membership, turnout was around 22%. But in relation to all European citizens who share Green values, this turnout is of course a much smaller proportion. At the same time, the participation rate for a Green congress is normally *"between two hundred and three hundred"* (interview with a campaign manager). With that in mind, the participation in the online voting process is much higher. Nonetheless, the campaign manager is not satisfied with the final number of voters: *"the number of participants, 22,000, a little bit more, was not too satisfied for us. It was ok but we hoped for more."* About the expected 100,000 voters, he replied: *"It was not an official number [. . .] But in terms of participation, we were not totally happy"* (interview with a campaign manager).

It is hard to evaluate the cost-effectiveness of the online Green Primary. Some argue this is certainly too much for a "flop": *"If you have 200,000 divided by 20,000 participants, that makes it 10 euro per vote. That feels to me as a bit too much, right? [. . .] The problem is of course that the fixed costs are enormous"* (interview with a researcher). Deutsche Welle reflects: *"How were these relatively unknown politicians supposed to lure European voters to the computer? Their strategies for the European elections hardly differed."*[4] Others underline positive achievements in the Green Primary. The National Democratic Institute (2015: 73) for instance: *"Functionally, the Green Primary was successful. The EGP empowered national parties to nominate candidates, constructive debates were held across Europe, citizens could engage the candidates and the online voting period lasted nearly 80 days."*

---

[4]https://www.dw.com/en/online-voting-flops-for-european-green-party/a-17395839, accessed 15 October 2018.

In addition, as one of the goals was to boost the campaign of the EGP and its member parties, it can be seen as a positive result that 39.75% of the participants (9014 voters) subscribed to newsletters. And the Green Primary has attracted public attention (Committee of the European Green Party 2014, Cremers in Put et al. 2016). The Committee of the EGP counted 4000 media reports about the two leading candidates from across Europe. The researcher we interviewed, concluded: *"in terms of awareness and exposure it has of course been an ideal instrument, because it generates much attention and the party mobilizes its own members and militants."* But, on the other side, the researcher worried that the openness of the election online made the Green Party vulnerable for opponents who can misuse the opportunity to vote, to manipulate the election in their own interest. This not only leads to failed elections, but also to bad press.

The conclusion of Beck et al. (2014: 95) might summarize these remarks in an overall judgement: *"The careful framing of the Green Primary as an experiment in European inner-party democracy turned out to be a wise choice. Attempting to involve people in choosing top candidates who were unfamiliar to them proved to be an uphill battle."*

In the end, with regard to the presidency of the European Commission, the final result was that Jean-Claude Juncker got the position, since the People's Party won a plurality (29%) in the 2014 elections.

11.2 Voting in Elections in Estonia

11.2.1 Introduction

Several objectives propelled the introduction of Internet voting in Estonia: one was to increase the efficiency of the public sector using digital information and communication technologies, another was to enhance user friendliness and effectiveness (Maaten 2004). Others were to increase or at least halt the decrease in electoral participation rates, to make elections more attractive to young people, and to improve accessibility for people with disabilities and for Estonians living abroad (Maaten 2004; OSCE/ODIHR 2007; Pammett and Goodman 2013). According to Solvak and Vassil (2016: 10), Internet voting *"was seen as an additional means to increase the convenience by which citizens can participate in political life and therefore constituted an extension of an already started motion to develop modern e-governance"*.

Before Internet voting or i-voting was introduced on the national level, several tests were carried out at lower levels. The first trials had already been conducted in 2004 and, as no problems were identified, the way was clear for the first binding use of Internet voting at the local level in 2005. After these elections were considered successful and secure, there were no more barriers to Internet voting at the national level for the parliamentary elections in 2007 (Trechsel 2007). In 2009, the Internet option was offered for the European elections in June, and again for local elections in

October. In March 2011, it was possible to cast a vote via the Internet for the second time for the national parliamentary elections; another online election took place in October 2013 on the local level, and another in spring 2014 for the European elections. Online voting was also offered for the parliamentary elections in March 2015, and the most recent i-voting took place in October 2017 at the local elections.

The kind of Internet voting discussed in this case study is remote voting via the Internet without any kind of supervision by official authorities. The use of voting machines, either at polling stations or public places such as libraries, kiosks or shopping malls, is excluded because these forms of voting focus on increasing the efficiency of the voting process, while remote Internet voting mainly aims at improving the convenience for voters. Internet voting in Estonia is one channel of many and follows the "double envelope voting method" of offline voting. The following steps illustrate the i-voting process[5]:

- Voter inserts ID card into the card reader.
- Opens the i-voting website (www.valimised.ee).
- Downloads and runs voter application.
- Identifies himself/herself by entering PIN1 code.
- Views the displayed list of candidates in the voter's electoral district.
- Makes his/her choice.
- Confirms his/her choice by digital signature (by entering PIN2 code).
- Receives a notice that the vote has been accepted.

The general principles of Internet voting in Estonia are: i-votes can be cast from the tenth day until the fourth day before the Election Day; i-votes can be recast as often as a voter wants because only the last vote counts; an i-vote can always be overwritten by a vote cast at the polling station; and the same rules and election principles apply to Internet voting as to regular offline voting.[6]

The usual election procedures also apply to the outcome of the Internet channel; there is no difference to the presentation of the results from other voting channels. Detailed information about Internet voting, including election results, is provided online on the website www.valimised.ee.

In Estonia, the general responsibility for conducting elections lies with different electoral committees, that is, the National Electoral Committee (NEC), county electoral committees and voting district committees. Until 2012, the National Electoral Committee (NEC) was in charge of overseeing Internet voting and ensuring its smooth operation. As a reaction to complaints about the capability of the NEC to deal with Internet voting issues appropriately (OSCE/ODIHR 2011), a separate Electronic Voting Committee was established in 2012 and has since been responsible for conducting Internet voting. The technical requirements are still established by the NEC, but the system itself is administered by the Electronic Voting Committee.

---

[5]https://www.valimised.ee/en/internet-voting/internet-voting-estonia, accessed on 2 January 2019.
[6]Ibid.

When the Internet option was offered for the first time in 2005, the legislative regulations for e-voting were very brief. In 2012, a large part of the electoral law was revised as the share of e-voters had been steadily increasing, and the authorities wanted to improve the legitimacy and transparency of e-voting (Solvak and Vassil 2016). In general, the regulatory framework consists of several statutes at different political levels, the Local Government Election Act, the Referendum Act, the European Parliament Election Act, the President of the Republic Election Act and the Riigikogu Election Act. Another central legal building block of Internet voting is the law regulating the use of digital signatures, the Digital Signature Act (DSA) of 2002. All Estonians have an identification card, which includes a digital certificate (signature).

However, all these regulations have not been adopted without contestation: Concerns about secrecy were raised, but overcome by reference to the possibility of overwriting the vote and casting a ballot as often as the voter wants (Drechsler and Madise 2004). In 2005, the Estonian Supreme Court decided that the possibility of casting a vote as many times as the voter wants appropriately balances all electoral principles (Supreme Court of Estonia 2005).

The idea of introducing Internet voting surfaced around 2000 and was supported by politicians and the public administration from the beginning. The initial proposals for Internet voting were made by the Estonian Prime Minister (Mart Laar) and the Minister of Justice (Märt Rask) at the time. Their initiative provided high-level support and helped to overcome the initial hurdles to implementing Internet voting. Nevertheless, not all parties were or are in favour of Internet voting; there has always been opposition (Pammett and Goodman 2013). When the first drafts of the revised election acts were discussed in parliament, several points were raised (Drechsler 2003): for instance, issues of unconstitutionality, proneness to fraud or possible inequalities resulting from digital divides.

11.2.2 Participants

The target group for Estonian Internet voting is the Estonian electorate of about one million citizens. In fact, the size of the electorate varies depending on the type of election, for instance, non-citizens are not allowed to vote in national elections (Solvak and Vassil 2016). In order to be able to vote, a person must be entered on the registered list of voters, must be at least 18 years of age and living at an address entered in the population register.

In general, the tool is accessible to every member of the target group. The main requirements are possession of a digital ID, Internet access and access to a computer. Owning a digital ID is compulsory for all Estonian citizens and public Internet access is widely available as are computers, which can be used in a public institution, for example, a library. The only minor potential obstacle for voters in terms of user-friendliness is that the usual browser cannot be used for online voting; a specific application has to be downloaded and installed instead. *"With regard to this procedure there might be room for improvement, but as we cannot trust the browsers, it is necessary for security reasons"* (interview with an administrator).

While at the beginning, when Internet voting was first introduced, the e-voters indeed showed particular sociodemographic, attitudinal and behavioural characteristics, in the meantime, Internet voters are non-distinguishable from other voters (Solvak and Vassil 2016). Vassil (2015: 2) stated that *"since 2011, we cannot talk about a typical e-voter because chances of online voting are the same for the young and old, educated and less educated, PC-literate and less PC-literate. In other words, Internet voting has diffused"*. In addition, Vassil et al. (2016: 458) state that *"technology has the potential to bridge societal divisions and ease political participation, not only for the already connected and resourceful, but also for the less privileged, who have fewer resources and remain at the periphery of rising modern technologies"* and that *"the potential enabling effects did not surface immediately in the electoral realm after the introduction of the new voting technology, but required a period of at least three elections to appear"*. According to one interviewee, *"Internet voters had slightly higher educational status, a bit more Estonians than Russians who live here, a bit more urban than rural voters. But after three elections, these tendencies faded. [...] Therefore, we cannot say who the e-voter is, it is rather a normal voter, who is just using it"* (interview with an administrator).

To start with, the introduction of Internet voting was accompanied by a special communication and engagement strategy in order to spread information about the system and the additional voting channel. As awareness of the system is now very high after eight elections involving Internet voting, a special strategy is no longer required (interview with an administrator).

11.2.3 Participatory Process

For the case of e-voting, the participatory process can be equated with the normal voting process. With regard to the sort of input participants can give, the same ballot is cast by the Internet voter as at the election booth. Citizens can e-vote in local, national and European elections. If one chooses to vote online, a special voting application has to be downloaded to the computer. The voter identifies him- or herself using digital ID and a PIN. If the citizen is eligible to vote, he or she can cast a ballot and use a second PIN to confirm their choice (Solvak and Vassil 2016). The votes are aggregated, and candidates are elected on this basis. The e-vote is deleted if the citizen later casts a paper ballot.

Debates about the secrecy of e-voting in Estonia emerge on a regular basis: in 2011, for instance, a student claimed that it would be easy to manipulate the system and sought the nullification of the election results (which was rejected by the Constitutional Review Chamber, because no fraud was detected and the possibility for manipulation is not sufficient reason to nullify the results; Sivonen 2011). The elections of 2014 were also accompanied by a debate about security issues. It is a major challenge for Internet voting to guarantee the secrecy and transparency of the voting process at the same time. The democratic principles of equal, free, direct, secret and universal suffrage apply to Internet voting as they do to paper-based voting. Asked about his opinion regarding security aspects of Internet voting in Estonia, one interviewee stated the following: *"We can never be 100 percent secure. No one can ever be 100 percent secure. But we are ready to work with the problems. Before and after every election we conduct several procedures. We don't use the same system as in 2003, we update it before and after each election. We keep up with the times. [...] We are not 100 percent secure, because you can never be 100 percent secure, but we are pretty confident that everything works out"* (interview with an administrator). Privacy and data protection issues in particular are addressed by *"public-private key-pair crypto and full anonymization according to electoral provisions [...], additional features such as end-to-end verifiability are being developed"* (interview with an administrator).

11.2.4 Results

In the case of Internet voting, there is an obvious relation between the citizens' contribution and the outcome of the decision-making process because the votes are aggregated and define the election outcome together with the non-Internet votes. Since the introduction of e-voting, Estonia has held nine elections, in which the entire electorate could use Internet voting as an additional voting method. The first opportunity to use the i-voting option was in the local elections in October 2005 and resulted in an overall voter turnout of 47.4%.[7] Back then, only 1.9% of the voters used the option to vote online. The turnout for the 2007 national elections was approximately 62%, a figure reportedly higher than in the previous two elections held in 2003 (58%) and 1999 (57%). The percentage of voters making use of the Internet option in the 2007 election had increased to 5.5%. The European Parliament election in June 2009 was the third occasion, where Internet voting was an option. In total, 43.9% of all Estonians participated, compared to approximately 27% in the 2004 European Parliament election. In the 2009 European election, almost 15% of all voters voted online. The local elections in 2009 showed a voter turnout of approximately 60%, of which almost 16% used the Internet option. In the national elections in March 2011, 63.5% of eligible voters participated, of which 24.3% voted online. The local elections in 2013 showed a voter turnout of 58% and a share of 21.2% Internet voters. In the European Parliament Election in 2014, 31.3% of all participating voters used the Internet option (turnout was 36.5%). In the parliamentary election in Estonia in 2015, the share of Internet voters among participating voters was 30.5%. In the most recent local elections in 2017, the share of i-voters

---

[7]https://www.valimised.ee/en/archive/statistics-about-internet-voting-estonia, accessed on 2 January 2019 (the other statistics in this section are also cited from this source).

was 31.7%. Regarding the use of Internet voting by Estonians living abroad, it can be observed that about 90% of the Estonian votes from abroad are now cast online (Solvak and Vassil 2016).

Assuming that the system has not been hacked and election fraud has not taken place, the results of the online votes represent the will of the online voters just as is the case for offline voters.

Regarding the question of whether Internet voting has the potential to increase participation, there are no clear indications for an increase in voter turnout when looking back over the relatively long period of Internet voting in Estonia at different election levels. What can be seen, however, is a trend towards an increasing share of voters using Internet voting over time (Goos et al. 2016). One interviewee (administrator) states that *"after 10 years we can say, [Internet voting] keeps the level of voter turnout. It does not increase automatically or drastically. But what we can say now is that it leads to an increase of some percentage points for the people who stay outside of Estonia, the expats. [...] And those people who have used it once, will use it again. So, we should see it differently: if we discontinued Internet voting, we would lose a lot of people. Therefore, we can say it has an effect of about 3–4 percent. But it does not particularly contribute to an increase as there are so many other impacts on voter turnout, such as conflicts in politics or policy."*

11.3 Voting in Elections/Referenda in Switzerland

11.3.1 Introduction

The main reasons for the introduction of Internet voting, a project called *vote électronique* in Switzerland, were to speed up vote counting, reduce the number of invalid votes and facilitate voting for Swiss citizens living abroad and for people with disabilities (Braun et al. 2003). Another rationale is the endeavour to play a leading role in the race for digital leadership in electronic democracy. In addition, *"the political institutions want to get ready for a potential future within a digital society"* (interview with an administrator).

In Switzerland, e-voting has been offered for many years, and was sometimes contested, both at the beginning and over the course of its application. While in Neuchâtel, for instance, there was no political opposition, in Zurich, regular, strong doubts have been voiced regarding its costs and cost efficiency. Geneva even suspended e-voting for a while, but then reintroduced it after a referendum on e-voting, where it was supported by 70%. Switzerland considers itself as still being in a test phase. Its motto is "security before speed" (Federal Chancellery 2019), so the introduction is a slow and careful process.

The Confederation defines the framework and requirements for e-voting, and the cantons are responsible for the operational level. Hence, provisions for e-voting are adopted on the Federal level, and the cantons decide on their own if and how they want to introduce e-voting. Furthermore, *"there are these external audits and companies who have nothing to do with it, have a look at it and write their reports. Based on [these reports] the Federal Chancellery decides, because it is the responsible authority for the approval [of an e-voting system] [...]"* (interview with a researcher).

The first trials in the three cantons of Neuchâtel, Geneva and Zurich were conducted between 2004 and 2005 for Swiss citizens living in Switzerland. In a second round of trials between 2007 and 2010, some cantons included Swiss citizens living abroad. While e-voting was only offered for referenda on the local, regional and federal levels until 2011, in October 2011, it was used in Federal elections for the first time (Goos et al. 2016). In 2015, out-of-country voters were able to vote online for the second time in Federal elections, in-country voters for the first time.

Today, two different e-voting systems are in place: First, the "Geneva system" CHVote, which is the result of a cooperation between the State Chancellery and the General Directorate of Information Systems of the canton and is therefore developed and hosted by Geneva. Other cantons can and do use this system, but it is remotely operated from Geneva. The second e-voting system in Switzerland was developed by the Swiss Post and the private company Scytl and has been in place since 2016 (Der Bundesrat 2017). A third system, the so-called consortium system, originally developed for the pilot canton Zurich, was abandoned in 2015 after an external audit discovered security vulnerabilities with regard to the secrecy of voting.

In order to vote, one has to be entitled to vote, and needs access to a computer. No particular software is required; the voter receives an individual ID number that is used to verify his/her identity on the election web page. Then, the ballot is cast and must be confirmed using a second individual code, which has been sent to the voter in advance. During the actual voting process, depending on the system in place, voters can cast their online ballots between 2.5 and 3.5 weeks prior to the day before the actual Election Day. (This description applies to the Geneva system; other systems work slightly differently.)

Switzerland is following a gradual approach to the implementation of Internet voting, and its legal basis was defined by the Swiss Federal Council and the Parliament in the Federal Act on Political Rights (*Bundesgesetz über die politischen Rechte, BPR*) (Art. 8a), the Regulation on Political Rights (*Verordnung über die politischen Rechte, VPR*) (Art. 27a) and in the Regulation of the Federal Chancellery on electronic voting (*Verordnung der Bundeskanzlei über die elektronische Stimmabgabe, VEleS*). For instance, the Federal Act on Political Rights defines minimum standards, for example, that it is only allowed to conduct Internet voting trials as long as they are limited in scope and time. Furthermore, it is stated that the eligibility to vote, the secrecy of the vote and the elimination of misuse need particular attention. The VPR goes into more detail and specifically regulates the prerequisites for conducting Internet voting trials. For instance, it is clearly defined how and under what conditions a canton is granted the permission to implement Internet voting. The legal framework for e-voting is adjusted on a regular basis. In 2013, for example, there was a special focus on the verifiability and certification of the e-voting systems in place.

In the early 2000s, e-voting in Switzerland was strongly promoted by the chancellor of Geneva, who then formed a coalition with Zurich and Neuchâtel. One of the interviewees (researcher) characterizes the chancellor at the time of Geneva as a *"policy entrepreneur, [...] an individual who strongly pushed Internet voting [...]. We want to be modern, we want to push it. Particularly because we have so many referenda in Switzerland"*.

Though initiated by the cantons, the introduction of Internet voting in Switzerland was also embedded in a broader Federal strategy from the beginning, the "Strategy for an Information Society in Switzerland". In cooperation with the Federal Council of Switzerland, three e-voting pilot projects were launched in 2004 and 2005. These three cantons were particularly suitable for an introduction of e-voting because of the organization of their political rights: Geneva has a centralized electoral register, Zurich a decentralized system, and Neuchâtel already had an e-government portal. After these pilots were declared successful, the Federal Council decided on the gradual introduction of Internet voting for local, cantonal and national referenda.

11.3.2 Participants

As every canton has its own citizens' rights defining who is entitled to vote, the target groups for e-voting differ respectively. During the pilots, the focus was on a selection of Swiss citizens living in Switzerland, but this focus has since shifted to expatriates who are registered in their home canton and people with disabilities. Meanwhile, the long-term objective is the nationwide introduction of Internet voting for out-of-country voters and ultimately for the entire electorate (OSCE/ODIHR 2012). The reason for this *"is clearly the cost-value ratio. The idea was from the beginning on to offer the vote electronique for the whole population. The target groups 'people with disabilities' and 'Swiss people living abroad' were clearly defined groups which strongly benefit from electronic voting and were also suitable for a trial phase"* (interview with an administrator). When exactly this is supposed to happen is not yet clear, because the implementation plans are regularly adapted. At one point, the medium-term aim was to allow Internet voting for all Swiss citizens living abroad in the national elections of 2015 (Schweizerischer Bundesrat 2013), but this was then postponed to 2017 and has since been postponed again. *"These goals and dates have changed constantly. If you read the e-government roadmaps, the e-government strategy, it has been adapted continuously"* (interview with a researcher). The current (not binding) aim is that two-thirds of the cantons should offer e-voting to out-of-country voters by 2019 for national elections. However, because the cantons are autonomous in their decisions to implement e-voting and to whom they offer it, their strategies are in a constant state of flux and it is not foreseeable what e-voting will look like in the future. In sum, currently a maximum of 3% of those entitled to vote have the possibility to vote online.

Several studies show that younger voters tended to use Internet voting in Switzerland more often than older voters, particularly the age cohort 30–39 years (Serdült et al. 2015). However, age loses its significance when controlled by ICT variables such as Internet usage and skills. Furthermore, education seems to be positively correlated with Internet voting—the higher the level of education, the greater the probability that someone votes online. Serdült et al. (2015: 130ff) concluded that *"Swiss voters' socio-demographic profile points to the conclusion that Internet voting has, at least to date, primarily been a service to the young and privileged [...]"*, but also *"that it is not these variables per se that make voters more likely to vote online, but rather their relationship with ICT variables, such as the frequency of Internet usage and trust in Internet transactions"* (Serdült et al. 2015: 131).

With regard to a potential increase in voter turnout, studies in Switzerland show that there is no indication that Internet voting has had any impact. However, analysing the electoral register has revealed a substitution effect between postal voters and Internet voters. *"We see a substitution effect, from postal voters. [...] We were able to verify this by analyzing data of voter registries. So this is not based on surveys, but we can say quite certainly which age groups, which sex, in which community, which people use the Internet. And we can say that some [voters] completely move to the Internet channel, but the largest part switches between Internet vote and postal vote"* (interview with a researcher).

Belonging to the target group is a requirement for voting online and, for expatriates, being registered in one of the respective home regions. Out-of-country voters have to register themselves in any case, regardless of whether they want to vote online or by post. The lack of a computer may be a potential obstacle to actually using this voting channel. On the other hand, according to one of the interviewees, surveys show that the user-friendliness of the e-voting process is perceived to be very high. In order to acquaint citizens with the online voting process, test websites were installed, and a hotline is available in case any problems occur during the voting process.

As e-voting in Switzerland has a rather long history, it can be assumed that most people are now aware of the fact that this voting channel is offered. At the beginning, the regular practice of automatically sending voting documents to the whole electorate by post was used to reach and inform the target group about the e-voting option. *"[In Switzerland], everything is sent via mail to the home of everyone. I.e., every man and every woman can see it in the letterbox. If you live in a municipality where Internet voting is offered, you will realise it. In addition, there was an active information strategy of the cantons, information events were organised, flyers were distributed at marketplaces, in shopping centres"* (interview with a researcher).

11.3.3 Participatory Process

The input participants can give are votes in elections and referenda. Votes are counted, representatives are elected. Legislation can be reaffirmed or rejected in referenda.

Internet voting requires particular security measures because the stakes are high. Voting is an essential element of democracy, so any hint of fraud could undermine the results of an election. The requirement of the anonymity of a vote while guaranteeing that voters vote only once poses particular challenges. Therefore, issues of security and privacy have been discussed since the very beginnings of Internet voting. One interviewee (researcher) states the following: "*I think, 100 percent security is never possible. You hear that quite often. On the one hand, we have IT specialists, the leading internet security and computer specialists from the US, who say 'hands off', 'there will never be enough security!'. And in Europe the attitude is rather [...], 'we have an operational security, which is very high'. It is never 100 percent, but the effort and the necessary know-how to control all elements and the server is really difficult. And then one really has to decrypt the virtual ballot box. The encryption is so strong; this is almost impossible at the moment. We know it would take years to accomplish that [...]. Maybe one can decrypt the current data in 10, 15, 20 years. That is a risk we accept at the moment [...].*" Another interviewee also agrees that "*100 percent security does not exist. Not in the case of postal voting. Not in the case of paper voting. And not in the case of electronic voting. What is relevant for electronic voting is that if it is possible to manipulate one vote, it is possible to manipulate all votes. The scale of manipulation is very central. Therefore the requirements for electronic voting are much higher than for postal voting or paper voting [...] It is important to take the right measures to keep the risks as low as possible*" (interview with an administrator).

11.3.4 Results

In the case of Internet voting, there is an obvious relation between the citizens' contribution and the outcome of the decision-making process, because votes are aggregated and define the election or referendum outcome together with the non-Internet votes. Communicating the results of the e-votes does not differ from the usual election procedures. In general, the Federal Chancellery presents the results of the e-voting trials and other related material on its website (Federal Chancellery 2016).

Due to the various provisions with regard to e-voting, a comparatively low number of the Swiss electorate can potentially vote online. Legal provisions and the step-by-step implementation process followed have resulted in relatively high standards. Accordingly, the absolute numbers per canton are comparatively low as well. For instance, in the referendum in September 2016, 5.3 million Swiss citizens were entitled to vote, and the turnout in absolute numbers was approximately two million votes (Federal Statistical Office 2016). The whole online electorate consisted of 153,838 eligible voters (102,036 Swiss people living in Switzerland, whereas 51,802 out-of-country voters), of which a total of 22,752 voters decided to vote online (Federal Chancellery 2016).

An inherent challenge of Internet voting is that the inner mechanisms of the computer-based voting process are not observable. Compared to traditional voting, e-voting lacks the possibility of counting the votes in public, as is practised in Switzerland, because the cryptographic procedures and information technology are hidden. *"In Switzerland, the votes are traditionally counted in the communities. In the big cities, such as Geneva, this is not the case, but usually lay persons and representatives of political parties count the votes by themselves or watch others count. [...] There you have direct control, you see every paper that is counted. That is omitted [in the case of Internet voting]. [...] That is the big question, how will it work in the future, when you cannot see anything? The technical solution actually [...] lies in universal and individual verification"* (interview with a researcher). Individual verification allows the voters themselves to verify whether their votes have been transmitted correctly. Universal verification allows the voters to verify whether their votes have been registered and tallied correctly. In the future, a technical solution could be used to make the whole e-voting process transparent through the use of encrypted vote transmission and a public bulletin board, where all the encrypted votes are displayed, and everyone can check whether the vote has been cast as intended. One of our interviewees (interview with a researcher) classifies this as a *"technical substitution for the missing transparency"*, though he also admits that trust in the system is a basic requirement for use and it is still a challenge to make the e-voting process comprehensible for lay persons. One measure to build up trust is that *"on election day, when the ballot box is decrypted, a ceremony takes place"* (interview with an administrator). In addition, *"[a commission, as representation of the electorate,] supervises all processes and looks if all procedures are correctly followed"* (Interview with an administrator).

References

Beck, C., Groizard, J., & Sellier, G. (2014). The next democratic revolution: From the Green Primary to European lists. *Green European Journal, 9*, 92–95.

Braun, N., Heindl, P., Karger, P., Krimmer, R., Prosser, A., & Rüß, O. (2003). *e-Voting in der Schweiz, Deutschland und Österreich: Ein Überblick: Arbeitspapiere zum Tätigkeitsfeld Informationsverarbeitung und Informationswirtschaft*. Accessed January 2, 2019, from epub.wu.ac.at/388/1/document.pdf

Committee of the European Green Party. (2014). *Annex to the political evaluation of the common campaign 2014 European elections - for information*. Evaluation of the GREEN PRIMARY 2014. Accessed October 15, 2018, from https://europeangreens.eu/content/political-evaluation-2014-common-election-campaign

Der Bundesrat (2017). *Faktenblatt – Vote électronique*. Accessed January 2, 2019, from https://www.bk.admin.ch/dam/bk/de/dokumente/pore/Faktenblatt%20E-Voting.pdf.download.pdf/Faktenblatt_DE.pdf

Drechsler, W. (2003). *The Estonian e-voting laws discourse: Paradigmatic benchmarking for central and Eastern Europe*. Accessed 2-01-2019, from http://unpan1.un.org/intradoc/groups/public/documents/nispacee/unpan009212.pdf

Drechsler, W., & Madise, Ü. (2004).. Electronic voting in Estonia). In N. Kersting & H. Baldersheim (Eds.), *Electronic voting and democracy: A comparative analysis* (pp. 97–108). New York: Palgrave Macmillan.
Federal Chancellery. (2016). *Versuche mit E-Voting*. Accessed January 2, 2019, from https://www.bk.admin.ch/bk/de/home/politische-rechte/e-voting/versuchsuebersicht.html
Federal Chancellery. (2019). *E-voting*. Accessed January 2, 2019, from https://www.bk.admin.ch/bk/en/home/politische-rechte/e-voting.html
Federal Statistical Office. (2016). *Eidgenössische Volksabstimmungen: detaillierte Ergebnisse*. Accessed January 2, 2019, from https://www.bfs.admin.ch/bfs/en/home/statistics/politics.assetdetail.335643.html
Goos, K., Beckert, B., & Lindner, R. (2016). Electronic, Internet-based voting. In R. Lindner, G. Aichholzer, & L. Hennen (Eds.), *Electronic democracy in Europe. Prospects and challenges of E-publics, E-participation and E-voting* (pp. 146–198). Springer.
Hobolt, S. B. (2014). A vote for the President? The role of Spitzenkandidaten in the 2014 European Parliament elections. *Journal of European Public Policy, 21*(10), 1528–1540.
Maaten, E. (2004). Towards remote e-voting: Estonian case. In A. Prosser & R. Krimmer (Eds.), *Electronic voting in Europe* (pp. 83–100). Technology, Law, Politics and Society, Workshop of the ESF TED Programme together with GI and OCG, July, 7th-9th, 2004, in Schloß Hofen / Bregenz, Lake of Constance, Austria, Proceedings. LNI 47, GI 2004.
National Democratic Institute. (2015). *Technology – A planning guide for political parties*. Tech4parties.org. Accessed October 15, 2018, from https://tech4parties.org/wp-content/uploads/2015/09/Tech4PartiesFullPDF.pdf
OSCE/ODIHR. (2007). *Republic of Estonia Parliamentary Elections 4 March 2007: OSCE/ODIHR Election Assessment Mission Report*. Accessed January 2, 2019, from http://www.osce.org/odihr/elections/estonia/25925?download=true
OSCE/ODIHR. (2011). *Estonia Parliamentary Elections 6 March 2011: OSCE/ODIHR Election Assessment Mission Report*. Accessed January 2, 2019, from http://www.osce.org/odihr/77557?download=true
OSCE/ODIHR. (2012). *Swiss Confederation Federal Assembly Elections 23 October 2011: OSCE/ODIHR Election Assessment Mission Report*.
Pammett, J. H., & Goodman, N. (2013). Consultation and evaluation practices in the implementation of Internet Voting in Canada and Europe. Ottawa: Elections Canada. Accessed January 2, 2019, from www.elections.ca/res/rec/tech/consult/pdf/consult_e.pdf
Put, G. J., Van Hecke, S., Cunningham, C., & Wolfs, W. (2016). The choice of Spitzenkandidaten: A comparative analysis of the Europarties' selection procedures. *Politics and Governance, 4*(1), 9–22.
Schweizerischer Bundesrat. (2013). *Bericht des Bundesrates zu Vote électronique, Auswertung der Einführung von Vote électronique (2006–2012) und Grundlagen zur Weiterentwicklung*. In BBI 2013 5069, 14.Juni 2013. Accessed January 2, 2019, from www.admin.ch/opc/de/federal-gazette/2013/5069.pdf
Serdült, U., Germann, M., Mendez, F., Portenier, A., & Wellig, C. (2015). Fifteen years of Internet voting in Switzerland: History, governance and use. In L. Terán, & A. Meier (Eds.), *ICEDEG 2015: Second International Conference on eDemocracy and eGovernment*, Quito, Ecuador, 8–10 April 2015, IEEE Xplore CFP1527Y-PRT, 126-132. Accessed January 2, 2019, from https://doi.org/10.1109/ICEDEG.2015.7114482
Sivonen, E. (2011). *Supreme court rejects last voter complaint*. News.err.ee, 21.3.2011. Accessed January 2, 2019, from http://news.err.ee/99529/supreme-court-rejects-last-voter-complaint
Solvak, M., & Vassil, K. (2016). *E-voting in Estonia. Technological diffusion and other developments over ten years (2005-2015)*. Johan Skytte Institute of Political Studies University of Tartu and Estonian National Electoral Committee. Accessed January 2, 2019, from http://skytte.ut.ee/sites/default/files/skytte/e_voting_in_estonia_vassil_solvak_a5_web.pdf
Supreme Court of Estonia. (2005). *Constitutional Judgement 3-4-1-13-05*. 1. September 2005. Accessed January 2, 2019, from https://www.riigikohus.ee/et/lahendid?asjaNr=3-4-1-13-05

Trechsel, A. (2007). *Internet voting in the March 2007 Parliamentary Elections in Estonia: Report for the Council of Europe.* Accessed January 2, 2019, from www.vvk.ee/public/dok/Coe_and_NEC_Report_E-voting_2007.pdf

Vassil, K. (2015). *Selected behavioral evidence on Estonian Internet voting.* University of Tartu. Accessed January 2, 2019, from http://www.ut.ee/kristjan.vassil/wp-content/uploads/E-voting-evidence.pdf

Vassil, K., Solvak, M., Vinkel, P., Trechsel, A. H., & Alvarez, R. M. (2016). The diffusion of Internet voting. Usage patterns of Internet voting in Estonia between 2005 and 2015. *Government Information Quarterly, 33*(3), 453–459.

Websites

Accessed 15 October 2018

https://europeangreens.eu/keywords/green-primary?page=1
https://europeangreens.eu/news/facebook-users-pose-questions-bové
https://www.dw.com/en/online-voting-flops-for-european-green-party/a-17395839
https://www.facebook.com/photo.php?fbid=709761329036958&set=a.277422362270859.78338.141366725876424&type=1
https://www.greenparty.org.uk/archive/egphustings/
https://www.greenparty.org.uk/news/2013/11/10/bringing-democracy-to-europe---the-european-green-primary-kicks-off-todayhas-begun
https://www.youtube.com/watch?v=e1NBkM01Oe0&feature=youtu.be

Accessed 2 January 2019

https://www.riigikohus.ee/et/lahendid?asjaNr=3-4-1-13-05
https://www.valimised.ee/en/Internet-voting/Internet-voting-estonia
www.valimised.ee

Open Access This chapter is licensed under the terms of the Creative Commons Attribution 4.0 International License (http://creativecommons.org/licenses/by/4.0/), which permits use, sharing, adaptation, distribution and reproduction in any medium or format, as long as you give appropriate credit to the original author(s) and the source, provide a link to the Creative Commons licence and indicate if changes were made.

The images or other third party material in this chapter are included in the chapter's Creative Commons licence, unless indicated otherwise in a credit line to the material. If material is not included in the chapter's Creative Commons licence and your intended use is not permitted by statutory regulation or exceeds the permitted use, you will need to obtain permission directly from the copyright holder.

Part III
Conclusions

Chapter 12
Assessing Tools for E-Democracy: Comparative Analysis of the Case Studies

Iris Korthagen and Ira van Keulen

Abstract Korthagen and van Keulen compare in this chapter the 22 case studies of digital tools discussed in part II of the book. They use Qualitative Comparative Analysis (csQCA) to study which conditions lead to actual impact of the tools on policy, (1) decision-making or (2) agenda-setting. Sixteen conditions identified from the literature review are compared. Ultimately, the most important conditions for successful e-participation identified by the authors are as follows: a close and clear link of e-participation processes to a concrete formal decision-making process should be available; the participatory process and the contribution of its outputs to the overall decision-making process have to be clarified to the participants from the start; feedback to the participants about what has been done with their contributions is an indispensable feature of the process; a participative process should not be limited to one event but should be imbedded in an institutional 'culture of participation'; and, finally, e-participation must be accompanied by an effective mobilisation and engagement strategy, involving communication instruments tailored for different target groups.

12.1 Introduction

In this chapter, the 22 case studies of digital tools discussed in part II of the book are compared. In the comparison, we analyse which conditions lead to impact on decisions or agenda-setting. The case studies were compared in a crisp-set Qualitative Comparative Analysis (csQCA). This was also the approach that Pratchett et al. (2009) used to compare different cases of e-participation (i.e. e-fora and e-petitions) in relation to the empowerment of communities influencing local decision-making. The foundation of csQCA lies in Boolean algebra. Hence, the scores of the cases on

---

I. Korthagen (✉)
Netherlands Court of Audit, The Hague, The Netherlands

I. van Keulen
Rathenau Instituut, The Hague, The Netherlands
e-mail: i.vankeulen@rathenau.nl

the different conditions and the outcome are dichotomised in the course of the procedure.

The number of conditions included in the QCA needs to be relatively low because the number of possible logical set-combinations quickly exceeds the number of cases (Berg-Schlosser and De Meur 2009). In other words, the empirically observed cases will occupy only a tiny proportion of the potential 'logical space' (3 conditions result in 8 possible logical combinations, 6 conditions lead to 64 possible combinations). Moreover, the fewer the number of 'causes' which are needed to explain an outcome, the closer we come to the core elements of causal mechanisms. A large number of conditions tend to individualise each case, which makes it difficult to find any regularity or synthetic explanation of the outcome across the cases. In our intermediate-N research design, working with a number of 4–7 conditions is advised in the literature (Berg-Schlosser and De Meur 2009: 28). The ideal balance between the number of cases and the number of conditions is found through trial and error.

The list of conditions we researched in our case studies is larger than the list of conditions that formed the configurations later on. The final conditions and outcome 'variables' are formulated in the last stage of the research, during which the variation of conditions and the outcome amongst the different cases is determined. At least one-third of the scores on a condition must be a one (1) or a zero (0); when conditions or outcome scores do not show enough variation amongst the cases, they are excluded or adjusted (Berg-Schlosser and De Meur 2009: 45). When a condition or outcome is difficult to score in too many cases (e.g. because of a lack of information, contradictory statements in the literature or from two interviewees in one case), it also cannot be used for further analysis. We based the scoring of the conditions and outcomes on the case studies. The data for the case studies was collected from (grey) the literature about the case, with both a standardised questionnaire and a semi-structured interview with two respondents per case. According to the design of the study, the two respondents are usually (1) a professional who is involved in the process of the case (i.e. organiser) and (2) an expert who studied the case (i.e. academic researcher).

The comparative analysis leads to two types of findings. First, a comparison of the conditions and outcomes of the cases. In Sect. 12.2 and 12.3, we introduce the conceptualisation of each condition—based on the literature review in Chap. 4—and provide a short analysis of how the condition is scored amongst the 22 cases. Where possible, we explain some of the underlying mechanisms of the conditions: why is the condition relevant to digital participation trajectories? This second part of the analysis identifies the conditions under which digital tools can successfully facilitate different forms of citizen involvement in decision-making processes, which answers the main research question. Success means that citizen involvement has led to either impact on decisions or impact on political or policy agendas. In Sect. 12.4, we analyse the configurations leading to impact on decisions as well as configurations that lead to agenda-setting. We distract a 'minimisation formula' as it is called. We conclude both sections by reflecting on what can be learned from the descriptive formulas and how impactful e-democracy on the European scale can be organised.

12.2 Assessment of the Different Conditions

Our complete study compares the 22 cases on 16 conditions and 2 outcomes (Korthagen et al. 2018). However, in this book we only report the results for the conditions that are part of the final configurations. These conditions concern whether cases use a combination of online and offline participation, a link is created with the formal decision-making process, the tool is sustainable, the participation process was clear from the start, a mobilisation and engagement strategy was in place, feedback was provided, voting was possible and interaction possibilities existed. The assessment of other conditions, such as the user-friendliness of the tool, moderation and whether the initiative is a governmental initiative ('invited space') or not ('invented space'), was less related to the outcome of impactful e-participation. In this section we discuss the nine conditions, their relevance to the outcomes, and identify the cases that score positively on each of the conditions.

12.2.1 Combination of Online and Offline Participation

This condition evaluates whether the participation process offers the opportunity to participate not only online but offline as well ('hybrid or blended format'). This condition can be expected to have an effect on the outcomes, since offering both online and offline possibilities encourages the inclusion of citizens. For example, a combination of online and offline channels to maximise inclusiveness is now state of the art in German participatory budgeting projects (Heidelberger 2009). Kies and Nanz (2013) evaluated different EU participation tools and recommend a combination of online and offline activities—an open online phase carefully connected with a phase of face-to-face consultations—to improve EU citizens' deliberation activities. By offering offline opportunities, everybody should be able to participate, even if they do not have online access or do not have sufficient digital skills. Or, as one of the interviewees of the participatory budgeting case in Berlin-Lichtenberg said: 'Because not everyone is comfortable with just one way [of participating]'. Another consideration for combining online with offline activities is that deliberation works better offline than online. The founder of petities.nl stated: 'The moral of the [online] medium is that you can endlessly 'fork' as we call it. If you do not agree, you move on to another website, another Whatsapp group, etc. Online there is no scarcity of space'. Kersting (2013: 278–279) is an advocate for a 'blended democracy combining online and offline instruments' because online spaces can lead to self-affirmation and in-group bonding. And yet another argument for a combination is that online activities which build on existing offline networks are more effective in mobilising 'real world' participation (Gibson and McAllister 2013: 21). However, online and offline participatory activities do not always have to complement each other. In cases of petitioning (petities.nl) or contacting politicians (theyworkforyou.com), the activities can substitute for one another (see Gibson and Cantijoch 2013).

In 14/22 cases, participants had the possibility to participate online and/or offline. The case of Wiki Melbourne, the crowdsourcing of a new constitution in Iceland and also the case of the European Citizens' Consultation (ECC) are classic examples of how digital instruments can contribute to democratic processes alongside offline participatory events. Those have been extensive and long-lasting participation processes consisting of different online and offline phases. For example, in the Wiki Melbourne case, existing offline networks have been used (and created) and perfectly integrated into the online process. Firstly, meetings with different stakeholders were organised to draw up a draft plan. This draft was then published as a wiki webpage, to which changes could be made online (although not yet by the public). A stakeholder consultation of 2 weeks was held in which changes in the document were made by specific stakeholders. A few weeks later, a month of public consultation was organised, in which the wiki was open for anyone to edit. Various meetings and events were organised to gather input for the document, making the project an actual combination of on- and off-line community activity. In other cases, like Futurium and Berlin-Lichtenberg, offline meetings such as workshops, public events, community meetings, etc., feed the online discussion, and vice versa. For political parties such as Podemos, the German Pirate Party and the Five Star Movement, offline meetings also play a vital role in the decision-making processes. Additionally, in several cases it was possible to vote online as well as offline (Participatory Budgeting (PB) in Paris, e-voting in Switzerland and Estonia), or to sign a proposal online or offline (European Citizens' Initiative, voting in Estonia, voting in Switzerland, Open Ministry—at least, for the Finnish Citizens' Initiative).

12.2.2 Link to the Formal Policy or Political Process

This condition reflects the official status of the digital tool and the participation process. It concerns the embeddedness of the tool in the formal processes of decision-making is organised. By designing such a link, the participation process and its outputs are clearly connected to what politicians or policy-makers are addressing at that time. A link to the formal decision-making process might therefore be of vital importance for the impact of the participatory input. For example, Font et al. (2016) looked at proposals resulting from participatory processes in Spain by studying 611 proposals from 39 different processes. They found that '[...] the odds that a proposal emerging from a participatory budget or other permanent mechanisms (e.g. citizen councils) is fully implemented double those of proposals coming out from a case of strategic planning or other temporary processes' (Font et al. 2016: 18).

A link to a formal process can be designed in several ways. It might be a policy or legal framework that prescribes what the participation process is about, its preconditions and how its results should be handled. An example of a prescription about how results should be handled is an obligation to provide adequate feedback on participative input. Such an obligation also creates pressure on the decisions to be taken, as it entails the acknowledgment of the participants as legitimate political actors (Badouard 2010). In Slovenia, proposals in Predlagam have to receive an official response from the competent authority of the government of the Republic of Slovenia, if at least 3% of the users active in the previous 30 days voted in favour of the proposal, and if there are more votes in favour than opposed. Official responses are also required in the cases of the Finnish and European Citizens' Initiatives.

Almost all cases had some sort of formal link to the decision-making process. We therefore demarcated the condition 'link to the formal policy or political process', so that it must be clear which formal decision-making process it concerns: the link has to connect the participation process to, e.g. a specific policy document, specific public funds, a specific internal democratic party process or an election. This means that although the Finnish Citizen Initiative is legally embedded in the parliamentary decision-making process by an amendment to the Constitution which allows citizens' initiatives to be submitted to Parliament, the participatory tool is meant to generate ideas for new policies and bills. Therefore, the tool does not link the citizens' input to a specific existing formal decision-making process on a certain topic.

A carefully designed link facilitates the political uptake of a proposal, request, or any other input from citizens. A link to the formal decision-making process does not necessarily signify that the outcomes of the e-participation initiative are legally binding. In fact, generally this is not the case. In the Berlin-Lichtenberg case, it is written in the 'Rahmenkonzeption' that citizens can suggest and discuss how public money should be spent, but that politicians will decide which suggestion will be included in the budget plan (Bezirksamt Lichtenberg von Berlin 2008).

We discerned two types of links, on the basis of their different roles in the policy cycle:

(a) Link to a formal currently existing agenda-setting process (10 of the 22 cases score positively);
(b) Link to a formal currently existing policy or political decision-making process (15 of the 22 cases score positively).

The cases score positively on either of these two conditions when the link facilitates the input of the participants to be taken up in one or both of these phases of the policy cycle. The cases that score negatively on condition (a) (agenda-setting process) are cases like the Dutch e-petition case, or the Slovenian Predlagam case, or the European cases ECI and ECC09. Positive scores are assigned to participatory budgeting cases (established link to existing political discussions about budgets) and political parties' cases (established link to the political agenda of the parties in question). More cases score positively on condition b than a. This is because some of the tools are just not agenda-setting tools, such as the e-voting cases and Belo Horizonte.

12.2.3 Sustainability

The sustainability of a digital participation tool was characterised by whether or not provisions for the future, like maintenance and improvement or expansion of the tool, are taken. For example, were user experiences used to improve the tool? This condition is taken from a study by Panopoulou et al. (2014) which attempted to determine the success factors for e-participatory projects, based on reviewed literature on e-government and e-participation success and on a survey of practitioners across Europe.

Badouard (2010) studied different EU participatory tools and concludes that important conditions for the sustainability of participative instruments are their official status and a legal framework on their position in the decision-making process. Sustainability was seen as a success factor in the literature as well as by the practitioners. There are different reasons why the sustainability of a tool is important for success, an important one being the attempt to improve the user-friendliness of the tool. Or, as one of the developers of the Betri Reykjavik tool said: 'We are always working on simplifying the process, in terms of how to participate. And that, I think, is in general a weakness of participatory processes, that they can be too complicated'. In other cases, improvements have been made over time to increase positive responses from government authorities. This is highlighted by the case of Predlagam, which introduced a lower limit of endorsing five or six proposals on a monthly basis to the competent authorities, so they now carry more weight and are more likely to succeed.

The majority of the cases (14/22) have a positive score for this condition: abgeordnetenwatch.de, theyworkforyou.com, PB Paris, PB Berlin–Lichtenberg, PB Belo Horizonte, Betri Reykjavik, E-voting Estonia, E-voting Switzerland, Five Star Movement, Your Voice in Europe, Futurium, Podemos, Dutch e-petitions and Predlagam. Cases of tools which have not been used repeatedly scored negatively, for instance, the European Citizen's Consultation (ECC09) or the Iceland constitutional crowdsourcing case. One interviewee is quite critical of the lack of sustainability of the ECC: *'They [European Union] are aware that we need to try to find new ways of involving citizens. So that's why they have been spending all this money. But then they are doing a one-shot experiment and they don't include it into the decision-making process. That is a problem. They don't think of a long-term solution for implementing citizen participation at the EU level. So it cannot work. Then it's better to do nothing'.*

Sometimes, tools which have existed for a longer period of time were not, or only marginally, improved and scored negatively on the sustainability condition as well. Such an example is the Dutch e-consultation website internetconsultatie.nl or—at least until more recent times, as evidenced by the proposal for revisions from September 2018—the European Citizens' Initiative. This might be explained by a lack of political urgency or willingness. Other reasons for a lack of sustainability can be a lack of funding, as in the case of the Open Ministry in Finland, which caused the downfall of the Open Ministry as a crowdsourcing service platform.

12.2.4 Communication or Engagement Strategy

This condition reflects on the communication or engagement strategies used to mobilise participants. Questions raised here are: Has the possibility to participate been effectively communicated to the target group? Have different strategies been used to attract different target groups? Has the strategy succeeded in mobilising different groups of citizens to use the tool? In Panopoulou et al. (2014), a 'promotion plan' was mentioned as a success factor for designing e-participation initiatives, defined in terms of utilising the most appropriate promotional activities for each stakeholder group. The engagement and communication strategy can thus be very significant in predicting the outcomes of the e-participation process. A lack of diversity amongst participants, and/or low representativeness of the participants, can result in decreasing interest from policy- and decision-makers in the input, and therefore in lower impact.

Mobilisation has proven to be one of the great challenges of participatory projects in general. One of the explanations is that citizens have low confidence that their input in such projects will have any real weight in the decision-making processes. When it comes to e-participation at the EU level, this scepticism appears to be well-founded, as is made clear in the literature review (see Chap. 4). Deliberative civic engagement tends not to be embedded in political decision-making, often being short-lived and temporary and focused on single issues. There can also be a lack of support and engagement from decision-makers. Other barriers preventing mobilisation are language problems and a low interest in European-level matters.

Some of the tools have facilitated different e-participation trajectories, such as the Dutch e-consultation website, Futurium, Your Voice in Europe and the ECI. In these cases, there is quite a lot of variation between the different trajectories. In order to assess the score for the communication and engagement strategy of these tools, we therefore took into account to what extent the tool/platform itself is well-known.

In half of the cases (11/22), an effective communication or engagement strategy was in place. The mass media are important mediators in several cases, and the attention of the mass media for the tool and the participatory process is generally important for mobilising participants. As in the case of abgeordnetwatch.de, the annual report of the monitoring website states media partners serve as important crowd-pullers, with one-third of visitors finding the platform through media. This can be seen in other cases, including Predlagam, German Pirate Party, Podemos and the Five Star Movement. Two of the participatory budgeting cases also received a lot of media attention (Belo Horizonte and Paris). However, in these 6/22 cases, media attention has not been constant. After the first buzz around the launch of the initiative, the attention of the media regressed.

Different target groups require different engagement strategies. In order to reach a high diversity of participants, it can be important to have an offline communication strategy as well. This might be easier to organise for local initiatives, like the participatory budgeting case of Berlin-Lichtenberg. The researcher and administrator interviewed for this case stated that decentralised meetings in community centres were an important way for community workers to reach new people every year and to get them involved in the participatory budgeting for the district.

In the other half of the cases (11/22), the general public appears not to be familiar with the tool, and lay citizens were not mobilised. This was the case for Predlagam, the Dutch e-consultation, theyworkforyou.com, Wiki Melbourne and Open Ministry (related to the Finnish CI). In the Dutch e-consultation case, the researcher interviewed noted that some civil servants did not have a problem with the tool being unknown to the general public; they did not want too many responses in the consultations and only wanted a few people who knew the ins and outs to react. Remarkably, all European-level cases also score low on their engagement strategy: the Green Primary, Futurium, ECI, Your Voice in Europe and ECC. In the European-level cases, not much effort has been invested in gaining a broader reputation amongst target groups other than the usual suspects (civil society organisations at European level).

Sometimes an active large-scale engagement strategy is not required to mobilise participants. The Dutch e-petition site gets about 2 million visitors per month without having to spend one euro on it. It gets its name and fame mostly through a snowball effect via social media, and more importantly—according to the founder—e-mail as well. The low threshold of participation in this tool—sign a petition by entering your name and e-mail address—plays an important role here, as well as easy ways to share e-petitions via social media and e-mail.

12.2.5 Clarity on the Process

This condition reflects how clearly the participation process has been organised (for participants) and to what extent expectations about the process are managed properly. Is it clear to participants from the outset what the goals of the process are? How far does their influence reach? What will be done with their input? Is it clear to participants which actors have responsibilities in the decision-making process? For example, an analysis of the ECC by Karlsson (2011) shows that members of the European Parliament (MEPs) as well as participating citizens have been disappointed in the participation tool. Karlsson found the design of the ECC project, at least in part, as being responsible for the failure. The procedure suffered from a lack of clarity over what inputs are desired by the MEPs and which inputs are expected from the citizens.

In 15/22 cases, clarity for participants had been adequately delivered on the participatory process: abgeordnetwatch.de, theyworkforyou.com, PB Paris, PB Berlin–Lichtenberg, PB Belo Horizonte, Betri Reykjavik, E-voting Estonia, E-voting Switzerland, Five Star Movement, German Pirate Party, Your Voice in Europe, Wiki Melbourne, Green Primary, Constitution Iceland and Open Ministry (Finnish Citizen Initiative).

The City of Paris provides extensive information about the participatory budgeting process. Firstly, the website provides infographics, FAQs and information, which explain the process of Budget Participative and how to participate. In the proposal submission phase, information regarding the legal framework and support on financial aspects is provided by the administration to the submitting participant(s). Also in the case of Melbourne, as well as in the case of participatory budgeting in Berlin, the expectations on the process were well-managed online as well as offline. The organisers in Melbourne were clear that: *'There is no guarantee that all suggestions can be incorporated into the Future Melbourne draft plan. A number of the recommendations fall outside the City of Melbourne's areas of responsibility'*. This kind of transparency did not seem to discourage participants.

In other tools, clarity was particularly lacking with regard to the decision-making process and how the input of participants is part of that process. One of the interviewees on Predlagam argued: *'The policy process is very complex. And citizens should be aware how complex it is. I don't think that they should be fooled. And in this case, in the case of this tool, I think they are being fooled, because there are still a lot of proposals and they are just going into a blackbox where nothing happens with them'*. For the European Citizens' Consultation 2009, the argument was that: *'So the process in itself was clearly presented and well communicated but the organisers were unable to say what would be the impact'*. And there are more cases like this. In the European Citizens' Initiative and Podemos, the official steps in the participation process are clear, but almost no proposal reaches the final stage. Politicians from Podemos claim to incorporate input from the online discussions in their considerations, but it is not clear how this indirect influence of participants actually works in practice.

Clarity on the process is supposed to encourage and empower participants, and ultimately it should prevent participants being disappointed. However, disappointment can be found in several cases. Beside the Podemos case, the digital budgeting case in Belo Horizonte is the most striking. The winning project in 2008 has not been finished because there is a problem in terms of land use and land ownership. After this disappointment, participation has fallen significantly: from 124,320 citizens in 2008, to 25,378 in 2011 and 8900 in 2013. Trust is hard to gain but easy to lose. In the case of the crowdsourcing of the constitution in Iceland, the transparency of the participation process seems to have created a lot of public appreciation and even a sense of co-ownership with the participants, according to one of the interviewees. Impact on decision-making is easier to achieve if it is clear beforehand exactly how the participatory process will contribute to the final decisions.

12.2.6 *Possibility to Interact with Other Participants*

We were also interested in how the diversity of views is managed within the different tools. Does the tool offer the possibility to deliberate? Deliberation is broadly defined here as the opportunity for participants to exchange views within the digital tool(s) available in the case.

The need for deliberative possibilities in e-participation projects is debated in the literature. Deliberation is supposed to enhance input quality when it comes to e-consultation (Albrecht 2012), and Albrecht advocates a model of deliberative e-consultations, which not only consists of collecting comments on a policy proposal but also allows for discussions on these amongst the participants and with representatives of the EU institutions concerned (see next condition). Organ (2014) points out that even if no legal outcomes of e-participation are achieved, the legitimacy of the policy agenda can be increased through the act of deliberation. However, deliberative civic engagement seems to be of a temporary nature, being employed for single issues and spanning only a short amount of time (Leighninger 2012). Kersting criticises the quality of online deliberative instruments, which appear to be '[...] *more oriented towards the construction of identity and community building than towards political dialogue and deliberation*' (Kersting 2013: 270). He also observes that web forums on the internet are low in deliberative quality, meaning that '[...] *they are not argumentatively-respectful and consensus-oriented, but are often pure monologues and frequently aggressive*' (Kersting 2013: 277). Another interesting argument against deliberation, but pro voting or signing, was made by a researcher who studied petities.nl: '*You can only sign or not sign. You cannot co-edit a text for example. At the same time, your voice is not lost as happens often in deliberative settings where a participant can take part in a discussion but where in the end it is difficult to ascertain where and how one's input has been used. With petitions, your voice just counts*'. The added value of participation in a digital tool thus seems to depend on how the deliberation is organised and the extent to which people use the options provided.

In 13/22 cases, it was possible to interact with other participants in the online tool. Where crowdsourcing was used to co-create a proposal, the tools facilitated deliberation between participants: Open Ministry related to the Citizens' Initiative in Finland, the constitutional crowdsourcing process in Iceland, Wiki Melbourne and Predlagam. Registered users of the political parties who are also aiming for collaborative decision-making (German Pirate Party, Podemos and Five Star Movement) have several tools at their disposal to debate issues. These include the European Citizens' Consultation 09 and the Futurium.

The four participatory budgeting tools include the possibility to comment on proposals to spend the municipal budget. This worked particularly well in the case of Betri Reykjavik, where the most popular arguments against the proposal were presented next to the most popular arguments in favour of it. One of the interviewees mentioned that by structuring the debate in this way, views are exchanged strictly by arguing for or against proposals, which helped to improve its quality: '*What we tried to do was to split the screen in two so people who support the idea can write points for it on the left side of the screen (...), and on the right side of the screen, people who are against the idea can put their points... And almost overnight (...) the quality level of the debate increased a lot*'. This approach minimises the extent to which a comment can refer to another comment rather than the proposal itself: '*If you see a point you don't agree with, there's no way to comment on it. You have to write a counterpoint*'.

In the case studies of Wiki Melbourne and the German Pirate Party, the exchange of ideas was seen as stimulating a more constructive mindset amongst participants rather than just approving or disapproving of ideas. However, the possibility to interact does not equal deliberative quality. In some cases in which interaction between participants was facilitated, like the PB in Berlin-Lichtenberg, the diversity of views on the different proposals appeared to be limited: only a few reactions can be found online. In the case of ECC09, the online deliberation varied widely between countries.

12.2.7 Possibility to Interact with Decision-Makers

This condition reflects whether the tool offers the possibility to deliberate with decision-makers. As with the former condition, deliberation in this context means the opportunity to ask questions and/or exchange views. Decision-makers can be administrators as well as politicians. Do they participate in the online tool? Barrett et al. (2012) mention that in order for deliberative civic engagement processes to be successful, one needs the engagement of public officials and politicians. Another example showing the same is OurSpace, an international project dedicated to improving the engagement of the youth of Europe with European decision-makers through the combination of ICT use, information and motivation to participate. The engagement of decision-makers was in the end an important factor in the success of the project (Parycek et al. 2014).

Interactions between decision-makers and participants contribute to a better match between the needs of decision-makers and citizens' input and to the quality of the input. Research on the case of ECC09 brought to light that politicians criticised participants for not understanding political reality and therefore recommends a 'meet and greet' between politicians—in this case MEPs—and participants at an early stage (Karlsson 2010). In this way they can exchange perspectives and knowledge before the content of the proposals is decided upon. The interaction between participants and decision-makers would thus improve the quality of the output (i.e. closer to political reality), and therefore probably the impact of the participatory input on political agendas or final decisions.

This same argument was made by the interviewed researcher who studied Predlagam, who claimed the tool was too open and recommended it should provide more information on what kind of input the government wants from citizens and should provide more such structures in its design. Furthermore, the initiator of Open Ministry proposed an improvement of the participatory process around citizens' initiatives, whereby citizens would work together with the parliamentary committee. The hope was that it would stimulate a discussion between citizens and politicians on the content of the proposal to increase mutual understanding which, in the end, might help to improve the legal quality of the law proposal.

In 8/22 cases, there is some form of interaction between the participants and the decision-makers. In 5/22 cases, this interaction takes place between participants and politicians, including in all four cases of the political parties, where public servants are involved (Five Star Movement, Podemos, German Pirate Party and—only in incidental Facebook chats—in the online Green Primary), as well as in the case of abgeordenetenwatch.de, where Q&As between politicians and citizens are moderated. In Wiki Melbourne a team of city officers answered questions by participants, corrected factual errors made in edits, linked citizens to relevant documents and updated participants on events and developments concerning the project. In the participatory budgeting cases of Berlin-Lichtenberg and Paris, policy officers also interacted with citizens about their proposals.

12.2.8 Quantitative Aggregation

Quantitative aggregation is easily done online, and the numbers provide an indication of the level of support for a proposal. This indication is relevant for decision-makers in considering the proposal. When a proposal is supported by many people, this might increase the chances for political uptake of these ideas. However, political willingness is also necessary. The crowdsourced constitution in Iceland gained the support of 67% of voters during a referendum (voter turnout was 49%), but still the constitution was not voted upon by the parliament due to political unwillingness. At the same time, one should be careful of giving too much weight and meaning to voting results in digital tools, taking into consideration that the representativeness of the participants could be low.

A total of 17/22 cases use some form of quantitative aggregation. To be able to make an appropriate comparison, we have further specified this condition by distinguishing between:

- *Voting on (or signing for) proposals with the aim to reach a certain threshold* (6/22 cases: Five Star Movement, German Pirate Party, Podemos, Finnish Citizens' Initiative and Open Ministry, Predlagam and European Citizens' Initiative)
- *Voting on proposals in order to prioritise individual proposals or decide on elections/referenda* (11/22 cases: PB Paris, PB Berlin–Lichtenberg, PB Belo Horizonte, Betri Reykjavik, E-voting Estonia, E-voting Switzerland, Five Star Movement, German Pirate Party, Green Primary, Constitution Iceland and European Citizens' Consultation)

The first type of votes, often in the form of signatures, is collected in the agenda-setting phase. An example can be found in the Predlagam case, where at least 3% of users that were active in the previous 30 days need to have voted in favour of the proposal. The cases of the political parties of Podemos and the German Pirate Party also show comparable procedures for individual ideas, which need to reach a certain level of support before the proposals are taken into further consideration. Other examples are the Finnish Citizens' Initiative or the European Citizens' Initiative, where 50,000 and 10,00,000 signatures are needed, respectively. When these thresholds are met, the Finnish parliament is obliged to discuss the proposal and vote on it, and the European Commission must examine the proposal for legislation and decide whether or not the initiative warrants taking legislative steps.

The second type of voting takes place in a later phase of the decision-making process. These are votes for specific proposals in order to prioritise the range of proposals, or votes in elections and referenda. An example of this second kind of voting is the participatory budgeting case in Berlin-Lichtenberg, where different budget proposals are voted upon by participants online and via surveys, resulting in a top ten. In the participatory budgeting case in Paris, the online and offline votes on specific proposals in the final phase of the process determine which projects receive the estimated budgets. Another example is the ECC09, where 88 recommendations from the national consultations were presented on each national website; the 1635 participants were asked to vote (online or by mail) for 15 recommendations that they wanted to become the final result of the ECC.

12.2.9 Feedback to Participants

This condition reflects the extent to which participants receive feedback from the organisers and/or the addressees, such as administrators or politicians, on (a) their contributions and (b) the final decisions (i.e. do they get informed about the way their contributions have been used?).

Feedback is significant because it relates to the trust participants have in the process and the political system. The interviewed organiser of Wiki Melbourne put it as follows: *'It is almost like you extend the respect to people as if they were sitting in a room talking to you. You would expect to have to respond to them. Otherwise it's just plain rude, right? [...] If you take that mind-set, you just leave a comment: 'I just moved this over to this section, because it seemed more appropriate over here'* or *'Sorry, that point, we're not legally able to change that part of the law, so I had to delete it. But I'll point you to the state government body who is responsible for that.' It is those types of contributions and changes that maintain the trust during the process'*. The organiser of Betri Reykjavik who was interviewed is also insistent about the importance of proper feedback, in terms of common courtesy. *'And obviously at the end, when the idea is agreed on or rejected, then everybody gets an email as well. It's super important [...]. Otherwise, you're really not respecting people's time'*. This is confirmed in a survey amongst participants of the Dutch e-consultation case, where participants indicated that participation should be rewarded more, for example by ensuring that responses are published on the site without delay.

Feedback, even if the message is that the participants' input is not going to be used, can increase the democratic value of the tool: *'It is more about participating in a democratic process. To me, a petition is also a success when the answer of a recipient is: 'sorry, that is not going to happen, for this and this reason.' After which the signatories might even agree'*, according to the initiator of petitie.nl. In the case of Predlagam, it turns out that despite the high amount of negative responses, users appreciate the feedback the ministry provides, as it shows it is giving adequate consideration to their suggestions. In contrast, in cases where participants perceive responses to be standardised, cynicism increases. Badouard (2010) argues in his study on EU participation tools that obligations to provide adequate feedback also create some pressure on the decisions to be taken and the recognition as a policy instrument, together with institutional accountability, and it brings the Commission to acknowledge the participants as legitimate political actors.

When the organisation is able to provide feedback to participants, it is a sign of a well-organised participation process. Feedback implies that the organisation knows how it can and will use the input of participants, or why it can't or won't. The impact on decision-making thus gets deliberated in the process. Such feedback was given in 14/22 cases. These were: abgeordenetewatch.de, Predlagam, Open Ministry and the Finnish Citizens' Initiative, constitutional crowdsourcing in Iceland, Wiki Melbourne, Berlin-Lichtenberg, Futurium, Five Star Movement, PB Belo Horizonte, PB Paris, Betri Reykjavik and the three e-voting cases.

The extent to which feedback was given differs amongst these cases. Some of them can be considered best practices when it comes to providing feedback. Digital tools can be very supportive in providing transparency about the participatory outcomes and final decisions. For example, the wiki tool used by the municipality in Melbourne to open up the vision document for input was an instrument to maximise transparency. All contributions throughout the process and the outcomes of offline activities were fed back into this wiki by City of Melbourne officers. The wiki tool manages revisions and shows participants what has happened with their contributions. Also in the case of Betri Reykjavik, the website forum, the municipality website and emails are used to inform citizens about developments in the decision-making process, as well as implementation and later developments (Bjarnason and Grimsson 2016): *'If there's an idea that is going into processing, people can track it on the website (...) and each time there's a status update, you know, it goes into a committee and is discussed and there are meeting notes, they are sent to all the participants'* (Interview 39, organiser).

When we look at the cases which score negatively on providing feedback to participants, it is striking that it is especially the tools at the EU level that often fail to provide proper feedback: ECI, Your Voice in Europe and ECC09. However, from the literature review, we know that the European Parliament Petitions Portal has been improved regarding this point. In November 2014 a new petitions web portal was introduced, possessing more feedback features on the status of petitions (alongside more information on the Parliament's areas of competence). In the case of ECI, the information supplied by the website itself is generally very good, with exceptions in the area of result feedback, where there is a lack of clear organiser feedback to supporting citizens due to a gap in the existing online collection system. The recent proposal for revision of the ECI addresses this by allowing organisers or the European Commission to collect email addresses to improve communication efforts. With Your Voice in Europe, a synopsis report on the outcomes of an e-consultation is required, but in many cases, it is not provided (yet). And in the case of ECC09, no feedback was given on the final outcomes of the process.

12.3 Assessment of the Outcomes

A common critique of e-participation practices at the EU level is that they are a successful civic instrument but not a convincing policy instrument (as Kies and Nanz 2013: 24, with regard to ECC). It seems to be an ongoing theme that e-participative projects might provide added personal value for participants and community capacity, but suffer from a lack of direct, or even indirect, political impact. Impact on the policy or political agenda, or on the final decisions made, have therefore been the focus of this study.

This study identified two key outcome factors defining a positive result for the different e-participation tools:

- Impact on the final decisions;
- Impact on policy or political agenda-setting.

12.3.1 Impact on Final Decisions

The outcome measure 'Impact on final decisions' reflects the extent to which the results of e-participation initiatives were taken up by the policy-makers and/or politicians and actually influenced their final decisions. Van Dijk (2012) calls the outcome 'influence on political decisions': *'The decisive touchstone of eParticipation in terms of democracy'*. The most relevant question we considered was as follows: Is the majority of the input suggested by the participants recognisably incorporated in law proposals, policy documents such as EU Communications, political party programmes or election results and/or implemented in municipal budgets, etc.? Did the participatory input have a substantive and/or repeated impact on decisions made?

In some cases, the participatory input entailed many different proposals/consultations, such as Predlagam, Open Ministry (Finnish Citizen Initiative), the Dutch e-consultation and Your Voice in Europe. In these cases, we scored whether the majority of the input had an identifiable impact. On the basis of desk research, questionnaires and interviews, it was assessed that there was a substantive impact on the final decision in 11/22 cases. That half of the cases show an impact on decision-making is a positive result, since in the literature it is generally concluded that few decisions of government, political representatives or civil servants have changed on account of the input of citizens through e-participation. Van Dijk (2010) concluded that *'scarcely any influence of eParticipation on institutional policy and politics can be observed yet'* (Van Dijk 2010). Millard et al. (2008: 76) wrote: *'Most administrations do not (yet) have mechanisms and capacities in place to cope with a significant increase in participation'*. This share of positive outcomes within the cases examined might be explained by the case selection. Many cases were individually requested in the project specifications, defined by STOA, in order to learn how to strengthen participatory and direct democracy.

The 11/22 cases which score positively on 'Actual impact on final decisions' are Wiki Melbourne, PB Berlin-Lichtenberg, Your Voice in Europe, German Pirate Party, Five Star Movement, PB Belo Horizonte, PB Paris, PB Betri Reykjavik, the Green Primary and e-voting in Estonia and Switzerland. It is interesting to note that all three of the e-voting cases and the four participatory budgeting cases have an impact on the final decisions. For the e-voting cases, this may not be that surprising, since voting is a legal right with direct impact. And the literature review predicted that when it comes to influencing decision-making, the area of e-budgeting has produced some of the strongest results.

12.3.2 Impact on Policy or Political Agenda-Setting

This outcome factor is related to the outcome factor of 'Impact on final decisions' but focuses on an earlier phase within the policy cycle: the agenda-setting phase. We assessed for each of the cases if the input to the online participation process has had a substantive and/or repeated effect on the policy or political agenda.

Impact on the policy or political agenda concerns the effects of the contributions from e-participation on the political or policy debate, without necessarily influencing the decision-making process per se. For instance, in the case of the Finnish Citizen Initiative, 15 legislative proposals by citizens reached the threshold of 50.000 signatures to be debated in parliament. These proposals were handled properly: initiators are heard by committees, and these committee hearings were open to all MPs and to the media (which was a novelty). However, only one of these citizens' initiatives has led to changes in the law: the gender-neutral marriage legislation. The input of citizens in the form of legislative proposals did have a significant and repeated impact on the political agenda, but the impact on final decisions lags behind. The Iceland case also scores positively on 'agenda-setting' while not having an impact on the final decisions. The Constitutional Council of 25 citizens presented its draft constitution to Althingi, the House of Representatives in Iceland, where it was discussed. However, the draft met resistance from politicians which led to troubled parliamentary deliberations. A referendum on the draft constitution followed, with a majority in favour of its adoption. However, the impact on the decision-making process remained zero, since in the end parliament never took up the proposed constitution, it was never brought to vote, and it never went into effect.

A total of 11/22 cases score positively on the outcome factor 'Impact on policy or political agenda-setting'. Two positive cases have already been mentioned: the Finnish Citizen Initiative (with the involvement of Open Ministry) and Iceland constitutional crowdsourcing. The other cases are The EC tool Your voice in Europe, the Dutch e-consultation, Wiki Melbourne, Futurium, participatory budgeting in Berlin, Paris and Reykjavik and the collective decision-making tools of the German Pirate Party and Five Star Movement.

12.4 Analysis of Configurations

Qualitative Comparative Analysis enables systematic analysis of the conditions that are necessary and/or sufficient to produce an outcome. In the previous section, the data collected was explored, scores assigned and the cases compared for the nine conditions. In this section the data is minimised by grouping the cases that have the same scores on relevant conditions and the outcome. The resulting tables, in which the cases that show similar configurations are clustered, are called *truth tables*. Through these steps, similarities and differences between cases on the conditions and outcome values come to light systematically. The different paths towards the outcomes 'Impact on final decision' and 'Impact on political or policy agenda' are assessed in the final steps of the csQCA.

12.4.1 Impact on Decision-Making

Two cases are eliminated from the analysis of configurations for the outcome impact on final decisions. The two monitoring websites do not aim to have an impact on final decisions and are therefore not included in this truth table. The six conditions included in the truth table appeared to have a stronger connection with the outcome than the other conditions we assessed in the case studies; these six conditions showed frequent presence in combination with the positive outcome (and non-presence in relation to the negative outcome) (Table 12.1).

Out of the 20 cases in this truth table, 12 show significant impact on final decisions. Seven of these twelve cases (7/12) score positively on all six conditions Participatory Budgeting (PB) in Paris, PB in Berlin-Lichtenberg, PB in Belo Horizonte, Betri Reykjavik, e-voting in Estonia, e-voting in Switzerland and the Five Star Movement. The findings suggest that having impact on final decisions involves:

1. Creating a link to formal decision-making (in these cases via embeddedness in the policy process, elections/referenda and official political representation)
2. A digital tool that has existed for a while and where several alterations have been made to improve the participatory process (sustainability)
3. An active mobilisation and engagement strategy
4. Clarity on the participatory process and its contribution to the overall decision-making process from the start (for the participants)
5. Providing feedback to participants
6. Including an option where participants can vote to decide via prioritising proposals or elections/referenda

The other five (5/12) cases show that not all six conditions are *necessary* to produce the outcome. The Pirate Party in Germany is positively rated on the link to formal decision-making (1), the mobilisation strategy (3), clarification of the

Table 12.1 Truth table with configurations for 'impact on final decisions'

	Link to formal decision-making	Sustainability	Mobilisation and engagement strategy	Participatory process and goals are clarified	Feedback to participants	Voting to consult/decide	Impact on final decision
PB Paris	1	1	1	1	1	1	1
PB Berlin-Lichtenberg							
PB Belo Horizonte							
Betri Reykjavik							
E-voting Estonia							
E-voting Switzerland							
Five Star Movement							
German Pirate Party	1	0	1	1	0	1	1
Your Voice in Europe	1	1	0	1	0	0	1
Futurium	1	1	0	0	1	0	1
Wiki Melbourne	1	0	0	1	1	0	1
Green Primary Constitution Iceland	1	0	0	1	1	1	C
Podemos	1	1	1	0	0	0	0
Open Ministry (Finnish CI)	0	0	0	1	1	0	0
Dutch e-petitions	0	1	1	0	0	0	0
Predlagam	0	1	0	0	1	0	0

European Citizens' Consultation	0	0	0	0	0	0
Dutch e-consultation	1	0	0	0	0	0
European Citizens' Initiative	0	0	0	0	0	0

participatory process (4) and the possibility to vote to (co-)decide (6). But the political opinion formation and decision-making software called Liquid Feedback—the backbone of online democratic processes within the German Pirate Party—appeared not to be sustainable, and insufficient feedback to participants was provided. Your Voice in Europe has positive scores on the link to formal decision-making (1), the sustainability of the tool (2) and clarity for participants on the participatory process (4), but not on the other three conditions. Futurium is linked to formal decision-making (1), is sustainable as a tool (2) and also provides feedback to participants (5). The path of Wiki Melbourne also includes a link to the formal decision-making process (1) and has a clearly communicated participatory process (4), and feedback is provided to participants (5).

One of the configurations is inconsistent: the combination of (1) a link to formal decision-making; (4) a clearly communicated participation process; and (6) the possibility to vote, corresponds with a positive as well as a negative outcome. These conditions are positively scored in the Green Primary case as well as in the case of the Iceland constitution. The contradictory configurations can be explained by a difference in the type of links to formal decision-making. Although the cases both have a link to the formal decision-making process, in the Iceland constitution case, the link still leaves a lot of room to the decision-makers in the Icelandic Parliament. The link entails a first parliamentary constitutional committee, which initiated the Constitutional Council with 25 member citizens from Iceland. Subsequently another governmental committee was established to prepare further decision-making about the new constitution. This committee published a provisional report in the spring of 2014, which identified the Constitutional Council's draft as *one of several possible alternatives for a new constitution*, thereby leaving the draft constitution on ice (negative impact on final decision-making). In the Green Primary the online voting result is directly translated into the election of two 'Spitzenkandidaten' (top-ranked candidates), which leaves no room to make a different decision (positive impact on final decision-making). This comparison of cases makes clear that there are different paths to impact on the final decision; different combinations of conditions can lead to the same outcome. The path with six positive conditions shows consistency and explains seven cases, which makes it an empirically stronger result than the five individual paths in which two or three of the conditions are lacking and where one path is inconsistent.

The minimisation of the configurations, without logical remainders (unobserved cases), leads to the following formula (Fig. 12.1):

The link to formal decision-making is present in all configurations with a positive outcome. The minimisation formula thus clearly shows that it is *necessary* to establish a link to the formal decision-making process that organises the potential uptake of the participatory input. Eleven of the twelve figurations also include the condition that the participatory process and its aims are sufficiently clarified from the start. Strictly speaking this is thus not a necessary condition since it is not present in all configurations. The importance of the condition of a clear process is however supported by the fact that none of the cases that have a negative outcome score positively on both of the conditions 'link to formal decision-making' and

12 Assessing Tools for E-Democracy: Comparative Analysis of the Case Studies   315

LINK*SUSTAIN*MOBIL* CLARIF*FEEDBA*VOTE	+	LINK*sustain*MOBIL* CLARIF*feedba*VOTE	+	LINK*SUSTAIN*mobil* + CLARIF*feedba*vote	
PB Paris, PB Berlin-Lichtenberg, Betri Reykjavik, Belo Horizonte, e-voting Estonia, e-voting Switzerland, Five Star Movement		German Pirate Party		Your Voice in Europe	→ IMPACT ON FINAL DECISIONS
LINK*SUSTAIN*mobil* clarif*FEEDBA*vote	+	LINK*sustain*mobil* CLARIF*FEEDBA*vote	+	LINK*sustain*mobil* CLARIF*FEEDBA*VOTE	
Futurium		Wiki Melbourne		Green Primary	

$$\text{LINK} \cdot \begin{bmatrix} \text{SUSTAIN} \\ \text{MOBIL} \\ \text{CLARIF} \\ \text{FEEDBA} \\ \text{VOTE} \end{bmatrix} \rightarrow \text{IMPACT ON FINAL DECISIONS}$$

Fig. 12.1 Minimisation formula for 'impact on final decisions'

'participatory process clarified' (excluding the case of the Iceland constitution discussed above). To emphasise its importance, only one other case with a negative outcome—Finnish Citizens' Initiative via Open Ministry—clarified the participatory process and its aims.

The link to formal decision-making, even in combination with the clarification of the participatory process, is however not *sufficient* to produce the outcome. To create impact on final decisions, it also helps to have a sustainable tool, which has been improved over time (9/12 cases), to have an active mobilisation and engagement strategy (8/12 cases), to provide feedback to participants (10/12 cases) and to include a possibility to vote (9/12 cases).

12.4.2 Conclusions: How to Organise Impact on Decisions at a European Level

What do we learn from this descriptive formula? The six conditions included in the configurations for impact on decision-making mostly have to do with a clearly organised participation process in which the expectations of participants and decision-makers are well-managed from the beginning. Interesting to note is that three of the six conditions are in fact easier to meet with *online* participation tools. For example, digital tools are very useful in creating transparency and accountability, providing (a) clarity on the participatory process and (b) feedback on the results. Furthermore, it is an advantage of online participation practices to combine deliberative processes with (c) voting processes.

This study is aimed at drawing lessons from the comparative analysis for the EU level. Are the observed conditions that contribute to impact on decision-making present in all the studied participation tools at the EU level? If not, could the factors be realised at the EU level, or do particular challenges arise at the EU level? We discuss the different factors below, ranked via frequency.

- Starting with what we identified as the most significant necessary condition: *a link to a specific formal decision-making process* (present in all configurations with a positive outcome). Two observed EU-level cases—Futurium and Your Voice in Europe—have such links established. When we look at the tool of Futurium, we see that the more recent consultations of the tool, such as 'eGovernment4EU' and 'Digital4Science' are linked respectively to the 'eGovernment Action Plan (2016–2020)' and the 'Future Horizon 2020 Work Programme (2018–20)'. The earlier consultation 'Digital Futures' was linked to the European Strategy and Policy Analysis System (ESPAS) and Horizon 2020's strategic programming exercise 2016–18. When we take a look at Your Voice of Europe, we see that participants are asked to deliver input through questionnaires for specific policy proposals, which are regularly influenced by the online input. In contrast, the Europeans' Citizens Initiative case scored negatively, since the ECI facilitates new ideas to be raised by participants, which do not necessarily relate to a specific existing formal policy. The European Citizens Consultation (ECC) case was also very broad in scope and not linked to a specific policy or political process, which makes it more difficult to create actual impact in policy or politics. Proposals that are too general do not match the needs of decision-makers, as we saw in the case of the ECC, as well as in the cases of Predlagam and the Finnish CI (Open Ministry). Moreover, without a link to a formal decision-making process, it is not clear who is responsible for processing the input in the decision-making process.
- The second most important condition is *clarity on the participatory process* and its contribution to the overall decision-making process from the start, particularly from the perspective of participants (present in almost all configurations with a positive outcome). This indicates that the participation process should be well-embedded in the decision-making process, and participants and decision-makers have to know what to expect. At the EU level, it can be challenging to offer clarity on the overall decision-making process since it can be very complex, involving many different actors. Moreover, European citizens are less knowledgeable about EU decision-making processes than they are about national or local processes. From the four observed EU-level cases, only Your Voice in Europe scores positively on this condition. Futurium has recently improved this clarity for its more recent consultations; however, the process of the 'Digital Futures' consultation that we were able to monitor from beginning to end did not show this clarity. Your Voice in Europe clearly has made an effort to explain the consultation process and its aims in an accessible way. Accessibility, however, does not imply that the process should be oversimplified. Oversimplification can be counter-effective, as in the case of Predlagam. Because Predlagam does not pay attention to the overall, complex decision-making processes, it might—in the

words of one of our respondents—'fool' people and will inevitably lead to disappointment of participants. In contrast, Wiki Melbourne and Berlin-Lichtenberg are best practices in being clear about the expectations participants can have. These platforms are also explicit in that there is no guarantee that each proposal will be implemented. The case of participatory budgeting in Paris shows how the use of infographics can help to clarify the participation process and its contribution to the final decisions.

- A third important condition in the observed cases that succeeded in having impact on policy or political decisions is providing *feedback* to participants. Providing feedback is a sign of a well-organised process in which it is clear how exactly the participatory input has contributed to the decisions made. In addition, feedback to participants is a form of accountability. To make participation processes rewarding for citizens, their proposals should be given adequate consideration. Otherwise, it will lead to distrust not only in the participatory process itself but also in the political system as a whole. This is thus all the more important in the European context, given the democratic deficit and the negative public discourse around the EU.

  Yet, of the four observed EU-level cases, only Futurium provides considerable feedback to participants: Every participant in the Futurium consultation 'Digital Futures' received an email with the final report. The 'eGovernment4EU' consultation that is now running on the Futurium platform will not only provide information about its progress and results on the platform, but participants (i.e. proposers) will also be notified about the decisions on the platform and how the actions will be implemented.

  The other three EU-level cases in this study lack feedback mechanisms to the participants (ECI, ECC09, and Your Voice in Europe). One solution at the EU level might be—as is the case in Predlagam for example—the obligation for government or political authorities to provide feedback. This can create pressure on the actions to be taken and acknowledges participants as legitimate political actors. However, procedures alone are not enough, as the Your Voice in Europe case and the Dutch e-consultation case illustrate. And such an obligation should not result in standardised responses to citizens about their contributions and their impact. Time investment is required to make an accessible report or to create another form of feedback, and it might help to implement feedback options in the design of the tool. An inspiring example is the Participatory Budgeting site of Berlin-Lichtenberg, in which decisions on proposals are motivated in short messages in a 'traffic light-format' (green for accepted proposals, orange for proposals in process and red for rejected proposals).

- A fourth condition that contributes to impact on final decisions is *sustainability*. It takes time to organise a digital participation process to run smoothly, which often implies adjustment over time. In Futurium the tool was made more user-friendly on the basis of their experiences during the first project, Digital Futures. DG CONNECT organised three public workshops in 2015 to collect best practices, ideas and feedback on how to engage with stakeholders online, especially through Futurium. This can be seen as best practice: the users'/citizens' perspective is greatly involved in the evaluation of the tool and broader process. With regard to the Your Voice in Europe tool, the aim is to unify the separate consultation pages to improve the process. This leads to central management of the page internally. In addition, YVIE strives for simpler visual guidance and explanation of where a particular initiative currently is in the policy-making process. In contrast, the European Citizens' Initiative has not made much improvement, although several evaluations have made suggestions. The one-time experiment of the European Citizen Consultation is problematic; it was not well-implemented in existing decision-making processes, and this could not be revised in time. Time to learn and improve the digital tool is important in order to create impactful participation. Experiments are riskier and have less chance of success.

- The possibility to *vote* was present in 9 of the 12 cases in which an impact on decisions made was detected. It is a particular advantage of online participation practices that votes can be easily collected and even combined with deliberative processes. The advantage of the combination of deliberation and voting is that it can show if the participative input is supported broadly, or not. The European Citizens' Consultation included such an option. The national consultations had resulted in 88 recommendations. Subsequently, participants were asked to vote for 15 recommendations that they wanted to be part of the final result of the ECC. However, because there was no link to a specific policy or political process, the results barely had any impact. The European Citizens' Initiative does include the option to sign a proposal, which also indicates the support for a proposal. But this sort of quantitative aggregation seems to have no significant impact, as other cases in our study illustrate (the Finnish Citizens' Initiative via Open Ministry, and the Dutch e-petitions case). This lack of impact can probably be explained by the link to the decision-making process: the signatures are collected in order to put a proposal on the agenda, but they leave all further interpretation to decision-makers.
- The sixth condition, an effective *mobilisation and engagement strategy (3)*, is probably one of the greatest challenges of e-participation, especially for the EU institutions. All the cases on the EU level, including the Green Primary, score low on the condition of an effective mobilisation and engagement strategy. The challenge to mobilise and engage EU citizens is even larger than it is to mobilise citizens on the national or local level, since:

    – EU citizens form a very large and diverse group of people, who generally do not share a sense of European citizenship
    – Mass media form an important mediator in mobilising the general public on the national and local level, but they cannot be expected to play a comparable role at the EU level (for instance, due to the negative discourse about the EU and the different national foci on EU decision-making, related to national interests)

    A lesson from the primaries of the European Green Party is that it might help to create commitment of partners at the national level, who can help mobilise the national publics. Another important point to note here is that different target groups require various mobilisation and engagement strategies, for which serious investments are needed. The possibilities that transnational social media offer could also be further explored in this regard.

12.4.3 Agenda-Setting

Only 16/22 cases are included in the truth table on agenda-setting. The websites abgeordenetenwatch.de and theyworkforyou.com are aimed at monitoring politics; the e-voting cases (including the Green Primary) and PB Belo Horizonte are aimed at making final decisions. These six cases (6/22) are therefore excluded from this analysis.

In the analysis of configurations for agenda-setting, five conditions are included. It appeared that these five conditions have a stronger connection with agenda-setting than the other conditions measured in this study (Table 12.2).

Eleven cases scored positively on the outcome agenda-setting. For five of these cases (5/11)—Participatory Budgeting in Paris, Participatory Budgeting in Berlin-Lichtenberg, the Five Star Movement, the German Pirate Party and Wiki Melbourne—the path towards agenda-setting involved:

1. A link to a specific existing formal agenda in policy or politics
2. Clarity on the participatory process and its goals from the start (for the participants)
3. The possibility to participate offline as well as online
4. The possibility within the tool to interact with other participants
5. The possibility within the tool to interact with decision-makers

Six cases that succeeded in setting the agenda (6/11) did not check all these boxes. The case of Betri Reykjavik, Your Voice in Europe and the Dutch ministerial e-consultation did not include the possibility to participate offline. In Betri Reykjavik and the Finnish CI (via Open Ministry), new ideas are raised by participants that do not necessarily relate to a specific existing formal agenda in policy or politics. In Your Voice in Europe and the Dutch e-consultation cases, interaction between participants is not facilitated by the tool. The tools of Open Ministry and the Finnish Citizens' Initiative, the Iceland constitution process, Betri Reykjavik, Futurium and the Dutch e-consultation do not offer the possibility to interact with decision-makers online. In the case of Futurium and the e-consultation in the Netherlands, it is not made sufficiently clear in the tool how the participation works and/or how the participatory input contributes to the decision-making process. Information on the participatory process and its aims for participants is lacking in these cases.

As this comparison demonstrates, in the truth table more unique pathways are identified for impact on agenda-setting processes than for impact on decision-making processes. The observed cases showed more variety in the paths towards political agenda-setting. The case of the Dutch e-consultation deserves attention

Table 12.2 Truth table with configurations for 'agenda-setting'

	Link to specific existing formal agenda in policy/politics	Clarity on participatory process and goals	Combination of online and offline participation	Possibility to interact with participants	Possibility to interact with decision-makers	Political/policy agenda-setting
PB Paris	1	1	1	1	1	1
PB Berlin-Lichtenberg						
Five Star Movement German Pirate Party Wiki						
Melbourne						
Constitution Iceland	1	1	1	1	0	1
Futurium	1	0	1	1	0	1
Betri Reykjavik	0	1	0	1	0	1
Open Ministry (Finnish CI)	0	1	1	1	0	1
Your voice in Europe	1	1	0	0	0	1
Dutch e-consultation	1	0	0	0	0	1
European Citizen Consultation	0	0	1	1	0	0
Podemos	1	0	1	1	1	0

12 Assessing Tools for E-Democracy: Comparative Analysis of the Case Studies

Predlagam	0	0	0	1	0	0
Dutch e-petitions	0	0	0	0	0	0
European Citizens' Initiative	0	0	1	0	0	0

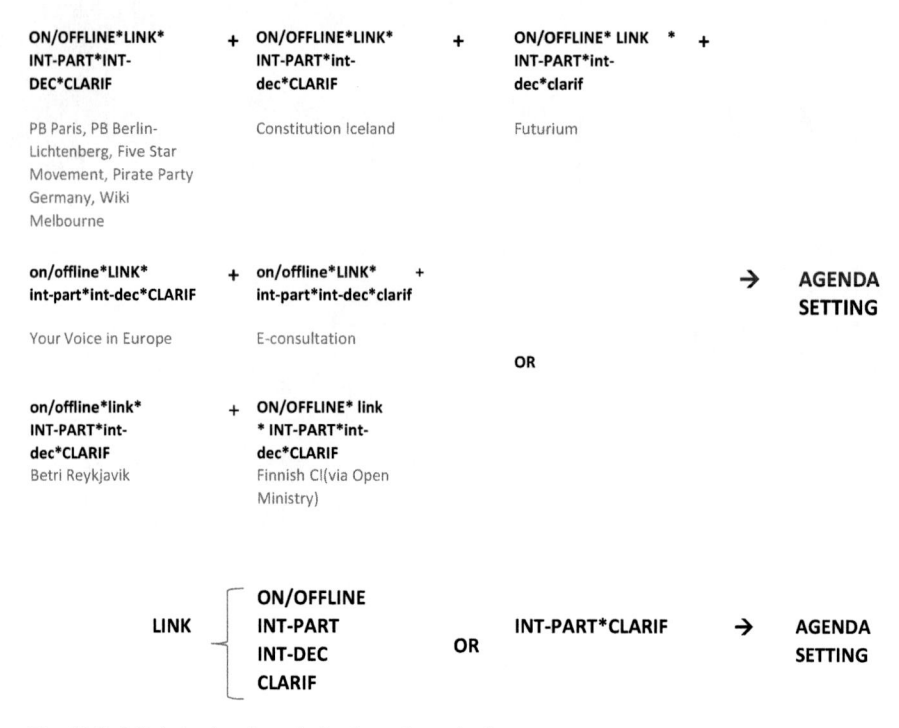

ON/OFFLINE*LINK* INT-PART*INT-DEC*CLARIF	+ ON/OFFLINE*LINK* INT-PART*int-dec*CLARIF	+ ON/OFFLINE* LINK * INT-PART*int-dec*clarif	+
PB Paris, PB Berlin-Lichtenberg, Five Star Movement, Pirate Party Germany, Wiki Melbourne	Constitution Iceland	Futurium	
on/offline*LINK* int-part*int-dec*CLARIF	+ on/offline*LINK* int-part*int-dec*clarif	+	→ AGENDA SETTING
Your Voice in Europe	E-consultation	OR	
on/offline*link* INT-PART*int-dec*CLARIF Betri Reykjavik	+ ON/OFFLINE* link * INT-PART*int-dec*CLARIF Finnish CI(via Open Ministry)		

LINK	⎡ ON/OFFLINE ⎢ INT-PART ⎨ INT-DEC ⎣ CLARIF	OR	INT-PART*CLARIF	→	AGENDA SETTING

Fig. 12.2 Minimisation formula for 'agenda-setting'

particularly, because this case only scores positively on the link to the formal decision-making process. Official policy around the ministerial e-consultation is that unless there is a valid reason why e-consultation does not suit the legislative process, it must be applied. Procedures also prescribe a report on the results of the e-consultation, which naturally facilitates an agenda-setting effect. However, this has only a modest impact on the policy agenda, which is not significant in all e-consultations. In some cases no input is collected. And in many cases, civil servants acknowledge they do not have much room to manoeuvre, as they are barely able to deviate from the law proposal that is already negotiated. Yet in other instances, knowledge from specialists or tacit knowledge is very valuable for policy-makers to improve the legislative proposal. Civil servants argue that in the majority of cases e-consultation improves the quality of legislative proposals that are subsequently discussed in parliamentary debate. Both interviewees in the case study on the Dutch e-consultation argue that as e-consultation is an obligatory step, and many civil servants are just doing their duty; this explains why the link to the formal policy agenda is such a decisive condition in this case. However, other non-observed conditions might also contribute to the agenda-setting effect of e-consultation, such as the available knowledge at the ministry on the subject and the quality of the contributions.

The minimisation of the configurations, without logical remainders, leads to the following formulas for agenda-setting (Fig. 12.2):

The minimisation results in two different formulas. The first formula represents nine cases (9/11) and has therefore a stronger empirical basis than the second formula which stands for two cases (2/11). The first formula indicates that it is *necessary* to create a link to a specific existing formal policy or political agenda. The links have different forms in the cases. Links are established that connect the digital participatory input through official municipal budgeting processes (PB Paris, PB Berlin-Lichtenberg, PB Betri Reykjavik). Other links are created through official political representation (German Pirate Party, Five Star Movement, PB Betri Reykjavik), or via a law on Citizens' Initiatives to parliamentary debate (Finnish CI via Open Ministry) and via consultation in official policy-making processes (Wiki Melbourne, Dutch e-consultation, Your Voice in Europe, Futurium). However, in most cases more conditions need to be met in order to set the agenda. This is also clear from the cases with a negative outcome; in four of these five cases, a link to the formal decision-making process is there, but is not enough to substantially or repeatedly affect the political or policy agenda (European Citizen Consultation, Predlagam, Dutch e-petitions, European Citizens' Initiative).

The second formula describes the combination of interaction between participants and a clarified participative process as necessary conditions to succeed in setting the agenda. This combination of conditions is not present in any of the five cases with a negative outcome.

In nine of the eleven (9/11) cases in which an agenda-setting effect is measured, interactions between participants are facilitated in the online tools. Deliberation might increase the quality of proposals and/or shows the social support for proposals. Clear goals and procedures contributed to the substantial or repeated effect on the political or policy agenda in nine of the eleven (9/11) observed cases, as well as a combination of online and offline participation tools (8/11 cases). A final interesting finding is that interactions between decision-makers and participants within the digital participatory process are facilitated in 5 of the 11 cases (5/11) with an agenda-setting effect, while this was only facilitated in 1 case without an agenda-setting effect.

12.4.4 Conclusions: How to Organise Impact on European Agendas

The outcome of the csQCA about agenda-setting is less clear-cut than the outcome of the csQCA about 'Impact on final decisions', but what can we learn from this descriptive formula? The five conditions included in the configurations that show an effect on the policy or political agenda mostly have to do with how the participation process is organised and the type of participation that is facilitated. Just as with the outcome 'Impact on final decisions', a link to an existing policy or political process, as well as the clarity of the participation process are important factors for 'Impact on agenda-setting'. Three further factors appear to contribute to an impact on agenda-setting. In the section below, we therefore address the following questions: Are these three factors present in the EU-level cases? And if not, could the factors be realised at EU level or do particular challenges arise at the EU level?

- First, the possibility *to participate* offline as well as *online*. A combination of online and offline participation improves the inclusiveness of the tool. Any method to improve inclusiveness is important at the EU level, since most EU citizens feel detached from the EU and generally there is a low level of interest in matters at European level. Combining online and offline participation is also important to overcome the digital divide, which is present in various EU countries, although with regard to access to basic broadband this no longer maps onto the underlying divides between richer and poorer regions of Europe (Negreiro 2015). Three of the EU tools in the cases already provide offline participation possibilities: Futurium encompasses many 'engagement activities', including offline meetings or workshops that feed the online discussions, and vice versa; ECC started off with an online phase to collect as many proposals as possible, which in their turn formed input to the national offline consultations; ECI offers the opportunity to sign an initiative offline (alongside the online collection system certified by national authorities in the Member States).
- Second, the possibility within the tool to *interact with other participants*. In the literature there is an unresolved debate about the need for deliberation in online participatory processes. In this QCA configuration, the possibility to interact with other participants seems to contribute to an effect on the political or policy agenda. Deliberation could enhance the quality of the input, and better proposals might more easily find their way to the political or policy agenda, but it does not seem to be a decisive condition. Deliberation between participants is facilitated in both Futurium and in the European Citizens' Consultation, but not in Your Voice in Europe or ECI. The different consultations on the Futurium platform has an interactive design, and participants can react to one another's input; according to the interviewed developer, it resembles a social network. During the online first phase of the ECC, participants had the opportunity to discuss one another's contributions, but how much deliberation actually took place differed per national website. Deliberation between participants from different EU countries was not possible, which is an often-heard critique of the ECC. This draws attention to a challenge that arises at the EU level: deliberation between participants from different EU countries is difficult to organise, particularly because of language barriers. Technological measures, like translation software, are not yet able to overcome this barrier. Futurium uses English as the common language, which suits a professional target group, but excludes many European citizens.
- A third condition is the possibility within the tool to *interact with decision-makers*. A good connection between the input from participants and the political reality would increase the chance of citizens' input being incorporated in the political or policy agenda. Interaction between participants and decision-makers can enhance this connection and can be realised online. Good practices in this regard are the Wiki Melbourne case, in which a vision document was co-created

between citizens and officials, and the PB Paris case. In the phase of project assessment, there is room for the Paris municipality to combine, pair and interpret the proposals of citizens. This phase was opened up for citizen involvement in 2016: 'We *made a big effort to involve citizens into the merging phase and really encouraging them to go together and defend the project together. First of all, to have less projects to deal with but also to have more comprehensive projects and finally because we need people to get more involved in the campaign phase*', the interviewed organiser explained. The four observed digital participation tools at the EU level lack the possibility to interact with decision-makers. This might be less problematic in the e-consultations of Your Voice in Europe or Futurium, where participants' input is interpreted by officials related to the specific policy. However, in relation to the more open tools of ECI and ECC, the interaction between participants and decision-makers would contribute to a better match between citizens' input and the reality and practices at the political and policy level. And last but not least, online interaction can also contribute to an increase in transparency and accountability.

12.5 In Sum: Digital Participation Is Not a Quick-Fix

A long-standing and continuing democratic deficit of the European Union is detected in both public and scholarly debate. This democratic deficit is explained by the complex and mutually reinforcing mix of the institutional design features of the EU and is held to contribute to the lack of a sense of European citizenship and the negative and national-oriented public discourse around the EU.

It is still believed by many that the perceived democratic deficit of the European Union indicates the need to foster a European public sphere as a space of debate across national public spheres. Moreover, there is a consensus that the new modes of political communication and participation via the internet can play a role in this respect. Redressing the democratic deficit is obviously a daunting task which cannot be accomplished through the introduction of e-participation tools alone. Far-reaching expectations of a fundamental reform of modern democracy through the application of online participatory tools are vanishing after two decades of e-democracy. However, if properly designed and implemented, e-participation has the potential to contribute to accountability and transparency, the transnationalisation and politicisation of public debates, and the improvement of exchanges and interactions between EU decision-making and European citizens.

A common critique of e-participation practices at the EU-level is that they are a successful civic instrument but not a convincing policy instrument. It seems to be an ongoing theme that e-participative projects might provide added personal value for participants and community building, but suffer from a lack of direct, or even indirect, political or policy impact. In our comparative case study, we therefore focused on the factors within e-participation practices that contribute to impact on the political or policy agenda or on the final decisions made. The most important factors for successful e-participation identified in the report are:

- A close and clear link between e-participation processes and a concrete formal decision-making process
- Clarity of the participatory process and the contribution of its outputs to the overall decision-making process for participants from the start
- Feedback to the participants about what has been done with their contributions
- E-participation that must be accompanied by an effective mobilisation and engagement strategy, involving communication instruments tailored for different target groups
- Participative processes that should not be limited to one event but should be embedded in an institutional 'culture of participation'

To realize these conditions in practice requires serious investments (in time and costs) and the commitment of all actors involved; digital participation is not a quick-fix.

References

Albrecht, S. (2012). E-Consultations: A review of current practice and a proposal for opening up the process. In E. Tambouris, A. Macintosh, & O. Saebo (Eds.), *Electronic participation* (pp. 13–24). Berlin: Springer.

Badouard, R. (2010). Pathways and obstacles to eParticipation at the European level. *JeDEM, 2*(2), 99–110.

Barrett, G., Wyman, M., & Schattan, C. V. (2012). Assessing the policy impacts of deliberative civic engagement. In T. Nabatchi, J. Gastil, M. Leighninger, & G. M. Weiksner (Eds.), *Democracy in motion: Evaluating the practice and impact of deliberative civic engagement* (pp. 181–206). New York: Oxford University Press.

Berg-Schlosser, D., & De Meur, G. (2009). Comparative research design: case and variable selection. In B. Rihoux & C. C. Ragin (Eds.), *Configurational comparative methods. Qualitative comparative analysis (QCA) and related techniques* (pp. 19–32). Thousand Oaks, CA: Sage.

Bezirksamt Lichtenberg von Berlin. (2008). *Rahmenkonzeption zum Bürgerhaushalt in Berlin-Lichtenberg ab 2010*. Berlin: Bezirksamt Lichtenberg von Berlin.

Bjarnason, R., & Grimsson, G. (2016). *Better neighbourhoods 2011 to 2016 – Participatory budgeting in Reykjavik*. Presentation material.

Font, J., del Amo, S. P., & Smith, G. (2016). Tracing the impact of proposals from participatory processes: Methodological challenges and substantive lessons. *Journal of Public Deliberation, 12*(1), Article 3.

Gibson, R., & Cantijoch, M. (2013). Conceptualizing and measuring participation in the age of the internet: Is online political engagement really different to offline? *Journal of Politics, 75*(3), 701–716.

Gibson, R. K., & McAllister, I. (2013). Online social ties and political engagement. *Journal of Information Technology and Politics, 10*(1), 21–34.

Heidelberger, C. A. (2009). Electronic participatory budgeting: Supporting community deliberation and decision-making with online tools. *Conference Paper Midwest Decision Sciences Institute Conference*, Miami University, Oxford, OH, April 16–18.

Karlsson, M. (2010). A panacea for pan-European citizen participation? Analysis of the 2009 European citizen consultations. In E. Amna (Ed.), *New forms of citizen participation: normative implications* (pp. 97–112). Baden-Baden: Nomos.

Karlsson, M. (2011). Connecting citizens to the European parliament: E-consultations as a tool for political representation. In Z. Sobaci (Ed.), *E-parliament and ICT-based legislation: Concept, experiences and lessons* (pp. 80–102). Hershey, PA: IGI-Global.

Kersting, N. (2013). Online participation: from 'invited' to 'invented' spaces. *International Journal of Electronic Governance, 6*(4), 270–280.

Kies, R., & Nanz, P. (Eds.). (2013). *Is Europe listening to us? Success and failure of EU citizen consultations.* Farnham: Ashgate.

Korthagen, I., Van Keulen, I., Hennen, L., Aichholzer, G., Rose, G., Linder, R., Goos, K., & Nielsen, R. O. (2018). *Prospects for e-democracy in Europe: Part II case studies.* Brussels: EPRS/STOA.

Leighninger, M. (2012). Mapping deliberative civic engagement. In T. Nabatchi, J. Gastil, M. Leighninger, G. M. & Weiksner (Eds.), *Democracy in motion: Evaluating the practice and impact of deliberative civic engagement* (pp. 1–23). New York: Oxford University Press.

Millard, J., et al. (2008). *eParticipation: Overview of issues and research questions.* Deliverable D5.1a to European eParticipation, Study and supply of serviced on the development of eParticipation in the EU.

Negreiro, M. (2015). *Bridging the digital divide in the EU.* European Parliamentary Research Service, PE 573.884.

Organ, J. (2014). Decommissioning direct democracy? A critical analysis of commission decision-making on the legal admissibility of European citizens initiative proposals. *European Constitutional Law Review, 10*(3), 422–443.

Panopoulou, E., Tambouris, E., & Tarabanis, K. (2014). Success factors in designing eParticipation initiatives. *Information and Organization, 24*(4), 195–213. https://doi.org/10.1016/j.infoandorg.2014.08.001.

Parycek, P., Sachs, M., Sedy, F., & Schossboeck, J. (2014). Evaluation of an E-participation project: Lessons learned and success factors from a cross-cultural perspective. In E. Tambouris, A. Macintosh, & F. Bannister (Eds.), *Electronic participation, Epart* (Vol. 8654, pp. 128–140). Berlin: Springer.

Pratchett, L., Durose, C., Lowndes, V., Smith, G., Stoker, G., & Wales, C. (2009). *Empowering communities to influence local decision making: Systematic review of the evidence.* London: Department for Communities and Local Government.

Van Dijk, J. A. G. M. (2010). Participation in policy making. In *Study on the social impact of ICT. Report for European commission, information society and media directorate-general* (pp. 30–70). Luxemburg: European Communities.

Van Dijk, J. A. G. M. (2012). Digital democracy: Vision and reality. In I. Snellen, M. Thaens, & W. van de Donk (Eds.), *Public administration in the information age: Revisited* (pp. 49–61). Amsterdam: IOS-Press.

Open Access This chapter is licensed under the terms of the Creative Commons Attribution 4.0 International License (http://creativecommons.org/licenses/by/4.0/), which permits use, sharing, adaptation, distribution and reproduction in any medium or format, as long as you give appropriate credit to the original author(s) and the source, provide a link to the Creative Commons licence and indicate if changes were made.

The images or other third party material in this chapter are included in the chapter's Creative Commons licence, unless indicated otherwise in a credit line to the material. If material is not included in the chapter's Creative Commons licence and your intended use is not permitted by statutory regulation or exceeds the permitted use, you will need to obtain permission directly from the copyright holder.

Chapter 13
Options for Improving e-Participation at the EU Level

Rasmus Ø. Nielsen, Leonhard Hennen, Iris Korthagen, Georg Aichholzer, and Ralf Lindner

Abstract In this chapter, Nielsen et al. propose options for improving e-participation at the EU level without changing underlying legal frameworks. In response to the challenges to e-participation, which arise out of current institutional designs, the authors make creative use of the research results presented earlier in the book to suggest 'low-hanging fruits' for practical reform. The challenges addressed include the relative weakness of individual citizens' participation compared to that of CSO's, the weakness of the Parliament in the legislative process and the continued de-coupling of the EU policy process from the will of the European citizens. While the chapter proposes no easy fixes, it points to some obvious practical steps forward. To improve existing participation mechanisms, the authors recommend providing improved support to citizens using the ECI, investing in the back-office support needed for the EP Petitions Portal to realize its potential and improving the scalability of Your Voice in Europe through advanced data analysis. They also make four novel proposals, first among which is to experiment with participatory budgeting in relation to the Regional and Social Funds. The chapter ends with a plea for a long-term vision of a unified European participation structure to gather and harness the potentials of individual mechanisms.

R. Ø. Nielsen (✉)
The Danish Board of Technology Foundation, Hvidovre, Denmark
e-mail: rn@tekno.dk

L. Hennen
Institute of Technology Assessment and Systems Analysis, Karlsruhe Institute of Technology, Karlsruhe, Germany
e-mail: leonhard.hennen@kit.edu

I. Korthagen
Netherlands Court of Audit, The Hague, The Netherlands

G. Aichholzer
Institute of Technology Assessment, Austrian Academy of Sciences, Vienna, Austria
e-mail: aich@oeaw.ac.at

R. Lindner
Fraunhofer Institute for Systems and Innovation Research, Karlsruhe, Germany
e-mail: ralf.lindner@isi.fraunhofer.de

This section of the book discusses options for improving e-participation at the EU level. The discussion makes creative use of the findings of the previous sections. The first step is to outline the challenges that the specific institutional arrangements of the EU present in relation to the development and implementation of e-participation. Our main emphasis, however, is on options for improving participation through digital means within existing institutional frameworks. Therefore, the second step of this section is to revisit already existing mechanisms and discuss options for additional ones.

To identify immediate options for strengthening EU institutions' rapport with European citizens through e-participation, we added two additional sources of information to the findings from the review of the state-of-the-art of research and the case studies (Part I and Part II of this book). The first additional source of information is experience. It is a well-established principle in pragmatist social science to rely on the first-hand experiences of the actors involved in a given social system, to identify the paradoxes and potentials for development of such systems (e.g. Flyvbjerg 2001). The other source of additional information is the outcome of creative brainstorming. Developing new tools and mechanisms for the functioning of institutions relies to a great degree on the ability of people who are positioned at the intersection between different institutional spheres to creatively combine elements of the different organizational practices to which they are exposed (see, e.g. Campbell 2004).

To allow our analysis to be influenced by these additional sources of information, we engaged with a small number of stakeholders to gather and generate ideas for immediate improvement of participatory practices at the EU level. All interviewees involved in the local-, national- and EU-level case studies were asked to elaborate on their ideas on how the tools, about which they were being interviewed, could be applied at the EU level. These inputs are reported in part in each individual case study. We also invited a small group of institutional and nongovernmental stakeholders and experts to a day of co-creation at a workshop held in Brussels on November 21, 2016. At this workshop, the authors of this report and the expert group discussed ideas for improving existing participatory tools at the EU level, as well as immediate options for going beyond these tools, for example, by adopting some of the new tools described in the case selection earlier in this report. Following these steps of stakeholder engagement, we have used the most clearly apparent consensus positions among the stakeholders as starting points for recommendations, which have been supplemented by the evidence gathered in the literature review and case sections of this report. Rather than attempt a systematic presentation and evaluation of all logically possible applications of the tools in use at national level, which were analysed in the previous section, we attempt to use the findings from the case studies to identify the 'low-hanging fruits' for EU-level participation. We take such low-hanging fruits to be those changes or additions to EU-level participation mechanisms that might make a significant difference without demanding changes to existing institutional mandates.

The section ends with a discussion of how a unified approach to e-participation could provide a common access point, not only to participation in the processes of the EU institutions but in the entire multilevel construction of European governance. Along the way, we seek to provide concrete suggestions for small steps towards such a unified approach and to take into account risks and potential pitfalls to be avoided.

13.1 EU's Institutional Architecture and the Need for e-Participation

Identifying suitable approaches and tools for e-participation at the European level demands first of all that we recapitulate EU's specific institutional architecture and the prevailing patterns of governance in the European Union, which need to be taken into account. Established institutional structures and procedures represent important enabling and constraining conditions not only for formal opportunities for citizens to influence European decision-making but also for the potential uptake of e-participation tools and practices.

In many ways, the European Union is a political system sui generis. As such, the EU combines elements of a supranational body, a joint federation of states and a few characteristics of genuine statehood. At this stage, the EU is not a fully sovereign state, and whether it will ever be so is a matter of fundamental contestation (e.g. Nicolaïdis 2013). This unique setting is reflected in EU's institutional structure and its related decision-making processes. Among the most notable characteristics is EU's duality as a union of citizens and a union of Member States (Sturm 2010). This duality is expressed in the roles of the European Parliament—the representative body of the European citizens—and the Council of the European Union, which represents the Member State governments. Another striking feature of the European Union is its multilevel governance, which blurs in everyday practice the distinction between national, international and federal governance. EU's complex institutional design is not based on a constitutional blueprint but is the result of numerous integration steps and incremental reforms, often accompanied by contention and tough negotiations between the Member States (Wallace et al. 2010: 70ff.).

We identify three features concerning the relations between the European institutions and their constituency. These are coupled to the specific institutional setting and the procedural rules of the European democratic system, which can be regarded (and actually are regarded by the European policymaking bodies) as problems or deficits of the democratic set-up of the EU; it is against this background that e-participation is perceived as an option for strengthening the ties between European citizens and the EU policymaking bodies.

- **Citizens have fewer rights to voice and consultation than civil society organizations (CSOs)**

    Before the enactment of the Lisbon Treaty in 2009, the often-cited democratic deficit and the legitimacy crisis of the EU (see Part 1 Sect. 3.3.2) had triggered discussions on how to better involve European citizens in the decision-making processes of the EU. At first sight, this 'participatory turn' (Saurugger 2010) seems to be more than mere rhetoric, as the aim for more and better involvement of civil society and citizens has entered a number of official policy documents, most prominently EC's White Paper on Governance (Commission of the European Communities 2001). Yet, a closer look at both the debate and the formal framework within which such increased participation could take place cautions us not to expect too many advances in citizen participation. First and foremost, it is important to note that according to the Lisbon Treaty (TEU, Art. 10), the EU is explicitly based on principles of representative democracy. Second, Art. 11 of the TEU contains a number of provisions complementing the principle of representative democracy. In clause 1, citizens and associations are given a right to voice their views. And clause 2 requires the institutions to 'maintain an open, transparent and regular dialogue with representative associations and civil society'. Comparing the two provisions, citizen involvement is explicitly defined as voice and consultation and remains rather noncommittal. This gives citizens fewer rights in decision-making processes when compared to civil society organizations (CSOs), which receive a formal guarantee to be heard and involved in dialogue (Fischer-Hotzel 2010: 340). Against this background and taking into account the debate, Fischer-Hotzel (2010: 339) points out that for many, 'participatory democracy' at the EU level actually means 'associative democracy' and the inclusion of CSOs in the processes of decision-making. It is a common critique of (digital) participatory processes that they are monopolized by established political actors (parties, associations or movements), and that ordinary citizens are not heard as much. In 11 of the studied cases, we found that both established organizations and professionals are strongly involved in the digital tool; this includes all four of the cases at the EU level (Voice of Europe, European Citizens' Initiative, European Citizens' Consultation, Futurium).

- **Improved legislative functions of the European Parliament, but still no right to directly initiate legislation or ability to effectively hold the European Commission politically accountable**

    Structures for representation at the EU level have arguably improved considerably over time. The Lisbon Treaty addressed many of the institutional problems that were frequently raised in debates about the EU. Most importantly with regard to the democratic deficit and related legitimacy problems of the EU, the position of the European Parliament (EP), which is EU's only directly elected institution, was considerably strengthened. Clearly, the Lisbon Treaty has taken substantial steps towards an effective parliamentarization of the EU. For the most part, the EP has become an equal player in legislative processes and spending decisions, thus significantly increasing at least the formal democratic legitimacy of most European regulation (Oppelland 2010: 87f.). Still missing, however, is the right to directly initiate legislation—a function that continues to rest with the European Commission (EC). In addition to the improved legislative functions, the EP gained important electoral functions, as the President of the EC, and the European Commissioners need to be approved by a majority of the EP. Any nomination for EC presidency by the European Council has to take into account the majority situation in the EP. However, EP's ability to effectively hold the EC politically accountable remains weak, as the threshold to dismiss a Commission with a vote of non-confidence is extremely high (2/3 majority). It is unusual that the threshold for non-confidence is higher than the requirements for election. One rationale for this atypical design feature might be that the EC President does not have the prerogative to dissolve the European Parliament (Oppelland 2010: 88).

- **Continuing de-coupling of the European political system from the processes of political will-formation of the European citizens**

    While important institutional improvements have been achieved, the political processes of the European Union still do not sufficiently fulfil key functions of representative democracy. Most importantly, election campaigns for the EP continue to be primarily driven by national perspectives. In addition and related to this observation, the political parties and parliamentary factions in the EP are currently not divided into recognizable majority and opposition groups competing for different policy solutions. The dominance of informal grand coalitions of the largest parties in the EP makes it difficult for the public and the citizens to hold the members of the EP and their parties accountable. This points to the current most crucial deficit of the European Union, as emphasized by, e.g. Habermas (2008: 98f.): the continuing de-coupling of the European political system from the processes of political will-formation of the European citizens. Noteworthy improvements in this regard have been achieved with the introduction of the so-called 'spitzenkandidaten' (top candidates) of the main political party families participating in the EP elections in 2014. From this perspective, the next logical step would imply that not only the President of the EC would be backed by a majority of the EP but also that the EC President and Commissioners are more often than not elected from the parliament, thereby establishing a more visible linkage between parliamentary majority and the executive actions of the EC. However, care needs to be taken that this type of party politicization of EU politics remains compatible with the requirements of negotiation between different Member State interests (Lippert 2013: 13) and sufficiently takes into account the interests particularly of smaller Member States.

Howsoever one views the state-of-play of European integration, there are good reasons to explore pragmatic options for citizens to voice their concerns and ideas. The long-standing and continuing democratic deficits of the EU are rooted in a complex and mutually reinforcing mix of institutional design features, lack of a genuine European public sphere, and insufficient politicization of European politics as such. Redressing these problems is ultimately a constitutional matter and far outside the range of what e-participation can achieve alone. However, if properly designed and implemented, e-participation has the potential to contribute to promising solutions in the areas of accountability and transparency, transnationalization and politicization of public debates and the improvement of exchanges and interactions between EU decision-making and European citizens.

13.2 Challenges Specific to e-Participation at the EU Level

Beyond the above-mentioned problems in the relation between the EU policymaking system and its constituency are a number of other challenges arising from the specific institutional structures of the EU, which must be taken into consideration for any attempt at improving channels for e-participation at the European level.

13.2.1 Language

A major challenge to e-participation at the European level is language. With 24 official languages, translation is a major element of the running costs of the EU. Several of the European-level cases address this in different ways (Part II). The institutionalized mechanisms range from relying on English as a working language to full translation of all major content into all official languages. Your Voice in Europe clearly privileges English speakers by treating English as a *de facto* lingua franca. The platform provides all consultations in English and only a few additionally in one or more of the major languages (German, French, Italian, Spanish). Written contributions are accepted in all official EU languages. But with the English-only availability of core information, such as the questions to be answered, the platform has a clear choice built-in that decisively shapes a priori the demographic of possible participants. The European Citizen Initiative (ECI) strikes a middle ground. The platform provides all information about the mechanism in all official languages. The platform also accepts initiatives written in all official languages. Translation into other languages was previously the sole responsibility of the initiator, but with a new agreement reached in December 2018, initiators will now also be able to ask for help from volunteer supporters contributing through an online collaboration platform.[1] The previous system clearly favoured well-organized campaigns over more loosely affiliated individual citizens as initiators. With the addition of the collaboration platform, one can hope that individual citizens and small groups will be better able to be heard as others volunteer their resources. The European Parliament's Petitions Portal is clearly the most multilingual of the institutionalized mechanisms. The portal allows submission of petitions in all official EU languages, and summaries of the petitions are translated into all official languages and made available to the public. Furthermore, video of meetings in the Petition Committee, where petitions are discussed and petitioners are sometimes invited to make their case, are made available online with the option to select interpretation in each of the official languages. It should be noted that the working language in these meetings is typically English. It is also important to note that that the translation efforts of the EP, from which the e-participation platform benefits, would take place in any case,

---

[1] http://europa.eu/rapid/press-release_IP-18-6792_en.htm

so that the e-participation mechanism is thus able to piggy-back on already allocated translation practices and resources.

There seems to be a pattern whereby e-participation platforms at the European level mimic the underlying institutional working mode with regard to working languages and resources committed to translation. This tendency is corroborated by the single example among our case studies in which a non-EU e-participation mechanism makes use of multiple languages, namely the Swiss e-voting platform. On this platform all information is made available in all official languages, which is traditional for the underlying Canton institutions. In this case, the translation workload is lightened considerably by the fact that the mechanism is a voting mechanism without deliberation.

It is a well-known dilemma of the European Union that full inclusiveness demands considerable investment in translation, while full efficiency privileges English as a working language. Considerable investments in new tools for digital translation have therefore been ongoing since at least the first Framework Programme for Research and Development (1984–87). However, the promises of digital translation have long seemed a mirage; always on the horizon and never quite as good as expected. Despite these setbacks, a new wave of optimism exists around translation software based on artificial intelligence and so-called deep learning (www.ec.europa.eu/citizens-initiative). One recent paper thus claims that a new version of Google's translation software was scored by observers to have a degree of fluency in the translation of random sentences from English to Spanish, which was very close to that of human translators (5.43 on average compared to 5.55 for humans). It is outside the scope of this report to assess the plausibility of such claims and the implied hopes for a more multilingual Internet that comes with it. However, there is no doubt that while digital translation into the major languages of the world are seeing massive investment, the European Union and its Member States will be forced to add their own investments on top of those of private actors if all of the official languages of the EU are going to have comparable degrees of support. Less ambitious results may be useful, of course. We would thus expect the availability of digital translation into the few most widely spoken languages in Europe to greatly improve the accessibility of EU-level e-participation mechanisms.

13.2.2 Multilevel Governance

An often-discussed challenge is the multilevel nature of European governance. It is well-known that governance complexity rises proportionally with the many levels of governance that the European system encompasses. With the upper echelons of this system having often only indirect connections with national representative democracies, it is easy to assume that e-participation at the EU level will automatically inherit the democratic deficit/'no demos' problems of the governance system as a whole. However, examples such as the UK Democratic Dashboard (see Part II, Chap. 2) show that it is possible to construct a common access point to a multinational and multilevel governance system, even if not all potential users have access to participation in all of the channels of participation. The digital infrastructure of the Five Star Movement similarly shows that a common infrastructure for local-, national- and European-level political participation can provide much-needed advice, guidance and overall structuration for citizens wishing to participate in decision-making (Part II, Chap. 10). Of course, the fact that the construction of such common infrastructures is technically possible means neither that it is necessarily, politically feasible nor that developing a well-functioning system is easy. Our point here is only that the constitutional difficulties of European democracy do not by necessity translate into roadblocks for a common European e-participation platform.

13.2.3 Digital Divide

As regards the so-called 'digital divide' (Mossberger et al. 2003, 2007), there are good reasons to revisit some of the assumptions underlying the traditional discussion of the divide between advanced and less advanced regions of Europe, given the development infrastructures for Internet access over the last decades. Granted, Europe-wide patterns of exclusion of the elderly, citizens with lower levels of education and citizens with disabilities from digital platforms of e-government and e-democracy remain (as discussed, e.g. by Van Dijk 2012 and Panopoulou et al. 2014). But these patterns are not specific to the EU level: they affect opportunities for e-participation at all levels of government. More importantly, with regard to access to basic broadband they no longer map onto the underlying divides between richer and poorer regions of Europe (Negreiro 2015). While the digital divide as traditionally understood is thus a challenge to be addressed by any e-participation platform, this challenge is not exclusive to participation on decision-making at the EU level. Rather, it is a reminder that all efforts at increasing citizens' participation in policymaking should beware of an online-only strategy; face-to-face participation processes supported by effective mobilization efforts must remain in the toolbox.

If an EU-specific digital divide is to be considered a relevant challenge for e-participation at the European level, it is the cultural divides between Member States with a great deal of trust between governments and their populations regarding the sharing and recording of personal data such as ideological standpoints, and those Member States which—for good historical reasons—do not have the same degree of trust. This cultural divide concerning degrees of digital openness presents a real challenge to the plausibility of common European approaches to e-government under any form, including e-democracy and e-participation.

Keeping these qualifications in mind, the following sections will present and discuss suitable e-participation approaches at the EU level in greater detail, while taking into account some of the above-mentioned institutional characteristics and weaknesses.

13.3 Ways of Improving Existing Participatory Mechanisms

The EU institutions already have a range of well-established mechanisms for digitally supported citizen participation. In our co-creative workshop, we focused on three of them: the European Citizens Initiative, the Your Voice in Europe consultation platform and the European Parliament Petitions Portal. The consensus position among stakeholders and scientific observers with regard to these mechanisms seems to be twofold. There is a general agreement that these platforms and the underlying legal mechanisms hold great potential as first steps in the direction of opening up European decision-making and governance to citizens' participation. However, the net result of the legal mandates, their interpretation and their practical and technical implementation is that ordinary European citizens are still without simple and transparent channels to engage with the EU institutions.

To make this consensus position more concrete, the work underpinning this report repeated an exercise performed by Lironi (2016) to facilitate a SWOT analysis (Strengths, Weaknesses, Opportunities, Threats) for each tool. Using this technique in dialogue with a large number of individual stakeholders, Lironi et al. corroborated the existence of the above-outlined consensus positions. In order to go beyond the findings of Lironi et al., our analysis placed special emphasis on ways of improvement. We thus deployed the SWOT analysis in the above-mentioned co-creative workshop, where participants were able to feed off one another's ideas to come up with recommendations to improve the existing mechanisms.

13.3.1 Improving the European Citizens' Initiative

At the time of writing (February 2019), a vote by the European Parliament on a European Commission proposal to improve the European Citizens' Initiative (ECI) is imminent. A reform proposal was made by the EC in September 2017, which sought to respond to a number of critiques and suggestions put forward by stakeholders, including some of those discussed below; the multi-NGO ECI Campaign welcomed EC's proposal as an 'overdue step' in the right direction.[2] The proposal went through interinstitutional negotiations in late 2018 and thus currently awaits a parliamentary decision. Our analysis of the ECI in this section takes the ECI as it existed before EC's proposal as a reference point.

As the first transnational e-participation tool for policy agenda-setting, which has an institutional embedding as strong as the one provided by the ECI in the Lisbon Treaty's §4, the platform is both unprecedented, and still unparalleled in terms of the advancement of participatory democracy at transnational level (cf. Part I, Chap. 4).

---

[2] See http://www.citizens-initiative.eu/commission-launches-legislative-proposal-improve-eci/

In formal terms, the ECI gives citizens a powerful agenda-setting tool, given the conditions that a proposal must fall within the remit of the European Commission and gather 1 million signatures. Ideally, the mechanism would both allow citizens to take collective actions and allow decision-makers within the EU institutions to gain greater insight into citizens' concerns. Furthermore, the ECI platform has arguably grabbed the attention of organized civil society and thus created an existing user base, which could help to propel the platform forward in the case of a process of revisiting and expanding its reach.

Despite these positive notes, there has been widely shared criticism of the ECI mechanism as implemented. The consensus position here seems to be that not only could the digital platform itself and the digital support tools be made more user-friendly but more importantly that the underlying legal constraints and the way they are interpreted by the EC block a culture of open involvement and engagement with citizens.[3] Since the ECI was implemented, over 70 proposals have been submitted, of which only four have been successful in passing the entrance demands, with a fifth on its way. The submission of proposals has been declining, likely due to the poor success rates of their predecessors. Of the failed proposals, roughly a third failed to gather the necessary support, another third were retracted by the submitters, and the remainder were rejected on formal grounds.

From a constitutional point of view, this should come as no surprise. As mentioned above, the Lisbon Treaty is explicitly based on principles of representative rather than participatory democracy, and it favours organized interests over individual citizens. These principles are mirrored in the conditions under which the ECI functions. The demand that the proposal submitted must fall within EC's competencies to act places a heavy burden of regulatory insight on those wishing to formulate and submit proposals. And the demand that proposals must gather one million signatures, with its various technical and security requirements, places a burden of organizational capacity and resources on proposers. In terms of the above-mentioned conditions for successful participation, a central weakness of the ECI is thus that although it provides an opportunity to participate, it fails to support this opportunity with a strategy for mobilizing and engaging citizens.

It is, therefore, no surprise that reform is now underway. However, the limited rights to 'voice' and 'consultation' established in §11 of the Lisbon Treaty could, in a practical context, be interpreted much more widely than is currently the case for the ECI. It would be legal and also practically possible to support citizens to formulate citizens' initiatives and ensure that proposals meet the terms of EC's competencies to act. The Finnish Open Ministry platform, for example, makes active use of volunteer experts, who support the formulation of citizens' initiatives to ensure that they fall within the remits of the body to which they are addressed (see Part II, Chap. 7). In lieu of such support having been provided for the ECI, NGOs have had to coalesce around the ECI Campaign, where they have attempted to provide citizens with some

---

[3]For an updated summary of these critiques, see http://www.europarl.europa.eu/RegData/etudes/BRIE/2017/614627/EPRS_BRI(2017)614627_EN.pdf

measure of support.[4] Part of the ongoing reform debate is, therefore, the question of where the responsibility lies for supporting citizens' participation via the ECI. Receiving little or no support from the EU institutions in their efforts to use the ECI mechanism, it would be no surprise if non-organized citizens suspect that the ECI in its original form was intentionally designed as a half-measure. The ECI has arguably set the stage for an unfortunate outcome where almost all proposals fail to qualify, either by falling outside the scope of EC's remit or by lack of mobilization and support.

Another important aspect of the ECI debate is what happens to proposals once they pass the qualification criteria. What exactly is the formal process for treating successful proposals, and how are they used in decision-making processes? The presence of such clarity is one of the most important conditions for the positive impact of participatory mechanisms and tools on decision-making and agenda-setting processes.

The EC's earlier strategy of achieving improvements within the existing framework has also been effective to some extent and should be pursued further as a complementary path to current reform attempts. Our analysis thus points to several opportunities to improve the mechanism through decisive action by institutional leaders.

Among the most obvious opportunities for improvement are greater support for proposal formulation and better follow-up regarding the processing of proposals after submission. Furthermore, following the success of the Five Star Movement (Part II, Chap. 10), to support mobilization efforts by ECI initiators, the ECI digital platform could be broadened to allow organized civil society to use it as a mobilization and campaigning platform, for example, by integrating online community functions as well as functions to support offline meetings.

More broadly, it is important not to fall into the trap of believing that improving the ECI is simply a matter of finding the right technical or legal 'fix'. The challenge of opening up the ECI platform to active engagement with European citizens is more than a matter of the adoption of new digital tools and new legislation. Getting the ECI to work for citizens is just as much a matter of organizational culture and leadership commitment. If a relaunch of the ECI was to take place, it would be essential that the process should not be one-sided. Instead, the relaunch process itself should seek to embody a new openness and a willingness to engage in mutual learning along the way. It would, therefore, be important to open up the implementation process to user involvement and to work actively with local and national governments as well as NGOs to draw on their experiences (Table 13.1).

---

[4]See www.citizens-initiative.eu

Table 13.1 SWOT analysis of the European Citizens' Initiative in its current form

European Citizens' Initiative (ECI)	
Strengths	*Weaknesses*
• The first transnational participatory agenda-setting tool in the world that has institutional embedding (art 4, Lisbon Treaty) • Has attention and an existing user base to build on • Allows decision-makers to get a grasp of issues citizens talk about and how they talk about them • Encourages active participation and citizenship	• Usability (of the mechanism in a broad sense, not only the web portal) • Not really designed for citizens—demands regulatory Competence and organizational capacity; the financial resources required are too high • No formal schema for impact on decision-making • Unclear informal impacts on decision-making—creates disillusionment • Unclear whether the initiatives generate new knowledge • Not cost-effective
Opportunities/improvement options	*Threats*
• Current EU crisis is a window of opportunity • Use the opportunity to make the ECI a bridge between citizens and EU institutions • Strengthen representative democracy by enhancing participation; stronger elected officials; and stronger citizens • Work with local/national platforms and/or NGOs to improve the ECI (and other mechanisms) • Seize the opportunity to improve the legal structure to address weaknesses (impact; transparency) • (Use as a tool for) mobilization and campaigning. • (Use as a tool to achieve) transparency in lobbying.	• Current crisis response is too chaotic to make good use of opportunities • The crisis of Europe, including the weaknesses of the ECI, lead to frustrated citizens • Pseudo-legitimacy • An ineffective ECI (and other mechanisms) easily backfires, leading to increased Euroscepticism and nationalism • An ineffective ECI leaves the door open for negative advice in the form of referenda, a type of input which is very difficult to handle

13.3.2 Improving Your Voice in Europe and the European Parliament Petitions Portal

In the following, we treat the common consultation platform of the European Commission alongside the European Parliament (EP) Petitions Portal. Although both these tools have a formal link to the decision-making process, there are still some important weaknesses to alleviate.

Albrecht (2012) reviews the e-consultation practice at EU level with a focus on the Your Voice in Europe platform, building on analyses of other scholars (cf. Quittkat and Finke 2008; Quittkat 2011; Tomkova 2009). His main points are as follows: online consultations have become a well-established instrument regularly used by practically all Directorate Generals (DGs). This has increased existing participation opportunities and brought more frequent public participation, especially of diverse interest groups, resulting in broader input into EU policymaking and the extension of its knowledge base. However, serious flaws include opaque and sometimes inadequate processing of contributions; a shift of focus on to closed question formats; little evidence of mutual learning; lack of feedback to participants on the use of their contributions, entailing frustration; one-way formats of communication with no opportunities to debate contributions; limited use of technologies (general purpose instead of specific e-participation and web 2.0 tools); and a lack of integration of new arenas for debate, e.g. the political blogosphere (Albrecht 2012: 15 ff.).

Albrecht advocates a model of deliberative e-consultations, which not only consist of collecting comments on a policy proposal but also allows for discussions both among the participants and with representatives of the EU institutions concerned. This is supported by our comparative case-analysis, where these two conditions—interaction with other participants, and interaction with decision-makers—appear to be very important in order to have an impact on the agenda-setting process. However, the implementation of such a model is confronted with a number of unresolved problems, such as how to adapt a face-to-face format to a large-scale setting, high costs, a minority of participants being willing to engage more deeply, the need to facilitate the process and to inform and support the participants and the reluctance of officials and policymakers to participate. With regard to improvements in technological support, natural language processing and argument visualization technologies are regarded as interesting candidates, although evaluation results to date are mixed. A third approach is to integrate e-consultations with 'third places' in new ways, i.e. social media platforms such as the blogosphere and popular social networking sites, in order to counter the dominating top-down flavour of existing EU channels. The assumption is that a good deal of exchange on these sites includes political talk and that the separation between political content and life world is increasingly blurred. Several EU projects have already experimented with linking e-consultations to social media (cf. Albrecht 2012: 19). Taken together, the strategies outlined show some promise to develop e-consultations to a model which is more open and effective than existing practice, and which will also enhance the quality and legitimacy of policy decisions with the help of tools such as Your Voice in Europe.

With regard to the EP Petitions Portal, Tiburcio (2015) examined 'The Right to Petition' in the European Parliament for the Committee on Petitions and made recommendations for the EU petition system. Tiburcio notes that recent studies on petitions tend to neglect the petitioning system of the European Parliament, referring to it as being a 'well-embedded process to deal with petitions' (Tiburcio 2015: 12). In his study Tiburcio comes to the following conclusion:

> [...] the petition system of the European Parliament compares well overall with the petition systems of Parliaments of Member States. In terms of conventional features, it scores well in all dimensions: ensures direct access (and not intermediate) by citizens; it's highly inclusive and open to both national citizens of Member States as nationals from third countries, if they reside within the EU territory; it offers possibilities for greater involvement of citizens, including through frequent hearings, followed by public debate in committee. (Tiburcio 2015: 40).

Nevertheless, the EP Petitions Portal is also a prime example of how the institutional peculiarities of the European Union can make it difficult to transfer experiences from the national to the European level. The limited powers of European parliamentarians to set the political agenda, combined with the subsidiarity principle, thus bear directly on the usefulness of petitioning MEPs. One workshop participant observed the difference that this creates in comparison with, for instance, the Dutch petitions platform petities.nl: *'The petition has to be about European laws and regulation and in particular the implementation of it by the Member States. It has to be about issues where the European Union has exclusive competence'* (interview with researcher, our translation). This is one of the reasons why so many filed petitions are rejected because the subject they are addressing does not fit this condition. By early 2019, more than 10,000 petitions had been received. Of these, one third turned out to be inadmissible.

Working within these limitations, it would nevertheless seem reasonable to make some use of the inputs gathered through the platform. The Petitions Committee could, for instance, make an inventory of what people ask for in inadmissible petitions, which could be distributed among MEPs and perhaps even national parliaments. Taking this idea one step further, the Petitions Portal could gradually be expanded to serve as a multilevel petition system with connections between the existing local, national and European institutions. This would give an enhanced basis for understanding issues which are stirring among European citizens, compared with top-down tools such as consultations and polls.

Comparing the Petitions Portal to Your Voice in Europe is illustrative in a number of ways. Your Voice in Europe exemplifies a one-stop-shop for EC consultations, which is a great advance on previous decentralized approaches. However, the consultation formats have not yet been harmonized across the different DGs, which makes the process less transparent for users than it could be. Upfront clarity about use of the inputs gathered through the platform could be improved. And there is a lack of feedback to citizens about the outcomes. The EP Petitions Portal, by contrast, has relatively clear feedback mechanisms, although this often comes late. The Petitions Portal has even less upfront transparency about what citizens may expect to happen to their input than the consultation platform. Information management is a concern with regard to both platforms. Petitions produce not only quantitative data but also potentially vast amounts of qualitative statements. Aggregating such input is both time consuming and politically risky; especially because there is no mechanism for the approval or disapproval of aggregation choices made by Commission services and by the people who provided the input. This leaves a great deal of power to shape the outcomes of consultations in the hands of the secretariat functions of the DGs. Similarly, the lack of transparent curation of petitions submitted to the EP Petitions Portal, along with the lack of clarity about the use of the inputs submitted, gives leeway for selective interpretation to the EP Petitions Committee. In terms of user experience, both platforms suffer from typical ailments of online participatory tools: a lack of interactivity; a lack of deliberation; and a lack of mobilization efforts. Together, these weaknesses produce results that may be recognized across a broad array of e-participation cases: over-population by organized interests and elites; and a lack of publicity.

Despite these shortcomings, we believe that relatively simple measures could considerably improve the socio-technical functionality of the platforms.

Your Voice in Europe could:

- **Provide feedback via e-mail**

    Once consultations are submitted, the results which are processed and fed into internal decision-making processes could easily be communicated to participants, thereby increasing their sense of transparency and involvement. For example, the synthesis report—which is a mandatory follow-up to each consultation—could be e-mailed to each participant in addition to publication on the website.
- **Make use of data analytics to aggregate qualitative inputs**

    Several data analytics companies, as well as DG Connect, have developed tools that help to make systematic and transparent decisions about the aggregation of qualitative data. Deploying such tools in the internal processing of results would help to improve the dependability of the process.
- **Improve scalability through technological support**

    The current difficulty of treating qualitative data represents a bottleneck, which from a resource perspective could actually serve as an incentive to maintain low participation numbers; how would EC services handle a 10-, 100- or 1000-fold increase in data? Big data technologies, such as machine learning whereby algorithms improve in step with the data amounts processed, might hold some answers to scalability.
- **Open up back-end data**

    If consultation data and the tools used to process it were made available to the public, the process of making use of the input would become transparent and would establish a hotspot for public dialogue on EU policy decisions.

The **EP Petitions Portal** could:

- **Benefit from more back-office resources**

    Whether through additional staff, additional technological support, or a mix of both, users would gain a much livelier experience of interacting with MEPs if the necessary back-office resources were available to ensure swift and qualified responses and interactions with users.
- **Use simple tools to educate and mobilize**

    Simple additional tools such as updates via text or e-mail, education on issues via video messages, ad hoc inputs via mini-polling and visualization of data and policy mechanisms would help to keep the attention of citizens and qualify their input.
- **Provide communication and mobilization support to petitioners**

    Since the EP Petitions Portal is more successful than the two other established tools in attracting the attention of non-organized citizens, it would be highly useful to provide these citizens with basic tools to mobilize support for their petitions (handbooks, free publicity mechanisms, etc.). The Dutch petition platform, for example, contains information that addresses how to get traffic to the petition, start a campaign website or blog with more information, write and spread a press release, get in touch with local or national TV or radio broadcasting centres and place a widget (so people can sign the petition from another social network site or campaign site). The Portal might also be provided with crowdsourcing functionality in order for campaigns to collect finances to hire a public affairs professional or to collect citizen volunteers for support.

- **Add various functions for online deliberation**

  A lot of the pressure to respond directly to questions and petitions could be taken off back-office staffers and MEPs if options for deliberation between participants were added to the Portal, e.g. debate options, options for collaboration on petitions, voting both for and against, etc. This would make it possible for citizens and interest experts to share knowledge in the ongoing process of developing and sharing ideas for petitions. Wiki Melbourne is one case in which such functions were embraced with enthusiasm by citizens and officials alike.

Such deliberative functions can be more or less structured. The 5SM makes use of debate platforms that are open to everyone, while voting on proposals is for registered users only. The Petities.nl platform has a structure where users cannot comment directly on proposals, but must make counter-proposals; the 'debate' between opposing proposals is then settled by voting. How to balance openness and structure is a question to be settled through experiment and experience. The major criterion is not to reinvent the wheel, but to keep working on the platform to improve its usefulness and popularity while drawing on experience from others along the way. This is underlined in the comparative case analysis by the fact that the condition of sustainability—improving the tool over time—contributes considerably to impact on final decision-making (Table 13.2).

13.4 The Low-Hanging Fruits: Obvious Steps to Improve EU-Level e-Participation

The discussion about increasing openness and participation at the EU level often centers around regulatory reform. However, no matter which regulations are put in place, openness in administration is as much a matter of culture as it is one of the formal structures (Torfing et al. 2012). To address the space of possibilities available to European institutions within existing formal structures, we have put together—with great help from experts and stakeholders engaged in our efforts—the following four suggestions for 'low-hanging fruits' of participation, which institutional leaders should be able to harvest while relying only on their existing remits.

Table 13.2 SWOT analysis of your voice in Europe and EP petitions portal

Your voice in Europe		EP petitions portal
Formal anchorage (in the EC, a better regulation approach)	S	Embedded in official structure (in Committee of Petitions, hearings, etc.)
One-stop-shop for all DGs		Relatively clear feedback
Consultation formats and procedures not harmonized across DGs	W	Lack of publicity; no focused communication strategy
Rules not clear, e.g. no clarity about the use of inputs, no mechanism for feedback		No strategy for engagement (i.e. mobilization) of supporters
Difficult information management		No clarity on the use of inputs
No deliberation		No curation of petitions
No interaction		Great delay in feedback
Over-populated by organizations		
Easy to improve using simple tools, e.g. feedback via e-mail	O	Assignment of more back-office resources
Use of data analytics to manage input (summarization) (e.g. using the DORIS system developed by DG CONNECT).		Use simple tools to educate and mobilize (video, SMS alerts, mini-polling, visualization, etc.)
Opening back-end data		Provide help to petitioners regarding their communication strategy (handbook, free publicity)
Scalability through technological support (e.g. machine learning, which improves summarization algorithms as more data goes through the system)		Add more deliberation (opportunities to debate and improve petitions; possibility of voting for and against petitions)
Drawing on the crowd for learning and ongoing improvement (beta testing, design thinking, UX development)		Add functionality for gathering funds for hiring professional assistance
Great overlap between 'smartification' and e-participation		Add functionality for volunteering where citizens can help each other develop and communicate petitions
Lack of agility in development of tools	T	Lack of agility in development of tools
Structural separation between problem owners and tool developers		Structural separation between problem owners and tool developers

13.4.1 Experiment with Participatory Budgeting in Relation to the Regional and Social Funds

This idea is that given the positive experiences with participatory budgeting methods by European cities, regions and Member States, there must be areas of EU spending where such methods could help to enhance citizens' participation. Current best practices such as described in, e.g. the Belo Horizonte and Paris case studies (Part II, Chap. 10), show that an e-participatory element is essential for scaling-up such methods. At the same time, however, face-to-face interaction and a certain rootedness in local situations is characteristic of all successful cases of participatory budgeting. Finally, the general conditions for the success of e-participation also apply here. For example, the Belo Horizonte case shows that failure to achieve a clear understanding among the participants concerning the mandate given to the process is lethal. In this case, the participation rate decreased enormously over time, in 2006 172,938 participants online and in 2013 8900. This was due to the failure to implement the winning project in 2008, after which people lost their trust in the procedure, despite other projects having been implemented. The question is therefore as follows: Given the complexity of the European decision-making process, can participatory budgeting even be conceived of at the level of the common European budget? Or should methods of participatory budgeting be seen as a means to making a connection between citizens and the EU at the local and regional level?

There is no doubt that setting aside a certain percentage of the total EU budget to be distributed by citizens would be a powerful symbolic gesture. However, there are many ways in which such a mechanism could go awry from the beginning. Allocating funds at the discretion of citizens would demand the implementation of some methodology to avoid simply reproducing current patterns of influence of different Member States. The participants at the workshop pointed to the Horizon 2020 EU research framework programme as an example of an allocation mechanism which is constructed to avoid simply reproducing national interests and focuses instead on the excellence and societal relevance of projects. The EU-funded CIMULACT project[5] provides an example where citizens have been involved, albeit indirectly, in the allocation of funds through the Horizon 2020 mechanism. Their role is to produce visions, priorities and calls for projects. A similar role might be conceivable if a budget was allocated to participatory budgeting at the EU level. One participant suggested such a mechanism might be thought of as an Erasmus programme for entrepreneurs, i.e. a platform where young entrepreneurs could submit ideas and compete for funding from participating citizens. Other participants underscored that such an allocation mechanism ought to be flexible and oriented towards pressing problems, such as—in these years—migration, climate change and improved education. Experiences from city-level cases show that participatory budgeting methods that start with small but realistic setups have a better chance of achieving longevity than those that make big promises, but do not follow through. For this reason, one participant suggested that it would be useful to start small and allow for an ongoing process of community-building to take place around the mechanism, which might then grow over time.

The EU already has well-established mechanisms for reallocating EU budgets to local initiatives and concerns through the Structural Funds. The Regional Development Fund as well as the Social Fund both already assign significant decision-making authority about the spending of these funds to the local or regional level. Building on lessons learned in cases ranging from Belo Horizonte to Paris (Part II, Chap. 10), it is not at all hard to imagine a unified framework for participatory budgeting being implemented as part of these budgeting processes. The availability of good projects and the willingness to back them would be crucial. But given the

---

[5]See http://www.cimulact.eu/

local development ambition of these funding programmes, and taking into account the much smaller scale of application, it would be feasible at this level to implement more open co-creation processes which reached organically from idea formulation to project application, funding decisions and implementation. In the wider perspective of regional development policy, it is conceivable that the input and throughput stages of participatory budgeting could bring together decision-makers, citizens and local organizations and businesses in a process that may help to create a common focus point for the community.

13.4.2 Expand Online Engagement with MEPs Beyond Petitions

This idea is to expand the palette of online engagement tools available to citizens to interact with Members of the European Parliament (MEPs) (and vice versa), beyond those that are currently available via the Petitions Portal and the EP website. Such tools could include:

- Availability of voting records for each MEP
- Public functionality to pose questions to MEPs and their staff
- Consultation functionality for MEPs to gather input from citizens
- Blogging functionality where MEPs can share work-in-progress and receive input from interested citizens

Most of these tools already exist (see Part II): votewatch.eu is an example of how voting patterns can be recorded and made public; WriteToThem and Abgeordenetenwatch both include an example of how posing questions to MEPs could be implemented; Your Voice In Europe already has the functionality needed to enable MEPs to post online consultations; and some MEPs have already adopted personal online blogging platforms to share work-in-progress and engage with citizens. The technical challenge is thus very minor in providing such tools to MEPs.

For such additional tools to have an effect on the relationship between European citizens and their MEPs, such tools would have to be both technically and strategically integrated with social media. Our case studies of TheyWorkForYou in the UK and Abgeordenetenwatch in Germany show that such functionalities in and of themselves tend to reach mainly organized interests and journalists, while social media provide a bridge through which ordinary citizens may also become involved. This reflects a tendency in which social media have grown to act as central hubs for communication and social networking in contemporary society; hubs that enable decentralized production and co-creation of ideas and even societal movements (Skoric et al. 2016). For most contemporary organizations, this tendency has produced a shift in online presence strategies from an emphasis on drawing traffic to the organization's website, to a focus on producing content that gains traction on social media platforms. Making this same shift in the EP would imply providing MEPs and their staff with the tools needed to send their 'fish hooks' into the whirlpool of social media debates in order to draw citizens onto their own platform for debate and co-creation (Dahlgren 2013).

Our case interviews indicate that initially some parliamentarians will see this as an 'extra' workload. The argument could be made, however, that online engagement is not going away, but is rather a new element of the changing role of the parliamentarian: from that of a representative of societal groups to that of a figurehead for an 'affective public' (Papacharissi 2015). In any case, it is clear that increased online engagement will make new demands of MEPs and that—as argued earlier—supporting services must go beyond a compliance mindset to one of exploration and co-creation. At the same time, for online engagement with MEPs to work, it is also necessary that parliamentarians and their parties accept a certain loss of control as the price to pay for a more vibrant interaction with (the most active parts of) their constituencies.

13.4.3 Create a Platform for Monitoring Member States' Actions During European Council Decisions

This idea is that the contributions and votes of each Member State in relation to decisions made in the Council of the European Union should be made publicly available in an easily accessible form.

Our discussion (Part I, Chap. 3) of the democratic deficit of the EU touched briefly on the Council's 'black box' function in European decision-making. This function is one of many factors that makes the EU seem to many citizens to be an outside force acting on the conditions for national policy. While there is some truth to this perception, increased insight into the actions taken by national governments in the context of the Council would help to dismantle those elements of this perception that rest on illusion or disinformation. It would also help to hold national policymakers accountable for the positions taken in the Council.

Much of the information needed to establish such accountability is already available, through the common EU web-platform, civil society services such as votewatch.eu and the web portals of national governments and parliaments. It is thus possible for the highly intrepid citizen to put many pieces of the puzzle together and to get an outline of the positions taken by nationally elected politicians in the European arena. However, not only does this place an unfair, and for most people prohibitive, burden of information gathering and analysis; key information is simply not available through ordinary channels.

Providing clear insights into the contributions and voting patterns of Member States is less a technical problem and more a question of procedure and culture. Where the line between the two is drawn, i.e. how much additional information could be made available without formal changes to the rules, is outside the scope of this report. Nevertheless, providing such information qualifies as an 'easy' step towards overcoming the division between an opaque European policy arena and the national public spheres. It would also, quite naturally, strengthen the ability of European citizens to participate in an informed basis in other, more active forms of e-participation.

13.4.4 Enable Crowdsourcing of Policy Ideas for the European Commission

This idea is that there is a gap in the policy formulation processes of the European Commission, which could be filled by a mechanism for crowdsourcing policy ideas. 'Crowdsourcing' is a highly ambiguous term. In this context we mean a process of gathering ideas through informal and frank exchanges of experiences and views, which is not bound to a specific phase in the decision-making process at the European level. Even assuming that both the European Citizen Initiative and Your Voice In Europe were revamped and relaunched, there would still be a gap between the functions of these two mechanisms, where early-stage policy development could benefit from open and frank sharing of ideas between European Commissioners, their staff and citizens. This early stage of pathfinding is especially vulnerable to lobbying activities by organized interests. While an online debate platform would not be a safeguard against such dominance, it would at least provide ordinary citizens with a space to engage with EU institutions in an informal manner that is otherwise only possible for lobbyists and other organized actors. The web portal Debatingeurope.eu provides an example of how such a crowdsourcing approach to the interaction between European citizens and decision-makers could be structured in an informal manner.

The creation of an informal crowdsourcing platform would help the EC to seize an otherwise missed opportunity to create a space for policy debate with a more transparent and ordered structure than the one currently provided for European citizens by social media. A crowdsourcing mechanism could also help to gather ideas for how the EC should interpret and weigh different expert and stakeholder inputs. For example, tools such as Futurium produce a wealth of expert ideas, but no clear synthesis. Here, a crowdsourcing mechanism could provide a space for follow-up discussions in the wake of foresight exercises, where less expert participants could become involved and help to develop ideas for policy strategy. By giving decision-makers and their staff a forum for gaining immediate feedback on tentative ideas and considerations, a crowdsourcing tool could also help to create more transparency in the policy formulation process, simply by making it possible to understand the thinking that went into more formal documents.

There are obvious risks to a more open platform. The Predlagam platform (Part II, Chap. 8) is an example to learn from. On this platform, which is an initiative of the Slovenian government, participants can add a proposal on current regulation or propose new regulation. There is room for voting and deliberation both between participants and with policymakers and some feedback from the government on the proposals since they are obliged to react. Impact is low, however, partly because many of the proposals would be difficult to achieve (see examples in the case study). Interesting criticism from one of the interviewees was that the format of the tool is too open and that it should be more structured, with more information given on what kind of input the government wants from citizens. This, of course, goes hand in hand with limiting the scope of participation and bureaucratizing the manner in which a proposal must be made. The interviewed researcher was of the opinion that the open structure of the Predlagam.vladi tool would not be an issue if there were sufficient staff to process the ideas: *'The policy process is very complex. And citizens should be aware how complex it is. I don't think that they should be fooled'*. Taking the lessons learned in Slovenia into account, our proposal is not to develop a stand-alone crowdsourcing platform, which would in itself risk becoming a 'black box'.

However, a crowdsourcing platform would perhaps be the ideal starting point for a one-stop-shop for online participation in European policy processes. While an online crowdsourcing platform could provide valuable input in and of itself, its main usefulness from a citizens' perspective would be as a springboard for deeper involvement, e.g. through Citizens Initiatives, EC consultations or EP petitions. From the perspective of the EU institutions, the input gathered from crowdsourcing could serve as inspiration alongside more formal expert group and stakeholder consultations. This could also help to hone the framing of consultations opened on Your Voice in Europe.

There are good reasons to explore this idea. Lironi (2016) argue that crowdsourcing platforms may enhance participation by involving civil society beyond typical stakeholder groups, as well as reaching young people, which may contribute to a learning process where both citizens and decision-makers broaden their understandings of a given topic and the range of opinions that exist on that topic. This argument is at least partially supported by our case studies of the Finnish Open Ministry and Wiki Melbourne, which both reached young people to a greater degree than is typical in participatory exercises (Part II, Chaps. 7 and 8). However, both of these case studies also showed clear tendencies towards over-representation of white, male, highly educated citizens. The main expectation of a less formal crowdsourcing platform should therefore not be that it will create a representative picture of what 'people' think. Rather, crowdsourcing is an opportunity to broaden debates by going beyond the implicit bounds that may arise in the Brussels 'bubble'.

To reap the benefits of crowdsourcing, an explorative mindset combined with ongoing commitment is a prerequisite. It would be of the highest importance that the design and implementation of such a platform go beyond mere compliance with some underlying legal mechanism. And it would also be necessary for platform development and learning to take place under relative resource stability. The case of the Finnish Open Ministry platform shows this quite clearly. The Open Ministry platform builds on an underlying legal mandate for citizens' initiatives and provides online functions to submit these initiatives. However, in its first years, the platform went far beyond the minimum requirements necessary for those functions. The Open Ministry platform thus aimed to provide a deliberative environment in which many spillover effects could be gained from the process of formulating, debating and gathering support for citizens' initiatives. The platform provided facilities for commenting on proposals, debating their possible consequences, suggesting improvements and voting for or against proposals. The platform also provided support from volunteer legal experts to draft proposals compliant with formal criteria. Over time, however, the budget available for these activities was reduced, and as a consequence, the platform gradually reverted to a bare-minimum approach. The online activities of Open Ministry around legislative proposals are now more directed to supporting initiatives with signatures rather than on deliberating proposals, and citizens can no longer take advantage of the legal support. In the interview the researcher argued: *'There is a need for some sort of legal advice to ensure that the proposals actually achieve what they are supposed to. And that's a problem because of course most citizens don't have the knowledge that they would need to ensure this'*. This case shows that it is possible for online exchange platforms linked to formal procedures to grow beyond a compliance mindset and embrace a more exploratory approach, but also that the long-term success of such an approach is highly dependent on sustained support.

Other cases, such as the Five Star Movement (Part II, Chap. 10) and the Icelandic experience of crowdsourcing a new constitution (Part II, Chap. 8), show that once an online platform grows beyond a compliance mindset, it may gain vibrancy and take a decisive role in the democratic community. The Five Star movement, centering in part on online crowdsourcing of policy ideas and strategies, has thus successfully mobilized a base of support that not only rivals existing political parties but has also placed the movement as the second largest Italian party. The Icelandic case similarly shows that a crowdsourcing platform can come to play a central role in public policy discourse, but also shows that a successful e-participation tool is in itself not enough to ensure policy impact. Care must be taken to balance formal and informal structures and to be clear about the ability of citizens to influence (or not) the process of policy formulation. The recipe for success here seems to be honesty and straightforwardness.

While these cases provide grounds for cautious optimism and concern regarding the plausibility of establishing a crowdsourcing platform to supplement the ECI and Your Voice in Europe, it is necessary to take into account the limitations of online-only platforms with regard to the facilitation of deliberation. Earlier in this book, we reviewed recent literature on policy crowdsourcing and found some critical warnings that are of the highest relevance in this context (Part I, Chap. 4). Face-to-face deliberative processes for the delivery of citizens' input to policy are often marked by high citizen interest, are often quite cost-effective and—when supported by effective mobilization strategies—may even provide superior performance regarding the inclusion of marginalized people and the overcoming of prejudice (Collingwood and Reedy 2012). However, deliberation is no silver bullet and only provides such benefits in settings that live up to other quality criteria at the same time. One well-established 'fact' among observers and stakeholders is that clear outcomes only come from deliberation when it is combined with some form of aggregation. The possibility to vote (quantitative aggregation) was thus present in nine of the twelve cases in which an actual impact on decisions was detected. But many online systems that claim to reproduce the deliberative situation quite simply do not. Many such systems support the construction of group identity and community very well, but fail to facilitate a respectful and consensus-oriented political dialogue (Kersting 2013). For this reason, when the purpose of a participatory process includes mutual exploration and co-creation, many expert observations point to the necessity of mixing online and face-to-face participation in processes; even if no one expects the potential gains from such processes to come easily (e.g. Kersting 2013; Nabatchi and Leighninger 2015). Our comparative case analysis also shows that the possibility to participate both online and offline is an important condition to create an impact on the agenda-setting process.

We expect that this latter recommendation will fall on fertile ground in the European Commission, where a recognition of the necessity of blending online and offline elements seems to pervade those DGs that are currently experimenting with online engagement. The Futurium platform[6] is one example. This platform is developed by DG Connect to enable co-creative processes involving policymakers in explorative and creative deliberation of possible futures in Europe (Part II, Chap. 9). This platform blends a wide range of online options for debates with offline meetings and events in order to enable structured deliberation and knowledge exchange. The CIMULACT project funded by DG Research and Innovation is another example. This platform is developed by a consortium of organizations to enable citizens and experts to co-create visions of a future Europe and to formulate priorities and calls for research and innovation to support these visions. This project blends online consultations with offline co-creation processes to enable the broadening of participation in the formulation of research and innovation policy.

Together, these two examples show that the idea of using crowdsourcing as a feed-in to policy already has support among EC decision-makers. Given the precedence of creating a one-stop-shop for online consultations across the DGs (i.e. Your Voice in Europe), it seems to be a natural next step to seek to establish a parallel or directly connected one-stop-shop for policy-crowdsourcing.

13.5 Cross-Cutting Issues: Towards a European e-Participation Infrastructure

In the above sections, we have focused on individual mechanisms and platforms and their shortcomings and opportunities for improvement. A key cross-cutting issue is that while tools such as the ECI, Your Voice in Europe and the EP Petitions Portal have the potential to serve as vibrant bridges between different spheres of public dialogue, they fail to do so due to a number of shared failings. Firstly, none of the existing mechanisms are supported by a clear and effective strategy for mobilizing

---

[6]See: https://ec.europa.eu/futurium/en

citizens to participate (Part I, Chap. 4). Observers and stakeholders generally agree that in lieu of such support, these mechanisms easily come to serve as yet another platform for elite debate among 'the usual suspects', i.e. organized private interests and social movements (see also Part I, Chap. 3). Secondly, all three existing mechanisms fail to provide feedback on the impact of their contributions to participants. Altogether, not enough effort has been put into ensuring that participants—citizens as well as decision-makers—experience their engagement with these mechanisms as rewarding.

What is perhaps most striking from a cross-cutting perspective, however, may be the weakness of follow-up and learning efforts which characterizes the implementation of existing mechanisms and the development of new ones. As already stated, it may be prudent to pursue a strategy of ongoing improvement within existing formal mandates, which seems to be, for example, what the EC has been doing with the ECI. However, if we accept that a focus on implementation may be more productive in the short term than a constant return to the question of formal frameworks, this places a responsibility on the services to pursue an implementation strategy where the improvement efforts surrounding EU's institutional e-participation mechanisms lead the field. Such a strategy currently seems to be absent. Instead, the current implementations of e-participatory mechanisms seem in many respects to aim for the delivery of a bare minimum standard. As a consequence, decision-makers and citizens are forced to look outside institutionalized e-participation channels to build the bridges for dialogue that Europe needs. Parliamentarians are thus taking to commercial blogging and networking platforms, while NGOs are attempting to provide mobilization support around the ECI. The net total of these failings is very little actual forward momentum on the advancement of a participatory approach to European decision-making.

The core question for a strategy of improving participation while staying within existing formal frameworks seems to us to be: What is the common unifying vision? As long as each of the existing mechanisms and experiments, such as DG Connect's Futurium projects, or DG Research's various pilot projects (e.g. CIVISTI, VOICES, CIMULACT[7]) remain stand-alone mechanisms with discrete functions and implementation programmes, the EU will remain an opaque jungle to the average citizen. If, on the other hand, a unifying vision of moving gradually towards an organic European participation infrastructure was agreed upon by all involved actors, the currently separate efforts of the different institutions and services to open up European decision-making could begin to build on one another rather than carving out separate corners of a bureaucratic universe. Such unity, of course, is easier to dream up than to achieve. For that reason, we have gathered a number of practical pieces of advice, which we hope may serve as support and inspiration to ongoing work to enhance citizens' participation in European decision-making.

---

[7] See www.cimulact.eu, www.voicesforinnovation.eu, www.civisti.org

13.5.1 Unify Platform Design Around the User

- **A one-stop-shop for participation would provide synergy between the EU institutions**
  Parallel efforts in different parts of the EU institutional system to enhance opportunities for e-participation would all benefit from integration into a 'one-stop-shop' platform. Contemporary platform design has long since abandoned the traditional approach of mirroring underlying organizational divisions because it puts an undue burden on the user to decode the internal logics of the organization. Why should it be up to each individual European citizen to understand the interfaces and overlaps between the ECI, EC's consultations and the EP Petitions Portal? Conversely, why should each participation experiment have to restart the process of mobilizing citizens for participation? Why not gather these and other participatory opportunities together in a common platform? The UK Democratic Dashboard is an example of such an approach. A one-stop-shop approach could significantly reduce the risk of citizens becoming dissuaded from participation because of a mismatch between their initial impulse to do so and the specific mechanism they turn to.
- **Multi-level integration would help citizens to navigate European democracy more confidently**

  Participating in the European policy cycle is not only about participation in the policy process within EU institutions. Europe includes local, regional, national and transnational processes. In the long term, efforts to arrive at a unified participation infrastructure ought to include the ambition to integrate the multiple levels of European democracy in which each citizen is involved. Without it, the many separate channels of participation available to citizens all run the risk of failing to channel citizens' wishes and concerns to the right governance levels and arenas. Also here, the UK Democratic Dashboard could be a starting point for such integrative thinking.
- **User-centric design can help to keep development focused on real-world usefulness**

  Due in part to the influence of legal expertise in public sector organizations, public sector online services tend to prioritize compliance with formal frameworks over user experience. E-participation platform designers therefore need an explicit mandate to put user experience first. Of course, this is not to say that online platforms should be anything other than compliant with formal demands. However, in terms of design processes, achieving compliance with legal requirements should be a secondary objective downstream from the development of an engaging user experience. A similar note should be made about the approach of the technical staff and contractors developing online platforms and other digital support systems for citizens' participation. A unified approach should not be read as a *technically* unified 'super-system'. Rather, unification should be understood from the user perspective, as a unified form of access and a homogenous user experience. Underlying such an experience may well be a number of heterogeneous systems; from the user point of view, this makes no qualitative difference.

13.5.2 Integrate Participation Processes

- **Formal and informal dialogue and consultation are points on the same spectrum**
  From a legal perspective, the different existing participatory mechanisms are distinct processes with discrete flows of information. From the point of view of citizens and decision-makers, however, it is more intuitive and useful to consider existing mechanisms and emerging experiments as points on a spectrum. Strategy formation in the EC services and the European-level political parties could benefit equally from the opportunity to engage in informal dialogue with citizens. Such dialogues could help to build momentum around European citizens' initiatives, and direct citizens to participate in consultations. Those issues that have no place in either might be taken up in petitions aimed at parliamentarians. A myriad of other connections is conceivable, which could be much more easily drawn in an organically overlapping e-participation infrastructure than by discrete stand-alone platforms focused strictly on each mechanism.
- **Expert and stakeholder consultations and citizen participation are part of the same process**
  Drawing on experiences from technology assessment and foresight, concepts such as 'Policy Making 3.0' have sought to consolidate the insight that policy formation processes that integrate evidence gathering, interest negotiation and democratic dialogue in a structured and transparent way can provide both greater input and output legitimacy. Again, a legally oriented approach to these processes will focus on the existing rules concerning expert and stakeholder consultation and seek first and foremost to ensure compliance with these rules. However, an approach which does not take into account the need for informal overlaps between these processes and risks pushing informal dialogues into the dark. A more integrated approach would present new challenges, but would also open up opportunities for more transparency in the policy formation processes of the EU.
- **E-participation and e-government are parts of a greater whole**
  E-participation and e-government should be viewed as part of the same movement towards a twenty-first century public sector. Europe cannot afford to consider e-government as a 'need to have' while e-participation is considered as merely 'nice-to-have'; both are equally necessary.

13.5.3 Learn As You Go

- **Starting small can help build trust**
  The road to the digital public sector of the future is by most accounts paved by trial-and-error and building on small successes rather than top-down planning of 'super-systems'. The guiding motto for the Swiss e-voting system—*safety before speed*—applies here in a broad sense: better to build on good and stable results

towards a long-term goal than to overreach and fall short. To be sure, this is not a recommendation for further stand-alone experiments. As discussed before, sustainability and tenacity are essential for citizens to have trust in institutions' efforts to build platforms for participation and patterns of governance around them. With long-term commitment, stand-alone experiments can in some cases do more harm than good to the relationship between EU institutions and European citizens.

- **Co-creation beats perfect planning every time**

  The standard operating mode of public sector institutions, including the European institutions, is to separate decision-making and implementation. In projects involving external contractors, this separation is most often a formal requirement. This means that well-proven approaches to the building up of online communities—e.g. starting small with simple services that are obviously helpful and easy to adopt and ongoing user involvement and crowdsourcing of ideas— are very difficult to implement. This operating mode also makes it very difficult to engage in dynamic partnerships with, for instance, media organizations that might help to create traffic to participatory platforms. It is a standard complaint concerning public sector ICT-development that this separation between the project owner and the developer favours planning over agility and top-down decision-making over bottom-up co-creation. Most leading advisors (from the EC Expert Group on Public Sector Innovation (EC 2013) to the OECD (2015)) therefore agree that innovative solutions to, for example, e-participation demand a new mindset. Central to such a new mindset is a focus on co-creation and a reinterpretation of formal and informal rules governing development efforts.

13.5.4 Organizational Support Is Necessary

- **High-level support and coordination**
  None of the above recommendations will be possible without high-level, crosscutting political support, guidance and investment. A high-level coordination group with cross-institutional participation and authority could thus be established to ensure that the efforts of different administrative bodies towards a unifying vision and strategy on e-participation work in the same direction.

13.6 Final Remarks

We end, then, on a note that is perhaps more positive than the conclusions drawn in our literature review. In the literature review, we saw that e-democracy, as it exists today, has not lived up to earlier expectations. Despite the Internet having produced vast improvements in the access to information on political decision-making, there has been little to no forward momentum in the direction of an online sphere of deliberation on diverse ideas and shared decision-making. Instead, the many-to-many communication, which the Internet makes possible, has become structured in a way that has accelerated the circulation of intentional and unintentional misinformation and tends to lock citizens into patterns of pre-existing preferences reinforced in the 'echo chambers' of subpublics. But even as this sobering state-of-play has weighed on our analysis, we have not taken for granted that the development of e-democracy in Europe has reached the end of the road. On the contrary, having delved into the detailed mechanics of specific cases of e-participation and e-democracy we have come to realize that *current* practice and *best* practice are still quite far apart.

There are basic rules of thumb for e-democracy implementation, identifiable in the comparison of empirical cases, which are too often ignored. Our analysis shows that e-participation cannot stand alone but must be embedded in an actual decision-making process, that the role of the participation mechanism in this process should be clear to participations, and that it is a good idea to tell participations what came out of their input once their participation is over. These and other examples show that where e-democracy fails is very often in the very same places that democracy in general fails. The core conclusion of our literature review—that e-democracy has failed to bring citizens much deeper into the decision-making processes of public institutions—thus seem valid. But our empirical findings indicate that this failure is less a consequence of the 'e' aspect of e-democracy than it reflects the underlying relationship between democracy as such and the decision-making culture of public institutions. As long as e-democratic solutions continue to be tacked on to existing institutionalized decision-making processes, without changing the business-as-usual of those processes, it is almost a matter of mechanical certainty that participating citizens will continue to be delegated to the limited roles that were available to them beforehand.

We take this insight to be good news for the prospects of e-democracy in Europe. Because when we see that the apparent failure of e-democracy to live up to its potential has little or nothing to do with anything inherent in the new world of digital communication and everything to do with the lack of openness of institutional decision-making processes, then we are able to land our investigation in the home court of European decision-makers: in the politics of European institutional design. In a nutshell, there is no technological mystery to be solved, 'only' an institutional one. The recommendations provided in this last chapter provide some obvious starting points.

Looking forward and looking for practical steps to advance e-democracy through institutional action, our recommendations should not stand alone. In our attempts to identify the low-hanging fruits of e-democracy, we have deliberately limited the scope of recommendations to actions that could be taken by the EU institutions within their existing institutional remits. Even without going into the possibilities that might arise in the event of a future revision of the Lisbon Treaty, European regulators could take a second look at the private sector actors who provide the contemporary world with its digital infrastructure. The question that looms over current debates on the future of democracy is: What can we as a society expect of

Silicon Valley? Does there not accrue some public service obligation to commercial providers of digital communication platforms similar to that of the media of the past? When newspapers, radio stations and TV stations have had a monopoly position—whether de jure or de facto—states have imposed editorial obligations for ensuring a fact-based and open public sphere. As social media platforms grow to become critical infrastructures for democratic governance, is there a positive argument for not imposing similar obligations on the Facebooks, the Twitters and the Snapchats of the world? We expect that this will be a second leg of future discussions, necessary to improve the prospects of e-democracy in Europe.

References

Albrecht, S. (2012). E-consultations: A review of current practice and a proposal for opening up the process. In E. Tambouris, A. Macintosh, & O. Saebo (Eds.), *Electronic participation* (pp. 13–24). Berlin: Springer.
Campbell, J. L. (2004). *Institutional change and globalization*. Princeton University Press.
Collingwood, L., & Reedy, J. (2012). Listening and responding to criticisms of deliberative civic engagement. In T. Nabatchi, J. Gastil, M. Leighninger, & G. M. Weiksner (Eds.), *Democracy in motion: Evaluating the practice and impact of deliberative civic engagement* (pp. 233–259). New York, NY: Oxford University Press.
Dahlgren, P. (2013). *Do social media enhance democratic participation? The importance-and difficulty of being "realistic"*. Policy Paper 04/2013.
Fischer-Hotzel, A. (2010). Democratic participation? The involvement of citizens in policy-making at the European Commission. *Journal of Contemporary European Research, 6*(3), 335–352.
Flyvbjerg, B. (2001). *Making social science matter: Why social inquiry fails and how it can succeed again*. Cambridge: Cambridge University Press.
Habermas, J. (2008): *Ach, Europa. Kleine politische Schriften XI*, Frankfurt.
Kersting, N. (2013). Online participation: From 'invited' to 'invented' spaces. *International Journal of Electronic Governance, 6*(4), 270–280.
Lippert, B. (2013) *Die EU zusammenhalten – aber wie? Überlegungen zur Zukunftsdebatte*. Arbeitspapier der FG 1, 2013/Nr. 01, March 2013, SWP Berlin.
Lironi, E. (2016). *Potential and challenges of E-participation in the European Union. Study for the AFCO Committee, European Parliament, Policy Department for Citizens' Rights and Constitutional Affairs*. Brussels: European Parliament.
Mossberger, K., Tolbert, C. J., & Stansbury, M. (2003). *Virtual inequality: Beyond the digital divide*. Washington, DC: Georgetown University Press.
Mossberger, K., Tolbert, C. J., & McNeal, R. S. (2007). *Digital citizenship. The internet, society, and participation*. Cambridge, MA: MIT-Press.
Nabatchi, T., & Leighninger, M. (2015). *Public participation for 21st century democracy*. San Francisco: Jossey-Bass.
Negreiro, M. (2015): *Bridging the digital divide in the EU*. European Parliamentary Research Service, PE 573.884.
Nicolaïdis, K. (2013). European democracy and its crisis. *Journal of Common Market Studies, 51* (2), 351–369.
Oppelland, T. (2010). Institutionelle Neuordnung und demokratisierung. In Leiße, O. (Ed.), *Die Europäische Union nach dem Vertrag von Lissabon* (pp. 79–96), Wiesbaden.
Panopoulou, E., Tambouris, E., & Tarabanis, K. (2014). Success factors in designing eParticipation initiatives. *Information and Organization, 24*(4), 195–213. https://doi.org/10.1016/j.infoandorg.2014.08.001.

Papacharissi, Z. (2015). *Affective publics: Sentiment, technology, and politics*. New York, NY: Oxford University Press.
Quittkat, C. (2011). The European Commission's online consultations: A success story? *Journal of Common Market Studies, 49*(3), 653–674.
Quittkat, C., & Finke, B. (2008). The EU Commission consultation regime. In: B. Kohler-Koch, D. De Bièvre, & W. Maloney (Eds.), *Opening EU-Governance to Civil Society*. Gains and Challenges, CONNEX Report Series No 05, University of Mannheim, Mannheim Centre for European Social Research (MZES), Mannheim, pp. 183–222. Accessed on 7-11-2016, from http://www.mzes.unimannheim.de/projekte/typo3/site/fileadmin/BookSeries/Volume_Five/Chapter08_Quittkat_Finke.pdf
Saurugger, S. (2010). The social construction of the participatory turn: The emergence of a norm in the European Union. *European Journal of Political Research, 49*(4), 471–495.
Skoric, M. M., Zhu, Q., Goh, D., & Pang, N. (2016). Social media and citizen engagement: A meta-analytic review. *New Media and Society, 18*(9), 1817–1839.
Sturm, R. (2010). Der Vertrag von Lissabon. In *Bundeszentrale für politische Bildung* (Ed.), Vertrag von Lissabon, Bonn, pp. 15–30.
Tiburcio, T. (2015). The right to petition. In *Policy Department C: Citizens' Rights and Constitutional Affairs* (Ed.), Brussels.
Tomkova, J. (2009). E-consultations: New tools for civic engagement or facades for political correctness? *European Journal of ePractice, 7*, March.
Torfing, J., Peters, B. G., Pierre, J., & Sørensen, E. (2012). *Interactive governance: Advancing the paradigm*. Oxford University Press.
van Dijk, J. A. G. M. (2012). Digital democracy: Vision and reality. In I. Snellen, M. Thaens, W. van de Donk (Eds.), *Public administration in the information age: Revisited* (pp. 49–61). Amsterdam: IOS-Press.
Wallace, H., Pollack, M., & Young, A. (2010). *Policy-making in the European Union*. Oxford: Oxford University Press.

Website

www.ec.europa.eu/citizens-initiative (accessed 7.02.2019)

Open Access This chapter is licensed under the terms of the Creative Commons Attribution 4.0 International License (http://creativecommons.org/licenses/by/4.0/), which permits use, sharing, adaptation, distribution and reproduction in any medium or format, as long as you give appropriate credit to the original author(s) and the source, provide a link to the Creative Commons licence and indicate if changes were made.

The images or other third party material in this chapter are included in the chapter's Creative Commons licence, unless indicated otherwise in a credit line to the material. If material is not included in the chapter's Creative Commons licence and your intended use is not permitted by statutory regulation or exceeds the permitted use, you will need to obtain permission directly from the copyright holder.